LANGUAGE BEHAVIOR:
A BOOK OF READINGS IN COMMUNICATION

JANUA LINGUARUM

STUDIA MEMORIAE
NICOLAI VAN WIJK DEDICATA

SERIES MAIOR

41

1970

MOUTON

THE HAGUE · PARIS

Elwood Murray

LANGUAGE BEHAVIOR

A BOOK OF READINGS IN COMMUNICATION

Compiled by

JOHNNYE AKIN
UNIVERSITY OF DENVER

ALVIN GOLDBERG
UNIVERSITY OF DENVER

GAIL MYERS
MONTICELLO COLLEGE

JOSEPH STEWART
U.S. PUBLIC HEALTH SERVICE

1970

MOUTON

THE HAGUE · PARIS

LIBRARY OF CONGRESS CATALOG CARD NUMBER: 77-110948

Printed in The Netherlands by Mouton & Co., Printers, The Hague.

For Elwood Murray
On the Occasion
of His Retirement

If I have seen farther than
    other men, it is because
I have stood on the shoulders
    of giants.

                        Isaac Newton

PREFACE

Elwood Murray once described the communication edifice as "... an elaborate old mansion built on some extremely valuable property in the midst of a projected urban redevelopment project". The old mansion he referred to still stands, and the property on which it was built is more valuable than ever. Moreover, during the past few decades the dwelling has undergone such dramatic changes in both structure and function that even some of its tenants have trouble recognizing it. The mansion is no longer the same because of scholars like Elwood Murray.

When Elwood Murray became Director of the School of Speech at the University of Denver in the early 1930's, college programs in communication were largely limited to training in fundamental skills such as voice, diction, and bodily action. Much attention was also given to oratory, debate, oral interpretation, and similar performance activities. Advanced courses and a great deal of the research in communication at that time focused on the history and theory of 'speechmaking'. Semantics, linguistics, group communication and the diagnosis and treatment of communication disorders received little emphasis.

Professor Murray had no objection to curricula designed to improve communication skills and platform effectiveness. Indeed, he was very much aware of the value such training has for the individual and his society. He was convinced, however, that to be meaningful, communication training should be concerned with all factors that influence the communication process and not merely with a few. He also felt that the speech educator has a responsibility to bring about comprehensive and long lasting changes in the speech personality of his students, changes that would be reflected in the students' casual interaction as well as in their more formal speaking performances.

One cannot broaden the goals of speech or communication training without also expanding the speech teacher's responsibilities as a student and a scholar. The teacher of public speaking, for example, should be well grounded in rhetoric and, among other things, have a good understanding of platform techniques. But this knowledge must be supplemented with relevant theory and research in the behavioral sciences if he is to encourage his students to develop more general communication skills. Conversely, one cannot broaden the interests of the communication scholar without also modifying his goals as a teacher. It was this expanded view of the responsibilities of the communication specialist that caused Elwood Murray to enlarge his communication study and research interests and to offer course work in many new areas. To identify the speech curriculum he pioneered in general semantics, group and organizational communication, linguistics, and language disorders. Murray used the phrase 'Communication Methodology'.

During the past few decades our knowledge of communication has been expanding on three fronts simultaneously: the technological, the psychological, and the method- ological. We have made rapid progress in our technical ability to transmit and receive messages and the body of theoretical and empirical literature dealing with the psychological aspects of communication has grown considerably. Advances on both of these fronts have provided the basis for developments in the third area, communication methodology.

Daniel Katz observed a few years ago that the physical barriers to communication have all but disappeared. Our technical and mechanical ability to get information from one place to another is dramatically demonstrated by one scientific achievement after another. Satellites can beam live television programs to any part of the earth where an antenna and receiver await. Direct dialing telephone systems make it possible for one human to literally press a button to get the ear of another human in a vast number of places on the globe. Information storage and retrieval systems based on computer operations are already beginning to replace the older library systems. Because of the technological advancements of the past few years, man's voice is capable of vast amplification; his written word capable of vast multiplication.

Who is listening? Here is the second front, the psychological human being who not only sends his messages by these marvelous technical systems, but also receives messages and treats them, somehow, in his nervous system. Let's repeat: 'treats them, somehow'. Message processing involves the perceptual, cognitive, associative, and other functionings of the human nervous system. What we know about that 'somehow' today is far in advance of what was known even a few years ago. Psychology, neurology, chemistry, sociology, linguistics, anthropology, philosophy, and many other disciplines have contributed theoretical constructs and research findings on which we can base a substantial understanding of human communi- cation.

On the psychological front a wealth of data is available about how a person learns, associates symbolically, thinks, reacts, performs with groups, adjusts his personality, copes with his dissonant and changing environment, and generally manages to move about effectively in a world of expanding information and technology. Much of the information has been around for a long time, ignored in many cases by the communication student because it happened to be cloistered in journals of psychology or reported in medical or other scientific publications. Fortunately, academic chau- vinism is today being challenged by the interdisciplinary scholar. Useful research data in many areas are available to point the direction for further study of man as a communicator.

Two things become apparent. First, human communication is not the exclusive province, for example, of the speech professor or the psychologist; we can learn much by pooling our interests and our research. Second, by making use of this pooled knowledge we can learn a great deal more about the psychological aspects of communication than we ever would have guessed before. What this means is that the second front, psychological considerations, is moving very nearly as rapidly as the first front, technological advance. It will continue to progress if we avail ourselves of the resources from the many disciplines.

We now come to the third front: methodology, the link between our knowing about communication and our putting this knowledge to better use.

Here we appear to be lagging. Here is the workaday regimen of trying to achieve more effective human communication. Methodology may be the never-never land between the statistical significance of an isolated piece of research and the gimmickry and glad-handing associated with getting along gracefully, if not genuinely. If we have the technology, and if we have a better grasp than ever before of the psychology of communication, how do we put these to work? How do we train a generation of people to agreeably make more sense with one another? How do we replace harmony for dissension in the family group? How do we move communities to minimize prejudice and discrimination? How do we keep nations talking with one another instead of shooting?

Answers to these questions will not be found in the pigeon-pecking laboratory nor in the antiquated declamation-oriented speech department of the last century. It may be argued that both have made contributions to our understanding of the communication process. Nevertheless, we have progressed beyond that point. Sophisticated methodologies for teaching, for disseminating the collected data on the propensities of human interaction, for effectively reconstituting a rational order out of the communicative chaos, are needed. Practitioners of these methodologies should not only train the new generation, but also move into government, industry, and any of the established human institutions as leaders with the powers of precept and persuasion. Slowly, effective methodologies are being developed. Imaginative use and creative extensions of these methodologies will be carried forward by what we can call the 'communication methodologist'. He will be a scholar who will contribute to and be well grounded in the literature of communication and the behavioral sciences. He will be a 'behaviorist' in the sense that he will be aware of the effects his teachings have on the behavior of others. He will be a 'practitioner' in the sense that he will draw upon his knowledge and skill to help individuals, groups, and organizations repair and improve their communication.

This book in honor of Elwood Murray reflects his philosophy of communication. Its approach is interdisciplinary, its concern is with communication as a science as well as an art, and its emphasis is both on communication as a methodology and as an area of inquiry. The readings are all original, not reprints, and they were prepared specifically for this collection. The authors represent such fields as speech and communication, psychology, anthropology, business administration, English, sociology, linguistics, education, and mineralogy. The subjects discussed range from such theoretical concerns as communication models and theories of perception to such practical matters as speech and communication training for middle management and the diagnosis of communication disorders.

The book is divided into four parts. Each part is devoted to an important area of communication study and research that Elwood Murray helped integrate into speech and communication curricula: Communication Methodology, Group Communication, Linguistics, and Communication Disorders. The introductions to each section provide the reader with an overview of the specialty and acquaint him with the material to follow. They are written for the student who is just beginning his studies in speech and communication. The readings in each of the four sections vary considerably in focus, level, and content. Some are highly general and theoretical, others are rather specific and more data oriented. Some consist of a broad review of the literature while others deal with a very narrow aspect of some problem. The topics are treated with enough rigor to satisfy the specialist and collectively they cover sufficient ground to meet the needs of the novice or generalist for a look at some of the major and minor interest areas in speech and communication.

TABLE OF CONTENTS

Preface 9

I. COMMUNICATION METHODOLOGY

David Elkind, On Perceptual Development 21
Lee Thayer, On Theory-Building in Communication: Some Persistant Obstacles 34
Dean C. Barnlund, A Transactional Model of Communication 43
Gregory Bateson, The Message of Reinforcement 62
Bess Sondel, The Analogue Laboratory of Elwood Murray. 73
Wayne N. Thompson, Communication, Communication Theory, and Rhetoric 78
O. R. Bontrager, The Education of Our Teachers 95
Harry L. Weinberg, Science, Mysticism, and Logic 103
Kenneth Frandsen, Semantic Compatibility in an Interpersonal Communication
    Laboratory 112
Dan McLachlan, Jr., Communications and Civilization 127

II. GROUP COMMUNICATION

Kim Giffin, The Study of Speech Communication in Small-Group Research . 138
Rupert L. Cortright, The Uses and Abuses of Discussion 163
Jack R. Gibb and Lorraine M. Gibb, The Process of Group Actualization . . 171
Seth A. Fessenden, Using Sociometry to Discover Intra-Group Relationships 188
Eugene E. Rebstock, Education in Organizations 204
Louis E. Glorfeld, The Rhetoric of Science 213

III. LINGUISTICS

Samuel B. Stone, Toward a Psycholinguistic Theory of Teaching 228
Zell SoRelle, Segmental Phonology of Texas Panhandle Speech 245

Raven I. McDavid, Jr., On a Hierarchy of Values: The Clinician and the
    Dialectologist 250
Gordon E. Peterson, Toward a Theory of Symbolization 256
Ray L. Birdwhistell, Some Meta-Communicational Thoughts About Com-
    municational Studies 265
Robert B. Lees, A Morphophonemic Problem in Turkish 271
Heles Contreras and Sol Saporta, Phonological Development in the Speech of
    a Bilingual Child 280
Albert Upton, That Monster Custom 295

IV. COMMUNICATION DISORDERS

Gerald M. Phillips, A New Direction for the Speech Profession. 308
Paul H. Ptacek, General Semantics and the Evaluative Process in Speech
    Pathology 325
Wendell Johnson and Joseph L. Stewart, Stuttering and North American
    Indians 340

Index 347
About the Contributors 356

PART ONE

COMMUNICATION METHODOLOGY

Man's growing interest in communication might be described as moving along simultaneously on three fronts. The first is the technological: the development of tools and devices to improve message transmission and reception and to enhance feedback processes. The second advance is in the human realm. It is reflected by the rapidly expanding body of theoretical and research data dealing with the social and psychological aspects of communication. Related to the first two is a third front which is devoted to the discovery and testing of methodologies designed to facilitate human interaction. Elwood Murray gave the label 'communication methodology' to this third aspect of communication study, research, and application.

The word 'methodology' should not mislead the reader. It seems to imply a superficial concern with methods, techniques, or gimmicks. Such is not the case. The specialist in communication methodology is interested in more than practice or application. He may be a practitioner, but he is primarily a scholar who engages in communication study and research. An activity that distinguishes the methodologist from other communication scholars consists of analyzing relevant theory and research in the communication and social sciences to determine their methodological implications. The methodologist also formulates and investigates his own methodological theories and approaches.

Communication can be considered a methodology when it is used in a systematic manner to achieve specific ends. Thus, when psychotherapists, speech clinicians, debaters, oral interpreters, teachers, or discussion leaders, for example, attempt to fulfill their roles by following an implicit or explicit set of communication rules or principles, they are using communication as a methodology. On the other hand, when these same individuals interact with others in a less deliberate fashion under circumstances where formal roles and goals are less obvious they are engaged in communication but their acts are not methodological. Although communication methodologists place a particular emphasis on the study and development of methodological principles and approaches, they must maintain an interest in all aspects of communication if they are to base their formulations on a balanced understanding of the communication process.

The methodologies of interest to communication specialists are many and varied. They range from the more traditional rhetorical approaches such as persuasive speaking and debate to such recent developments as T-group training and ortha-chorics. General semantics and gestalt therapy are some of the communication methodologies available on an intrapersonal level. Dyadic methodologies include interviewing and the various speech therapies and psychotherapies. Brainstorming, reflective thinking, and PERT are task-oriented group methodologies and psycho-drama and sensitivity-training are process-oriented group methodologies. The case method, business games, parliamentary procedure, the incident process and scores of other procedures for improving interaction and achieving interpersonal goals are studied and employed by the communication methodologist.

A broad conception of communication and of the role of the communication methodologist greatly enlarges the 'span of the discipline', as Dean Barnlund once expressed it. It expands the communication curricula, increases the academic and research responsibilities of communication scholars, and demands that the student of communication develop a knowledge of relevant theory and practice in a wide variety of areas. The communication specialist must keep abreast of developments in information theory, communication theory, games theory, general systems theory, rhetoric, organization theory, and perception theory. He must know the viewpoints, findings and practice in semantics, general semantics, cybernetics, linguistics, psycho-linguistics, kinesics, psychotherapy, and communication disorders. His research should be theoretically oriented and should reflect a high level of competence in data gathering, data processing, and experimental design.

The first section contains readings of relevance to the student interested in the broad area of communication and communication methodology. Among other things, the selections deal with technological and mathematical constructs, with the effects on human interaction of the communication of others, and finally with specific methodologies.

For many years teachers and scholars identified with the field of speech thought of themselves as being concerned primarily with the 'art' of communication. This attitude has changed somewhat during the past few decades with the development of mathematical and scientific concepts dealing with information bits, redundancy, and more quantifiable aspects of message exchange.

We make a plea for broadening our conception of communication as human behavior. These articles provide insights into the theories and models of human communication with special emphasis on the psychological concepts of importance to the communication methodologist.

An excellent review of major perceptual development theories is provided by Mr. David Elkind. In 1964-65 Elkind traveled to Switzerland to study with Jean Piaget. His studies at the Piaget Institute certainly influenced the descriptions he provides of learning theory and his discussion of the relations between activity and perceptual development.

How we build our theories about communication is the subject of Mr. Lee Thayer's article. An interdisciplinary scholar and active methodologist in the training of business students, industrial clients, and teachers, Thayer brings to this volume a systematic review of major communication theories and how they were developed.

From the theories we build our models. Mr. Dean C. Barnlund's 'transactional' model of the communication process provides the methodologist with a theoretical approach to his subject that is useful on many levels ranging from the intrapersonal to the intercultural. By defining communication as the generation of meaning from within, Barnlund avoids the pitfalls inherent in theories that refer to messages that travel like an arrow from the head of the sender to the head of the receiver. Elkind's writing on perceptual development in children becomes even more meaningful when related to Thayer's theory-building and Barnlund's model construction.

Elkind, Thayer, and Barnlund have taken psychological constructs and suggested how they might be made useful to the experimenter or the methodologist. Mr. Gregory Bateson's "The Message of Reinforcement" provides the student of communication theory with a stimulating and provocative discussion of learning or "the receipt of information". According to Bateson, information can be 'hard' or 'soft', and an individual's 'search patterns' are likely to be 'hard'. As a result, one often sees what one expects to see; premises tend to be self-validating. Nevertheless, patterns of search are indispensable, and consequently, the relationships which an investigator can discover are rather restricted. Bateson discusses these restrictions and describes the pattern of reinforcement in which learning occurs.

In "The Education of Our Teachers" O. R. Bontrager punctures many contemporary myths about education. The important question, he asserts, "is what are we trying to accomplish through the process of education?" His answers are as delightful as they are profound.

The final writers deal with communication as methodology. Professor Bess Sondel, whose work in interpreting the communication implications of cybernetics is widely recognized, analyzes a special kind of advanced study laboratory developed by Elwood Murray. In his Analogue Laboratory, Murray has brought together outstanding representatives of various disciplines to construct analogues of the underlying themes and structures of human knowledge. In her analysis of the Analogue Laboratory, Sondel defines analogy and reviews the assumptions behind this laboratory and its implications for understanding human and machine communication.

Like Bess Sondel, Kenneth Frandsen also analyzes a laboratory developed by Elwood Murray. However, Frandsen focuses on Elwood Murray's Laboratory in Interpersonal Communication, one of the most attractive courses Professor Murray developed. Mr. Frandsen is one of the leading quantitative researchers in the speech-communication discipline and he provides interesting information about the effects of participation in an interpersonal communication laboratory on semantic compatibility.

Dan McLachlan, Jr. is a physical scientist who has long been interested in communication theory. At one time, he and Elwood Murray jointly taught a course in communications. In his paper McLachlan shares some of his thoughts about individual development, civilization, and communications.

DAVID ELKIND

ON PERCEPTUAL DEVELOPMENT

The problem of perception has sometimes been posed by the phrase, "Why do things look as they do?" (Gibson, 1950). Why do objects have form and position, depth and distance and why do they look right up or upside down? From a developmental point of view this question must be rephrased to read, "How do things come to look as they do?" This question presupposes the fact that the perceptual world of the child differs from that of the adult and that the transformations of the child's perceptual world can be described in terms of general principles of development. The aim of this paper will be to describe the developmental rules which seem to determine how things come to look as they do.

DIFFERENTIATION

Perhaps the most fundamental transformation which the perceptual world of the child undergoes is that of differentiation. It is true that shortly after birth the neonate can make a variety of crude sensory discriminations (Bridger, 1961; Gesell, Ilg & Bullis, 1949) and that by the age of three or four months he can be trained to make what appears to be discrimination between geometrical forms (Zaporozhets, 1965). Pattern discrimination is also an apparently early development (Fantz, 1961). Compared to the refined discriminations of the normal adult, however, these elementary neonatal behaviors must be regarded as relatively crude and global. It is not, for example, until the age of three that children can match a variety of geometric forms (Stanford Binet, 1960), and the ability to reproduce more complex patterns such as those of the Bender Gestalt Test (in which some of the figures overlap one another) does not appear until middle childhood (Koppitz, 1964). The articulation of perceived forms is thus a gradual development.

It should not be assumed, however, that the recognition of more complex forms in later childhood is entirely due to modifications in the visual apparatus and associated cortical centers — area 17 — which serve it. There is more and more evidence these days to support the notion that from the very beginning visual perception is aided and abetted by the motor system. The young infant, as Piaget (1952) and more recently White *et al.* (1964) have shown, looks for the things he touches and hears so that visual discrimination is guided by kinesthetic stimulation. Work in the field of perceptual 'rearrangement' with the aid of distorting lenses and prisms by such investigators as Kohler (1964), Ewert (1930), and Stratton (1934) lend vivid evidence for the contention that motoric factors play a large role in determining the way things look. When wearing lenses that invert the visual field, it is the objects which are most often handled and used that are adapted to most readily (Kohler, 1964). Visual exploration and discrimination is thus from the first day of life linked with motor investigation and stimulation.

The differentiation of form is only one of the ways in which the perceptual system becomes more discriminating in the course of development. One finds in addition an increasing appreciation of depth and distance. The well-known work of Gibson and Walk (1960) utilizing the VISUAL CLIFF suggests that depth discrimination comes into play quite early in life. In the visual cliff situation the child is encouraged to cross a plate glass bridge between two tables. The child's reluctance to cross the 'bridge' is an index of the fact that he sees the difference in depth between himself and the floor. The results of the visual cliff experiments suggest that the infant can discriminate depth as soon as he can crawl. This discrimination is, nonetheless, only with reference to relatively near objects and patterns. Discrimination of far depth or distance relationships emerges later in development. In a laboratory setting Updegraff (1930) found that four-year-old children were less proficient in distance discrimination than were adults. When distance discrimination was tested out-of-doors, with more cues than those available in the laboratory, even four-year-olds showed good distance discrimination. This suggests that one aspect of distance perception is the recognition of the essential cues for correct distance judgments.

Stereoscopic vision, or three-dimensional perspective, has also been explored in children. Work with the stereoscope by Carr (1935) and by Gesell, Ilg and Bullis (1949) suggests that such vision improves with age beyond the age of five years. Such research is, however, difficult to interpret since ability to comprehend instructions and to focus the stereoscope may play a part in the child's response. A study by Johnson and Beck (1941) avoids these difficulties by an arrangement such that, if three-dimensional vision is present, an illusory doll is seen between the child and the screen. The child's reaching for the illusory doll in the intervening space where it is located is the clue to whether or not the child has experienced the phenomenon. With this apparatus even two-year-olds gave evidence of tridimensional vision and Munn (1965) says that Beck in personal communication told him that even one-year-old children reached for the illusory doll. Apparently then three-dimensional perspectives are present by the end of the first year.

Still another aspect of the adult perceptual world which appears to derive from the principle of differentiation is what has been called perceptual constancy. A friend seen at a distance looks no smaller than after he has approached us and is seen at close range. This is true despite the fact that the absolute size of the retinal image is much larger when the friend is near than when he is far. Unfortunately the evidence regarding constancy in infancy is difficult to evaluate because of the experimental difficulties involved. In a searching review of the literature on the subject Wohlwill (1960) concludes that size constancy is probably present by the end of the first year, and that it reaches adult-like values at about the age of five years after which there is apparently little further significant progress. A similar conclusion may well hold for size and brightness constancy.

The relative lack of differentiation in the perceptual world of the child gives rise to several interesting and often charming phenomena. In the first place the child's perception tends to be GLOBAL in the sense that a particular feature of the object tends to be taken for the whole object. Quite often this particular feature is form. Since many quite different objects are alike in form (say a world globe and a volley ball) children of nursery school age quite often come up with metaphoric-like expressions. The writer's son recently held up a potato chip and said "look daddy, like a butterfly!" On another occasion he called a small, oblong, gray stone a 'turtle'. These are of course not true metaphors since the awareness of symbolic likeness is absent in the child. Such metaphoric extensions arise because the child can ignore multiple perceptual differences and see essential similarities between what to the adult are quite disparate things. The crass psychologist calls this 'false generalization', but the intuitive teacher calls it 'imagination'.

Another phenomenon arising out of the child's relatively undifferentiated perception has been described by Vernon (1962). While the adult finds little difficulty in isolating elementary parts in more complex wholes, as say the quarterbacks in a huddle or the horse one has bet upon in a race, this is much more difficult for the child. Indeed, to the child the part often partakes of the whole and is frequently not recognized in isolation. Piaget's (1954) one-year-old daughter grew so accustomed to seeing him framed in the window of his workroom that she still looked toward the window when asked, 'where is Pappa' even though Pappa was standing in front of her in the garden! As Vernon (1962) points out, the situation is not that there are two Pappas but rather that Pappa in a new context seems new and unfamiliar. This part-whole phenomena can also work in reverse. Children who see strangers in familiar surroundings may accept them much more readily than if the context in which they were seen was also new.

Still another phenomenon associated with the lack of differentiation is what Werner (1948) has called PHYSIOGNOMIC PERCEPTION. Children often perceive things according to their dynamic value and not exclusively in terms of their static characteristics. Indeed, Werner claims that the child responds to the action qualities of things before he responds to the passive ones. Werner reports an experiment by Rubinow and Frankle regarding the adequate stimuli for the sucking response in the infant. Rubinow and Frankle observed five successive steps in this response. The reaction occurred 1) when there was a sudden movement of the object toward the mouth; 2) when there was a similar movement of a pointed object; or 3) of any object capped by a nipple or nipple shaped form. Later the response was evoked 4) only by the object, whether stationary or moving, and at about the age of eight months; 5) only by an object containing a white substance.

The great sensitivity of children to the dynamic character of things has been shown in a variety of ways. One of the most consistent findings of investigators studying stroboscopic or apparent movement (of which motion pictures are the best example) is that children perceive apparent movement at much lower rates of presentation than is true for adults (Gantenbein, 1952; Meili & Tobler, 1931). Children also perceive contact between moving objects when in fact there is not contact and when such contact is not perceived by adults (Piaget & Lambercier, 1958). Likewise Olum (1956), using a Michotte apparatus — which presents moving lines behind a screen with differently oriented slits so that the lines appear to be moving toward and away from each other — found that children give movement responses such as 'A passes B and B passes A' which are never reported by adults in a similar situation.

The dynamic character of the child's perception is also shown in his interests and in his verbalizations. How explain children's abiding interest in animals if not by the fact that they are dynamic, moving and alive? Observation also reveals that the child deals with objects in terms of their active qualities. A hole is 'to dig' and a bicycle is 'to ride'. This dynamic quality of the child's perception may also be in part responsible for the night terrors so often encountered during the nursery school years. When one awakens in the night and outlines are obscure and nothing is distinct, dynamically oriented perception paints the room with strange moving forms which frighten impressionable minds. If I may be excused for using still another example drawn from personal observation, the aforementioned three-year-old son recently told me, "Daddy, do you know why I cried last night? I thought there was a lion in the room but there was no lion". It is sometimes worth remembering that a dark room is an entirely different thing to the dynamically oriented perception of the child than it is to the more prosaically and statically oriented perception of the adult.

Differentiation is thus a general law of perceptual growth that in part determines how things come to look as they do. The gradual discrimination of forms, size, distance, depth and tridimensionality give increasing texture and body to the perceptual world of the child. Correlated with this growing differentiation is the gradual disappearance of those phenomena unique to childish perception, globality, part/context confusion, and dynamic intrusions. Differentiation, however, is but one of the laws that regulates perceptual development and now we need to look at another, namely, organization.

ORGANIZATION

It is to the Gestalt psychologists that we are mainly indebted for the notion 'perceptual'. By organization one usually means part-whole relationships. The well-known phrase that somehow adhered to any discussion of Gestalt psychology, namely, that the whole is more than the sum of the parts is, nonetheless, misleading. It suggests some quantitative lawfulness as if one were to say that two apples and two apples were more than four apples. On the contrary, *Gestaltqualitaten* recognized by von Ehrenfelds were in fact NEW qualities which emerged from the parts and that were qualitatively unlike them. Such properties as 'slender', 'round', 'angular', and 'harmonious' are words which refer to superordinate qualities of things which are qualitatively distinct from the parts that go to make them up.

One of the many contributions of Gestalt psychology to the question of organization or the resulting *Gestaltqualitaten* was a description of the principles regarding the stimulus characteristics which induce organization and give rise to these new qualities. In general things which are similar in appearance (dots, or squares, or dogs or cats) tend to be grouped together as are things which are near to one another. In addition, continuous figures tend to be seen as wholes more often than as discontinuous figures. So-called 'good' figures, those whose outlines are regular, symmetrical, etc., also tend to be organized more often than figures which lack these properties. Organization into figure and ground, into a part that stands out as clear and bounded and another which is unbounded, is another characteristic of perceptual grouping and organization.

Now the Gestalt psychologists (Koffka, Kohler, Wertheimer, and others) have argued that these rules of organization are more or less built into the organism and that they are primary in ontogenesis. The elementary sensations that were once thought of as the building blocks of more complex perceptual organizations were rather to be thought of as psychologically secondary resultants of intellectual analysis. From the point of view of Gestalt psychology, the elementarists committed an almost unpardonable psychological error, namely, that of identifying logical priority with psychological priority. In point of view of development, organization is the primary fact and elementary or single sensations must be abstracted out of this organized fundament rather than be built up out of them.

Granted the validity of the Gestalt position in its broad outlines, the developmental psychologist must still ask whether the laws of organization outlined by the Gestalt psychologists are the same for adults as for children or whether there may be quantitative or qualitative differences in the rules governing perceptual organization at different points in development. In general the research on this problem suggests that while the laws outlined by Gestalt psychology do indeed hold for children, their effect seems to be quantitatively weaker in children than it is among adults. The stimulus field must show more contiguity, similarity, proximity and good form to be organized by the child than is true for older children and adults.

A corollary to this is the fact that children seem to show a greater need to impose organization on a relatively unstructured field than is true for more mature persons.

In one of the most systematic studies in this area, Rush (1937) studied more than 9,000 subjects from Grade 1 through college. She used patterns of dots to explore the effects of proximity, similarity and contiguity in visual grouping as this was reflected in the perception of visual direction. She found that even the youngest children grouped the dots according to the Gestalt principles. Older children, however, arrived at more complex organizations than did the younger ones. For example, older children saw the dots going in two directions while younger children saw them going in only one direction. In terms of the relative strength of the various principles of grouping, Rush found that continuity was the strongest factor, direction was the weakest, and that similarity and proximity fell somewhere in between.

The increasing complexity of perceptual organizations with increasing age was also demonstrated by Piaget and von Albertini (1954). In this study children were exposed to intersecting figures (such as a line drawing of a diamond superimposed on a line drawing of a square) and to incomplete figures (made by cutting a portion out of a drawing of a whole figure). Children had little difficulty with the intersecting figures but had great difficulty with the incomplete figures where continuity was weak. A study by Gollin (1960) gave similar results. Children (2½ to 5½) were shown line drawings of common objects that varied in the completeness of the outlines. There was a regular decrease with age in the amount of completeness or continuity needed for correct recognition to occur.

Other results point in the same direction. Freeman (1929) showed adults and children dot patterns of varying numbers and asked them to estimate the number of dots. Adults were much more efficient than children when the dots were numerous and irregularly grouped. Freeman argued that this result was due to the greater facility of older children and adults in forming subjective groupings and organizations. This interpretation is given confirmation by the results of Slochower (1946) who required children from five to ten to make pencil reproductions and two-dimensional clay models of various simple shapes. She found that there was a considerable tendency to improve the structure of these reproductions in the direction of greater regularity, symmetry and rectilinearity than existed in the originals. Furthermore, this tendency was much stronger in young children than it was in the older subjects. The greater need among the young children to force structure upon the materials suggests the lessened ability to impose this structure subjectively or mentally.

Although it is not possible to go into all aspects of perceptual organization here, where only the highlights are being noted, it might be well to explode one myth about the perceptual organization of children before concluding this section. The myth is that children are less influenced by the spatial orientation of figures than are grownups. The myth derives in large part from the fact that children are often observed looking at picture books upside down without any apparent difficulty in recognizing the figures portrayed therein. The assumption is then made that orientation makes no difference to the child and that he can recognize things presented upside down as easily as he can recognize them when they are presented right side up. A considerable amount of research work shows, however, that this in fact is not the case.

In a simple direct test of the young child's facility to recognize inverted figures Ghent (1960) presented a series of realistic figures tachistoscopically in each of four orientations: right side up; inverted; turned 90° to the left and 90° to the right. The subjects were 3-7 year-old children. The youngest children, 3-4 years, recognized significantly more figures in the right side up position than in any other. The older children, 5-7, recognized the figures equally well regardless of the orientation in which they were presented. Brooks and Goldstein (1963) performed a similar experiment with a slightly different twist. Children from 3 to 14 years of age were shown pictures of their friends and were then asked to identify them. The pictures were of the head only and were presented in an upright orientation. In a second presentation, a week later, the previously identified pictures were shown upside down and the subjects were again asked to identify them. The overall results showed that the proportion of children in each age group who had scores above the median increased as a function of age. In short, the older children were better able to recognize inverted pictures of their friends than were the younger children. A study by the writer and his colleagues (Elkind, Horn and Schneider, in press) has shown that the ability to READ words printed upside down also increases with age.

These studies show rather clearly that the ability to recognize inverted figures far from being more prominent in younger children, tends to improve with age. It must be added, however, that this ability varies with the materials in question. As Gibson and Robinson (1935) have pointed out some figures are habitually seen in a single orientation. One rarely sees a tree or a car upside down. Other objects have no distinctive orientation and are seen in different orientations almost every time they are perceived. Such things as rulers, pens, pencils, etc., are used in one orientation but are seen and handled in a variety of orientations. The ease with which an object will be recognized in an inverted orientation is thus a function of the degree to which it has an habitual or accustomed position.

It nevertheless remains to ask why it is that children are observed to look at picture books upside down when research shows that they are less efficient in recognizing pictures upside down than older children. The myth seems to arise from the belief that the child sees the world in the same way that we do. Claparéde (1919) gives a charming illustration of how children can make the same discriminations as adults, only on an entirely different basis. Claparéde tells of a young child who could not read but who could nevertheless select from a pile of phonograph records the one that was mentioned to her. Since the child was clearly not reading the labels, how was she able to do it? It seemed clear that she was taking account of other cues such as the color of the label, the size of the type, the width of the grooved section, etc. Now the same thing probably happens when a child looks at a picture book upside down. What he is responding to are different cues than those habitually employed by the adult, clues moreover, that might well be independent of orientation, such as color or brightness. The child is thus not seeing things upside down at all, since for him the figure reorganized is a different figure. It is the adult who, from his point of view, sees the figure as upside down and who assumes it must also be so for the child. Once we recognize that the child is seeing a different configuration from what is seen by the adult, the fallacy of its upsidedownness is immediately revealed.

The rules of perceptual organization that have been described by the Gestalt psychologists thus seem to be operative in children. For little people, however, the characteristics of the stimulus which make for organization must be stronger for the organization to occur. Contrariwise the child exhibits a greater need to impose structure upon stimulus materials because he lacks the facility to make subjective groupings and thus must put the structure in the stimulus materials themselves. These results seem to thwart both the nativists and the empiricists. While the disposition toward organization seems to be present from the start of life, at the same time there are changes in organization which seem to be the result of maturation and experience. In a very real sense then perceptual organization is neither inborn nor acquired in the strict sense of either of those terms. On the contrary perceptual organization shows all the characteristics of a growth phenomenon and thus must be regarded as developmental in nature. We must now consider the last and least explored rules of perceptual growth and the one that promises to be at least as important as differentiation and organization.

PERCEPTUAL ACTIVITY

Still a third rule or principle which governs how things come to look as they do has been described by Piaget (1961) under the rubric, *perceptual activity*. In the infant and young child perceptual activity is limited to visual sampling of the stimulus field and to exploration both of which become more systematic and coordinated with increasing age. A second, more dynamic and organizing type of perceptual activity emerges somewhat later during the nursery school and elementary school years and might be called perceptual activity proper. This second form of perceptual activity involves transports (comparing two lines as to length which are separated in space); references (recognition of comparable forms separated in space or time); anticipations (the ability to predict the results of certain transformations of a stimulus); and schematizations (the ability to reorganize perceptual givens as evidenced by the ability to reverse figure and ground or to discover hidden figures). All of these activities enable the child to relate bits of perceptual information gathered at different times or at different places. Such perceptual activity inevitably involves cognitive and verbal processes as well as the perceptual system and is a highly adaptive development.

To illustrate the nature of perceptual activity consider the child's response to part-whole figures (Elkind, Koegler and Go, 1962). In these drawings more complex objects are made up out of simpler ones which themselves have independent and separate meanings. When nursery school children view these figures they almost invariably name the 'parts' and do not see the whole. At a somewhat older age (5-6) they begin to see both the parts and the whole but in alternation rather than in combination. Children at this age may say, for example, 'Fruit', and then 'A man', as if there were no connection between the two and as if seeing the one excluded seeing the other. Only toward the age of seven or eight do children begin to combine the parts and whole into an integrated figure which they call 'A man made out of fruit'. These responses neatly demonstrate the development of schematizations and also illustrate another aspect of the development of perceptual activity. As the child grows older perception not only becomes more active but also more RAPID. The young child sees parts and wholes as temporally distinct which the older child and adult see as a simultaneously integrated complex. It is important to distinguish this more rapid integration of perceptual givens in the older child and adult from the tendency to PROJECT activity into perceptual givens which is more characteristic of the younger child. The former refers to the activity of the subject, the latter to the activity of the object.

Development of perceptual activity can also be demonstrated with the aid of reversible figures such as the classic Rubin vase-profile drawings. In a series of studies the writer and his colleagues have shown that spontaneous figure ground reversal increases regularly with age (Elkind & Scott, 1962; Elkind, 1964) and that although training is effective in improving figure ground reversal it does not alter the age differential (Elkind, Koegler & Go, 1962). That is to say older children require fewer learning trials to attain a higher level of performance than do younger children.

What seems to occur in the case of figure ground reversal is that the contours of one figure are detached and 'transported' to the ground so that what was previously bounded and distinct becomes unbounded and formless ground while what was previously ground now becomes bounded, has form and emerges as figure. The same kind of explanation would account for the finding that older children show greater ease in discovering embedded figures than do younger children (Elkind, Horn and Schneider, in press). Embedded figures are those in which a simple figure shares contours with other figures in a complex whole. The state of Colorado is thus 'embedded' in the map of the United States since it shares contours with other states such as Utah and Wyoming.

Perceptual activity is also the underlying mechanism which permits visual comparisons. Vurpillot and Zoberman (1965), for example, presented children with drawings of houses in pairs with each house in the pair containing the same number of elements (such as a door, chimney, and windows) located in parallel spatial positions. Some pairs were equivalent in the sense that the parallel places were filled with similar elements. Other pairs were different in the sense that parallel places were filled with nonsimilar elements. Young children judged the houses on the basis of a single comparison between elements. Their success was thus variable. If the pair of houses were equivalent it made no difference which elements were compared and the child always judged correctly. But for the houses which were different, young children judged them to be the same or different, depending upon whether similar or nonsimilar elements were compared. By the age of six or seven, however, such variable comparisons were no longer made since the older children based their judgment on the basis of a comparison of all of the elements of the whole so that their judgements were invariably correct. Perceptual activity also underlies the diminution of certain illusions, such as the Müller Lyer, with age (Piaget, 1961).

The recognition of the role of perceptual activity in growth of perception has important practical significance. The writer and his colleagues, as an illustration, have begun to explore the role of perceptual activity as it pertains to reading. We have found that perceptual activity, as measured by the ability to unscramble words, to disembed figures, to recognize inversed words and to overcome illusions is highly correlated with reading achievement (Elkind, Horn, & Schneider, in press). In addition we have found that when children are matched for intelligence, slow readers not only manifest poorer perceptual activity but also profit less from training in this skill (Elkind, Larson, & Van Doorninck, 1965). Teaching techniques aimed at improving perceptual activity in children have already been devised (Elkind, in preparation) and are in use in some school systems along with other teaching methods.

Other practical applications of measures of perceptual activity have appeared in the field of mental retardation (Elkind, Koegler, & Go, 1965); in the field of limited-hearing children (Binnie, 1963) and in the area of cultural deprivation (Bryde, 1965). In all of these studies, patterns of normal perceptual development are used as a standard for assessing perceptual growth in atypical children or in children growing up in deprived environments. The work in this area has only just begun.

Although not directly related to our present topic, a pedagogical note might not be entirely out of place in this context. It is probably fair to say that with few exceptions very little attention is paid to training in perception in the course of the normal school curriculum. On the face of it, this is truly extraordinary. Perception plays such a central role in such activities as reading and concept formation which are at the heart of educational goals that it hardly seems possible that it could be neglected. Our own work has shown that perceptual activity can be improved with training and that such training is beneficial in a variety of learnings. Hopefully, systematic training in perceptual skills will become an accepted part of educational programs within our lifetime.

SUMMARY AND CONCLUSIONS

We began with the question as to how things come to look as they do and have explored the parts which differentiation, organization and activity play in this development. Far from being identical with the perceptual world of the adult, the visual world of the child is diffuse, disorganized and passive in comparison to what it will be later in life. By and large the transformation of the visual world of the child into that of the adult appears to be a spontaneous one and children are seldom given systematic training in this sphere. We have suggested the need for, and the value of, such training in public school education.

Our review of the principles which underlie perceptual growth also suggests that the ancient nativism — empiricism dichotomy — leaves out an important third factor which is perhaps more important than either of these components. This *tertium quid* is the activity of the subject. It is the activity of the subject which actualizes the inborn potentialities in relation to environmental givens. Perceptual activity thus plays the same role in mental development that the 'organizer' (Waddington, 1940) plays in the development of the organism. At each step in perceptual growth it is the activity of the subject which consolidates past gains and makes possible new acquisitions. It is not passive nurture or passive nature which guides development but rather the active subject. Only when we take into account the activity of the subject in constructing his perceptual world do we get a true grasp of how things come to look as they do.

UNIVERSITY OF ROCHESTER

REFERENCES

Binnie, C.A., "A comparative investigation of the visual perceptual ability of acoustically impaired and hearing children", unpublished master's thesis, (University of Denver, 1963).

Bridger, W. H., "Sensory habituation and discrimination in the human neonate", *American Journal of Psychiatry* (1961), 117, 991-996.

Brooks, R. M., and A. G. Goldstein, "Recognition by children of inverted photographs of faces", *Child Development* (1963), 34, 1033-1040.

Bryde, J. F., "A perceptual study of Sioux Indian children" (Paper presented at the 1965 Convention of the Rocky Mountain Psychological Association, Denver, Colorado, May 1965).

Carr, H. A., *An introduction to space perception* (New York, Longmans, 1935).

Claparéde, E., "La conscience de la ressemblance et la différence chez l'enfant", *Archives de Psychologie* (1919), XVII. Pp. 67-80.

Elkind, D., "Ambiguous pictures for study of perceptual development and learning", *Child Development* (1964), 35, 1391-1396.

Elkind, D., "Non-verbal exercises for remedial reading instruction" (in preparation).

Elkind, D., J. Horn, and Gerrie Schneider, "Modified word recognition, reading achievement and perceptual de-centration", *Journal of Genetic Psychology* (in press).

Elkind, D., R. R. Koegler, and Elsie Go, "Effects of perceptual training on unmatched samples of brain-injured and familial retarded children", *Journal of Abnormal Psychology* (1965), 70, No. 2.

Elkind, D., R. R. Koegler, and Elsie Go, "Effects of perceptual training at three age levels", *Science*, (1962), 137, No. 3532, 755-756.

Elkind, D., Margaret Larson, and W. Van Doorninck, "Perceptual decentration learning and performance in slow and average readers", *Journal of Educational Psychology* (1965), 56, No. 1, 50-56.

Elkind, D., and L., Scott, "Studies in perceptual development: I. the decentering of perception", *Child Development* (1962), 33, 619-630.

Ewert, P. H., *A study of the effect of inverted retinal stimulation upon spatially coordinated behavior*, (= *Genetic Psychology Monographs*, 1930, 7).

Fantz, R. L., "The origin of form perception", *Scientific American* (1961), 204, 66-72.

Freeman, G. L., "An experimental study of the perception of objects", *Journal of Experimental Psychology* (1929), 12, 340-358.

Gantenbein, Maria-Martha, "Recherches sur le dévelopement de la perception du mouvement avec l'âge (mouvement apparent, dit stroboscopique)", *Archives de Psychologie, Genève* (1952), 33, 197-294.

Gesell, A., F. L. Ilg, and Glenna E. Bullis, *Vision: its development in infant and child* (New York, Hoeber, 1949).

Ghent, Lila, "Recognition by children of realistic figures presented in various orientations", *Canadian Journal of Psychology* (1960), 14, 249-256.

Gibson, Eleanor J., and R. D. Walk, "The visual cliff", *Scientific American* (1960), 202 (4), 64-71.

Gibson, J. J., *The perception of the visual world* (Boston, Houghton Mifflin, 1950).

Gibson, J. J., and D. Robinson, *Orientation in visual perception. The recognition of familiar plane forms in different orientations* (= *Psychological Monographs*, 1935, 46, No. 6) (Whole 210).

Gollin, E., "Developmental studies of visual recognition of incomplete objects", *Perceptual and Motor Skills* (1960), 11, 289-298.

Johnson, B., and L., Beck, "The development of space perception: stereoscopic vision in pre-school children", *Journal of Genetic Psychology* (1941), 58, 247-254.

Kohler, I., *The formation and transformation of the perceptual world* (= *Psychological Issues* (1964), III, Monogr. 12).

Koppitz, Elizabeth M., *The Bender Gestalt test for young children* (New York, Grune & Stratton, 1964).

Meili, R., and Tobler, E., "Les mouvements stroboscopiques chez les enfants", *Archives de Psychologie, Genève* (1931), 23.

Munn, N. L., *The evolution and growth of human behavior* (Boston, Houghton Mifflin, 1965).

Olum, V., "Developmental differences in the perception of causality", *American Journal of Psychology* (1956), 69, 417-423.

Piaget, J. *The origins of intelligence in children* (2nd ed.) (New York, International Universities Press, 1952).

Piaget, J., *The construction of reality in the child* (New York, Basic Books, 1954).

Piaget, J., *Les mécanismes perceptifs* (Paris, Presses Universitaires de France, 1961).

Piaget, J., and Barbara von Albertini, "Recherches sur le developement des perceptions XIX observations sur la perception des bonnes formes chez l'enfant par actualization des lignes virtuelles", *Archives de Psychologie, Genève* (1954), 34 203-243.

Piaget, J., and M. Lambercier, "Recherches sur le developement des perceptions XXXIII la causalité perceptive visuelle chez l'enfant et chez l'adulte", *Archives de Psychologie, Genève* (1958), 36, 77-202.

Rush, Grace P., "Visual grouping in relation to age", *Archives de Psychologie* (1937), 217, 1-95.

Slochower, M. Z., "Experiments on dimensional and figural problems in the clay and pencil reproductions of line figures by young children I. Dimension", *Journal of Genetic Psychology* (1946), 69, 57-75.

Stratton, G. M., "Vision without inversion of the retinal image", *Psychological Review* (1934), 41, 341-360; 463-481.

Updegraff, R., *The visual perception of distance in young children and adults: A comparative study* (= *University of Iowa Studies in Child Welfare*) (1930), 4, No. 4.

Vernon, M. D., *The psychology of perception* (Baltimore, Penguin, 1962).

Vurpillot, E., and N. Zoberman, "Rôle des indices communs et des indices distincts dans la différenciation perceptive", *Acta Psychologica* (1965), 24, 49-67.

Waddington, C. H., *Organizers and genes* (Cambridge, Cambridge University Press, 1940).

Werner, H., *Comparative psychology of mental development* (Chicago, Follet, 1948).

White, B. L., P. Castle, and R. Held, "Observations on the development of visually-directed reaching", *Child Development* (1964), 35, 349-364.

Wohlwill, J., "Developmental studies of perception", *Psychological Bulletin* (1960), LVII, 249-288.

Zaporozhets, A. V., "The development of perception in the preschool child", In P. H. Mussen (Ed.), *European research in cognitive development* (= *Monographs of the Society for Research in Child Development*, 1965, 30, No. 2), 82-101.

LEE THAYER

ON THEORY-BUILDING IN COMMUNICATION:
SOME PERSISTENT OBSTACLES*

It is now some three-and-one-half years ago that I first became concerned with the condition of concept- and theory-building in communication.[1] At that time, I described a number of conceptual obstacles that, in my opinion, were likely impeding the development of a comprehensive and viable theory of human communication. My purpose then, as now, was simply to share my observations on some potential pitfalls and barriers to theory-building in communication which are evident in the ways we approach the phenomena we are interested in — insofar as those pitfalls and barriers are evident in the literature. The question I asked of our theories and our concepts, explicit or implicit, and of our metatheoretical assumptions, is this. What is there in the ways in which we come to conceptual grips with our phenomena that might be standing in the way of the development of a more useful, comprehensive, viable theory of human communication?

Now, from the perspective of those intervening years, it seems worthwhile to report on what, in my opinion, are some continuing and persistent barriers to theory-building in communication. These might be viewed as second generation observations on the condition of the conceptual-theoretical foundations of the 'field'. Their usefulness is necessarily personal. This is not an exercise in treatment or repair, but in provocation. How well one succeeds in conceptualizing those phenomena of the world with which he is concerned depends upon how carefully examined are his implicit conceptual approaches. I would like to provoke a measure of dispassionate re-examination of some of the common and implicit assumptions and conceptual orientations that may be impeding more effective theory-building in communication.

(For all good reasons, one who would cast himself in the role of commentator upon the condition of his field's theorizing ought to be able to offer more than Freudian interpretations of his motives. Mine are fairly simple and straightforward. FIRST, as a human being, I am often not able 'to communicate' with others and

* An earlier version of this paper was presented as a talk at the Annenberg School of Communications, University of Pennsylvania, November 1, 1965.
[1] First presented as a talk before the Summer Conference of the National Society for the Study of Communication, Purdue University, August 27, 1962.

'to be communicated' with by others as effectively or as efficiently as I would like. Our models and 'theories' of human communication are not as helpful to me as I think they should be. So I wonder, "Why aren't they?" SECOND, as a teacher, I continue to experience a great gap between what's possible and what actually occurs in the classroom. Again, our so-called 'theories' of human communication seem inadequete to the task. THIRD, I believe that a comprehensive, viable theory of human communication is the most significant need in the science of man — either as a much-needed bridge between the disciplines[2] or as an integrating discipline in its own right. I believe that those seriously engaged in the business of trying to understand the processes of human communication have a destiny to fulfill — and this, either well or poorly. One needn't stumble on his own shoelaces while looking for a place to set his feet down.

SOME CONCEPTUAL PROBLEMS[3]

In an earlier paper, I proposed that we take a cautious look at a number of conceptual problems that might be impeding the building of a viable theory of human communication. Those observations, as useful context for this paper, can be briefly rephrased as follows:

1. We seem to be treating 'communication' as a thing *sui generis*, as something to be set apart from and not basic to other domains of human behavior or its artifacts. Closely related, our endowment of 'communication' with noun-ness, and of 'communicates' with verb-ness has all-too-often functioned to our conceptual detriment. Our hypostatization of 'communication' as thing DONE rather than as event OCCURRING may be serving as a barrier to a potentially more useful understanding of the process. Similarly, the phenomena of human communication have typically been approached as a problematical situation to be corrected rather than as neutral event to be understood. This orientation has had its unfortunate consequences for theory-building.

2. We seem to be very careless in handling our UNITS and LEVELS OF ANALYSIS. We commonly discourse on 'mass communication' or 'interpersonal communication' or just plain 'communication' from non-differentiated or poorly distinguished conceptual stances. Sociological phenomena may not be amenable to the same conceptual framework as that employed to comprehend psychological phenomena. This carelessness may also be serving as a persistent impediment to whatever theoretical progress we might be making.

3. We cling to OUTMODED AND DISADVANTAGEOUS NOTIONS OF CAUSALITY. We exhibit a tendency to over simplify our perspectives, to cast for explanations rather

---

[2] D. M. Mackay, "The Science of Communication—A Bridge between Disciplines", Inaugural Lecture, University of Keele, February 23, 1961.
[3] This summary is based upon an earlier paper: Thayer, Lee, "On Theory-Building in Communication: I. Some Conceptual Problems", *Journal of Communication*, December, 1963.

than for understandings. We seem to misread the principle of parsimony and pay the price of toting around a clutch of part-theories that don't fit together at their edges. We seem to have been victimized by our own 'physical sciences thinking', an important point I'd like to return to below.

4. I often see in our literature the implicit and UNCRITICAL ASSUMPTION THAT 'COMMUNICATION' BEHAVIOR IS ESSENTIALLY CONSCIOUS AND/OR WILLED, an assumption which has lured us far from potentially more profitable conceptual perspectives.

5. We have suffered from an OVER-EMPHASIS ON ONE ASPECT OF HUMAN COMMUNICATION (e.g., language) with concomitant neglect of other aspects of the same event (e.g., institutionalized expectations, intention, etc.).

6. Perhaps as one consequence of our neglect of the full scope of the phenomena we are interested in, we have surreptitiously REIFIED some of our media and elements, such as WORDS AND MESSAGES. It is commonplace in the literature that messages 'do things' to people, rather than vice versa, or that the effective 'stimulus' was someone's words. These orientations to our phenomena could well be impeding the development of more viable concepts and theories.

7. There is evident the NORMATIVENESS OF OUR CONSTRUCTS and models, and our head-nodding semantic 'blackmail' of each other, even in the use of our central term, 'communication'.

8. Implicit in much of what is said about the phenomena of human communication are a number of MYTHS that we cling to at a metatheoretical level — particularly the myths of objectivity and rationality. To subscribe conceptually — if implicitly — to a position which is empirically untenable is not especially rational! But this we seem to do — and then we expend our energies doing conceptual battle with these self-constructed but invisible obstacles.

9. Finally, I noted the ILLUSION OF MEANING which stands behind much of what is written under the banner of 'communication'. (There is, too, our often mystical quest for meaning's meaning. Analogically, one might ask how illuminating it would be for a physicist in quest of the meaning of electricity, to ask, "What does electricity REALLY mean?")

These do not exhaust the list of potentially disadvantageous modes of thought and approach to which we seem to be peculiarly susceptible. Nor are these pitfalls in our thinking mutually exclusive.

At the same time, I realize full well how easy it is to stand back and second-guess the authors of published documents. But it is more than an exercise in one-upmanship. If the field is to achieve its full growth and vitality, it must be conceptually healthy. To that end, I'd like to offer some additional observations on what I take to be some persistent obstacles to theory-building in communication.

SOME PERSISTANT OBSTACLES

These observations on the condition of theory-building in the field may seem to be in addition to my earlier observations, or to overlap them in one way or another. No matter. If they 'communicate' to your advantage, the logic of their order is unimportant.

FIRST, and almost just in passing, because it is so obvious (perhaps so obvious as to permit of a truly significant impediment), there is the popularity of the term, the universality of concern with the subject, the ubiquitousness of the phenomenon itself. 'Communication' is a catchword of our times, 'communication problems' an apparent national pastime. As with other cultural shibboleths, however, that universal and popular concern with matters of human communication may well preclude the building of empirical inroads for a good many years to come. Add to this the insularity and the ownership of the part-theories of those established disciplines having some stake in the study of communication. How do we put these pieces together into a meaningful whole, when to do so is a loss of empire for one or another of our constituent disciplines? This equivalent of nationalism amongst established scientific and normative disciplines contributes political and economic as well as semantic barriers. By contrast to our problem of theory-building across established and traditional disciplines, an international government would be a simple and painless achievement.

The term is a lay term as well, as always to the great disadvantage of those who would use the term particularly rather than generally. 'Communication' is something everyone 'does'. The process is 'understood' through its doing. (This offers the same kind of disadvantage to the development of empirical understandings of the process as did the obviousness of the earth's flatness to the layman and the scientist some millennia ago.) We 'get by'. Implicitly, we must therefore 'understand' the process. And our very 'getting by' — our taking the process for granted, obscures those elements which might lead to more fruitful explanations of the obvious.

But we can't attribute all of this semantic confusion to the uninitiated. Apparently even communication experts take the term for granted. Those who are 'in' the field perhaps engage in a little 'head-nodding' when the term is used. As a result, it's not at all clear what the term is supposed to refer to. To illustrate that careless ambivalence, I have drawn these diverse uses of the term from a recent award-winning book in the field:

"...what gets communicated..."
"...communication about..."
"...tended to communicate in...mode..."
(And incidentally, these three were taken from the same paragraph!)
"...amount of communication..."
"...they often regard the communications which come to them..."
"Communication with such a person may often be..."

"These are clearly social facts about the existing system of communications..."

"...on other issues, they wanted more communication..."

"...(those) who by their manner, communicate their need for communication..." (!)

"...the role of the communications process..."

(Then, if we add an adjective to communication and/or communications, and permute...)

"...purposive communication activities going beyond a review of the day's news..."

These are admittedly out of context. But, even so, specifically what is it that is being referred to when everyone 'understands' something — when it's so obvious, so universal — that something doesn't get its appropriate scrutiny, doesn't get finely honed for use as a seminal conceptual tool.

SECOND, and most importantly, perhaps, is an obstacle of almost infinite ramifications: what I would like to call our 'physical sciences thinking'. It is probably apparent that communication theorists and researchers, like those in many other of the normative fields of inquiry, struggle (or frolic) under the yoke of scientism. (Let me quickly add parenthetically here, however, that it is perhaps equally apparent that so much that passes for communication theory and research suffers from an opposite kind of burden — that of intuitivism or 'anectodalism'.) But by 'physical sciences thinking' (which, incidentally, is much less prevalent in the physical sciences today than in the so-called behavioral sciences), by 'physical sciences thinking' I wish to refer to more than just an insidious scientism or an equally insidious normativism or philosophism. By 'physical sciences thinking' I want to refer to a basic mode of thinking which seems to permeate our conceptual stances vis-à-vis our phenomena at metatheoretical levels — at the very foundations of our orientations to our task.

'Physical sciences thinking' is at best an amorphous notion. But as a style or mode of thinking which pervades the literature, it is itself as amorphous as it is pervasive. Perhaps some specification of its inadequacies for the task of conceptualizing the processes of human communication will serve to characterize this barrier to theory-building in the field.

A. The probabilistic approaches of modern science are inappropriate for conceptualizing human communication phenomena. Human communication is time and place (and other dimensions) specific, and is not situationally replicable.[4] Most of our 'models' of the human communication process are heavily imbued with this sort of physical sciences thinking — inadequate and disadvantageous as it is to our task. If I leap from behind a tree and seize a pretty girl and mutter "I love you!" she will undoubtedly take me for a clown or a nut. But, if a young fellow has designs, and the young lady has mutual designs, then after the appropriate number of dates,

---

[4] For a crystallization of this dimension of our 'physical sciences thinking', I am indebted to Jurgen Ruesch, in a personal letter.

with a little moonlight and a little music, that grandaddy of all clichés works like magic. Now what caused what? Which is the 'independent variable' my psychologist friends are so fond of? What are the PROBABILITIES that THAT stimulus (whatever the other demographic or countable variables) would produce THAT response? From the impetus of 'physical sciences thinking', we seek those "If A, then B" relationships. In following this causal approach, we often fail to exercise that which we have gained empirically — perhaps in part because much of our empirical data is not easily reduced scientistically. In human communication, as today for much of the frontier of the physical sciences, the variables are patently systemic as well as demographic, are emergent as well as *a priori*, idiographic as well as nomothetic.

B. Another example of our vicitimization by our 'physical sciences thinking': we've travelled — and still seem to be travelling — a tortuous (and unnecessary) path in our attempts to account for the NECESSARY and the SUFFICIENT conditions of the phenomena with which we are concerned. Like our psychologist colleagues — who have had literally to outlive the stranglehold of S→R (and even S→O→R) METATHEORIES — we will likely have to outlive a succession of indefensible and downright disadvantageous 'models' of our phenomena, beginning with the message as sufficient condition, then through a second-generation of models in which the receiver is the sufficient condition, and so on. None of the 'push-pull' models take account of the SELF-ORGANIZING aspects of the organism, of interpersonal encounters, or of organizations. To be more than academically useful, to be viable, our theories are going to have to accomodate such obvious conditions of the processes we want to understand and explain.

C. Too, our underlying 'physical sciences' orientations seem to facilitate our emphasis on the 'countable' dimensions of our phenomena — senders and receivers, messages, words, repetitions, sense modalities, 'noise' and 'feedback', etc. — to the exclusion of our attention to some of the 'uncountable' aspects [5] of those same phenomena — such as intention, mutuality, "naming" and "knowing", competence, and so on.[6]

As one consequence of our allegiance to our implicit 'physical sciences' orientations, we languish conceptually (and hence theoretically) under the onus of a monstrous illusion. It's almost as if we were to build an engine which runs on gasoline, and then stood in amazement at this phenomenon of the running engine before falling to work feverishly on a massive research effort to determine how the gasoline 'communicates' to the engine. In the same way, we systematically build into each other more or less 'appropriate' reactions to our messages, and then set about studying those 'messages' to determine how it is that they (a) cause, or (b) don't

---

[5] For a delightful explication of the moral, "Not everything that can be counted counts", William Bruce Cameron, *Informal Sociology* (New York, Random House, 1963).
[6] A further treatment of this problem will appear in my paper "On Intention, Mutuality, and Competence in Human Communication" (in preparation).

cause, the 'appropriate' responses! In the former instance, if they work, we point
to the 'message' as the sufficient cause of another's appropriate response; in the
latter, if they don't, to his stupidity or obstinancy. Success in the first instance may
in fact have been in spite of my utterances, in the same way that my failure in the
latter instance may have been in spite of my utterances.

Our 'physical sciences thinking' sets us to looking at the world and to explaining
it according to the inadequate physical sciences analogies and models we have in
our conceptual sleuthing kits. And that very mode of thinking obfuscates and per-
petuates the grand illusion.

It would be impossible to circumscribe all of the implications of this pathology
of our thinking. But perhaps this brief characterization of this fundamental flaw in
our thinking will pique the reader's imagination.

THIRD, lest I seem to be unduly prejudiced in the degree of exception I have taken
to the physical sciences thinking implicit in much of the communication literature,
let us consider an opposite sort of obstacle to theory-building in communication.
I believe our conceptual approaches to human communication phenomena are
unjustifiably mentalistic, unrealistically conscious-istic, unnecessarily symbolic, and
awkwardly teleological. We don't take adequate account of the empirical data we
do have; e.g., most of what goes on intraorganismically when communication occurs
is essentially programmatic — that is, occurs outside of psychological (as such)
intervention or control. While one may view either inputting or outputting as serving
one of two broad purposes — instrumental or consummatory — he is still stuck
with the fact that WHAT'S POSSIBLE for the organism is incipiently programmed into
it in the form of its over-all organization and in the form or organization of currently
activated subsystems that serve as immediate bases for both its information and
energy processing. It is likely that internal behavioral 'control' is both similar to
and different from the sort of thinking the cyberneticist engages in when he plies
his trade in man/machine systems.

Space does not permit a complete development of the implications of this potential
fault in our thinking about communication. But we need to accomodate the fact
that most human behavior — considering both its complexity and its magnitude —
are automatistic. MOST of what we do is simply not 'mentalizing' as such. Most of
our behavior is nonconscious. Our internal behavior and our transactions with others
is not necessarily symbolic. And our 'communication' behavior may have as purpose
no more than our capacity to do it. If we limit 'communication' behavior by these
exceedingly restrictive and causal criteria, we thereby exclude from our models a
broad range of human behavior that might be essential for providing the kinds of
insights into the processes of communication we need in order to develop a more
viable and comprehending theory.

One consequence of these arbitrary exclusions is our disinclination to look upon
language, writing, words, speech, documents, etc., as part of our technology of
communication. Because we have disenfranchised some of the essential behavioral

functions in our models we end up by reifying our instruments to make the whole process go, to give it a mechanism.

Similarly, we are easily duped, by these and other inadequate and inappropriate parameters of our models, into confusing prose or speech with communication, confusing the word for the thing (e.g., confusing the word 'communication' with an as-yet-unspecified event of the world), confusing agreement with effectiveness, equating communication with meaning, and so on.

FOURTH, and in a somewhat related way, our theorizing languishes for want of an adequate cross-disciplinary language with which to conceive and structure our phenomena. We suffer no dearth of terms coined for special occasions; these occasional words envelop us like quicksand. We choke on our verbal coin and risk asphyxiation at the hands of the word merchants of every discipline. We don't lack words. Our lack of an appropriate, an adequate, language is our lack of a taxonomy for fixing those aspects of our phenomena we want to think about and manipulate in our 'laboratories'. Relating the elements of our phenomena in the way of theory- or model-building before we have agreed upon those elements is undeniably standard practice in the field. But that exercise reveals the vast and unconscionable immaturity of our theories. While ambiguity is the rich soil from which the hard grain of theory must evolve, there comes a time when one reaches for his own conceptual boot straps to pull himself up out of the muck of his own thinking. Difficult as forging a common language — a taxonomy — may be, without it we are destined to continue on in conceptual confusion.

The structuralists and the harbingers of scientism, along with the anecdotalists, have long dominated the literature. As one consequence, we have failed to discriminate the several possible FUNCTIONS of human communication. Thus we are faced on the one side with part-theories as a result of the disciplinary compartmentalization of knowledge, and on the other by gross, structural models within the field of communication itself which may be obstructing the development of those part-theories that would indeed be advantageous to our theoretical growth and maturity.

If we had a common language, if we could learn to talk with each other more productively, these obstacles would likely vanish. But I don't see any evidence yet that there has been even any tacit agreement as to what our shibboleth itself — 'communication' — is supposed to refer to. We seem to have a 'communication problem' of our own.

It is possible that these are the sorts of obstacles to theory-building in communication which would fade from consideration if the diverse and far-flung interests in human communication were brought together within a single scientific discipline. There are increasingly more of those activities here and abroad which — intentionally or unintentionally — would hasten the emergence of COMMUNICATION as a discipline in its own right. Even so, there is a bit of the old chicken-and-egg dilemma here. It is not so much which IS to come first, but which MUST come first. Without a clearly circumscribed discipline, conceptual difficulties such as those I've described here are likely inevitable. Yet, unless these inadequacies of approach are overcome, the emergence of COMMUNICATION as a discipline is far from inevitable — and, perhaps, short of possible.

There is no single, nicely-bounded theoretical heritage to which human communication scholars may turn. They must dip into some part of a score of disciplines for relevant data. And the present conceptual confluence of systems theory, information theory, cybernetics, general semantics, and the so-called 'third force' in psychology has spotlighted the communication scholar — and has thus cast into deep relief the fallacies of his traditional thinking.

One should not challenge without encouraging. Science evolves of its own laws, perhaps. It has frequently been observed that while the most complex problems of a man are also those of greatest relevance to him, they will be the last to be systematically or scientifically comprehended. If this be true, then surely the development of viable and comprehensive theories of human communication will be among the ultimate achievements of man's understanding of his world.

So perhaps I lean too heavily. Even so, if one has some place to go, he serves himself ill if his faulty thinking precludes his getting there expediently.

UNIVERSITY OF MISSOURI AT KANSAS CITY

DEAN C. BARNLUND

A TRANSACTIONAL MODEL OF COMMUNICATION

Men have advanced from myth-making to mathematical equation in search of better ways of communicating their understanding of physical and social realities. For centuries investigators were content to rely upon ordinary language as a means of conceptualizing their hunches about reality. Not long ago the physical scientists became disenchanted with words as a vehicle for thought and turned to the language of mathematics; today, behavioral scientists reflect the same dissatisfaction and search for more suitable symbol systems for coping with their emerging problems.

The reason for this widespread discontent is not difficult to locate. Any hypothetical statement in sentence form must fit the categories of language and obey the rules of grammar. This is no handicap as long as the investigator deals with situations in which the elements are discrete and more or less constant, or where their influence upon each other is a linear or additive one. Descriptive statements about such events can be a reliable way of postulating what is known, for language is a splendid instrument for handling stable elements and sequential or additive relationships.

There is serious doubt, however, whether or not the simplistic explanations demanded by language serve the ends of research sufficiently well if more dynamic forces and more complicated relationships are involved. This seems to be the case today. Both the problems that interest the behavioral scientist, as well as the perspective from which they are attacked, have changed radically. According to Peter Drucker there has been a quiet revolution in scientific thought during the past few decades. "An intelligent and well educated man of the first 'modern' generation — that of Newton, Hobbes, and Locke — might still have been able to understand and make himself understood up to World War II. But it is unlikely that he could still communicate with the world of today, only fifteen years later."[1] The contemporary scientific world has quietly replaced the two related premises of the Cartesian, or mechanistic, view of the universe — that the whole is the sum of its parts and causality the ONLY unifying order — with a world view that emphasizes process. This has brought about a theoretical revolution of such proportion that "virtually

[1] Peter F. Drucker, "The New Philosophy Comes to Life", *Harper's Magazine* (August, 1957), p. 36.

every one of our disciplines now relies on conceptions which are incompatible with the Cartesian axiom, and the world view we once derived from it".[2] Appeals for fresh approaches to the problems of matter, life and mind are no longer the exception in scientific journals.[3]

One evidence of the changing perspective is seen in the new vocabulary of science. To convey their discoveries biologists resort to neologisms like ecology and homeostasis; psychologists analyze human personality in terms of drives and syndromes; rhetoricians find themselves talking about communication and meaning. All are terms that reject an atomistic or elementalistic approach in favor of a systemic or holistic one.

> It is the whole of speech, including not only the words left unsaid but the whole atmosphere in which words are said and heard, that 'communicates'. One must not only know the whole of the 'message', one must also be able to relate it to the pattern of behavior, personality, situation, and even culture with which it is surrounded.[4]

Another sign of the search for new modes of attack on the problems of matter and mind can be found in experimentation with other modes of conceptualization. One of these innovations is the scientific model. As a theoretical tool the model is not an entirely unique instrument in that many theoretical statements can be translated into models, and some models, in turn, may be restated as theories. Yet, while admitting this, the scientific model remains one of the more promising ways of treating the complexities of human behavior and a method of representing its inner dynamics that deserves careful study.

THE NATURE OF MODELS

A model is an attempt to recreate in physical or symbolic form the relationships alleged to exist among the objects or forces being investigated. It may consist of a complex arrangement of wires and relays built by a neurologist to reproduce the reflex loops of the nervous system, or an elaborate structure of sticks and wooden balls arranged by a chemist to duplicate the DNA molecule. Although models are as diverse as the questions men phrase in their search for knowledge, they can be classified broadly as to purpose and material.

Structural models are designed to show the formal properties of any event or object. They serve to identify the number, size and arrangement of the discrete parts of a system. A miniature solar system, charts indicating levels of management, diagrams of the components of an electronic computer illustrate the formal model.

---

[2] *Ibid.*, p. 37.
[3] See L. L. Whyte, *Accent on Form* (New York, Harper, 1954) and J. F. T. Bugental, "Humanistic Psychology: A New Break-Through", *American Psychologist* (September, 1963).
[4] Drucker, *op. cit.*

In other cases the model is designed to replicate function. The designer attempts to represent the forces that comprise the system and establish the direction, volatility, and relation of their influence. Functionally isomorphic models need not resemble the event they simulate, but they must operate in essentially faithful ways. Walter's 'tortoise' and Ashby's 'homeostat' do not look like the cerebral cortex, but each duplicates some important function of the human brain.

Models also differ in the material of which they are made. Some are built of wood or steel or papier-mâché, and are constructed so that they can be manipulated or dismantled according to the whim of the investigator. Tangible models include prototypes of the human skeleton, replicas of assembly lines, clay mock-ups of new pieces of equipment. Models may also be symbolic in character, consisting only of lines or shapes on a piece of paper. Lewin's vector drawings and Korzybski's structural differential are examples of symbolic models.

Our interest lies in the symbolic rather than physical model, and with the functional rather than structural model. It may become possible for future investigators to create mathematical models of human communication rivalling those of the physical scientists, but in the absence of sufficiently discrete variables and with current complications in measurement of these variables, this hope seems premature. The diagrammatic model seems best suited to accomodating our current level of knowledge about communication and, at the same time, providing an improved mode of conceptualizing over that secured through verbal statements alone.

VALUES AND LIMITATIONS

Several features of the diagrammatic model recommend it as a means of 'picturing' the communication process. The complexity of communication has long been regarded as the major impediment to the study of human speech. Yet this obstacle may be unduly exaggerated, with much of the pessimism deriving from an outmoded strategy. When social scientists try to isolate and order all of the elements of a complex event — that is, when they approach such a system analytically — the results are often unmanageable. As Ashby has observed, "If we take such a system to pieces, we find we cannot reassemble it!"[5] The temptation, then, is to junk the whole idea and fall back upon over-simplified aphorisms and maxims. We may, as Grey Walter suggests, be able to do better than that.

The number of observed facts is the exponent of the number of possible hypotheses to relate them. When there are few facts and many impossible connections the subject may be understood without great difficulty, but when there are many facts from diverse sources and nothing can be assumed impossible special tactics must be used to permit an ordinary mind to see the wood rather than the trees. Perhaps the simplest and most agreeable device

[5] W. Ross Ashby, "The Effects of Experience on a Determinate Dynamic System", *Behavioral Science* (January, 1956), p. 36.

in such a situation is to construct models, on paper or on metal, in order to reproduce the main features of the system under observation.[6]

One advantage of the model, then, is the ease with which it handles a multitude of variables and relates their effects upon each other in highly complicated ways, thus preserving the integrity of events under study.

To this must be added the heuristic or clarifying advantage of the model. The designer of a model is forced to identify variables and relate them with a precision that is impossible for the writer to achieve because of the stylistic demands of effective writing. A diagram or formula can portray at a single glance, and with great transparency, the assumptions and properties of a new theoretical position, thus stimulating the study of alternative approaches.[7]

Closely associated with the clarity of the symbolic model is its critical vulnerability. It simplifies the job of the critic who needs to identify innovation, who must discover the strengths, ambiguities and omissions of new conceptual positions. More models of human behavior might be produced if models were not so critically vulnerable for even the architect cannot overlook the deficiencies of his own model. This, of course, is precisely what recommends it as a means of theoretical communication.

Not to be overlooked in these days of editorial compression is the compact nature of a model. Short of a mathematical equation, it is the most cryptic form in which a theoretical position can be communicated. While verbal description must supplement most models, once understood, the model is usually sufficient in itself to serve as a framework for empirical or experimental research.

Yet a model is no more than an analogy. As such it is subject to all the risks as well as opportunities latent in any comparison. Factors that appear in real life may be overlooked or distorted in the model. The relationships claimed may not parallel the dynamics of the observed event. The model may be oversimplified or overelaborated; both errors can be contained within the same model. Some model makers are carried away by what are essentially esthetic, rather than empirical, considerations. And there is always the danger of becoming so entranced with the construction of models that the arduous search for new and irreconcilable data is neglected. In short, no model can rise above the empirical data and theoretical assumptions on which it rests.[8]

The construction of any model proceeds in a circuitous way. One postulates what one can verbally, then translates these assumptions into diagrammatic form. This, in turn, reveals omissions and distortions that must be eliminated by modifying assumptions, making further changes in the drawings, and so on. The following

[6] Grey Walter, "Theoretical Properties of Diffuse Projection Systems in Relation to Behaviour and Consciousness", in E. D. Adrian (Ed.), *Brain Mechanisms and Consciousness* (Thomas, 1954), p. 367.
[7] Considerable light is thrown upon communication theories of the past by making this sort of translation from text to model although a critical review of traditional theories of communication is beyond the limits of this paper.
[8] See Alphonse Chapanis, "Men, Machines, and Models", *American Psychologist* (March, 1961).

postulates, constituting the theoretical foundation of the proposed models can be derived from them, but it may be helpful to state them verbally and see to what extent they are realized within the diagrams that follow.

COMMUNICATION POSTULATES[9]

COMMUNICATION DESCRIBES THE EVOLUTION OF MEANING. While we are born into and inhabit a world without meaning, we rapidly invest it with significance and order. That life becomes intelligible to us — full of beauty or ugliness, hope or despair — is because it is assigned that significance by the experiencing being. Sensations do not come to us all sorted and labeled, as if we were visitors in a vast but ordered museum. Each, instead, is his own curator. We learn to look with a selective eye, to classify, to assign significance.

The word 'communication' stands for those acts in which meaning develops within human beings as neuro-motor responses are acquired or modified. It arises out of the need to reduce uncertainty, to act effectively, to defend or strengthen the ego. Its aim is to increase the number and consistency of meanings within the limits set by attitude and action patterns that have proven successful in the past, emerging needs and drives, and the demands of the physical and social setting of the moment. It is not a reaction to something, nor an interaction with something, but a transaction in which man invents and attributes meanings to realize his purposes.[10] It should be stressed that meaning is something 'invented', 'assigned', 'given', rather than something 'received'. The highly idiosyncratic character of our meanings is richly documented in studies of perception, particularly in the interpretation of projective tests. Flags, crowns, crosses and traffic signals do not contain meanings; they have meanings thrust upon them.[11] Our physical and social environment, including the messages to which we attend, can be regarded only as placing some sort of upper limit upon the number and diversity of meanings we invent.

It is clear that communication, in this sense, occurs in a variety of settings traditionally neglected by students of communication. Meanings may be generated while a man stands alone on a mountain trail or sits in the privacy of his study speculating about some internal doubt. Meanings are invented also in countless social situations in which men talk with those who share or dispute their purposes. But no matter

---

[9] Some of the material in this section is drawn from an earlier paper. See Dean C. Barnlund, "Toward a Meaning-Centered Philosophy of Communication", *Journal of Communication* (December, 1962).

[10] The most recent writing on transactional psychology is found in Franklin Kilpatrick (Ed.), *Explorations in Transactional Psychology* (New York University Press, 1961).

[11] This may explain why information theory which has so much to contribute to the study of message transmission has so little relevance for the study of meaning. The analysis of message 'bits' neglects the semantic import of the message units which must be the target of the communicologist.

what the context, it is the production of meaning, rather than the production of messages that identifies communication.

COMMUNICATION IS DYNAMIC. The tendency to treat communication as a thing, a static entity, rather than a dynamic process occurring within the interpreter, seems to be an assumptive error of long standing and one that has seriously hampered the investigation of human communication. As Walter Coutu has stated so succinctly, "Since meaning is not an entity, it has no locus; it is something that occurs rather than exists... Despite our Aristotelian thought forms, nothing in the universe 'has' meaning, but anything may become a stimulus to evoke meaning by way of inducing the percipient to give self instructions on how to behave in relation to it."[12]

Both entity and process are circumstantial, that is, contingent upon the surrounding milieu, but an entity is at the mercy of external conditions while a process changes from moment to moment according to its own internal law or principle. The latter condition, according to Kenneth Boulding, clearly characterizes man as a communicator. "The accumulation of knowledge is not merely the difference between messages taken in and messages given out. It is not like a reservoir; it is rather an organization which grows through an active internal organizing principle much as the gene is a principle or entity organizing the growth of bodily structure."[13] This 'internal organizing principle' in the case of man is commonly referred to as abstracting, a capacity or potentiality shared with all living organisms.

The process of abstracting is set in motion by a perceptual discrimination of some sort, the detecting of a difference between ourselves and others, between figure and ground, between phenomena that are similar or contiguous. It is carried on by focusing attention on arbitrarily selected cues, by grouping and assigning potency to these cues, and by linking them with the whole array of past experience. Although some aspects of perceptual set are currently understood, the dynamics of the internal manipulation of cues and the attribution of meaning to them is still largely unfathomed.

COMMUNICATION IS CONTINUOUS. Communication with the physical world, or with other human beings, is not a thing, nor even a discrete act, but a continuing condition of life, a process that ebbs and flows with changes in the environment and fluctuations in our needs. "It is only the imperfection of the fit, the difference between organism and environment, coupled with the perpetual tendency to improve the fit, that allows the working parts to work and makes them continue to work."[14]

This process has no beginning nor end, even in sleep or under conditions of sensory deprivation, for man is a homeostatic rather than static mechanism.

[12] Walter Coutu, "An Operational Definition of Meaning", *Quarterly Journal of Speech* (February, 1962), p. 64.
[13] Kenneth Boulding, *The Image* (Ann Arbor, University of Michigan Press, 1961), p. 18.
[14] Whyte, *op. cit.*, p. 120.

The brain works as naturally as the kidneys and the bloodvessels. It is not dormant just because there is no conscious purpose to be served at the moment. If it were, indeed, a vast and intricate telephone exchange, then it should be quiescent when the rest of the organism sleeps... Instead of that, it goes right on manufacturing ideas — streams and deluges of ideas, that the sleeper is not using to THINK with about anything. But the brain is following its own law; it is actively translating experiences into symbols, in fulfillment of a basic need to do so. It carries on a constant process of ideation.[15]

The dynamic equilibrium of a mobile by Alexander Calder, in which the movement of each pendant upsets the balance among all the others until a new equilibrium is achieved, is an artistic expression of the 'internal organizing principle' of which Boulding writes. Each new meaning derived from communication is both relieving and disturbing to man, leading to a ceaseless search for new ways of coping with our surroundings. Only in the organically deficient or the functionally disturbed, where rigidities in perceiving and abstracting are extreme, is this process retarded or temporarily arrested.[16] For most, communication begins at birth or before and continues without serious interruption until death.

COMMUNICATION IS CIRCULAR. Defining communication as a continuous process of evolving meanings leaves the communicologist in the position of facing an altogether new problem with an outmoded vocabulary and strategy. The usual starting point in the analysis of any communicative act is to identify the critical elements. Normally this leads to categorization of a 'sender', a 'message', and a 'receiver'. Having defined the problem in structural terms, the investigator is then obliged to continue his analysis within the framework of this assumption. It is obvious, largely because grammar suggests it, that the elements must fall into some sort of pattern: A, then B, then C. It is not long before the conclusion is drawn that these entities not only occur in sequence, but that they are causally related. A sender causes, by means of a message, certain effects in a receiver. Communication originates with the speaker, it terminates in a listener.[17]

No matter how appealing this may appear in its clarity and simplicity, it generates more problems than it solves. A structural approach, with its static elements and terminal implications, does not fit a process like communication. "There is", according to Arthur Clarke, "no demarcation of a boundary between the parts in a com-

---

[15] Susanne Langer, *Philosophy in a New Key* (Mentor, 1942), p. 33.

[16] The tendency to talk about abstracting in static rather than dynamic terms is found even in some psychiatric literature where traumas are sometimes regarded as psychological injuries with a well-defined locus in childhood. It seems plausible that many perfectly ordinary events actually become traumatized by continual abstraction of these episodes in a nervous system with narrow or illusory assumptions until the original event becomes so shocking in its meaning that it can no longer be admitted to consciousness. Indeed, if experiences did not continue to be processed in the nervous system, there would be no possibility of cure for the disturbed individual.

[17] Recently, through the influence of writings in cybernetics, another causal link, the reverse of the above, has been added to include the feedback of information in the opposite direction. This addition, while compensating for some of the naïveté of the earlier explanation, has not produced a radical change in the mode of analysis employed in studying human interaction.

munication process."[18] To erect such 'lines of demarcation' cannot help but obscure the circular character of communication.[19]

New conceptual opportunities may arise if functional terms, such as sending and receiving — or better, encoding and decoding — are substituted for the former labels. It is clear, then, that these are operations and that, as such, they may assume a variety of patterns: symbolizing and interpreting may go on in a single person when he is alone; meanings may develop in two or more communicants simultaneously; messages, in the absence of either a source or receiver, may generate effects; meanings continue to flourish or deteriorate long after they are initiated, and so on.[20] There is a temptation to borrow the term 'transceiver' from the engineers for it summarizes the way encoding and decoding functions may be accomodated within a single organism. Communication seems more accurately described as a circular process in which the words 'sender' and 'receiver', when they have to be used at all, serve only to fix the point of view of the analyst who uses them.[21]

A structural approach seems ill-adapted to handling the internal dynamics of this complex process. If the actual variables were discrete and independent of one another, complexity in their relations would not be a deterrent, for the functional formula, $Y = f(a, b, c...)$, is available for handling such data. But if one has to cope with variables that are not only unstable, but that are interdependent as well, new modes of analysis are needed. Linear causality, with its sharp demarcation of independent and dependent variables, no longer gives sensible structure to observation.

We now merely note that methodologically the complexity that is added by reciprocal control may be denoted by the loss of a clear separation between independent and dependent variables. Each subject's behavior is at the same time a response to a past behavior of the other and a stimulus to a future behavior of the other; each behavior is in part dependent variable and in part independent variable; in no clear sense is it properly either of them.[22]

When signals must be treated simultaneously as both cause and effect, or where the communicative variables have reciprocating influences, a change in approach is necessary. A kind of 'interdependent functionalism' might be proposed by tampering with the functional formula so that each variable becomes a function of all other variables. For example, $Y = f[a = f(b, c...), b = f(a, c...), c = f(a, b...)]$. But

---

[18] Arthur Clarke, "Messages from the Invisible Universe", *New York Times Magazine* (November 30, 1958), p. 34.

[19] Structural terminology is not outmoded, of course, when structural aspects of communication are studied. The earlier terminology would seem to continue to be of value in research on public address where there is considerable stability in the roles of speaker and audience.

[20] See John Newman, "Communication: A Dyadic Postulation", *Journal of Communication* (June, 1959).

[21] A striking parallel is found in research on leadership in face-to-face groups. As long as investigators phrased their problems in terms of leaders and followers, that is in terms of persons, little progress was made during several decades of research. As soon as leadership was defined operationally, in terms of functions, important advances were made at once in describing various patterns of influence.

[22] John Thibaut and Harold Kelley, *The Social Psychology of Groups* (Wiley, 1959), p. 2.

the statistical complications associated with such an elaboration of the formula when combined with the difficulties in measuring communication variables underscore the need for alternative approaches. Diagrammatic rendering of the interdependence and circularity of encoding and decoding processes may constitute such an alternative.

COMMUNICATION IS UNREPEATABLE. The distinction being suggested here is between systems that are deterministic and mechanical, and those that are spontaneous and discretionary. In the former, the output of the system can be predicted as soon as the input is identified for the system obeys a rigid logic that was built into it and which it is incapable of revising in its own interests. The system operates with minimal degrees of freedom. Repeat the input conditions and obtain identity of output. In an information handling system of this type one can speak of the 'same message' producing the 'same effect' for the system does not have autonomous control of its own programming.

In the case of spontaneous systems, one that more accurately fits the communication of men, the system is governed by internal organizing principles which are themselves subject to change. There are substantial degrees of freedom which give the system a certain element of caprice, otherwise circularity would imply repeatability. In a spontaneous organism it is dangerous to assume that identical inputs will lead to the same output because the system has some control over its own internal design. One may start an engine over and over again, or return to the same office repeatedly. But one cannot expect the same message to generate identical meanings for all men, or even for a single man on different occasions. The words of a message, even when faithfully repeated upon request, may provoke new insight, increase hostility, or generate boredom.

This is not to say that man never behaves in the same way on separate occasions. Carried to an extreme the principle of unrepeatability would require totally erratic responses. This, in turn, would make a science of man virtually impossible. People do display consistency in behavior; the degree of the consistency reflects the rigidity of the assumptions required by the personality to maintain itself in encounters with reality. But, while behavior patterns may reappear from time to time, normally they do not repeat themselves precisely, nor are they triggered by identical environmental cues. Perhaps more central to developing a science of 'healthy human behavior' is the recognition that modification rather than repeatability is inherent in the human organism and that the exploitation of this capacity of the personality may be an important measure of its performance.

COMMUNICATION IS IRREVERSIBLE. Even in those systems that are autonomous there is the question of direction. Some processes are not only repeatable, but reversible as well. Heat will convert a block of ice into water, and finally into steam; a drop in temperature will liquefy the gas, and return it to a solid state. Transposing the terminals on a storage battery can reverse the direction of chemical changes within. Reversible systems can return to earlier states by simply retracing the steps by which they reached their present condition. A number of bodily functions such as breathing involve reversible processes.

Some systems, however, can only go forward from one state to another, from one equilibrium to a new equilibrium, never returning to their original state. "The basic cycles of nutrition, waking, and sleeping, and work and play must be maintained but they should be complemented by an adequate degree of one-way processes: of growth, reproduction, learning, and constructive or creative activities. With every breath, in and out, we grow older, but this can be complemented by a small residue of cumulative achievement."[23] One can speak of the human skeleton as evolving from infancy to adulthood without the possibility of returning to earlier developmental stages. The same holds for human experiences. Our communication with ourselves and the world about us flows forward inexorably. Recent investigations of psychical phenomena through neurosurgery seem to bear this out.

Let me describe what seems to happen by means of a parable: Among millions and millions of nerve cells that clothe certain parts of the temporal lobes on each side, there runs a thread. It is the thread of time, the thread that runs through each succeeding wakeful hour of the individual's past life... Time's strip of film runs forward, never backward, even when resurrected from the past. It seems to proceed again at time's own unchanged pace.[24]

Here a figurative phrase, the 'stream of consciousness', attains literal truth. Human experience flows, as a stream, in a single direction leaving behind it a permanent record of man's communicative experience. Interruptions may mar the record as in the case of amnesia, or injury reduce its efficiency as in aphasia, but there is no 'going back'. One cannot start a man thinking, damage his self-respect or threaten his security, and then erase the effects and 'begin again'.

COMMUNICATION IS COMPLEX. Enough has already been said to suggest the complexity of human communication. If any doubt remains after considering the continuous, interdependent, irreversible and sometimes elusive functions of encoding and decoding, one has only to add the vast array of communicative purposes, social settings, and message forms at the disposal of any communicant. There is communication with self, with the physical environment; there is communication with others in face-to-face, organizational and societal contexts. The drives that require communication for their fulfillment stretch all the way from overcoming physical and psychological isolation through the resolution of differences, to catharsis and personality reorganization. In addition, the evolution of meaning is a process that goes forward at many levels of the personality, sometimes conscious, other times preconscious or subconscious; there are even channels of 'crosstalk' linking these levels that still baffle and elude us. It is a rare message that does not contain both manifest and latent meanings, that does not illumine internal states as well as external realities.

---

[23] Whyte, *op. cit.*, p. 117.
[24] Wilder Penfield, "The Permanent Record of the Stream of Consciousness", *Proceedings of the 14th International Congress of Psychology* (June, 1954), pp. 67-68.

And the verbal symbols of a message are often played off against a backdrop of significant gestures and nonverbal accompaniments that may contradict, elaborate, obscure or reinforce then. The study of man's communication with self and others seems both complicated and, at the same time, central to the full appreciation of what it is to be a man.[25]

A PILOT MODEL

A pilot study is an 'experimental experiment' in which an investigator attempts a gross manipulation of his variables to determine the feasibility of his study, clarify his assumptions and refine his measuring instruments. The drawings that follow are 'pilot models' in the same spirit for they are preliminary experiments in diagramming self-to-environment, self-to-self and self-to-other communication.

Intra-Personal Communication

It may help to explain the diagrams that follow if the abstract elements and relations in the models are given concrete illustration by using a hypothetical case. Let us assume a simple communicative setting. In Figure 1, a person (P_1), let us say a Mr. A, sits alone in the reception room of a clinic waiting to see his doctor. As a communication system Mr. A decodes (D), or assigns meaning to the various cues available in his perceptual field by transforming sensory discriminations into neuro-muscular sets (E) so that they are manifest to others in the form of verbal and nonverbal cues. Evidence is not available which will permit us to establish if encoding and decoding are separate functions of the organism, successive phases of a single on-going process, or the same operation viewed from opposite ends of the system, but it is reasonable to assume until we have solid proof that they are closely articulated and interdependent processes. The spiral line connecting encoding and decoding processes is used to give diagrammatic representation to the continuous, unrepeatable and irreversible nature of communication that was postulated earlier.

The meanings presented in Mr. A at any given moment will be a result of his alertness to, and detection of, objects and circumstances in his environment. The lines terminating in arrows on Figure 1 can be used to indicate either the different stimuli that come into focus as Mr. A's attention shifts from moment to moment,

---

[25] Man has been variously described as a symbolizer, abstracter, culture-creator, time-binder, and communicator. More recently system theorists, reflecting current interests in cybernetics and information theory, have characterized him as an 'open system'. The parallel between the communication postulates above and the criteria for identifying open systems is striking. Allport specifies that in such systems there is "intake and output of matter and energy, achievement and maintenance of homeostatic states", an "increase in complexity and differentiation of parts", and "there is more than mere intake and output of matter and energy; there is extensive transactional commerce with the environment". Gordon Allport, "The Open System in Personality Theory", *Journal of Abnormal and Social Psychology* (Volume 61, 1960), pp. 303-306.

or that a single 'experience' may be a mosaic of many simultaneous perceptions. The direction of the arrows illustrates the postulate that meaning will be assigned to, rather than received from, the objects admitted to perception.

There are at least three sets of signs — or cues — to which Mr. A may attribute meaning in this setting.[26] Any of them may trigger interpretations or reactions of one kind or another. One set of cues derives from the environment itself. These cues are identified in Figure 1 as public cues (C_{PU}). To qualify as a public cue any object or sound or circumstance must fulfill two criteria. First, it must be a part of, or available to, the perceptual field of all potential communicants. Second, it must have been created prior to the event under analysis and must remain outside the control of the persons under observation. Two types of public cues can be distinguished. Natural cues, those supplied by the physical world without the intervention of man, include atmospheric conditions of temperature and humidity, the visual and tactual properties of minerals, the color and forms of vegetable life and climatic crises such as hurricanes and rainstorms. Artificial cues, those resulting from man's modification and manipulation of his environment, include the effects created by the processing and arranging of wood, steel and glass, the weaving and patterning of clothing, the control of climate through air or sound conditioning.

As Mr. A glances about the office he may be aware of the arrangement of furniture, a worn carpet, a framed reproduction of a Miro painting, a slightly antiseptic odor, an end table covered with magazines. To any of them he may attach significances altering his attitude toward his doctor or himself. In some instances the cues may be authored and edited by a number of persons. The painting, for example, is a message from Joan Miro, its framing a message from the decorator, its choice and location a message from the doctor. All these cues are available potentially to anyone who enters the reception room. The perception of any specific cue, or the meaning assigned to it, however, will be similar for various people only to the extent that they possess the same sensory acuity, overlapping fields of perception, parallel background experiences, and similar needs or purposes.

A second set of cues consists of those elements or events that are essentially private in nature, that come from sources not automatically available to any other person who enters a communicative field. Private cues might include the sounds heard through a pair of earphones, the sights visible through opera glasses, or the vast array of cues that have their origin in the taste buds or viscera of the interpreter. In the case of Mr. A, the private cues (C_{PR}) might include the words and pictures he finds as he riffles through a magazine, the *pot pourri* of objects he finds in his pocket, or a sudden twitch of pain he notices in his chest. Public and private cues may be verbal or nonverbal in form but the critical quality they share is that they were brought into existence and remain beyond the control of the communicants.

Although no one else has yet entered the communicative field, Mr. A has to

---

[26] The more generic term of cues has been adopted to avoid some of the difficulties that attend the sign-symbol distinction.

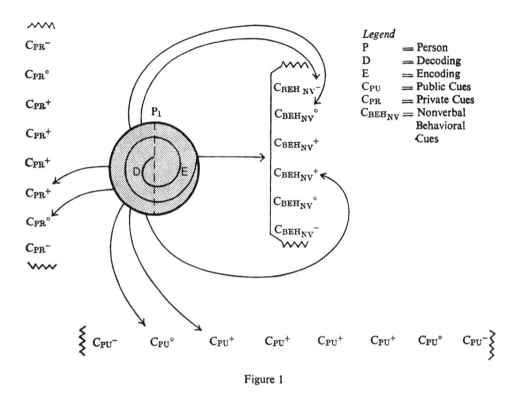

Figure 1

contend with one additional set of cues. These, however, are generated by, and are substantially under the control of, Mr. A himself. They consist of the observations he makes of himself as he turns the pages of his magazine, sees himself reflected in the miror, or changes position in his chair. The articulation and movement of his body are as much a part of his phenomenological field as any other cue provided by the environment.[27] Indeed if this were not true he would be incapable of coordinated acts. To turn a page requires the assessment of dozens of subtle muscular changes. These cues are identified in Figure 1 as behavioral, nonverbal cues ($C_{BEH_{NV}}$). They comprise the deliberate acts of Mr. A in straightening his tie or picking up a magazine as well as his unconscious mannerisms in holding a cigarette or slouching in his chair. They differ from public cues in that they are initiated or controlled by

---

[27]   While this sort of intra-personal communication is usually identified as feedback, the connotation of this term may be unfortunate when applied loosely to human communication for it suggests a sender-receiver dualism where there may be none, and implies that a person receives information about his performance from his environment. Actions, however, are incapable of sending meanings back to the source. The individual acts and as he acts observes AND interprets his own behavior. As long as this is understood the term need not cause difficulty but this does not always seem to be the case in the literature on communication.

the communicant himself. When public or private cues are assigned meaning, Mr. A is free to interpret as he will but his meanings are circumscribed to some extent by the environment around him. Where his own behavior is involved, he controls (consciously or unconsciuosly) BOTH the cues that are supplied and their interpretations as well. Two sets of lines are required in Figure 1 to reflect the circularity of this communication process, one to indicate the encoding of meaning in the nonverbal behavior of Mr. A, the other to show interpretation of these acts by Mr. A.

The jagged lines ($\wedge\wedge\wedge$) at either end of the series of public, private and behavioral cues in Figure 1 simply illustrate that the number of cues to which meaning may be assigned is probably without limit. But, although unlimited in number, they can be ordered in terms of their attractiveness, or potency, for any viewer. Men do not occupy a neutral environment. The assumptive world of Mr. A, a product of his sensory-motor successes and failures in the past, combined with his current appetites and needs, will establish his set toward the environment so that all available cues do not have equal valence for him. Each will carry a value that depends upon its power to assist or defeat him in pursuit of adequate meanings. Tentative valences have been assigned to the public, private, and behavioral cues in Figure 1 through the addition of a plus, zero or minus sign ($+$, 0, $-$) following each of them.

The complexity of the process of abstracting can readily be illustrated through the diagram simply by specifying the precise objects which Mr. A includes or excludes from his perception. Research on dissonance and balance theory suggests the direction followed in the discrimination, organizing and interpreting of available cues.[28] Unless other factors intervene, individuals tend to draw toward the cues to which positive valences can be assigned, that is toward cues capable of reinforcing past or emerging interpretations, and away from cues to which negative valences are attached or those that contradict established opinions and behavior patterns.

By a balanced state is meant a situation in which the relations among the entities fit together harmoniously; there is no stress towards change. A basic assumption is that sentiment relations and unit relations tend toward a balanced state. This means that sentiments are not entirely independent of the perceptions of unit connections between entities and that the latter, in turn, are not entirely independent of sentiments. Sentiments and unit relations are mutually interdependent. It also means that if a balanced state does not exist, then forces toward this state will arise. If a change is not possible, the state of imbalance will produce tension.[29]

Successive diagrams of a particular communicative event could be made to demonstrate in a cognitively dissonant setting how a person avoids negatively loaded cues, maximizes or minimizes competing cues, or reassigns valences in order to produce consonance.

[28] See Leon Festinger, *A Theory of Cognitive Dissonance* (Row Peterson, 1957) and Fritz Heider, *The Psychology of Interpersonal Relations* (Wiley, 1958).
[9] Heider, Ibid., p. 201.

An illustration, even though oversimplified, will suggest the course of Mr. A's communication with himself. At the moment he is faintly aware of an antiseptic odor in the room which reinforces his confidence in the doctor's ability to diagnose his illness (C_{PU+}). As he glances through a magazine (C_{PR0}) he is conscious of how comfortable his chair feels after a long day on his feet (C_{PR+}). Looking up, he glances at the Miro reproduction on the wall, but is unable to decipher it (C_{PU0}). He decides to call the nurse. As he rises he clumsily drops his magazine ($C_{BEH_{NV}-}$) and stoops to pick it up, crosses the room ($C_{BEH_{NV}0}$), and rings the call bell firmly and with dignity ($C_{BEH_{NV}+}$).

Interpersonal Communication

The communication process is complicated still further in Figure 2 by the appearance of a second person (P_2), let us say Dr. B, who enters the reception room to look for his next patient. The perceptual field of Dr. B, as that of Mr. A, will include the public cues supplied by the environment (C_{PU}). These cues, however, will not be identical for both persons, nor will they carry the same valences, because of differences in their backgrounds and immediate purposes. Dr. B may notice the time on the wall clock or the absence of other patients, and he may assign different valences to the disarray of magazines on the table or to the Miro print. In addition, Dr. B will be interpreting private cues (C_{PR}) that belong exclusively to his own phenomenological field, such as his own fatigue at the moment, and these may alter the interpretations he attaches to Mr. A's conduct. Finally, there are the behavioral cues ($C_{BEH_{NV}}$) that accompany his own movements to which he must be tuned in order to act with reasonable efficiency.

Even before any verbal exchange takes place, however, there will be a shift in communicative orientation of both individuals. As Mr. A and Dr. B become aware of the presence of the other (sometimes before), each will become more self-conscious, more acutely aware of his own acts, and more alert to the nonverbal cues of the other as an aid to defining their relationship. Each will bring his own actions under closer surveillance and greater control. The doctor, as he enters, may assume a professional air as a means of keeping the patient at the proper psychological distance; the patient, upon hearing the door open, may hastily straighten his tie to make a good impression. A heightened sensitivity and a shift from environmental to behavioral cues identifies the process of social facilitation. Men do not act — or communicate — in private as they do in the presence of others. While audiences represent a special case of social facilitation, and mobs an unusually powerful and dramatic one, the mere appearance of a second person in an elevator or office will change the character and content of self-to-self communication in both parties.[30]

At some point in their contact, and well before they have spoken, Mr. A and Dr. B will have become sufficiently aware of each other that it is possible to speak of

[30] See Erving Goffman, *The Presentation of Self in Everyday Life* (Doubleday Anchor, 1959).

behavioral cues as comprising a message (M). That is, EACH PERSON WILL BEGIN TO REGULATE THE CUES HE PROVIDES THE OTHER, EACH WILL RECOGNIZE THE POSSIBLE MEANINGS THE OTHER MAY ATTACH TO HIS ACTIONS, AND EACH WILL BEGIN TO INTERPRET HIS OWN ACTS AS IF HE WERE THE OTHER. These two features, the deliberate choice and control of cues and the projection of interpretation, constitute the criteria for identifying interpersonal messages.

Dr. B, crossing the room, may initiate the conversation. Extending his hand, he says, "Mr. A! So glad to see you. How are you?"[31] At this point, despite the seeming simplicity of the setting and prosaic content of the message, Mr. A must solve a riddle in meaning of considerable complexity. In a non-clinical environment where the public cues would be different, perhaps on a street corner (C_{PU}), Mr. A would regard this message (C_{BEH_V}) as no more than a social gesture, and he would respond in kind. This on the other hand, is a clinic (C_{PU}). Is this remark, therefore, to be given the usual interpretation? Even here, the nonverbal cues ($C_{BEH_{NV}}$) of Dr. B, the friendly facial expression and extended hand, may reinforce its usual meaning in spite of the special setting. On the other hand, these words (C_{BEH_V}) may be interpreted only as showing the sympathetic interest of Dr. B in Mr. A. In this case, the message requires no answer at all but is a signal for Mr. A to come into the office. In spite of the clinical setting (C_{PU}) and the gracious gesture ($C_{BEH_{NV}}$), however, the last phrase (C_{BEH_V}), because of a momentary hesitation just before it ($C_{BEH_{NV}}$), might be an invitation for Mr. A to begin giving an account of his symptoms. In deciphering the meaning, Mr. A will have to assign and reassign valences so that a coherent interpretation emerges. (No valences are assigned in Figure 2 because their positive, negative or neutral value would depend upon the interpretive decisions of Mr. A and Dr. B.) All three contexts, the environmental, behavioral and verbal will have to be scanned, assigned meanings, and compared in order for Mr. A to determine a suitable response.

Meanwhile, Dr. B is involved in weaving some interpretations of his own out of the cues he detects and the valences he assigns to them. Mr. A smiles back and says, "Nice to see you again, too. I wish the circumstances were different." At this moment Dr. B turns his attention from the carpet which needs repairing (C_{PU}) to Mr. A. How should he interpret this message? Since they are in a clinic (C_{PU}) it is not surprising that Mr. A should speak of the 'circumstances' of his visit. Yet, could this be a warning that the visit concerns a serious medical problem rather than a trivial one? Mr. A's relaxed posture ($C_{BEH_{NV}}$) does not reinforce the former meaning, but his flushed face does ($C_{BEH_{NV}}$). Or could this remark be no more than a semi-humorous reference to a past episode on the golf links (C_{PR})? In any case, Dr. B,

---

[31] We do not have, as yet, in spite of the efforts of linguists and students of nonverbal behavior, an adequate typology for identifying message cues. In the case of this simple remark, is the unit of meaning the phoneme, morpheme, word, or phrase? And, in the case of nonverbal cues, is it to be bodily position, gesture, or some smaller unit? Until we have better descriptive categories the careful analysis of communicative acts cannot proceed very far.

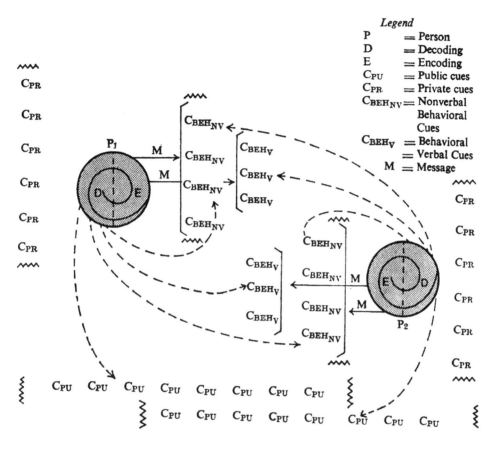

Figure 2

like Mr. A, must reduce the ambiguity in the situation by experimentally assigning meanings to public, private, nonverbal and verbal cues, relating them to the surrounding conditions of time and place, and determining the extent of congruence or incongruence in the meanings given them. Not until further verbal and nonverbal cues are supplied will Dr. B be confident that he has sized up the message properly.

This analysis suggests that meanings are assigned to verbal cues according to the same principles that govern the interpretations of all other cues. Indeed, this seems to be the case.[32] Meaning is cumulative (or ambiguity reductive) and grows as each new cue, of whatever type, is detected and assigned some sort of valence. Verbal cues are distinctive only in the sense that they constitute a special form of behavior are finite in number, and are presented in a linear sequence.

[32] James M. Richards, "The Cue Additivity Principle in a Restricted Social Interaction Situation", *Journal of Experimental Psychology*, (May, 1962), p. 452.

One further clarification must be added concerning the transferability of cues. A public cue can be transformed into a private cue by manipulating it so that it is no longer available to all communicants. Mr. A may refold his coat so that a worn cuff cannot be seen by Dr. B, or the doctor may turn over his medical chart so that Mr. A cannot read his entry. Private cues may be converted into public ones. Mr. A may want Dr. B to see a cartoon in the *New Yorker* he has been reading or Dr. B may choose to show Mr. A the latest photograph of his daughter. Sometimes an action on the part of a communicant involves manipulating or altering an environmental cue. Dr. B may unconsciously rearrange the magazines on the table while speaking to Mr. A and, in this case, environmental and behavioral cues merge.

The aim of communication is to reduce uncertainty. Each cue has potential value in carrying out this purpose. But it requires that the organism be open to all available cues and that it be willing to alter meanings until a coherent and adequate picture emerges. Conditionality becomes the criterion of functional communication which, according to Llewellyn Gross, "involves the attitude of thinking in terms of varying degrees and changing proportions; the habit of acting provisionally and instrumentally with a keen awareness of the qualifying influence of time, place, people, and circumstances upon aspirations and expectations; the emotional appreciation for varieties and nuances of feeling".[33]

What is regarded in various academic fields as an 'error of judgement', or 'a communication breakdown', or a 'personality disturbance', appears to be a consequence of a sort of communicative negligence. The nature of this negligence is intimated in what a British psychiatrist has called "The Law of the Total Situation".[34] TO THE EXTENT THAT A PERSON IS UNABLE TO RESPOND TO THE TOTAL SITUATION — BECAUSE HE DENIES CRITICAL CUES FROM THE ENVIRONMENT, DISTORTS VERBAL OR NONVERBAL CUES FROM THE OPPOSITE PERSON, FAILS TO REVISE INAPPROPRIATE ASSUMPTIONS REGARDING TIME AND PLACE — TO THAT EXTENT WILL IT BE DIFFICULT, OR IMPOSSIBLE, FOR HIM TO CONSTRUCT MEANINGS THAT WILL ALLOW HIM TO FUNCTION IN PRODUCTIVE AND SATISFYING WAYS.

The observance and disregard of the Law of the Total Situation can be documented again and again in human affairs, at the most intimate interpersonal levels, and at the most serious public levels. Since communicative negligence is so omnipresent, it might be refreshing to consider an instance that illustrates a sensitive observance of the Law of the Total Situation.

Betty Smith, writing in *A Tree Grows in Brooklyn*, tells of a neighborhood custom. On the night before Christmas a child could win a tree if he stood without falling while it was thrown at him. When Francie was ten and Neeley nine, they went to the lot and asked the owner to throw his biggest tree at the two of them. The small

[33] Llewellyn Gross, "The Construction and Partial Standardization of a Scale for Measuring Self-Insight", *Journal of Social Psychology* (November, 1948), p. 222.
[34] Henry Harris, *The Group Approach to Leadership Testing* (London, Routledge and Kegan Paul, 1949), p. 258.

children clasped each other to meet the force of the great tree. For just a moment the man agonized, wanting simply to give it to them, but knowing that if he did he would have to give away all his trees, and the next year no one would pay for a tree. Realizing he must do it, he threw the tree as hard as he could. Though the children almost fell, they were able to withstand the impact and claimed the tree. As they started to pick it up Francie heard the man shout after them: "And now get the hell out of here, you lousy bastards". There was no doubt about what he said. But Francie was able to hear beyond the rough words. She knew that this tone of voice, on Christmas Eve, from one who had no other language really meant: "Merry Christmas, God bless you." The man could not have said that, and Francie recognized it. He used the only words he had and she was able to understand him, not from his words alone, but from the totality of time, place, personality, and circumstance.

The complexities of human communication present an unbelievably difficult challenge to the student of human affairs. To build a satisfactory theory about so complex an event through sole reliance upon the resources of ordinary language seems less and less promising. Any conceptual device which might give order to the many and volatile forces at work when people communicate deserves attention. The value of any theoretical innovation, such as a symbolic model, may be measured by its capacity to withstand critical attack, its value in prompting new hypotheses and data, or finally, by its contribution to the improvement of human communication. The pilot models described here may not fulfill any of these criteria completely, but they will have served a useful purpose if they prompt the search for better ways of representing the inner dynamics of the communication process.[35]

SAN FRANCISCO STATE COLLEGE

---

[35] Only slight modifications are needed to adapt these models for use in representing the dynamics of mass communication.

GREGORY BATESON

THE MESSAGE OF REINFORCEMENT*

> Nature has no Outline, but Imagination has. Nature has no Tune,
> but Imagination has. Nature has no Supernatural, and dissolves:
> Imagination is Eternity.
>
> <div align="right">W. Blake: <i>The Ghost of Abel</i>, 1822.</div>

1. *Information, Messages and Redundancy*

In this essay, these words will be used as follows: If from any PART of a sequence of events an ideal receiver can make better than random guesses at other parts of the sequence, I shall say that the part contains 'INFORMATION' or a message about the remainder, and that the sequence as a whole contains REDUNDANCY.

If A says to B "it is raining", this verbal event PLUS the raindrops outside the window together constitute a redundant sequence for B. If B looks outside, he will get less information from the falling drops than he would have got, had he not heard A's message. He could have guessed with better than random success that he would see rain.

The case of the receiver who is not 'ideal' — i.e. who does not already know about all the redundancy patterns of the observed system — is more complicated. Under certain circumstances he may acquire information about sorts of redundancy of which he was previously unaware. I shall say that such information about patterns of redundancy is of higher order or higher logical type than that which the ideal observer can acquire. The latter, like the hypothetical player of a Von Neumannian game, is by definition incapable of such learning.

2. *Definition of Learning*

Let us define LEARNING as the receipt of INFORMATION by an organism, a computer, or any other data-processing entity. This definition is intended to include all sorts and orders of information, ranging from the single bit which we suppose to be

* This essay was prepared under N.I.H. Career Award No. HEW 7K3-MH-21,931-02 and U.S. Naval Ordnance Test Station Contract No. N.123-(60530)53792A.

received in the single firing of a single neural end organ to the building up of complex chunks of information — i.e. constellations of neural structures and events — about relationship, philosophy, religion, mechanical systems, etc. The definition also will include internal learning — the building up of information regarding the changing states and characteristics of the learning entity itself. After all, there are many parts of any learning entity which are themselves concerned with the processing of information, so that what I am calling 'internal learning' is, in fact, the receiving of information by such parts.

The purpose of this definition will be to provide some clue to the structure of contexts of 'learning', (in the more conventional sense) and in particular to consider what sorts of information are provided by those events or experiences which are called REINFORCEMENT.

It is important to note that this definition says nothing about consciousness. If a man speaks correctly in a given language, we shall say that he 'contains' information about the grammar of that language. If he KNOWS that he has that information, we shall say that he contains information of a higher logical type.

3. *Classification of Information*

From this definition, the next step is to consider how information shall be classified, remembering that the purpose of the classification is to understand the phenomena of 'learning' as above defined.

Two alternative methods present themselves: a. Classification based upon Russell's Logical Types; and b. Classification based upon the location and status of the information in the program and circuitry of the organism or computer.

Other sorts of classification could, of course, be examined. It would be orthodox, for example, to classify information according to its relevance and usefulness for the various 'needs' of the organism. The result would be a system of categories resembling 'instinct' theory. A large amount of speculation and pseudo-explanation is already associated with this way of thinking in economics, 'functional' anthropology, and animal ethology. Masses of data have been dissected into this procrustean bed but it still seems to me that the explanatory principles, i.e. 'instincts' invoked in these studies resemble the 'dormative principle' proposed by Molière's learned doctors to explain the physiological effects of opium.

In this essay I shall therefore confine myself to the more tangible types of explanation — the logical types of Russell and the status of information in programs. The first, it will be noted, is a set of characterizations inherent in the actual items of information, while the second is descriptive of methods of storage and use of that information. Neither of these classifications can be pushed very far in the present state of our knowledge but it is instructive to examine the resemblance and contrast between the two systems.

In regard to the logical types, it is sufficient here to call attention to the fact that contrasts of logical typing, derived from the abstract world of logic, have implications for the real world of learning and organization. But the logical model must be used with caution because there are also important differences between the real world and that of logic.

In the world of logic, the statement of a grammatical rule for a given language tells the logician nothing about what a speaker of that language is saying at a given moment but in the real world, knowledge of the grammar may help a man to decipher a text in that language. Moreover, in the real world, there may be some sort of conflict between items of information of contrasting type. Teachers of language believe today that the study of grammar actually interferes with learning to speak a foreign language and do their best to prevent the would-be learner from using his own language as a model when he attempts to speak the new language; and yet nobody doubts that some (perhaps unconscious) knowledge of grammar is useful to a writer or that a knowledge of Italian is useful to the learner of French. Above all, it is evident that the (almost undescribable) experience of having learned one foreign language will enable a man to learn another more quickly and easily.

These considerations suggest that in the natural history of learning the functional relationship between (e.g.) grammar and speech is not merely a matter of formal logic and the theory of types but is also shaped or colored by some other factor. It appears that information about grammar (i.e. information of higher type) is under certain circumstances most useful when least 'conscious'. This suggests that not only the logical typing of a piece of information but also its location and status in the circuitry of the organism may affect its usefulness in learning.

This problem of natural history is not precisely the same as any that the logician encounters. For him, there are strict and definable limits to what propositions can be arrived at by induction or deduction from a given set of propositions of given types. For an organism, the limits are perhaps less sharply defined and, above all, are of a different kind. The organism does not ask, "What conclusions are logically supported by this given set of premises?" He asks, rather: "What in the light of these premises is worth trying?" He operates by TRIAL AND ERROR, and the information provided by past experience or by the genome determines the SET of alternatives among which he will make random trial. In many cases, the organism will appear to be more rigid than the logician: The set of alternatives available to the organism may seemingly contain only one member, where the logician would have seen many. On the other hand, sometimes the organism will arrive by trial and error at discoveries which the ideal logician, who may not guess, could never have allowed himself to make. "Life", it has been said, "is the art of drawing sufficient conclusions from insufficient evidence."

In addition, the task of classifying messages, and meaningful actions of the real world in terms of the theory of logical types is complicated by another matter which, ideally, should not concern the logician. At least in theory, a logician, after spending many years examining the ramifications of a given tautology (say Euclidian geometry) based upon a given set of axioms and definitions, should be able without perseveration to turn around and start to build another tautology based upon another set of premises. An organism cannot do this and of course, insofar as logicians are themselves organisms, they cannot achieve freedom from this perseveration. The most abstract premises — and especially those of which the logician is least conscious — are likely to remain unchanged even when he thinks he is making a new start.

In all real entities capable of processing information, some sorts of information are necessarily more deeply and irreversibly built into the computing system than are others. In the language of the computer engineer some parts of the program are 'hard' while others are 'soft'. 'Soft' items can easily be changed when the program is to be adapted for some other related use but to change the 'hard' items may involve an almost total restructuring of the program.

The writer of a computer program has some choice as to how he builds his program. He can, within limits, decide which items he will permit to be 'hard' and which he will keep 'soft'. He will be guided in this choice by his expectations regarding future applications of the program. If he foresees that certain components of the program will have to be altered in future applications he will be wise to represent these components in ways that can easily be changed. Other, expectably constant, components he will permit to be 'hard'.

Inevitably and ideally, there will be a correlation between degree of generality on the one hand and constancy on the other. General propositions and propositions about form will rarely need to be changed but propositions regarding specific details or content will expectably vary from one occasion of use to the next. From this it follows that there will be a tendency for the programmer, guided only by pragmatic considerations, to classify his instructions and items of informations AS IF he were guided by the theory of logical types. Items of higher, more abstract and general type are likely to be programmed 'hard'; while items of lower and more specific type are likely to be programmed 'soft'.

An analogous phenomenon is recognizable in the learning organism. Indeed the very human logician, mentioned above, who had difficulty in changing his most basic premises, is an example. He permitted those premises which had been true for him for a long time to become hard. He then could not change his program without pain.

Another example is provided by the phenomenon of 'transference' in psychoanalysis. The patient attempts to structure his relationship to the analyst on the model of early relationships which he has experienced with parents or other character-forming persons, i.e. the patient will bring to the new situation abstract premises about RELATIONSHIP derived from his past. These premises have commonly the characteristic that they are self-validating (Ruesch and Bateson, 1949). In most transactions the holder of the premise can act in such a way as to make the premise appear true. It follows from this characteristic that the premise will have SEEMED true to the patient throughout a long sequence of experiences, so that when he finally comes to analysis, the premise will be already programmed 'hard'. In the picturesque language of Wilhelm Reich the premise will be 'armoured', i.e. it will now have, connected with it, a whole network of interdependent premises from which, if the primary premise were somehow excised, it could easily be regenerated.

The learning organism, however, differs from the system composed of programmer PLUS computer in that while the programmer is influenced by his expectations, the organism is a product of its past. Habit formation has sorted out the constant from the changeful so that that which for a long time has seemed recurrently true has become deeply embedded in the circuitry of the organism while the changeful remains under flexible control.

What mechanisms may lie behind habit formation we do not know, but certainly this continual sorting and sifting of sorts of propositions within the learning organism has many parallels in other evolving stochastic systems. In the learning organism an essential function of this sorting process is economic: the more flexible circuits must be reserved for dealing with the more changeable phenomena (cf. Bateson, 1962). The decisions of the programmer are economic in the same sense.

All in all, it appears that, if we are to classify information in a way that shall be appropriate in a study of learning processes, we must be guided by the following considerations:

a. that it is desirable to discriminate those items of information which are 'hard' programmed in the organism from those which are 'soft';

b. that in the ongoing life of the organism there is a process of sorting, which in some of its forms is called 'habit formation'. In this process, certain items, which have been learned at 'soft' levels, gradually become 'hard';

c. that this process must in general be guided by the constancy of the apparent truth of the items to be learned — the more constant being, in general, selected for hard programming;

d. that constancy is likely to correlate with generality, so that information about forms is more likely to be hard programmed than information about their contents. (In general, items of higher logical type are likely to become hard programmed.)

e. that the converse of 'habit formation', i.e. the disruption of hard programmed items, is a form of learning which is always likely to be difficult and painful and which, when it fails, may be pathogenic (cf. Bateson *et al*).

4. *The Distribution of Information*

It is evident that information is 'unevenly' distributed in the perceptual universe of any organism. This unevenness of distribution is exemplified by the subjective experience of an English speaker who must learn a language like German or Latin, in which the verbs are commonly placed at the ends of the sentences. He must learn to wait for the information contained in the verb which, when the sentence finally reaches its end, will tell him not only what the action was but how the other items of the sentence are interrelated. Certain sorts of information are aggregated in the verb and the learner of German is conscious of lacking this information which he had expected to receive earlier. The verb when it is finally reached seems to illuminate (i.e. contains special information about) the earlier parts of the sentence. (Native speakers of German are perhaps not conscious of this phenomenon.)

A more formal illustration of unevenness in the distribution of information is provided by Attneave's elegant experiments (Attneave, F., 1959) on the outlines of visible forms. A picture in three colors is created by coloring the squares of a grid. Such a picture will have areas of, say red, white, and blue, each area containing many squares of the grid. A similar but blank grid is given to a human subject who is asked to guess the color of each square in turn. If he guesses wrong, he must guess again, so that he finally knows the color of each square and can mark it appropriately with a crayon on his blank grid. Rather rapidly the subject discovers that the distribution of the colors contains redundancy — the communication theorist's word for regularity or pattern. Thereafter his errors occur most frequently at the boundaries of the colored areas. A map of these errors becomes, in fact, an outline drawing of the colored picture. This experiment illustrates two important (if tautological) platitudes: that information about shape is aggregated at boundaries, and that the inside of an homogeneous set contains no information except for the repeated affirmation of homogeneity.

5. *The Distribution of Classes of Information*

We now ask: does the unevenness of distribution of information in the experiential universe contain any regularities which might relate to that classification of information whose outlines we considered above? Specifically: if we classify what is to be learned according to either its constancy or its logical typing, shall we find that the resulting classes of information are differently located in the experiential universe? Is information about form distributed in the universe in a way which is different from the distribution of information about content?

But, these questions are already partly answered by the examples of uneven distribution given above. In Attneave's experiments a certain SORT of information was shown to be concentrated at those boundaries or outlines which delimited areas of uniformity; and this information at the boundaries is clearly more formal and more general than the information to be got from single colored squares within the uniform patches.

But these boundaries have, in a sense, no real existence, being made up only of squares of color exactly like the other squares which they surround. As Blake puts it, "Nature has no Outline." In other words, among aggregates or sets of similar items, those particular items which happen to be on a boundary come to transcend their individuality as members of the set and carry information about the set as a whole. In natural history, certain members of a class, differing from their fellow members only in being located in a 'boundary' come to stand as labels or names for their class. (This contradiction of Russell's rule — that no member of a class can be the name of that class — is apparent rather than real. In communication theory and in the theory of logical types there are, of course, no things: only MESSAGES carried by these objects or events. A single object can carry many messages and these may be of various types. Russell's rule insists only that a name or message of a given type shall not be classified as a name or message of a different type. The map is not the territory, even when the physical territory is the only embodiment of the map.)

The same phenomena can be considered in terms of constancy of informational content. While the perception of each item of an aggregate of red squares carries or proposes the fact of that square's redness, the marginal squares when encountered by the experimental subject propose a new constancy or 'rule': that now the subject will be well advised to guess 'red' for each succeeding square until he again encounters a change at a new boundary.

It is at the point or moment of CHANGE that new constancies are proposed.

6. *Patterns of Search*

But all this is accessible and useful to the experimental subject ONLY if he can acquire information of a still higher order, namely the information that the total system of colored squares contains redundancy, such that squares of similar color tend to be aggregated in patches. (At the start of the experiment he is given no reason to believe this. For all he knows, the colors could be randomly distributed or their distribution might be governed by any kind of simple or complex patterning.)

We must ask then about the location of this still higher order of information, though no complete answer can be given.

If, however, we consider the Attneave experiments more precisely, a part of the answer will emerge. The subject was asked to guess the color of each square and arrived at information about the rules for distribution of these colors. But clearly how soon he arrives at this abstract information will depend upon the ORDER in which his sample of data is collected. In the actual experiments, he is asked to guess the color of successive squares in order, following their ranking in the grid. If, on the other hand, he had been asked to guess squares in a random order, he certainly would not have achieved his inductive step so soon. He would have had to scatter errors randomly over the grid until the acquired information rather clearly showed that similar squares were aggregated in patches. In the final completed map of his errors, the boundaries of the patches of squares of uniform color would be less clearly marked.

In sum, the ability of an organism to acquire information about patterning and redundancy in the world must always depend upon certain characteristics of habits of the organism itself. In the total system, organism PLUS environment, there is a necessary interplay between the patterns of redundancy in the environment and the SEARCH PATTERNS of the organism. Certain sorts and orders of redundancy will be more accessible to certain search patterns but more inaccessible to others. Indeed this generalization follows as a truism from the unevenness of distribution of information in the phenomenal world. The organism must, IF IT CAN learn to look in the right places, in the right order, for the right sorts of information. Consequently, it is caught in a limited view of the universe by its search patterns, insofar as these are rigidly defined and unchanging. No pattern of the universe which cannot be discovered by these patterns can exist for that organism.

We noted above, however, that it is precisely the self-validating premises that are likely to become hard programmed, and it is clear that search patterns because they cannot commonly be disturbed by that which they cannot discover are likely to become hard programmed.

In spite of the tendency to become hard programmed, search patterns can certainly be learned and possibly unlearned, and this phenomenon has been variously named 'set learning' (Harlow), deutero-learning (Bateson), or more generally, 'learning to learn'. The precise synonymy of these terms is still obscure but certainly the learning of patterns of search is an acquisition of information of a rather high abstract order. This information is both subtly related to that information which is to be acquired by the search and subtly related to the structuring and redundancy patterns of the universe in which the search is to be conducted. The universe may contain many sorts of patterning other than those sorts which interest the organism. These irrelevant patterns may, however, complicate or restrict the process of search.

It may well be that any particular pattern (or redundancy) in the method of search will necessarily blind the searcher to certain possible patterns in the universe; and that only RANDOM search can ultimately catch all possible regularities. This ideal will be achieved, however, only by a searcher with infinite time and in a universe which makes available infinite series of data.

Real organisms in real environments will necessarily have to resort to particular patterns of search, and this restriction of search will be accompanied by a corresponding restriction in the patterns which can be discovered.

7. *The Triad of Learning*

We are now ready to think about the curious circumstance that the study of 'learning' in the psychological laboratory is usually structured around a triad of events: Stimulus-Response-Reinforcement. In the past, I have often suspected that this triad is only an artifact of the laboratory, useful because it provides a vocabulary for talking with psychologists, but harmful insofar as it restricts discourse to what can be said in this vocabulary. But the matter is not so simple.

After all, to say that the triad is an artifact of the laboratory, would mean that it is derivative from the SEARCH PATTERNS of the psychologists. Now it is probably true that every search pattern restricts what can be found and what can be discussed in terms derivative from that pattern. But it is also true that certain obscure, but coercive, regularities must govern the learning or evolution of such patterns. The psychological experimenters are, themselves, organisms. They possess 'Imagination' in Blake's sense and, therefore, they too seek for and recognize 'Outlines'. Their search patterns, BECAUSE they are self-validating, must be somehow related to the structures of the data field.

I have implied above that all learning, above the very simplest level (at which, for example, the colored square proposes only the fact of its own color), is in truth acquisition of information about 'outlines'.

The question of the 'reality' of the stimulus-response-reinforcement triad thus becomes a question about outlines of the second order or meta-outlines. The psychologist seeks to discover outlines among the phenomena of animal learning — but this learning is itself the discovery by the animal of outlines in its experience.

8. *The Sliding Triad*

The triadic pattern CAN be imposed upon any three events in a human interchange. If, for example, A and B interact to give the sequence ... a b a b a b a b ..., where a and b stand for interactive behaviors of A and B respectively, then any ... a b a ... or ... b a b ... CAN be regarded as such a triad. There are no primary outlines which would tell us whether a given ... a ... is 'stimulus', 'response', or 'reinforcement'. But, at least in occidental cultures, the individuals concerned do seem to have opinions which would classify interactive behaviors as parts of such triads. Lacking primary outlines, they are often in disagreement about how the sequence should be punctuated. A will assert that a given ... a ... was only a response to some previous ... b ...; but B will say that ... a ... was an example of A's initiative and spontaneous aggressivity. And so on.

These diasgreements clearly support the idea that the triadic structure of the learning sequence can be 'real' for organisms other than psychologists. It would seem, however, that while some need or process of logic may compel the organisms to perceive their interaction as structured in triadic sequences, there is no similar compulsion which will determine precisely how this sequential structure is to be imposed on the series of interactive behaviors.

The program is 'hard' and, as we might expect, it determines form but not content.

9. *The Triad as a 'Context'*

The fact that the triadic pattern does not require particular content is, however, not a sufficient explanation of the curious floating or sliding characteristic of the triad. It is characteristic of all patterns that they define form but not content. This particular pattern is unusual in being both (presumably) valuable to the organism and indeterminate as to its beginning and end. The wider notion of 'context' has, however, this same sliding characteristic. A 'context' can be imagined around ANY event by grouping neighboring or 'related' events along with it within an imaginary temporal boundary. And indeed the triad which we are discussing would seem to be a special case of 'context'.

The notion of 'context' is primary and fundamental for all communication. No message or message element — no event or object — has meaning or significance of any kind when totally and inconceivably stripped of context. Without context, an event or object is not even 'random'.

When the notion of context is admitted it becomes evident that every context has its meta-context, and so on *ad infinitum*. Insofar then as every event carries information about its context, we must grant that every event is relevant, i.e. carries information about every step of that infinite series which is the hierarchy of contexts. In this sense, every event becomes INFORMATIONALLY relevant to the whole universe (which is not the same as causally relevant). Here we shall limit discussion to those orders of information which occur within the learning triad and within the interactional sequences which immediately surround that triad.

In the simple case of the Attneave experiments, the boundary squares carry two sorts of information. Not only does each boundary square propose its own color, it also proposes (when appropriately encountered) a CONTEXT within which the subject gathers that he will do well to guess that succeeding squares are of that same color. The 'set' for which the boundary square is a 'label' is not just an aggregate or list of items; it is partially structured or ordered (relative to the search pattern) in such a way that the boundary squares become 'context markers', i.e. signals which give information about sameness or change, i.e. RELATIONSHIP among other signals.

10. *The Messages of Reinforcement*

In the more complex case of the triadic context of 'learning', we ask therefore which components carry meaning or information about which others.

In terms of the conceptual framework which I have built up it is clear that the event which is called the 'reinforcement' carries information of at least five sorts:

a. The event called reinforcement proposes the fact of its own occurrence. It is perceptible.

b. It proposes certain characteristics ('rightness' or 'wrongness') in the sequential relation between 'stimulus' and 'response'. And, if reinforcement is metacommunative to the relationship between the other two components of the triad, it follows that 'learning' will usually depend upon at least a triad of events. Three events are necessary if one is to be a message about a relationship between others. We may say that the triad is REAL, in the sense that it is, for certain sorts of information transmission, a minimum.

c. It proposes that a certain contingency pattern among the three components in sequence is or shall be characteristic of the ongoing interchange.

d. It proposes the even more abstract notion that the ongoing flow of interactive behavior is, in general, divisible into segments having some sort of contingency pattern.

e. It proposes that the SEARCH PATTERN of the learning subject is 'right' in the sense that this search pattern will discover this particular triadic patterning.

Any event carrying these five types of information can, appropriately, be called a reinforcement.

But the matter does not end there. The normative information (b. above) about 'rightness' and 'wrongness' is such as would explain the enhancement or extinction of the given 'response' in presence of the given stimulus, but the information (c. and d.) which proposes the patterns of contingency is more profound and more necessary. WITHOUT IT, the enhancement or extinction of response could not be expected. For 'learning', (as the word is ordinarily used in psychological laboratories) to occur at all, the organism must, either by experience or phylogeny, have become capable of receiving information (c. and d. above) of rather abstract types.

It is also important to note that both the information which reinforcement carries in regard to the contingency pattern within the triad, and the information (e.) about the search patterns of the learner are non-normative. At these levels, even 'negative' reinforcement may become desirable and may be SOUGHT by the learning organism. If the organism is unsure about what contingency patterns are expectable in a given interaction, he may be reassured when he encounters punishment.

As a schizophrenic patient once put the matter: "If it's not the way I want it, I'll prove it."

OCEANIC INSTITUTE, HAWAII

REFERENCES

Attneave, F. (1959), *Applications of information theory to psychology* (New York, Henry Holt and Co.).

Bateson, G., D., Jackson, J. Haley, and J., Weakland, (1956), "Towards a Theory of Schizophrenia", *Behavioral Science*. Vol. 1, No. 4, pp. 251-264.

Bateson, G., (1962,) "The role of somatic change in evolution", *Evolution*. Vol. 17, pp. 529-539.

Ruesch, J., and G. Bateson (1951), *COMMUNICATION: The Social Matrix of Psychiatry* (New York, Norton and Norton).

BESS SONDEL

THE ANALOGUE LABORATORY OF ELWOOD MURRAY

The Analogue Laboratory of Elwood Murray grew out of his conviction that just as there is unity in the world of nature, so, also should there be unity in man's knowledge of the world of nature. It was his conviction, further, that the integrative process is essentially a semantic process and that the analogue design is the appropriate formative mode by which to establish significant relationships between apparently disparate areas of experience.

Following Korzybski, Murray adhered to four basic assumptions. ORDER in the universe is probably the fundamental assumption of thinking man, along with the assumptions of universal PROCESS, of absolute UNIQUENESS of individuals and individual events, and of universal RELATEDNESS. Murray insisted, also, that RANDOMNESS is one of the facts of life and physical nature that can be understood only as we relate randomness to the basic order that exists in all of nature, from atomic structure to cosmos.

How shall we discover unity in a process world in which all things, all events, etc., are unique and which is characterized by universal relatedness? Unity can be approached only through knowledge of relationships in nature. The Analogue Laboratory of Murray rests, therefore, upon the discovery and coordination of congruent patterns in diverse systems in nature. The first task is, therefore, to enumerate the kinds of symbolic patterns with which we must deal to be able to discover isomorphism where it exists.[1] The following symbolic patterns are referable to patterns in nature:

THE TIME PATTERN
This pattern follows the calendar; hours, days, months, years, centuries, aeons, etc.
THE SPACE PATTERN
This pattern follows the map, the graph, the blueprint, the constellations, etc.
THE BONA FIDE CAUSE TO EFFECT PATTERN
This symbolic pattern is referable to actual recurrent causal patterns in nature.

[1] Bess Sondel, *The Humanity of Words* (New York, World, 1958), pp. 152-153, 176, 179, 180, 184, 194; Bess Sondel, *Power-Steering With Words* (Chicago, Follett, 1964). PS/W is a cybernetic approach to communication. The index will indicate references to the various kinds of verbal patterns.

THE IMPUTED CAUSE TO EFFECT PATTERN

This pattern has its place mainly in the social sciences where all the evidence cannot be in. This pattern describes probable causal relationships on the basis of incomplete evidence.

THE MEANS TO END PATTERN

This pattern is a program that is calculated to move from the present state of affairs to a more desirable goal-state. This pattern cannot be verified either before or after the fact of accomplishment when it involves human beings. It is invaluable, however, as a developmental construct.[2]

THE SECTIONAL PATTERN

This pattern is made up of parts (sections) that belong within a given frame of reference. The sections may be conjunctive (joined by the conjunction 'and'); disjunctive (separated by 'or' or 'but not'); equivalent (joined by $=$); proportional (A is to B as C is to D); analogical; etc.

Elwood Murray became interested early in his career in the use of verbal patterns by which to stabilize the otherwise variable communication process. It was he who gave critical attention and invaluable advice to me in my experimental work in the classrooms of the University of Chicago. It was he who extended theory and practice in the use of the analogical symbolic design, not only to advance knowledge but to unify apparently divergent areas of experience.

It is the analogical sectional pattern that we shall investigate in this paper as a preface to Murray's objectives in the Analogue Laboratory at the University of Denver.

ANALOGY DEFINED

'ANALOGY' MEANS STRUCTURAL CORRESPONDENCE. Norbert Wiener says that two patterns are identical when there is a one-to-one correspondence of elements (parts) and a one-to-one correspondence of the kind of relationship between the elements.[3]

Korzybski states that when two patterns are identical, they have all their logical characteristics in common.[4] And Ogden and Richards state that when a symbolic pattern accurately represents an actual pattern in nature, the symbolic pattern is both true and logical.[5]

Analogy means LIMITED structural correspondence. Analogy between two processes accrues from the perception of actual structural correspondence between two systems, but analogy does not mean identity of the two systems. The test by which we dis-

[2] John Dewey, *Logic, The Theory of Inquiry* (New York, Holt, 1933), pp. 50, 511. Harold Lasswell, "The Policy Orientation", *The Policy Sciences*, Daniel Lerner and Harold D. Lasswell eds. (Stanford, Calif., Stanford University Press, 1951), p. 5.
[3] Norbert Wiener *The Human Use of Human Beings* (Boston, Houghton Mifflin, 1950), p. 3.
[4] Alfred Korzybski, *Science and Sanity*, 4th ed. (Distributed by Institute of General Semantics, Lakeville, Conn.), p. 60.
[5] C. K. Ogden and I. A. Richards, *The Meaning of Meaning* (New York, Harcourt, 1938) 5th ed., pp. 82, 87.

criminate between a good analogy and a false analogy consists in the determination of the extent of actual structural correspondence.[6]

Plato's *Republic* is an historic exemplar of analogy. In *The Republic*, Plato draws an analogy between man and the State. The body politic, Plato argues, is LIKE man in certain structural features. Therefore, from knowledge of man, it is possible to draw inferences concerning the conduct of the State. The test of Plato's analogy lies in the extent of structural correspondence of the two. A good analogy should lead, moreover, to inferences that are subject to operational proof.

The greatest analogy of our time is, without doubt, that drawn between man and the machine — between *God and Golem, Inc.*, as Norbert Wiener puts it.[7] Wiener explored this analogy systematically in an earlier work, *Cybernetics, or Control and Communication in the Animal and the Machine*.[8] The analogy between man and the machine is worth exploring in this context because Murray proposes, in the Analogue Laboratory, to use communication as the means by which to coordinate the various facets of human experience. Such coordination is, of course, an ideal. Such coordination is, of course, an experiment in the effort to find analogies that will bring together such vast areas of experience as science, the arts, and religion.

Murray's project in the Analogue Laboratory at the University of Denver will require, first, that the separate facets of each of these three major classifications be analyzed, and, if possible, coordinated. Pertinent analogies will need to be drawn between the biological, the social, and the physical sciences.[9] Pertinent analogies will need to be drawn between the arts — all the arts — such that common formal features of design will emerge.[10] Pertinent analogies will need to be drawn between all religions such that religions, irrespective of differences, will have a common core.[11] And, finally, this task will require that in science, art, and religion there will be found significant analogies that will make their unity such as to move toward the convergence of all knowledge.[12]

Such an epistemology would derive from symbolic design in which words become speculative instruments by which to reach the ultimate goal of man's search for unity. This is the great and never-ending enterprise of philosophy. This is the noble endeavor to infuse abstract and quantitative design with qualitative attributes of man.[13]

[6] Karl W. Deutsch, "Communication Theory and Social Science", *Selected Papers on Psychotherapy, Purpose, and Communication* (New York, American Orthopsychiatric Association, 1952), pp. 469-483.
[7] Norbert Wiener (Cambridge, Mass. Inst. of Technology Press, 1964), title.
[8] Norbert Wiener (New York, Wiley, 1948).
[9] Aldous Huxley, "The Humanist Frame", in *The Humanist Frame* (New York, Harper, 1961), pp. 11, 48.
[10] Suzsanne Langer, *Philosophy in a New Key* (Cambridge, Mass., Harvard U. Press, 1957), pp. 96, 99-101.
[11] Norman Cousins, *Who Speaks for Man* (New York, MacMillan, 1953).
[12] I. A. Richards, *Speculative Instruments* (Chicago, U. of Chicago Press, 1955).
[13] *Ibid.*

To exemplify penetration into analogy, let us now explore Wiener's analogy between communication in man and the machine.

COMMUNICATION IN MAN AND MACHINE

We shall explore the analogy between man and the machine by attention to the structure of three factors: (1) Calculation; (2) Memory; and (3) Control

(1) CALCULATION in man is dependent on what is in his memory and on his ability to retrieve information that is required as an instrument of reasoning. We can repeat this in identical language with respect to the machine. In so far, there is correspondance of operational structure.

(2) MEMORY is stored information. This is true of man and the machine. In so far, there is correspondence of structure. In man, however, information is stored on various levels of accessibility. Relevant information may or may not be subject to immediate recall. The human memory stores the history of a life lived, much of it not subject to volitional recall. This is at once a weakness of man's memory and yet an advantage. It is a weakness in that relevant information may be inacessible when needed. It is an advantage in that the resources of man's memory are deeply ingrained in his nervous system. REMEMBERING IS NOW THOUGHT TO BE AN INHERENT PSYCHOPHYSICAL PROCESS OF RELATING OTHERWISE ISOLATED BITS OF DATA.

It is generally conceded that THINKING is a process of relating bits of data, that KNOWLEDGE is understanding of relationships in nature, that INTERPRETATION of incoming stimuli is the process of fitting stimuli into the patterned reservoir of experience of the interpreter. In the human organism, INFORMATION is not isolated bits of data but patterned input that is relevant to the goal-state of that human organism. In the human organism, RELEVANT INFORMATION, when not subject to wilful recall, may, and indeed often does, coalesce with other such 'forgotten' information spontaneously and emerges to mesh with present input to create new symbolic 'compounds'.

In the machine, everything that is stored under its proper 'address' is accessible instantaneously, however complex the information may be, however great the volume may be. But everything that is relevant cannot be stored. The machine cannot 'know' what the programmer has 'forgotten'. The machine cannot know what lies buried in the programmer's deep unconscious.

(3) There is structural correspondence between CONTROL of programmed information in man and in the machine. Both make use of the feedback loop. In man, the communicator corrects deviation between the actual state of affairs and his goal-state by the use of negative feedback. In man, when positive feedback runs wild, as Murray has indicated in lectures, it is likely to generate its own constraints, its own restraints. This happens on the conscious level when the CONSEQUENCES of the communicator's words and actions are used by the communicator as new infor-

mation by which to steer his subsequent output. Just so, the machine can be programmed to correct possible predictable errors. Concerning control, however, there are important differences between the structured operations of man and the machine. In man, the output-input-output continuum is a connected and inseparable cycle. This is not so in the machine. Input and output are two separate operations. In the machine, therefore, the control is not a continuous cyclic transaction.[14]

In biological systems, control of behavior depends on inherent modes derived from past experience, whereas the machine is dependent on programmed inputs. In the human organism, the direction of control is from the inside outward; in the machine, from the outside inward. Control in the behavioral organization of man is cumulative and pervasive; in the machine, control of the program is specific and singular with respect to the predetermined goal-state.[15]

To conclude this brief analysis of the analogy between man and the machine, let me extrapolate on the value of analogical analysis in general and on the Analogue Laboratory of Elwood Murray in particular.

Since man's nervous system is, for the most part, the prototype of the machine, this analogy illuminates differences as well as similarities. With the passing of time, it is Murray's hope that these differences may be minimized, thus to improve the operations of the machine and to advance man's fulfillment of his potentials.

In the machine, the programmed feedback loop gives attention to possible errors inimical to the goal-state. Man is not so careful to program his own behavior. Man is so intent on his output that he is likely to ignore input, i.e., perception of favorable or unfavorable consequences of his words. This means that his valuatory mechanism is not functioning efficiently, and this means that he cannot know what, if any, deviation exists between the actual state of affairs and his goal-state. He cannot, in other words, make full use of negative (corrective) feedback.

MURRAY'S ANALOGUE LABORATORY

Murray's thesis is this: We are goal-seeking creatures. Man is an exquisitely complex system in pursuit of goals. Man's works are many and varied, all of them directed toward self-fulfillment. His efforts are vitiated when his resources are scattered or pigeon-holed. His powers are mobilized when the separate facets of his experience — conscious and unconscious — converge to supplement and to reinforce each other.

Murray's brilliant life-work, his whole life through, is an exemplar for others to emulate. The Analogue Laboratory of Murray shows the way. It is for us to follow.

ILLINOIS INSTITUTE OF TECHNOLOGY

[14] Peter H. Greene, "Discussion, Some Biological Ideas", *Bionics Symposium, Living Prototypes, the Key to Technology*, Sept. 13-15, 1960. Air Force Systems Command, U. S. Air Force, Wright-Patterson Air Force Base, Ohio, pp. 496-497.
[15] *Ibid.*

WAYNE N. THOMPSON

COMMUNICATION, COMMUNICATION THEORY, AND RHETORIC

Communication and rhetoric, according to two panelists at a Central States speech convention, are synonymous or nearly so. Both of these men were mature, respected, generally knowledgable scholars, but in this instance their responses, so the writer believes, were not based upon careful thought.

The point of the story is that an essay elaborating on differences between communication theory and rhetoric is no belaboring of the obvious. On the contrary, a need exists for a detailed explication of the meanings of the terms, both of which are critical to intelligent thought and discussion about both written and oral discourse. The method will be the empirical, not the investigative, with not a single datum quantified and not a *t*-test or a correlation. Nor is this a reworking of definitions derived from dictionaries or other sources. Rather, the writer has called upon the sum of all of his past reading and thinking for the purpose of elaborating the differences and the implications of the terms RHETORIC and COMMUNICATION THEORY as they are commonly used. Like the lexicographers who prepare new dictionaries, he is not creating definitions arbitrarily but is developing those extended definitions that follow logically from an analysis of common usage in the scholarly community.

The problem in present usage is peculiar. At the level of definition the view that rhetoric and communication are synonymous[1] is widespread, but at the level of detailed usage the two terms encompass territories that differ fundamentally. The purpose of this paper is to point out these differences.

Presumably general conceptions (or maps) should represent detailed applications of terms (or territories) as closely as possible, and presumably those who use words without much appreciation of the referents confuse both themselves and others.

Three other preliminary points are necessary. First, whereas RHETORIC commonly refers both to a field or method of study and to a process in which human beings engage, COMMUNICATION THEORY is the analogue for the former and COMMUNICATION

---

[1] A. Craig Baird uses almost this precise language. "Rhetoric, oral communication, and public speaking are synonymous". *Rhetoric: A Philosophical Inquiry* (New York, The Ronald Press Company, 1965), p. 31.

for the latter. Comparisons in this paper, therefore, sometimes employ the former term and sometimes the latter. Second, communication theory, unlike information theory, is not a precise term referring to a set of definite postulates and formulations; rather it is a generalized, somewhat formless composite of notions whose boundaries are indistinct. The use of this term, nevertheless, seems justified, for agreement about the general territory that it covers is sufficient to make the expression meaningful to most scholars. Third, RHETORIC in this paper refers to the traditional or classical form — that is, the referent here is the one that is the most common among scholars in the field of speech.

The distinctions between RHETORIC and COMMUNICATION or COMMUNICATION THEORY fall into four groups.

ACCURACY VERSUS EFFECTIVENESS

First, communication theory focuses upon the accuracy of transmission; rhetoric upon the effectiveness of discourse. In the former the fundamental objective is a one-to-one relation, meaning that ideally the recreation in the mind of the listener is an exact replica of whatever was in the mind of the speaker. "The degree to which the receiver's comprehension or reaction corresponds to the original idea or intent of the sender is a fair index of the 'effectiveness' ... regardless of the 'value' of what is communicated."[2] Moreover, the numerous attempted models of the communication process are striking demonstrations of this point that accuracy of transmission is at the heart of the usual notion of the meaning of COMMUNICATION. "So the communication is like overlapping rings: on the left is what I meant, and you didn't get; on the right side is what you got, and I didn't mean; and the overlapping part in the middle is all we can ever hope to convey."[3]

Still further evidence of this one-dimensional emphasis in communication lies in the nature of the major criticisms directed against it as an influence in contemporary education. Two passages suggest the nature of this attack:

The consequences for teachers of composition of these changes in contemporary thinking is to raise questions about communication courses in which the emphasis is on language in its referential aspects and where the ideal of writing is the 'objective' report written in 'neutral' language. The idea is an artficial one and does not prepare students for real life situations. Neutral exposition is relatively rare; as I. A. Richards, in *The Philosophy of Rhetoric* pointed out.[4]

---

[2] John B. Hoben, "English Communication at Colgate Re-examined", *Journal of Communication,* IV (Fall, 1954), p. 77.

[3] M. W. Thistle, "You Can Change the Past", in *Proceedings of the* 1959 *Institute in Technical and Industrial Communications,* eds. Herman M. Weisman and Roy C. Nelson (Fort Collins, Colo., Institute in Technical and Industrial Communications, 1960), p. 26.

[4] Aerol Arnold, "Points of View in the Philosophy of Communication", *College Composition and Communication,* X (Oct., 1959), p. 149.

And from the field of speech comes this complaint:

We have almost starved rhetorical language with the doctrine of clarity (or better, 'non-ambiguity') which, by an unfortunate perversion, has led us toward an ideal of language usage variously described as 'scientific', 'logical', or 'neuter'. ...We have suffered glorification of the DENOTATIVE quality of language at the expense of the CONNOTATIVE. We have celebrated the LITERAL, DESIGNATIVE function of language, yet allowed the SYMBOLIC function to fall into decay.[5]

Joshua Whatmough, late Professor of Comparative Philology at Harvard, also is critical of the attempt to restrict the study of language to its designative function.[6]

The prevailing conceptions that I. A. Richards was attacking when he called for a new rhetoric that "would be a study of misunderstanding and its remedies"[7] are still far removed from the communication that Arnold, Baker and Eubanks, and Whatmough are criticizing. Although beginning speech courses may include units in informative speaking and although *docere* was listed as a speech purpose as far back as Cicero, advanced courses give but limited attention to the accuracy of transmission, and the problems that the rhetorical critic sets for himself almost always are the estimation of effectiveness and the analysis of the rhetorical factors in reference to success or failure.[8] Perhaps somewhere in the professional literature there exists a study seriously concerned with why some speaker did or did not secure expository success, but the association of rhetoric and effectiveness is so strong that such critiques are rare, if not nonexistent. Aristotle's definition of rhetoric as "the faculty of observing in any given case the available means of persuasion",[9] has been the dominant conceptualization of the term RHETORIC, partly because Aristotle has been revered and partly because the major rhetorical concerns in all ages have been the persuasive problems of the preacher, the counselor in the court of law, and the speaker on matters of public policy.[10] With such practical concerns foremost, a strong slanting in rhetorical writings toward persuasion has been inevitable.

[5] Virgil L. Baker and Ralph T. Eubanks, "Democracy: Challenge to Rhetorical Education", *Quarterly Journal of Speech*, XLVI (Feb., 1960), pp. 76-77.
[6] I. A. Richards, *Language: A Modern Synthesis* (New York, St. Martin's Press, 1956), pp. 88-90.
[7] I. A. Richards, *The Philosophy of Rhetoric* (New York, Oxford University Press, 1965), p. 3. Richard's lecture, however, was delivered in 1936.
[8] "Informative discourse is not usually associated with rhetoric, either historically or at present. It is true that a high proportion of the current textbooks on public speaking contain treatments of exposition, but the subject is so uniformly absent in the rhetorical theories of the past and the rhetorical criticism of the present that its presence in textbooks can be attributed to expedient or commercial considerations". Edwin Black, *Rhetorical Criticism: A Study in Method* (New York, The Macmillan Company, 1965), p. 11.
[9] *Rhetoric*, i.2. 1355b 25-27.Plato, although differing greatly from Aristotle in the attitude toward rhetoric, did not disagree on definition and purpose. "Must not the art of rhetoric, taken as a whole, be a kind of influencing of the mind by means of words?" (*Phaedrus*, 261A). "The function of oratory is in fact to influence men's souls" (*Ibid.*, 271C).
[10] Adresses of display for ceremonial purposes have received extensive treatment from rhetoricians. This interest is the only major exception to the general truth that practical, persuasive problems have dominated the thinking of the authors of rhetorics.

Even the accurate observation that contemporary textbooks for beginning speech courses and the classes themselves include substantial units on informative speaking does not constitute refutation of the generalization that persuasion is the preoccupation of traditional rhetoric. First, this balance between effectiveness and learning as outcomes of discourse, as pointed out by Edwin Black in footnote eight, does not characterize advanced courses and research. Second, the source of this material in the beginning course is not classical rhetoric. To some extent communication theory is responsible for this modern development, but basically communication theory and the presence of expository units in speech courses are effects of a single cause. The highly complex world of twentieth-century business and industry has resulted in a realization that the clear conveying of information is a function that in its essentiality to society deserves a place along with the services of the preacher, the lawyer, and the political debater.

Comparisons of rhetoric and communication as operative concepts do not deal with absolutes to which there are no exceptions, but in general the conclusion of Russell H. Wagner is sound:

To most of the classical authorities rhetoric was practically synonymous with persuasion. Aristotle, in his definition, makes the finding of the means of persuasion the whole objective of rhetoric. It was the ultimate end or purpose of the orator to Cicero, to which other purposes such as teaching or delighting were subordinate. Quintilian, while refusing to make rhetoric the art of persuasion, everywhere assumes persuasion to be the grand object of oratory.

Different Attitudes Toward Language

These disparate concerns — accuracy for communication theory and effectiveness for rhetoric — lead to several essential differences, one of which is the way in which language is viewed. Both regard it as an all but indispensable constituent of their processes, but the respective substrata make the detailed analyses of the linguistic element vastly different.

More specifically, the concern of the communication theorist is with the denotative, nonaffective aspects of language — with the extent to which a word or a phrase is free from ambiguity and leads the listener to recreate the idea that the speaker had in mind. A strong secondary interest is the efficiency with which language functions. Redundancy is to be avoided. Connotative aspects are of but slight interest and then only because they are a sort of nuisance increasing the hazards of the communicative process.

The rhetorician, in contrast, approaches language through an awareness that it is a force that can affect mightily the hearer's attitude toward the speaker's thesis. The emotional shadings of words, thus, are almost as important as what Richard Weaver calls their nuclear meanings. Impressiveness, interest, and/or force are

[11] "Thomas Wilson's *Arte of Rhetorique*", *Speech Monographs*, XXVII (March, 1960), p. 14.

qualities that most rhetorical works treat as desirable attributes.[12] Clarity, commonly identified as the most important quality, holds this high place not so much because clarity is desirable *per se* (the reason the communicationist would place it first) as because clarity is necessary to the attainment of a persuasive goal.

The Traditional Canons

These differences in the role of style in rhetoric and in communication have their counterparts in the places accorded to two of the other canons, delivery and arrangement. Whereas these are significant in rhetorical theory because of their presumed close relationships to effectiveness, they interest the communication theorist only insofar as they affect the attainment of the one-to-one objective. Thus, in rhetoric delivery is viewed almost solely as a means of effectiveness, and the parts of the speech are analyzed for their contributions to the speaker's goals.

In communication theory, on the other hand, the introduction is attenuated to a consideration of feedforward, and other aspects of arrangement are likely to be omitted entirely. Delivery becomes a constituent of intelligibility, viewed like style and arrangement narrowly and in a highly specialized fashion.

Still more striking are the differences in respect to invention. Regarded by any true classicist as the most important of all the canons[13] and accorded the greatest amount of space in most traditional rhetorics, ancient and modern, it is without significance in communication theory. At the source of this movement are the physicists and the engineers, whose concern with the transmission of bits of information may lead to ignoring meanings entirely. "The word *information*", according to Warren Weaver, "is used in a particular sense ... not to be confused with its ordinary usage. In particular, information must not be confused with meaning."[14] As Dale Drum, a speech professor, observes, "To the engineer, a meaningless message may have more information than one packed with 'information' in the popular sense."[15] This approach to discourse leads to an atomistic analysis that would look out of place in a rhetorically based volume:

[12]   Aristotle gave a good bit of attention to the metaphor as a device for avoiding meanness and adding liveliness *Rhetoric*, iii. 10-11, 1411^{b}21-1413^{b}2. Among recent textbooks that have included one of these terms are A. Craig Baird and F. H. Knower, *General Speech: An Introduction* (New York, McGraw-Hill Book Company, Inc., 1963), pp. 142-146; Milton Dickens, *Speech: Dynamic Communication* (New York, Harcourt, Brace & World, Inc., 1963), pp. 215-220; Giles W. Gray and Waldo W. Braden, *Public Speaking: Principles and Practice* (New York, Harper & Row, 1963), pp. 504-522; Robert Oliver, Harold Zelko, and Paul Holtzman, *Communicative Speech* (New York, Holt, Rinehart and Winston, 1962), p. 189.
[13]   Two of the three books in Aristotle's *Rhetoric* deal with invention. "Content", writes A. Craig Baird, "is...emphasized in Aristotle and in subsequent rhetoricians". *Rhetoric: A Philosophical Inquiry*, p. 15.
[14]   Claude Shannon and Warren Weaver, *The Mathematical Theory of Communication* (Urbana, University of Illinois Press, 1949), p. 99. Italics are Weaver's.
[15]   "Change, Meaning, and Information", *Journal of Communication*, VII (Winter, 1957), p. 161.

The source and destination of a message are respectively the speaker's and hearer's brain. The message is made up of discrete units transformed into continuous form (speech waves) by the transmitter (the speaker); the signal is normally mixed with 'noise' (interference) in the channel, e.g. actual noise, a foreign accent, a bad cold; it is picked up by the receiver (the human ear) and decoded back into discrete units at the destination.[16]

MECHANISTIC VERSUS HUMANISTIC

A second group of specific distinctions as far reaching and striking as those arising out of the effectiveness-accuracy disparity are those resulting from the humanistic qualities of rhetoric and the mechanistic characteristics of communication theory.

As for the former, in the main stream from Aristotle to the present people have been its central concern. Aristotle, who regarded the personal character of the speaker as a powerful persuasive factor, gave much of Book ii to descriptions of audiences and to analyses of the nature of the emotions and of the opportunities afforded the speaker. The invention of arguments was an intellectual process, and intellectuality, according to the *Nicomachean Ethics*, is the most human of all characteristics. Treatments of disposition and style in the *Rhetoric* were based upon the presupposition that oratory pertained to listeners whose human and 'sorry' characteristics required prudent speakers to make adjustments to a purely logical presentation. Nor was all of this peculiar to Aristotle. For twenty-three centuries rhetorical works, often by explicit statement and always by implication, have been audience centered — i.e., rhetoric as an art concerned with the influencing of people has continued to derive its principles from an examination of separate constituents as they operate in the speaker-audience situation. Thus, the rhetorical act involves human beings in the most human of all relationships, the communication of ideas devised by the human mind. According to the traditional analysis of oratory as deliberative, forensic, and epideictic, rhetoric is an instrument for determining public policy, attaining justice, and praising (or blaming) fellow man. To many rhetoricians, more so in some eras than in others, oratory also is a medium for carrying forward the uniquely human enterprise of the pulpit.

Finally, rhetoric has been humanistic in that to varying degrees its theorists and practitioners have sometimes viewed it as a fine art. Both Greeks and Romans had this view, and especially in the Second Sophistic of the Roman Empire, because of the impossibility of public debate on political issues, oratory became largely a fine art in which performers were judged for their skills and not for their content.[17]

---

[16] Whatmough, p. 218.

[17] George Kennedy makes this statement about epideictic oratory: "This is a form of literature which has relatively few admirers today, but if we are to understand the Greeks thoroughly it seems necessary to understand, if not to share, their love for it." *The Art of Persuasion in Greece* (Princeton, N. J., Princeton University Press, 1963), p. 153.

Eugene Bahn gives this description of oral reading and declaiming in the Silver Age in Rome (14-138 A.D.): "Large halls were hired for the rendering of imaginary themes, and crowds pressed

Today the role in rhetoric of fineness of performance is unclear. Effectiveness, as judged by results, undoubtedly holds first place, and teachers and textbook writers praise highly the direct, clear, economical presentation. Yet, at least some place remains for something more. The oration persists as a forensic event — presumably because influential teachers and coaches find value in training students to express themselves with distinction — and although attending a speech for aesthetic purposes is uncommon, most rhetoricians probably would agree with Lester Thonssen that the quality of expression should be among the criteria for choosing the addresses that deserve to be singled out as outstanding from the thousands delivered annually.[18]

All such considerations are foreign to communication theory, which gives no attention to beauty of expression and little, if any, to ethics and logic. Humanness is recognized only to be deplored — as something that makes the transmission of bits of information a process less certain, controllable, and predictable than it would be otherwise.

These communicationists, to go further, are almost fiercely scientific. Structural linguists have been the most aggressive minority in the recent history of the field of English, and in speech, general semanticists, behaviorists, and group dynamicists have been energetic and persistent. Such exponents of 'new sciences' have been neither hesitant nor modest; in their own estimation, they have been saviors, the only true prophets. This zeal, perhaps, is a reason that so little synthesis of the ideas of rhetoric and communication theory has occurred.

The responsibility for this lack of useful dialogue, of course, is not one-sided. The communicationists may have pushed too hard, but the rhetoricians have been inflexible, and unprogressive. One of the few to recognize the limitations that compartmentalized scholarship imposes[19] is Elwood Murray:

Considerable reluctance prevents us from the breaking out of the old closed system of codes, rhetoric, phonetics, and linguistics. Our psychologists, group dynamics people, and sociologists tend also to remain within their own borders... There has been too little effort to explore the communication methodologies which are inherent in the works of many of the greatest of the philosophers of the past, and the tremendous potential in the organismal approaches from modern biology and space-atomic physics likewise has been neglected.[20]

---

their way to hear the great declaimers. The public baths were also rendezvous for declaimers and their admirers spent hours contemplating impossible ethical, moral and legal problems well adorned with emotional fervor and dynamic vigor. Hopeful declaimers attended these gatherings regularly, and studied the ways of arousing emotional reactions in writing and speaking." "Interpretative Reading in Classical Rome", *The Quarterly Journal of Speech*, XXIII (April, 1937), p. 208.
[18] "Does it [the speech] express the idea and mood with a measure of rhetorical distinctiveness"? *Representative American Speeches: 1959-1960* (New York, The H. W. Wilson Company, 1960), p. 4.
[19] That those who assert that communication theory and rhetoric are synonymous will synthesize the two approaches is hopeless. They don't even understand that rhetoric and communication theory are different.
[20] Elwood Murray "We Go, But Too Slowly", *Journal of Communication*, IX (Dec., 1959), p. 191.

Progenitors and Confreres

This humanistic-mechanistic disparateness, which leads to secondary differences, originates in the unlike sources of rhetoric and communication theory. The latter began with electrical engineering, mathematics, and the natural and behavioral sciences; and even the more humanistic sources, such as semantics and linguistics, are the fields within the humanities that are the most scientific in method and outlook. Rhetoric in contrast is derived from logic, ethics, politics, and philosophy. Aristotle specifically called it the counterpart of dialectic, which was an elaborate system of logical investigation, and relations with his other nonscientific works are easy to perceive. According to Richard McKeon, "Rhetoric is closely allied to logic, for it is the counterpart of dialectic, in Aristotle's analysis, and it has not infrequently been used by his successors to suggest improvements or substitutions for logical devices. It has a moral and political dimension.... It is finally a verbal art, the development of which, both before Aristotle's analyses and since, has been closely associated with the interpretation of poetry."[21] Consistent with this analysis is the listing of volumes by Alexander Grant, who divided Aristotle's writings into the theoretical and the practical-productive. The extant practical and productive works — i.e., those parts of the Aristotelian corpus belonging to the same general fields — are the *Rhetoric*, the *Nicomachean Ethics*, the *Politics*, and *On Poetry*.[22]

Nor are communication theory and rhetoric alike in their research procedures and scholarly habitats. The one, a product of the twentieth century, is scientific and investigative; the other, largely a creation of the fourth century B.C., is reflective and empirical. Thus, the modern theorist on the one hand seeks new knowledge by experimentation that often uses instrumentation to measure phenomena with precision. The location of his study is likely to be a laboratory, and his statistical procedures often require computers because of their complexity. With such a scientific orientation, he finds his colleagues for his research interests among the biologists, psychologists, physicists, electronic engineers, linguists, semanticists, and mathematicians.

Rhetoric, on the other hand, belongs primarily to those whose training is in rhetoric itself. The tendency is to perpetuate both the content and the methods, which throughout history have been observation, value judgment, intuition, and generalization. Since the object of study is human relationship, the locale of research is either those places where human beings are interacting or libraries, where books and other documents provide second-hand information on interactions. Aristotle's own method was to observe human nature and the speech events about him and to think philosophically.[23] Dealing with total events, he made no attempt to secure

[21] Richard McKeon, *Introduction to Aristotle* (New York, The Modern Library, 1947), p. 620.
[22] "Aristotle", *Encyclopedia Britannica: A Dictionary of Arts, Sciences, and General Literature*, 9th ed., Vol. II (New York, Samuel L. Hall, 1878), p. 520.
[23] Edward Copleston gives this account of the formulation of the *Rhetoric*: "Nothing is arbitrary, nothing gratuitous. Long experience with mankind, attentive observation of human nature in public

knowledge by an exact investigation of the small items that comprise the communicative act. This empirical-philosophical approach, despite the completion in this century of a large number of quantitative studies of rhetorical acts, to this day is the source of almost all OPERATIVE rhetorical doctrine.

Basic and Applied Sciences

These rhetorical doctrines essentially are items of advise concerning the speaker's behavior in various circumstances, whereas communication theory is largely a basic science. The goal of the one is to improve performance; the concern of the other is with understanding process. The very definition of rhetoric as "the faculty of observing in any given case the available means of persuasion" implies that the transmission of ideas is not a mechanistic process in which each act is a duplicate of its predecessor. Instead, the rhetorician's concern is with a variable art in which diverse and alterable circumstances necessitate judgmental applications of broad principles. Plato's writings on rhetoric include this description:

First, you must know the truth about the subject that you speak or write about: ...secondly, you must have a corresponding discernment of the nature of the soul, discover the type of speech appropriate to each nature, and order and arrange your discourse accordingly, addressing a variegated soul in a variegated style that ranges over the whole gamut of tones, and a simple soul in a simple style. All this must be done if you are to become competent within human limits, as a scientific practitioner of speech, whether you propose to expound or to persuade.[24]

In its general tenor Aristotle's *Rhetoric*, as well as other works in the classical tradition down to the most recent textbooks in public speaking, is practical. True enough, he gave a philosophic foundation to a subject that among the sophists had been entirely pragmatic, but the ultimate purpose in locating underlying explanations was that of helping speakers determine what would work the best for them. E. M. Cope states flatly, "Rhetoric is a *practical art*",[25] and other scholars classify it as practical or productive.[26]

Practicality also is attributable to communication, but the term does not mean the same here as it does for rhetoric. The explanation lies in the fact that the rhe-

---

and in private life, the political history of past times, and the occurrences of his own age, furnished him with the materials of this great work. In the course of inquiry, nothing is left untouched on which Rhetoric, in all its branches, has any bearing. His principles are the result of extensive original induction. *A Reply to the Calumnies of the Edinburgh Review against Oxford* (1810), pp. 26-27.

Others who describe the empirical processes responsible for the *Rhetoric* include W. H. Atkins, *Literary Criticism in Antiquity*, Vol. I (Cambridge, England: At the University Press, 1934), p. 136; E. M. Cope, *An Introduction to Aristotle's Rhetoric* (London, Macmillan and Co., 1867), P. xi and p. 6; Lane Cooper, *The Rhetoric of Aristotle* (New York, Appleton-Century-Crofts, Inc., 1932), p. XXXV.

[24]   *Phaedrus*, 277BC.
[25]   Cope, p. 19. The italics are Cope's.
[26]   Among these are Grant, p. 520, and McKeon, p. xxi.

torician, believing that the general principles already are known, is concerned solely with problems of application, whereas the communicationist still is searching for lawful generalizations. Put another way, communication theory is interested in communication *per se*, but rhetoric is interested in the communicative act as a link between man and his political and social environment. The former, as indicated earlier, began as a study of the transmission of bits of information without interest in the content or the significance or effects of the items. Rhetoric, in contrast, to use the words of Lester Thonssen and A. Craig Baird, "is, instead a practical skill serving as a direct link between the individual and his immediate social environment on the one hand and the larger political pattern of the state on the other. Logically, such a position argues for a close relation between the speaking art and the allied fields of social inquiry. The Aristotelian system provides for precisely such an interrelation."[27]

Again, such distinctions are not absolute but relative: Some workers in communication are interested in social control and seek to apply basic theory to practical situations. Characteristically though, communication theory partakes of the basic sciences and is a study of the act or the process itself; rhetoric, again to characterize broadly, pertains to applications and consequences.

THE BROADNESS OF THE TWO STUDIES

Third, the two terms differ in the broadness of the areas that they encompass, or, to put the matter more exactly, they do not possess the same kinds of broadness. The two earlier sections, which developed the accuracy-effectiveness and the humanistic-mechanistic comparisons, included some materials relevant to this analysis, but in the present section the topic of broadness is to be considered explicitly.

Media

If the number of media is the criterion, communication theory is the broader, for rhetoric is so preoccupied with the verbal code that all other media are unimportant. Far less limited is communication theory, which brings from engineering and the natural and behavioral sciences to the social sciences and the humanities a strong nonverbal influence. Such parts of the communication approach as cybernetics and kinesics, for example, are nonverbal sciences. Moreover, by most definitions[28]

---

[27] *Speech Criticism* (New York, The Ronald Press Company, 1948), p. 71.
[28] "[Communication includes] all of the procedures by which one mind may affect another. This involves not only written and oral speech, but also music, the pictorial arts, the theatre, ballet, and all human behavior". Jurgen Ruesch and Welden Kees, *Nonverbal Communication* (Berkeley, University of California Press, 1956), p. 1.
    "[Communication is] any means which links one mechanism or organism with another." Joshua Whatmough, "Mass Media and Mass Neurosis", *Logos*. II (Oct., 1959), p. 84.
    "[Communication is] all those processes by which people influence one another." Jurgen Reusch

communication includes 'all' media; and so far as the writer has observed, communicationists in practice think broadly, much as the definitions say that they do and should.

Finally, this looking away from the strictly verbal approach, though a product of the mathematical and engineering origins of communication, has influenced those communication theorists whose concerns are close to those of rhetoricians and who often work with them in the same college departments. Seth A. Fessenden, a speech professor, writes, "We consider a communication method to be any procedure or practice which promotes the interchange of thought and attitude."[29] Bess Sondel, a second example of a speech teacher who is a communicationist, also illustrates the multimedia outlook:

The word 'communication' is a very broad term. When you hear it, you may think it refers to Western Union or to the Morse code; to the Bell Telephone Company with its intricate network of wires; to the Pennsylvania Railroad and its system of tracks, its red lights, its green lights, its whistles; to the symphony; to the police siren; etc. Obviously, communication is a process that relates people and things.[30]

Rhetoric, although not unaware of the role of gesture and other nonverbal elements, both visual and auditory, clearly makes them subordinate,[31] and in many works, including the great ones of the classical period, the treatment is negligible. Moreover, insofar as nonverbal elements appear in traditional rhetorics, they do so as factors bearing upon effectiveness, and only rarely are they examined as carriers of ideas. As for the media of transmission, rhetoric has no interest in wires and circuits and electronics generally.

Feedback

A second point at which communication is broader and more complete than rhetoric is in the consideration of feedback. This major factor in the engineer's treatment of communication has also been of great interest to theorists outside the purely scientific fields. Complete accuracy may be unobtainable in human encounters, but when accuracy is the primary test the notion of self-correction through feedback is compelling. Bess Sondel observes that "... the communication process is a circular, and

and Gregory Bateson, *Communication: The Social Matrix of Psychiatry* (New York, W. W. Norton and Company, 1951), p. 6.
[29] Seth Fessenden, "Methodologies", *NSSC Newsletter*, III (May, 1, 1955), p. 10.
[30] Bess Sondel, *The Humanity of Words* (Cleveland, The World Publishing Company, 1958), pp. 21-22.
[31] For evidence of the overriding attention to language in traditional rhetoric, one can turn to almost any volume within this genre in any age. Of particular interest is the treatment by A. Craig Baird in his recent volume, *Rhetoric: A Philosophical Inquiry*. An examination of the section on "Meaning of Rhetoric" leads to the conclusion that rhetoric deals almost entirely with words, written or spoken (pp. 5-10), and Baird concludes his survey of the history of style as the third canon by writing, "Thus is maintained the central place of language, through the centuries, in the theory of rhetoric", p. 144.
Richard McKeon in characterizing Aristotle's *Rhetoric* writes, "*It is finally a verbal art*", p. 620.

not a linear, experience ... . There is ... an output-input-output-input continuum which causes changes at both poles."[32]

Pale by comparison is the treatment in rhetoric of feedback or any comparable doctrine. The much emphasized notion of audience adaptation is a unidirectional process, treated with little or no attention to a circular flow of sequential stimuli. With adaptation removed, scarcely anything is left in rhetoric that even appears to be comparable to feedback. Empathic response, also usually analyzed only as uni-directional, is not important in most books, and such advice as restating points that appear to be misunderstood or stopping argument when the thesis seems to be accepted does not go beyond prescriptive statement to any theoretical consideration. The role of such items in rhetorical advice as a whole, indeed, is small.

The relevance of the feedback concept to rhetorical problems, however, is being appreciated, and here is one of the few points that some integration of traditional rhetoric and communication theory may occur.

Content and Ethical Consciousness

As compared with rhetoric, communication theory is narrow and shallow in its approach to problems of content and ethics. Although Campbell and Whately stripped from rhetoric the fuller, nobler emphases upon invention, even the present watered down versions stress content far more than do the works of the communicationists.

One consequent of this difference in concern over content is that the analysis in rhetoric of kinds of materials is of no interest to communication theorists. That Aristotle created his *Rhetoric* for the purpose of providing a method of dealing with probabilities may be an exaggeration, but he did regard the probable nature of its materials as a factor distinguishing rhetoric from the sciences.[33] This approach persists to the present day when textbooks, particularly those on argumentation, speak of rhetoric as THE method of estimating truth when scientific verification is impossible. Rhetoric thus performs an investigatory service that, coupled with its service as a tool in political and juridical matters, makes it essential to the continued proper functioning of democracy.

Such major interests of rhetoricians of all ages have no counterparts in communication theory, which in anything approaching its pure form is unconcerned with both the content of the message and the purpose that is served.

Similarly, communication theory is nonethical, whereas rhetoric is ethically self-conscious. As stated earlier, the engineer is concerned with the efficient, accurate transmission of items of information and not with their truth, rightness, or probable

---

[32] Sondel, p. 205.
[33] "Rhetoric with few exceptions excludes the universal and necessary, and deals only with the probable; and this is the essential difference between it and the scientific or demonstrative processes.

consequences. Some individuals as individuals, of course, are concerned personally with both communication theory and ethics, but this is not an argument that the theory itself has an ethical dimension.

In contrast, rhetoric, excepting for some strayings from classicism, always has been ethically self-conscious. Plato's first rule for the orator was "First, you must know the truth about the subject that you speak or write about",[34] and similarly in Aristotle's list of the purposes of rhetoric the prevention of the triumph of fraud and injustice stands first.[35] In the words of Richard McKeon, speaking of the *Rhetoric*, "It has a moral and political dimension."[36]

As with invention, the role of ethics in contemporary rhetoric, although still far more important than any counterpart in communication theory, is watered down from classicism. The ethical consideration, which in Plato and Aristotle was inextricably bound up in the conception of rhetoric and was inseparable from it, now is something attached — a section or a chapter urging the student to be a responsible citizen and to persuade ethically. Such treatments rarely satisfy entirely, and the large number of articles on the ethics of speechmaking indicates both dissatisfaction with these recent efforts and a lively interest in the topic.[37] The ethical dimension at least remains prominent in rhetoric; in communication theory it never has existed.

OTHER DIFFERENCES

Beyond these three sets of differences — accuracy-effectiveness, mechanistic-humanistic, and kinds of broadness — lie three other areas producing important distinctions. These differences, like those already discussed, are discernible even for those groups within speech departments who derive their ideas and attitudes from communication and rhetoric respectively. If those from all departments who belong to these two groups are considered, the differences become still more striking.

---

[34]   *Phaedrus*, 277B.
[35]   I.1.1355a20-24.
[36]   P. 620. Robert T. Oliver says, "According to Aristotle, the purpose of the speaker is limited by two factors beyond his control: (1) truth and justice, which it is his duty to maintain; and (2) the emotional nature of auditors." "The Confucian Rhetorical Tradition in Korea During the Yi Dynasty (1392-1910)", *Quarterly Journal of Speech*, XLV (Dec., 1959), p. 363.
[37]   Since 1957 at least seven articles on this topic have appeared in the three publication of the Speech Association of America. Henry Nelson Wieman and Otis M. Walter, "Toward an Analysis of Ethics for Rhetoric", *Quarterly Journal of Speech*, XLIII (Oct., 1957), pp. 266-270; Hugo E. Hellman, "The Man with the Grey Flannel Mouth", *QJS*, XLIV (Feb., 1958), pp. 56-60; Franklyn S. Haiman, "Democratic Ethics and the Hidden Persuaders", *QJS*, XLIV (Dec., 1958), pp. 385-392; Edward Roge, "Evaluating the Ethics of a Speaker in a Democracy", *QJS*, XLV (Dec., 1959), pp. 419-425; Ernest G. Bormann, "Ethics of Ghostwritten Speeches", *QJS*, XLVII (Oct., 1961), pp. 262-267; J. Vernon Jensen, "An Analysis of Recent Literature on Teaching Ethics in Public Address", *Speech Teacher*, VII (Sept., 1959), pp. 219-228; Arthur N. Kruger, "The ethics of persuasion: a re-examination", *Speech Teacher*, XVI (Nov., 1957), pp. 295-305.

Interdisciplinary Relations

Both communication and rhetoric are interdisciplinary, but in different ways. The former is interested in a number of disciplines because of the belief that the several kinds of communicative acts and processes are comparable and because of the hope that the findings in one area, such as biology, may be relevant to an understanding of the acts and the processes in some other area, such as electrical engineering. Both the hope of finding THE first principle and a faith in the fruitfulness of reasoning through analogues make an interdisciplinary approach both desirable and necessary.

Rhetoric today does not go to logic, psychology, or philosophy for either of these two reasons. The purpose instead is to find new and better explanations for existing doctrine. In argumentation for example, the interest in *Toulmin's* logic is as an explanation of how reasoning occurs, and there are no important practical outcomes in the form of rhetorical guides. Likewise, cognative discourse is emphasized more in persuasion as an explanation of why changes in attitudes occur than it is as a source of rhetorical instruction. Possibilities exist for creating new doctrines, but as a rule they have not been realized. Better explanations, though worth seeking, should not be confused with new precepts *per se*.

Functions of Generalization

Still another difference between communication theory and rhetoric is in the way in which generalization functions as a means of securing useful knowledge; each employs this device in its own special way.

A major interest of communication theorists, as previously mentioned, is to find broadly explanatory principles. This process rests initially upon the discovery of numerous specifics, but even more important is the creativity needed to see the principle to which these details point. This whole process, aimed at developing a field theory, is much like Aristotle's search for a first principle as described in *Posterior Analytics*.[38] That communication theory in this respect has more in common with Aristotle's logical works than with his *Rhetoric* or his dialectic should not be surprising, for modern communication theory is primarily scientific.

Generalization as a method for developing rhetorical theory, however, functions quite differently than it does in communication. No one in any age seems ever to have thought of a field theory as a useful and tenable goal. The objective is not THE first principle but a large number of low- and medium-level generalizations pertaining to the many different facets of speaking and writing. The method is the simple, practical one of observing a number of rhetorical events and drawing con-

---

[38] See especially Book II, chapter 19. Richard McKeon includes these statements in his summary of the Aristotelian analysis of the relation of the individual item to the generalization: "We get to know first principles, therefore, by induction, but they are apprehended as principles by intuition...They are isolated in the repetitions of experience—in induction, abstraction, and analogy—until they are perceived as principles in intuition", p. XVII.

clusions; the purpose is not the creation of theory qua theory, but the generation of guiding rules for practical situations.

Progressiveness

Such conclusions as those in the two preceding sections suggest that traditional rhetoric in the last century has neglected to re-examine classical doctrines vigorously and to seek new precepts. The stimulating though controversial facts and theories of such fields as psychology, linguistics, and semantics at most have led to accretions or revised justifications of established doctrine. Communication theory, possibly excepting feedback, has had but little impact, and the relevant quantitative findings have led to little more than footnotes supporting the intuitively derived principles of Aristotle and his successors. Even the underlying spirit of inquiry that is basic to the quantitative endeavor has had but little influence: textbooks show the same confidence in unproved bits of prudential advice on speechmaking as they did before the methods of testing hypotheses under controlled conditions became well known.

Appearances of modernity, in the form of references to the recent scholarly literature, are abundant, and most textbooks have sections or even chapters with information on general semantics, cognitive dissonance, or something else that is more recent than Winans and Woolbert. Such materials, however, are self-contained sections that are minor additions to traditional instruction and they are not reworkings of rhetoric itself. Likewise, the inclusion in a single speech department of traditionalists, experimentalists, and general semanticists does not mean that classical doctrine is being rethought.

Whether communication theory will do better is uncertain, but its adherents are trying. In fact, its attractions include the encouraging atmosphere for theorizing and the stimulating belief that great discoveries are likely. Because of the prevailing assumption that knowledge is both incomplete and obtainable, those in one field, such as business, search enthusiastically through the writings of other communicationists for the basis for an analogue practical to their own interests. By studying system x, so it is believed, one may perceive something new about system y or at least develop a new hypothesis. False starts, frustrated hopes, and even mistaken conclusions characterize many of these ventures, but creativity is so rare and so precious that even one success outweighs a multitude of failures.

Three passages, from philosophy, business, and speech, illustrate the diversity and the vitality of this belief in the potential values of analogues:

There are certain obvious analogies between communication systems such as the telegraph, or systems using sound waves instead of graphemes, and human speech: the sender encodes a message by translating it into other signalling units, the message is carried over the channel, is received, decoded and reaches its destination. On the basis of these analogies, 'communication' theory is relevant to linguistics, to which, considered as a whole, it gives a mathematical foundation... We are entitled, therefore, to be optimistic about the possibility of connecting 'communication' theory more closely with linguistic theory, and especially that part of it which is concerned with structure; in other words, it provides a useful model of certain aspects of language.[39]

In industry, communication is a two-way system whereby objectives, policies, and orders are transmitted downward, and desires and dissatisfactions are transmitted upward. It is analogous to the nervous system through which various stimuli bring about a co-ordinated reponse. Lack of co-ordination, misdirection, and failure to move in any direction at all results from an imperfect system of communication.[40]

The human brain is also a model for human organization and communication in the structures of human societies, large and small. From it we may find the vital principles of two-way communication, homeostasis and feedback, of checks and balances, PRINCIPLES OF HEALING, whereby a society may heal itself, and stop the ever recurring tyrannies, corruptions, infections, and diseases which beset our social order. When two-way communication is impaired between the brain and an arm or a leg, spasticity results. A similar paralysis occurs where human enterprise, institutions and nations cut their lines of communication. In fact, for almost every corruption and breakdown in the human being, one does not have to look very long to find its analogue in human organizations and societies. And there is evidence that the obverse of this may also be true, that for long continued disorders in society, there are corresponding disorders in the human mind and spirit.[41]

This faith in the usefulness of analogues, along with the confident search for a field theory, is heady motivation for the communication theorist that is without a parallel in contemporary rhetoric. Perhaps nothing useful will result, but the spirit of progress and some promising methods, both so sadly lacking in traditional rhetoric, exist in communication.

CONCLUSION

Whether the argument prevails that communication and rhetoric are not synonymous is for others to judge. The differences, so the writer believes, are numerous, fundamental, and significant both theoretically and practically. Moreover, noticeable differences exist between those in speech departments nationwide who are by training and inclination rhetoricians and those who are communicationists. Both groups deserve respect, and the purpose of this paper is not to elevate one at the expense of the other. More rhetorician than communicationist, the writer laments those shortcomings that exist in both fields, but in both he finds more to esteem than to deplore.

The failure of the two groups to engage in extended and meaningful dialogue is a major cause for regret. Each could learn from the other, and the fields themselves would be the better. Which of the two should be the base for synthezized formulations is a judgment dependent upon personal backgrounds and inclinations. The

[39] Whatmought, *Language: A Modern Synthesis*, p. 200.
[40] Raymond W. Peters, *Communication Within Industry* (New York, Harper & Row, Inc., 1950), p. 163.
[41] Elwood Murray, "Corridors among the Ivory Towers", a lecture (mimeo.), pp. 35-36.

writer's personal preference is for a system based upon rhetoric but drawing fully upon communication theory for facts, hypotheses, and methods. The year 1970 is not the fourth century B.C., and a modified rhetoric, enlarged, enlightened, and revised should be possible. The need is urgent to search out new precepts and to examine old ones critically. Pursued with vigor, openmindedness, and intelligence, this process should produce new doctrines, modifications of old ones, and better explanations for those retained. Just as eighteenth-century British scholars brought renewed vigor to rhetoric by looking to natural law for explanations, so may the twentieth-century American scholars bring vitality to the field by drawing upon the related areas, including communication theory.

An essential prelude to such a forward step is the realization that rhetoric and communication theory are not synonymous.

UNIVERSITY OF HOUSTON

O. R. BONTRAGER

THE EDUCATION OF OUR TEACHERS

I began to teach nearly half a century ago. This was in the year we entered World War I. It was in the day of the Model T Ford. Very few states had a paved highway that crossed the state. The few airplanes in existence then were less trustworthy than a present day Piper Cub. The radio had not yet come in; it was to come a few years later, ushered in by KDKA in Pittsburgh, in November, 1920. Women had not yet dared to cut their hair. There were no nylons. At this time I had not yet seen lipstick. There were no cigarettes, except the occasional do-it-yourself type.

The formal education requirements for teaching (in Iowa) at that time were minimal: high school graduation plus two summer courses at the State Teachers College. I have forgotten what those courses were. I am sure they bore little relationship to the problems I had to cope with when I entered my first school — a one room rural school with fifty children.

At this time, very few people spelled education with a capital E. The giant beehives now called Colleges of Education did not yet exist. There were beginnings, to be sure, more frequently labeled departments than colleges. No one then dreamed that the time would come when the University of Chicago catalog would list more courses in education than in all of the sciences and applied sciences put together. This is by no means to suggest that we know more about teaching than our combined knowledge in all of the sciences.

This half century has witnessed a mushrooming of words about many aspects of education. These years could be quite appropriately designated as the era of logorrhea in education. For example, in the early 1930's I became intrested in children who had difficulty in learning to read. At that time I could find fewer than ten articles dealing with such children in the education books and journals. Less than twenty years later there came to me a bibliography listing over 8,000 such articles. Despite this fantastic proliferation of words, however, the very first article I read stated that reading 'problems' in schools were steadily increasing in number. Quite clearly the increase in wordage was not accompanied by a decrease in the number of 'problems'.

I have heard heated debates on whether education should be regarded as 'life' or 'preparation for life'; or whether education should be 'child-centered' or 'subject-centered'.

In psychology, I passed through the period of the 'IQ' and the white rat. Indeed, we have not got out of the white rat period yet despite the fact that I have never in a half century had to deal with a class of rats.

During the latter half of my half-century, Robert Maynard Hutchins has been assuring us perennially that the 'great ideas' of the past are the panaceas for the problems of the present. He has never told us how he knows this, nor has he ever made clear which one of these great ideas will solve present-day problems of over-population or water supply or wiping out all life in the age of the satellite and H-bomb.

I have heard solemn assurances that education should consist in part of something called 'general' education which in turn includes something called 'humanities' which includes courses in art, music, literature, philosophy and history, but should NOT include courses in mathematics or in any of the sciences. This despite the fact that Lancelot Hogben has characterized mathematics as the 'mirror of civilization'.

This period saw men debate something they called the 'transfer of training' which led people to ask, "Should Mary really take algebra, anyway?"

Over these years, volumes of words were written about 'individual instruction', 'homogeneous grouping', 'the platoon school', 'readiness', 'workshops', 'group process', (called group-think by someone), the atypical (who is not) child, 'sex', teaching the 'whole' child, human relations, and so on. 'Sex' in particular has a great fascination for many people, and, it might be added, for living forms other than people. The fact that only people need to have courses about 'sex' provides conclusive evidence for the superiority of the human class of life.

A man who, as far as I know, never taught a child to read and (I am told) did not even learn to read in this country wrote a book called *Why Johnny Can't Read* and created a tremendous disturbance, particularly among those people who have never read a book.

Professor Bestor and Admiral Rickover have persuaded themselves that some education is more 'basic' than other education, although they are not too clear on how they know this.

I have witnessed the cult of measurement come, even as it is now slowly passing out. I once knew a benighted member of this cult who was for a time a colleague of mine. As far as I know, he never earned more than $5,000 a year. He could never get a doctor's degree in a country where, as Jacques Barzun puts it, it is impossible to keep even a moron from getting one. Despite all this, for a small fee and an 'aptitude' test, he could divine for any and all comers where jobs could be had that would 'fit' them and that would pay anywhere from ten thousand dollars a year and up. It is not on record that he ever explained why he did not take one of these jobs.

Currently we hear verbalizations about 'team' teaching. This particular form of word magic seems to assume that one teacher in a class can not know enough; there must be at least two or three or even more. In the end, however, we can rest assured that each child will know as much as all of the teachers put together.

Then Sputnik came along. One irreverent commentator on the educational scene remarked that Sputnik transformed a lot of politicians into educational authorities and many of the latter into politicians. Angry voices were raised everywhere from barbershops to the offices of great corporations pointing to schools as the scapegoats responsible for the great anguish that Sputnik had brought upon us. What the voices did not mention was the obvious fact that, in the final analysis, schools can only reflect the wishes of the people who pay for the schools. Despite this, committees, local, state, and national were organized in great haste. These committees, often composed at least in part of members who would be hard put to solve a ninth grade algebra problem, issued solemn declarations to the effect that only some things called 'science' and 'mathematics' could save us. Curriculums were solemnly re-organized, (that is, new titles were affixed to old courses) although anyone familiar with the history of curriculum revision would find it difficult to put much faith in such performances.

Something called 'research' became an issue of great concern. 'Research' waxes and waxes greatly. It is probably not unfair to state that today the typical school administrator in higher education would sooner be caught with no clothes on than admit that he has no director of research. Moreover, as Jacques Barzun has astutely observed, it is much easier to discover the name of the director of research in an educational establishment than it is to get meaningful descriptions of the 'research' he is directing.

As the onrushing wave of technological developments accelerates at an ever-accelerating rate, the human family finds itself involved in relationships of increasing complexity: depletion of natural resources; strangulation of transporation arteries in mushrooming metropolitan communities; pollution of water and air; school drop-outs; poverty; slums and suburbs; how to live with atomic power; how to provide educational facilities for a population that has been increasing roughly 4 million each year since 1947; outmoded political subdivisions; problems of mental health; increasing crime rates; increasing forms of graft in governmental and private affairs; technological unemployment; and others too numerous to mention.

Accompanying the thunder of the wave, we hear the solemn pronouncements and prescriptions of Conant, Admiral Rickover, Woodring, Bestor, Koerner, Gardner, and all the others. These prescriptions have on thing in common: Not one of the prescriptions faces clearly the question, "What are we trying to accomplish through the process of education?" As one writer recently put it:

"When considerations of 'why' are dodged, we get prescriptions which simply cannot be appraised. One cannot truly evaluate the proposals made in widely read books which are characterized by indifference to aims and purposes in the early chapters and which then constantly smuggle in unanalyzed value assumptions through the remainder of the pages: Two knights entered in the educational jousting show this tendency: both the great and good James B. Conant and the provocative and prancing Martin Mayer.

"Conant, for instance, does not set forth aims for education in 'The American High School Today'. Yet he steadily makes assumptions as to what knowledge is of most worth.

"In 'Slums and Suburbs,' Conant says, 'It is after visits to schools like these that I grow impatient with both critics and defenders of public education who ignore the realities of school situations to engage in fruitless debate about educational philosophy, purposes, and the like. These situations call for action, not hair-splitting arguments.' Yet 'Slums and Suburbs' is permeated with proposals for action which must be based on philosophic assumptions." (7)

It is worth repeating that any and every proposal for action in education, the education of teachers included, is grounded in some assumptions about what is of worth. Any educational proposals that are not congruent with or relevant to the conditions of human existence will most certainly pass into oblivion.

Can we establish some of the conditions of human existence without resorting to speculation or without, so to speak, 'pulling rank?' Can we derive, from a consideration of these conditions, some clues regarding the form that teacher education must take? Gardner (5), who is a very wise man, has spoken cogently in behalf of 'The Pursuit of Excellence'. Unfortunately, however, he has not been too clear about what constitutes 'excellence'. He leaves unanswered the question, EXCELLENCE FOR WHAT? I like his emphasis on the importance of the individual, but he treats much too lightly those relationships that establish beyond doubt the FACT of that importance. He resorts to 'talent searches' although history records the abysmal failures of the 'searchers' in the cases of Thomas Edison, Albert Einstein, and countless others. He fails completely to realize that an 'individual' without a society could never get out of the cave.

Let us start where Gardner left off and see whether we can establish some criteria for 'excellence' for the HUMAN class of life. As a point of departure, I shall assume that 'excellence' for a dog or a white rat cannot constitute excellence for a human being.

The successful cultivation of any plant requires knowledge about the nature of the plant and about the environmental factors that will hinder or facilitate the growth of the plant. For example, we have learned that hybrid varieties of corn produce twice as much corn per acre than did the common varieties that were commonly cultivated when I was a boy. Some of these hybrid varieties will mature in a much shorter growing season. Some have a higher sugar content.

We also know that corn can be grown successfully only when such environmental factors as temperature, rainfall, the nature of the soil, the presence of nitrogen, etc., permit the plants to grow. Corn will not flourish where cacti thrive.

What we have said about plants is equally true about animals as any producer of chickens, hogs, or cattle can testify. Each plant, each animal, thrives only under suitable environmental conditions. Fish will not live on dry land. Corn and forests do not grow without water. The nature of the plant or the animal becomes a determining factor in the survival of each living form. The conditions that will insure life for one form will not necessarily insure life for another. Cattle cannot be successfully produced in accordance with fish nature or in fish environments.

In a similar way, the nurture and training of human beings, including teachers, will certainly fail if we do not differentiate clearly between the necessities for survival for plants; the necessities for survival for animals; and the necessities for survival for human beings.

At this point someone usually questions whether or not survival is so important anyway. There is also a sizeable cult of true believers in the hoary old Freudian myth of a supposed death 'instinct' among us. I have observed over many years, however, that those who talk loudest about a death 'instinct' quickly call a physician or race to a hospital at the first signs of a belly ache. The monumental costs of hospitals and medical facilities and hospital and medical insurance do not support beliefs in such myths.

The Darwinian theory of evolution performed a grave disservice for mankind through its overemphasis on what has been called the 'gladiatorial theory of survival'. This theory postulated brute, physical strength as the chief criterion for survival. Animals with larger horns, larger teeth and stronger jaws were able to domineer and ultimately kill off other forms. Of course, this is demonstrably not so. Men tame the elephants and put giant gorillas in cages. Simpson (6) and Eiseley (4) have both ably discredited the 'tooth and claw' explanation of survival.

Despite this, the teachings of perhaps the most widely disseminated system of psychology in the Western World today would have us accept hostility, sexual activity and irrationality as the cardinal characteristics of the human dimension of life. As I have shown elsewhere (1), these characteristics do not differentiate us from animals at all. They suggest instead animal models of behavior for human beings. The mythologies and histories of every culture consist in the main of accounts of military exploits. The children of the world are brought up in almost total ignorance of the less spectacular developments that have slowly lifted the human race above the levels of animals.

Example? Let us consider an extremely common article of commerce, a can of peas. There is hardly a grocery store in America where a can of peas could not be found. Most homes would, in all likelihood have one or more cans of peas.

Let us consider further some of the less spectacular developments that have been taking place over thousands of years that made cans of peas possible. These will turn out to be developments that are not celebrated in the mythologies and histories of cultures. Indeed, any reader who would undertake to trace back the origins of the knowledge — human knowledge — without which a can of peas would be impossible, would discover that he would not live long enough to do it.

A can of peas would not be possible without a knowledge of agriculture. If we trace back the knowledge of agriculture, we will eventually include: the discovery of what plants can be eaten; the discovery that seeds can be planted which will grow as plants that will produce other seeds; the discovery of seasons and a calendar; the creation of plow-like implements for cultivation; irrigation; plant breeding; the conquest of plant diseases; and a host of other items of knowledge.

That can of peas would not be possible without metallurgy. The taming of fire would be a part of the history of that can of peas. That history would include the creation of the wheel, without which peas could not be cultivated or transported. Knowledge of food preservation which has slowly accumulated over the centuries would make up part of the story. We would have to trace into the dim past the history of representation — speaking and writing — without which the knowledge necessary to produce peas today could never have been transmitted. That history would have to search out the development of economic and monetary systems and usages and all the other activities of commerce.

From this brief consideration of a can of peas, we are in a position where we can envision a HUMAN model of behavior and some guide posts for the education of teachers.

To begin, no dog's survival depends on his being able to go to a grocery store for a can of peas or other canned food. Our survival does.

We belong to a dimension of life that would quickly die if suddenly we should be cut off from knowledge acquired by our ancestors — back to the discovery of fire. No animal has ever learned how to control fire. Consider our plight should we suddenly lose our inherited knowledge about controlling fire. Every automobile, every truck, every locomotive, every airplane would suddenly stop. Engines are only devices for controlling fire. Let me repeat: No living dog depends for his survival on what an ancestral dog learned a half million years ago. No human being can long survive without such knowledge.

From these considerations, I am led to these conclusions regarding the nature of programs for the education of teachers.

First and foremost in this program, I put knowledge. Without knowledge gained from dead men, none of us would have survived beyond a matter of days after birth. Without such knowledge, not one of us could safely choose the next bite he will eat. The human family would starve in a very short time if some cataclysm forced it to subsist on nuts, buffalo, rabbits, fish, clams, wild roots, and berries — in short, only foods that do not come to us as the fruit of slowly accumulated human knowledge. To eat anything at all draws upon ages-old knowledge that has been transmitted to us about what we can eat that will not kill us. Remove all knowledge of metals, agriculture, uses of fire, the wheel, etc. and we all perish very quickly.

The education of teachers must insure, then, that they become, so to speak, custodians of knowledge, participants in the dissemination of old knowledge, and facilitators of the creation of new knowledge. Teachers must become knowledgeable on a broader scale than we have ever known; this is not to say that teachers must become 'know-alls'. On the contrary, I suggest as one of the prime items of knowledge, the knowledge that no one knows all about anything.

The old question about which educators have beat their gums together for years: which is more important, 'content' or 'method'? is thus quickly resolved. Without knowledge we die. But all the knowledge man has ever created is sterile and useless unless it is transmitted. To do this most effectively requires KNOWLEDGE of method. Thus to ask, "Is 'content' or 'method' more important?" is the precise equivalent of asking, "Is the ocean deep or wet?" The answer to both questions is YES. I have dealt with such issues at much greater length elsewhere (2). Viewed against the background of our common human condition, the criteria for 'excellence' for which John W. Gardner pleads so eloquently (5) are brought into much clearer focus. Excellence in knowledge about how best to inform ourselves about existing knowledge; excellence in knowledge about how to transmit knowledge; excellence in knowledge that will lead to better utilization of knowledge; excellence in knowledge about how to facilitate the acceptance of knowledge; excellence in knowledge about how to discard old knowledge no longer appropriate to changed conditions; excellence in knowledge of how we can develop a sense of responsibility in every human being to assume personal responsibility for all these things as well as for the creation of new knowledge — these are some of the specifications for the kinds of excellence our common condition demands.

These considerations etch in sharp outline the strategic position teachers must play in the unfolding human scene as well as the nature of programs for the education of teachers. For many years now, G.B. Chisholm, the first Director of the World Health Organization, has been going all over the world, telling people everywhere how tremendously important the teacher's role in survival has become.

"The most important thing in the world today is the bringing up of children. It is not a job for economic or emotional misfits, for frightened, inferiority-ridden men and women seeking a safe, respectable and quickly attainable social and emotional status, nor for girls filling in their time before marriage. Fortunately, there are recent signs of intellectual stirrings amongst teachers which give some hope. To be allowed to teach children should be the sign of the final approval of society. The present scale of values is clearly illustrated by the disparity between teachers' salaries and those of movie actresses or football coaches. I am reminded of a group whose responsiblity was the reclamation, training and rehabilitation of all the unmarried mothers in a certain community. The procedure was to have an 'I.Q.' done and then to train the girl according to a simple chart. The upper levels rated various types of useful training. Those at the bottom, not fit for anything else, were trained as nurse-maids, to bring up children." (3)

Up to now, we have paid far too little attention in teacher education to some of the things to which Doctor Chisholm calls attention. In the past, we have exposed our children to far too many emotionally insecure teachers at all levels in our educational programs. We have exposed them to far too many teachers who are abysmally ignorant about the most elementary facts of human existence in the world in which we all live. If we are to survive, we must quickly acquire more of the knowledge that already exists; we must rid ourselves of outmoded knowledge and beliefs that are no longer relevant to the present human condition; and, somehow, we must seriously set ourselves to the task of creating new knowledge, the necessity for which is forced upon us by the rapidly changing circumstances of existence.

No one can count himself out. We are all in this world together. Education must train a new generation of teachers who will stimulate a new generation of children to create the new knowledge we must surely have. Knowledge has ever come out of individuals. It is the ONLY place it has ever come from. Any educational program that overlooks this simple fact moves inexorably toward a dead end. At no time in history has the knowledge at one date sufficed at a date 100 years later. In the meantime, the only place that needed NEW knowledge could possibly come from was out of individuals.

The titanic changes that are taking place precludes the possibility that programs for the education of teachers will equip them with final sets of answers. Our teachers must be prepared to formulate for themselves the new solutions to the new problems that will surely arise in the wake of the unprecedented changes now taking place all over the globe. This is not the kind of education that can be terminated with a bachelor's or master's or doctor's degree in education, or anything else. From here on out, assuming our continued existence, it must be the kind of education that will go on and on and on 'till death do us part'. During half of my half century, it has been my great privilege to have been associated with Elwood Murray, a great teacher, who has played a vital role in facilitating movement in the directions I have indicated.

CALIFORNIA STATE COLLEGE AT LONG BEACH

BIBLIOGRAPHY

1. Bontrager, O.R., "General Semantics and Psychotherapy.", *General Semantics Bulletin*, Numbers 28 and 29 (1961/1962).
2. Bontrager, O.R., "Moral and Spiritual Values in the Schools", Chapter 9 in Belok, Michael *et al: Approaches to Values in Education* (Dubuque, Wm C. Brown Company, 1965).
3. Chisholm, G.B., "The Reestablishment of Peacetime Society", *Psychiatry* (February, 1946).
4. Eiseley, Loren, *Darwin's Century* (New York, Anchor Books, Doubleday and Company, 1961).
5. Gardner, John W., *Excellence* (New York, Harper Colophon Books, Harper & Row, 1962).
6. Simpson, George Gaylord, *The Meaning of Evolution* (New York, The New American Library, 1951).
7. Van Til, William, "Is Progressive Education Obsolete?", *Saturday Review*, Vol. XLV, No. 7 (February 17, 1962), pp. 56-57, 82-84.

HARRY L. WEINBERG

SCIENCE, MYSTICISM, AND LOGIC

I.

General semantics may be classified as a negative metalinguistic system which, through its emphasis on the negative, leads to a positive value system whose major goal is the preservation of the human race and predicated on the chance of our learning how to act more like human beings and less like animals.

The roots — the assumptions, axioms, implications — of the system are more intricate, varied, multivarious, and interwoven than that of any other systems of thought, science, philosophy, religions of which I am aware. Yet it is not isolated from these other systems for it borrows from all of them some of their bricks to build its own edifice.

We assume that man is a product of evolutionary development and therefore possesses both instinctive and learned behavioral patterns which are the means of adapting to, and surviving in his environments. But for reasons only dimly known, the proportion of instinctive behavioral patterns in man is much less than those he has to learn, be taught, if he is to survive. The reverse is true of all other forms of life of which we are presently aware. In short, animals are guided largely by instinct; man largely by learned behavior.

This reversal seems to be linked to his ability to use symbols—language. It provides him with the most flexible and fastest adaptive 'tool' yet discovered among living creatures. But the price we pay for this is very high and may prove fatal. Man is the great symbol-user and this is his main means of survival, but he is not born with any built-in rules (instinctual) for using symbols properly. He may, and has been known to use them against himself. As has been said in many ways and many times over the ages, man must study himself as a symbol-user to discover how to do the 'survival bit' most effectively. But to study himself, he must have the ability not only to be aware of his environment, which we infer the higher forms of animal life possess, but also the ability to be aware of his awareness. This ability, presumably, is linked to his symbol-using capacity. Thus, in a sense, he can talk to himself about himself and this in turn generates his ability to create a past, present, and future. Here, then, is the reason why Alfred Korzybski classified man as unique among all known living creatures — man is a binder. Through the use of symbols, he uses knowledge of the past in the present and passes it on to future generations. But what he takes from the past and uses now and passes on to others yet to be born may be false, untrue, deadly superstition.

Another burden, most probably linked to his symbol-using activity is his need to 'picturize', visualize, make 'models' of his own nervous system, his 'mind' and, along with this, the need to explain how and why things did happen, do happen, and should happen. In short, he has to create 'meanings'. Alfred Korzybski preferred that we substitute the 'semantic reactions' for 'meaning' because at different levels of awareness, and symbol-usings, meaning has different kinds of meaning. As soon as we talk about different levels, we, in effect, imply a hierarchical structure to our 'model of the kind'. I shall not attempt to explicate the many characteristics on this model, yet, because it implies a hierarchy of levels of language usage, it points to one of the unique factors of Korzybski's model — its negativeness. Put very, very simply, he emphasized that each level is different from the others and, therefore, he substituted the 'is not' for the 'is' of identification so common in other philosophies or models of man. Words, symbols, statements are not things (sensory perceptions, feelings, emotions), but are 'pointers' to explanations and inferences about them. So we have two great levels of abstraction in man; the verbal and the non-verbal and each of these levels has different orders or levels. For example at the verbal level we have factual statements (note: not facts, which are non-verbal happenings, perceptions), inferential statements and generalizations; inferences about inferences; generalizations about generalizations; hypotheses, laws of 'nature' — an unending process so long as we wish to keep talking.

The crucial point in Korzybski's model of the verbal process or model of the mind or model of man, whose uniqueness lies in his symbol-using potential, is this: whenever we confuse the different levels or orders of abstraction, we get into trouble with ourselves represented by various forms of neurosis and psychosis, and also with others with whom we communicate, be they mates, neighbors, or nations. Thus, through this negative stress that one level of abstraction or order of the hierarchical structure of sensing and symbolizing IS NOT the same as another, we create a 'positive value system'. It is stated as a value judgment, an 'ought to', a commandment, and not as a statement of fact. Thou shalt not confuse the levels and orders of abstraction for if you do you will, to some degree, diminish the survival chances of the human race, and we assume, with no attempt at a means of proof, that the survival of man on this earth is the greatest good, a many splendored and splintered 'thing' no matter how improbable and non-viable a 'thing' in the long reaches of time this may be.

On the basis of these preliminaries, let us turn for a moment to the title of this paper: "Science, Mysticism, and Logic". It violates some of the basic principles of general semantics in that it separates verbally that which cannot be separated non-verbally — labeled 'elementalism' by Korzybski. At the non-verbal level of feelings, emotions, perceptions, all these run together, are part of each other and necessarily so if they are to be meaningful; and felt-meaningfulness is the purpose of all humanness and the aim of education in developing a human being. It is linked to words and statements such as "aha, I see", "I get it", "now I understand it", etc. It zeros in on the ability to "see", "get", "feel" the picture as a whole or, in general semantics terminology, the order, structure, relationships of the parts as they create in a non-additive fusion the meanings of the 'big picture'. Using as an analogy the jigsaw puzzle, the structure of the whole put together lends meanings to the structure of the parts which in turn enable us to put the parts together to form the completed whole.

It is on the basis of many analogies of the above type that we can begin to understand the rather puzzling assertion of general semantics that the whole is more than, or other than, the sum of its parts. In a strictly arithmetical sense, the whole always equals the sum of its parts. Count the separated pieces of the jigsaw puzzle and they add up to the number of pieces when they are put together. Yet the meanings — our semantic reactions to it — of the completed picture are certainly not the simple additive meanings of each individual part as we react to them before putting the picture puzzle together. In effect, our hierarchical model of the abstracting process is representation of how we react to the world around us — the jigsaw of sensory perceptions, feelings, emotions, labels, theories, past experience, memories, hunches, intuitions, guesses which at each conscious moment we put together to produce what we can call the felt-meanings of each of our encounterings with the world in and around us.

Another burden of this complicated abstracting process is related to other differences between the verbal and non-verbal levels. The non-verbal is much more process oriented; all kinds of stimuli from all our sensory receptors and filters are constantly pouring in on us and changing all the time; which add to stimuli or sets of them, some to be attended to, some not; which filters — conscious, subconscious, unconscious — we use to make a sensed, meaningful structure of this deluge of stimuli cannot in any yet known way be added up arithmetically.

At the verbal level, things 'quiet down' a bit; it is more static and we can, if we wish, serialize it, make it more additive. Thus, when we write or speak, one word follows another, we cannot write or say two words or symbols at the same time, even though when these neat, serialized symbols 'descend' to the non-verbal levels or orders, their meanings become non-serialized, non-additive.

We come now to the ultimate problem of the symbol-using creature we call Man. How can we more effectively make the verbal and non-verbal levels more synergistic and less antagonistic? How can we make ourselves whole, rather than compartmentalized? How can we, to some extent, make the non-verbal and the verbal levels and orders work together rather than against each other? How can we become

'masters' rather than 'victims' of this enormously complex process of abstraction?
Who shall be the victor or victim — we or the word?

Having indicated that even the title of this article is a form of misevaluation due
to the serial, additive nature of the verbal levels when they are used, and have to be
used, to indicate the non-additive, non-serializable levels and orders of the non-
verbal worlds, how can we break out of these dilemmas and procedures which seem
to be inevitable when, as in writing, we are forced to confuse levels and forms of
abstraction?

One method is to acknowledge the existence of degrees and kinds of uncertainty
at every level of abstraction and, therefore, forego the expectation of any type of
knowledge or experience which we can represent as 'absolute', i.e., free of any
degree of uncertainty. This method is inherent in the general semantics system,
but is only one part of it. Very often, people not fully cognizant of the whole structure
of the general semantics system stop at this point and 'prove conclusively' that the
general semanticist asserts that since everything is uncertain, logic and mathematics
must also be filled with uncertainties and self-deluding methodologies. Or, if they
do have this high degree of certainty, it is obtained by their being meaningless
because of tautological reasoning, and therefore trivial games of little relevance to
the 'real' facts of and problems of life.

A fuller knowledge of the whole structure of the general semantics system, however, reveals that this is most certainly not the case, that 'pure' logic, 'pure' math,
'pure' science and even 'pure' mysticism can maintain their 'purity', and therefore
absolute certainty, by the very deceptively easy and simple device of learning and
understanding that, because of the hierarchical structure of our language and nervous
system what is very uncertain at one level of abstraction can be highly certain at
another; that both certainty and uncertainty, absolute and relative, are not antag-
onists, but necessary partners for promoting the creating of ourselves as human
beings. Just as the Yin and the Yang are the intertwining symbols for the whole
being in parts of Oriental philosophy, we can, perhaps, blow new life and meaning
into a very overworked cliché of Western thought — that there are two sides to
every coin — by the assertion that a coin, to be a coin, must have two sides in order
to be ONE coin and that the heads and tails of coins may be viewed as simple, even
antagonistic, logical opposites. In the general semantics system, they can be considered not only as two-valued, logical and equal opposites, but also as two QUALI-
TATIVELY different sides which combine non-additively to form the one whole structure we label 'the coin'.

The greatest occupational hazard I find in trying to be a reasonably competent
general semanticist is avoiding being sucked in to writing a whole book explaining
general semantics before getting down to the particular issue at hand. Thus far,
I discover myself once more dangerously near the 'eye' of the whirlpool and shall
now attempt to address myself to the topic of this article and console myself that
any perambulations that have preceded this point make enough sense so that what

follows sounds a little more sensible. We have assumed that the hierarchical structure of general semantics is of a negative character which leads to a positivistic, moralistic value system; that this hierarchical structure in some psycho-physiological way is analogous to the hierarchical structure of man's nervous system and that we can make these analogies, or models of ourselves to ourselves, because we have developed into creatures who are symbol-users.

My main point then is that we can learn to use this symbol-using ability more effectively, and along with this learning, we are enabled to control it, to focus it as best we can, from moment to moment at that particular level of abstraction which, as we proceed in the solving of some particular problem, seems most likely to lead to a solution.

II

Now we are ready to tackle the topic of "Science, Logic, and Mysticism". The first step, of course, as Wendell Johnson wrote, is to state the problem or question in such a way that it becomes an answerable question and not an unanswerable, or meaningless, one. The next step is to reread part I to see how much, if any, of this has been done. Having just done this, I discover that, to me, not only have I done this but, miraculously, have both posed the question and have solved the problem.

Science is the name we give to certain processes men have developed for solving many kinds of problems. If the problem is how to build a bridge from point A to point B, we call this a problem in 'applied' science. We use facts (observations of data recorded by the scientists in books of science and engineering) as well as scientific theories, high-order abstractions such as Newton's laws of gravitation, laws (all man-made) of relationships between stresses and strains of materials of certain crystalline structure, etc.

If the problem is of a much more theoretical nature, we tend to call it a problem in 'pure' science. For example, we may be trying to produce a theoretical model of the 'structure' of some atomic nucleus or 'nature' of electromagnetic radiations. As science becomes more sophisticated in both concepts and instrumentation, the relationship between pure and applied often becomes very difficult to define. Both employ various logics and forms of mathematics.

At first glance, it may seem that the science employed to build a bridge and that to build a new theory are very far apart on the abstraction ladder. A bridge can be seen, felt, heard, sensed — the bridge is at the non-verbal level. A theory, a law of nature, is purely verbal, a bunch of words, highly abstract, far from the non-verbal level. Yet, though the goals and achievements — the non-verbal bridge and the abstract, purely verbal, theory, even though they emphasize different levels of the abstraction ladder --- have a common anchor: the non-verbal, sensory level.

The bridge is a thing, a non-verbal. The criteria for judging its value lie in the future. How long will it hold up, what strains, expected and unexpected, will it withstand, will its usefulness fulfill what was expected and predicted, how does it fit into the landscape, is it a thing of beauty, does it represent an elegant solution to the problem bridges are supposed to be? In every case, each criterion is measured against what is observed as time passes. Always, the non-verbal test remains the ultimate, the last court of appeal. The map (verbal) must fit the territory.

What are the criteria by which we evaluate a new theory? In general, these are predictability, range of application, simplicity, fertility, elegance. Again note that the final and ultimate test resides at some non-verbal levels. Its predictability is always a sensing of some kind — an explosion, a reading on a dial, a sound, a taste, etc. To the sensing of the reading on a dial, we may have to add many inferences to supplement and fill out our explanations and understanding; but there must be predicted sensing of some type. If it does not occur, then the theory is discarded. Range of application is of a similar nature, for application eventually is tested against some non-verbal criterion. Simplicity and elegance are less easily defined, yet they too bow to the non-verbal judgment — felt-meaning — valued. Again, the map must fit the territory. Fertility can best be defined as a kind of sensed foresight. If a theory seems to close the door to future experiments and theories, if it does not seem to at least point to some new direction for contemplation, if it seems to bring us to a dead end, then it is a sterile theory and remains suspect, a kind of petrified verbal forest.

Turning now to logics and mathematics, we find it easier to place them at the various verbal levels. They need no anchors in the non-verbal. What counts most in them is the validity of the procedure. There must be no inconsistency in the reasoning, no self-contradiction, no violation of the rules of the game. It is how we handle the symbols that counts most. The rules are symbols, the manipulations are the manipulation of symbols. There seems to be no necessary anchorage to the non-verbal world; so, to keep the language straight we should say that in the sciences if the verbal maps do or do not fit structurally the non-verbal territory, then we can use the terms 'true' and 'false'. In logic and mathematics, the appropriate terms are 'valid', 'invalid', 'indeterminate'.

But even here we are not completely free from the non-verbal levels. Even though 'pure' logic and mathematics consist only of the manipulation of symbols, still, in the background lurk the tests of simplicity and elegance.

Many logical and mathematical problems above the very simple levels of complexity can be solved by a number of methods and give equally valid and identical answers. The answers can be identical because, being purely verbal symbols, identity can be possible. It is only at the non-verbal levels that no two things are identical — merely similar according to criteria we have set up whereby we agree that observed differences shall not make a difference unless, of course, upon further observation and testing, we discover that they do make a difference, whereupon we look for other variables or differences to observe.

But the experts in the games of pure symbol manipulation -- logic, mathematics, chess, have a 'feel' for the nuances of the method of solution, the beauty of it. And these are feelings or emotions at the non-verbal level. In the arts, no analytical procedures can tell us why we consider a work beautiful, great, art, elegant, or 'hack' work. For to analyze is to kill, to count is to kill; experience, knowledge, expertese, count but cannot be counted. Again, the old cliché; there can be no accounting for 'taste'. About the only criterion seems to be time and times. If many critics of many types, of many schools, over a period of about 300 years agree that, as an example of its class, this particular piece of art form is great art, then it is. It has, in some way, defeated fashions, schools, trends, individual matters of taste, manner, intuition; perhaps we can say it has defeated time or, rather, timing. It has endured the slings and arrows of outrageous fortune and it possesses, somehow, something of value.

III

Mysticism is the most difficult of the three to write about. More than any of the other two so far discussed, the negative outlook seems to me most important in the sense that the methods used are extremely important in that they constitute a positive, active, directed insistence on the learning of the 'is not'. The goal seems to be the learning, the deliberate arts and acts of extending the 'is not' to the point of being able to achieve at 'will' the active, actual control of the hierarchically structured symbol-using process which is the hallmark of man. The final step seems to be learning to 'shut off' all the verbal levels of the abstracting process: no factual statements, or inferences, or explanations, or theories, etc. It means the learning of silence at the verbal level. The minute we talk or explain in any way, i.e., using symbols, the felt mystic experience turns into its shoddy counterpart we call mysticism.

The next step seems to involve the shutting off of even ordinary non-verbal sensory feelings, sensations, emotions. It is somewhat analogous, perhaps, to the non-verbal experiences which occur when we become absorbed in some artistic creation to the point where we cease to be conscious of symbol-using in any way. Somehow we become part of the non-verbal happenings and, for a moment at least, have a sense of the explainable, of a oneness with the world.

What results is somehow akin to the non-verbal religious experience as opposed to any explanation of the experience; once again the verbalizing 'kills' and the resultant 'corpse' can now be safely labeled 'religious dogma'.

The closing down of both 'regular' or 'ordinary' verbal symbolizing and non-verbal sensing does not mean being unconscious or in some state of hypnotic trance. Rather, it seems that when we learn the 'art-science knack' of deliberate control over the abstracting processes, we open ourselves to a new type of experience, of being flooded in an all-enveloping acute awareness of the NOWNESS of things and a feeling of the absolute 'rightness' and goodness of a timeless and untimeable structurizing process.

One last-comment — a hunch, a guess, a pondering not yet worthy of even the label 'hypothesis'. Perhaps the achievement of this degree of deliberate control over the abstracting process at all levels may be the necessary balance to those errors of our growth toward humanness introduced by the development of symbol-using abilities in the creature we call 'man', analogous, perhaps, to the bad, unwanted, 'side effects' of some of the newly developed 'wonder drugs'. Even more difficult is that the 'wonder drug' of symbolizing ability which makes us human must be turned back on itself, so to speak, and used to control itself. It must be used as both a negative and positive feedback control mechanism so that we can achieve a dynamically balanced equilibrium which will prevent us from over-reaching any extreme state which can destroy our homeostatic balance. We must avoid the one extreme of over-valuing the 'nowness' experience to the point of seeking to dwell indefinitely in the hall-less halls of nowness; or the other extreme, sometimes represented by science and logic, of undervaluing the experience and dismissing it as being 'merely' hallucination, trance, self-hypnosis.

Perhaps it is another form of nature's balancing act. In the long term process of evolutionary development, we creatures with our symbol-using abilities have appeared upon the stage. This symbol-using ability can be used to turn things out of balance so quickly that the relatively slow, long-termed processes of adaptation through natural selection and survival of the fittest found in the so-called lower forms of life may be overwhelmed in us and lead to the destruction of the human race. We have been put in the position of having to learn how to live; we have to choose those courses of action which we hope will not lead to our self-extinction, so that some further development in the evolutionary processes may occur. At this point we cannot even imagine what this 'super-man', if he develops, will be like. But, this can be only a matter of hope or faith at this time.

A hope that the vast possible acceleration of the rate of entropy of man's adaptive abilities and, therefore, increasingly probable date of self-destruction brought on by the success of his symbol-using capacities in the areas of 'hard science' and 'hard technology' and relative slowness or lack of success in the areas of the 'soft sciences', 'soft technologies' we call sociology, psychology, humanities, etc., will somehow be brought into balance by the very same symbol-using ability.

So, in order to reinforce this hope, I shall paraphrase two well-known commentaries on the nature of things; one Biblical, the other the title of a book by the physicist-philosopher P.W. Bridgman: *The Way Things Are*. For all abstractions under the sun, there is a time; a time for observing and a time for describing; a time for inferring and a time for checking; a time for theorizing and a time for deliberate symbol-silencing; and may we always have the courage to proceed in the face of the knowledge that for each of us individually there is a time when there will be no more time; and that is the way things are.

TEMPLE UNIVERSITY

KENNETH FRANDSEN

SEMANTIC COMPATIBILITY IN AN INTERPERSONAL
COMMUNICATION LABORATORY

I. INTRODUCTION

Semantic compatibility in an Interpersonal Communication Laboratory may be desirable — or it may not. To be compatible semantically, that is, in terms of the relations among cognitions, referents, and words, is to agree with a person or a group. While it oversimplifies, the following example presents the basic notion. When I say ice cream, if some of your present cognitions can be described by the words good, soft, and cold, then we possess similar relations among some cognitions, a referent, and some words. To that extent we agree — we exhibit some degree of semantic compatibility.

Studies of semantic compatibility concern a specific kind of agreement. In these studies, compatibility is usually defined operationally as the amount of measured agreement concerning the location of a concept in a semantic space of n dimenions.

Concepts are located in semantic space according to an individual's responses to a form of the Osgood semantic differential. Check marks placed on seven-step graphic rating scales, anchored by bipolar adjectives, provide the raw data. Through a series of simple mathematical operations, the concept that elicited the original set of check marks can be represented as a point in semantic space. The coordinates of that point constitute the connotative meaning of the concept. The various dimensions of semantic space correspond to the fundamental aspects of a concept's emotionally or viscerally based meaning and describe the principal sources of variation in connotative meaning.

Repeatedly, studies have indicated that, although the possibilities seem infinite, three principal dimensions or factors account for almost all of the variation in connotative meaning (Kumata and Schramm, 1956; Osgood, 1957; 1962; 1963; Osgood and Suci, 1955; Suci, 1960; Triandis and Osgood, 1958). Analysis of responses indicates that the dominant dimensions or factors are: an Evaluation factor (represented by scales like *valuable-worthless*), a Potency factor (*strong-weak*), and an Activity factor (*active-passive*).

Since its appearance, Osgood's semantic differential has been used frequently and evaluated rigorously. Smith's 1962 bibliography reports over one hundred published studies and the flow of such studies has not subsided. In an evaluative review of behavioral research in Communication, Hartman concludes that "the Semantic Differential is flexible in its ability to assign meaning to stimuli; economical and efficient to administer, to score, and to interpret; and the only available procedure that provides a rationale for reducing a variety of meanings to a few basic components" (1963, p. 182).

With the measures provided by the semantic differential, the desirability of semantic compatibility can be determined empirically. Several studies suggest that semantic compatibility facilitates successful performance of various encoding tasks. Investigations of the encoding behavior of individuals (Triandis, 1960 a & b; Greenberg and Tannenbaum, 1962), debate teams (Allen, 1963), writing teams (Barrow, 1961), television production staffs (Greenberg, 1964), and high school students (Weaver, 1959), have shown that differences in effectiveness are reliably linked to differences in degrees of semantic compatibility.

Other studies have focused on changes or differences in group semantic compatibility during the production of a play (Tannenbaum, Greenberg and Leitner, 1963), in various group communication networks (Low, 1963), under different styles of direction (Rockey, 1964), and as the result of a speech training program (Williams, Clark and Sundene, 1965). According to Tannenbaum (1963), this second group of studies indicates that, following the performance of a specified encoding task, a group's level of semantic compatibility changes notably in the direction of increased harmony or agreement. Under conditions of extreme stress, e.g., a dress rehearsal, exceptions to this trend have been observed in a conventional theater setting but not in Readers Theater. While those exceptions support the claim of instrument sensitivity, they do not contradict Tannenbaum's generalization.

What the foregoing implies is simply this: (1) Group interaction regarding a collection of concepts relevant to a task produces a certain kind of agreement known as semantic compatibility. (2) Semantic compatibility is a desirable outcome of group interaction as measured by objective criteria.

II. RATIONALE

Experience in an Interpersonal Communication Laboratory might lead to semantic compatibility — or it might not. Predictable questions regarding semantic compatibility in such an environment are: About what? and Among whom? Before turning to those questions, however, a look at previous systematic investigations in similar, though not identical, settings is in order. While the laboratory experience is not a course IN general semantics, it IS a course WITH general semantics. Consequently, the following are considered relevant.

Claims regarding the value of a knowledge of general semantics are commonplace, but supporting evidence is scant and mostly subjective. Wendell Johnson (1961) concluded that the written comments of his students "seem particularly promising of continuing effects". Goldberg (1965) conducted a study of the effects of the Interpersonal Communication Laboratory to discover if Johnson's conclusions could be "supported by more formal measures". In his review of previous research, Goldberg acknowledges a recent survey by Coleman (1963) and cites "a relatively small number of systematic attempts to investigate the matter..." (Croft, 1960; Hansen, 1962; Johnson, 1961; Minor, 1964; and Treiner, 1938). Using standardized tests as measures of effect, Goldberg hypothesized that reductions in dogmatism, opinionation, authoritarianism, and rigidity would occur among participants in the laboratory. His predictions were confirmed, in part, by significant changes in dogmatism and rigidity.

Confronted by this dearth of evidence, the suggestion that we study semantic compatibility in the laboratory seemed timely. During the third term of the 1963-64 academic year, with the advise and consent of Professor Elwood Murray, we began the study.[1]

III. PROCEDURE

On each of four occasions, participants and their instructor were asked to rate five concepts on a series of nine bipolar, adjectival scales. The five concepts, selected to be representative of the field of general semantics, were: (A) Non-Allness, (B) Extensional Orientation, (C) Interpersonal Communication, (D) Consciousness of Abstracting, and (E) Non-Aristotelian Systems. The dimensions of connotative meaning indexed in this manner and the associated scales were: I. Evaluation (valuable-worthless, pleasant-unpleasant, and positive-negative). II. Potency (deepshallow, strong-weak, hard-soft), and III. Activity (active-passive, cool-warm,fastslow). In addition to the five concepts named above, participants also rated the concept 'Professor Elwood Murray' on the same series of scales each time.

Semantic differentials were distributed in booklet form at the beginning of the first, fourth, seventh and tenth weekly laboratory meetings. Participants (N-22) included both male and female undergraduates and graduate students at Southern Illinois University. Later, identical response booklets were completed by a comparable group of students at another university. This second group (N-22) had neither experience in nor any knowledge of the Interpersonal Communication Laboratory.

This procedure yielded slightly more than six thousand check marks. Each check mark was assigned a numerical value from one to seven according to its position on a scale and the resulting values were synthesized. Standard parametric and nonparametric statistical techniques were employed to answer the following questions:

[1] The author acknowledges the assistance of Professor Murray and the participants in the laboratory, particularly, Mr. James R. Rockey, who assisted with collection and tabulation of the data.

1. Where, in semantic space, are the concepts located for the two groups and what is the extent of agreement within groups regarding concept locations?
2. How congruent are the concept locations (a) when the instructor and the laboratory group are compared, (b) when the instructor and the outside group are compared, and does conceptual congruence vary over time?
3. How similar are the locations of each of the five general semantics concepts and the location of the concept, 'Professor Elwood Murray', (a) for the laboratory group, (b) for the outside group, and does conceptual similarity vary over time?
4. What is the pattern or structure of the set of concepts (a) for the laboratory group, (b) for the outside group, and what are the relations among these patterns?

IV. RESULTS

Synthesis of semantic differential data produces geometric information about the position of a concept in a three-dimensional semantic space. This 'space' is imaginary, but it is useful to think of it as an equilateral cubic area with edges that are seven units long. For an individual, the connotative meaning of a concept is a point in semantic space. Numerical values associated with the three dimensions of the cube index that point. In this study, as in others, the dimensions of the cube represent the fundamental sources of variation in the connotative meaning assigned to a concept — value, potency, and activity.

Concept Location and Extent of Agreement

For a group, the connotative meaning of a concept can be described as a cloud of points. Conventional measures of central tendency and variability, i.e., the mean and variance, indicate the location of a concept for a group and the extent of agreement among group members. Here, we can examine the locations and degree of agreement within two separate clouds — the outside group and the laboratory group — for each of the six concepts. Moreover, we can note how the clouds for the laboratory group change with time.

The data presented in tables I and II provide indexes of concept location and extent of agreement within groups measured by central tendency and variability. Responses to the semantic differentials for each concept by each group at various times were considered separately. These data suggest, for example, that the outside group assigned the concept, 'Non-Allness', considerably less value, potency and, activity than did the laboratory group at its initial meeting. The reverse of this comparison holds for the concept, 'Interpersonal Communication'. The outside group exhibited greater disagreement than the laboratory group regarding the

TABLE I.

Central Tendency of Group Locations for Selected G. S. Concepts in Semantic Space

CONCEPT:	FACTOR:	Outside Group	T_1	T_2 Laboratory Group	T_3	T_4
	I	3.59	5.68	5.68	5.99	5.86
A	II	3.73	4.99	5.23	5.55	5.59
	III	2.82	4.55	4.64	4.82	4.55
	I	5.55	5.50	5.64	5.99	6.45
B	II	5.86	4.99	5.14	5.36	5.59
	III	4.99	4.27	5.05	4.95	5.05
	I	6.27	5.55	6.27	6.32	6.59
C	II	5.82	4.99	5.73	5.82	5.95
	III	5.77	4.95	5.68	5.64	5.45
	I	5.09	5.60	6.14	6.09	6.18
D	II	5.27	4.95	5.36	5.68	5.77
	III	3.86	4.36	4.99	5.14	5.05
	I	4.41	4.82	5.60	5.14	5.41
E	II	4.86	4.68	4.77	4.86	5.05
	III	3.91	4.09	4.64	4.41	4.14
	I	4.45	5.45	6.36	6.41	6.64
F	II	4.41	4.99	5.73	5.82	5.73
	III	4.04	5.14	5.99	5.95	5.77

Concepts: (A) Non-Allness, (B) Extensional Orientation, (C) Interpersonal Communication, (D) Consciousness of Abstracting, (E) Non-Aristotelian Systems, (F) Professor Elwood Murray.

Factors I. Evaluation II. Potency III. Activity

concept, 'Non-Allness', but not about the concept, 'Interpersonal Communication'.

With a few notable exceptions, two general trends emerge from the laboratory group data. First, the value and potency of the concepts increased with time while the activity of the concepts reached a peak at the fourth or seventh meeting and then faded. Second, the laboratory group exhibited greater agreement than the outside group regarding the value, potency and activity of the concepts. Three of every four comparisons supported the second trend.

For the concepts, 'Interpersonal Communication' and 'Professor Elwood Murray', two specific trends appear in the laboratory group data. Agreement regarding the value of these two concepts increased steadily while agreement regarding their potency and activity declined.

TABLE II

Variability of Group Locations for Selected
G. S. Concepts in Semantic Space

CONCEPT	FACTOR	Outside Group	T$_1$	T$_2$	T$_3$	T$_4$
				Laboratory Group		
A	I	3.40	1.85	2.32	1.24	2.03
A	II	3.16	1.81	1.42	1.21	1.59
A	III	2.16	.83	1.67	2.10	1.59
B	I	1.12	1.69	1.86	1.43	.64
B	II	.98	1.62	1.65	1.58	2.06
B	III	2.48	.97	1.38	1.57	1.09
C	I	.97	1.69	1.45	1.18	.54
C	II	1.01	1.05	1.16	1.30	1.28
C	III	1.30	1.09	1.56	1.67	1.78
D	I	1.71	1.68	1.74	1.32	.73
D	II	2.14	1.28	1.67	1.18	1.14
D	III	2.31	.81	2.19	1.65	1.85
E	I	3.49	2.68	1.59	1.74	1.21
E	II	3.27	.99	1.99	1.84	1.19
E	III	2.37	.94	1.29	1.11	1.27
F	I	1.88	1.59	1.00	.73	.53
F	II	2.35	.99	1.26	1.20	1.73
F	III	2.24	1.03	1.33	.81	1.71

Concepts: (A) Non-Allness, (B) Extensional Orientation, (C) Interpersonal Communication, (D) Consciousness of Abstracting, (E) Non-Aristotelian Systems, (F) Professor Elwood Murray.

Factors: I. Evaluation   II. Potency   III. Activity

Conceptual Congruence as a function of Time

In addition to the clouds of points representing the outside group and the laboratory group at different times, a set of 'anchor points', or locations at various times, represent the instructor's connotative meanings for the five concepts. To determine the extent of agreement between the instructor and the laboratory group or between the instructor and the outside group, the generalized distance statistic, D^2, was employed (Osgood, 1957, pp. 90-104; cf. Tannenbaum, Greenberg, and Leitner, 1963). As a measure of the multidimensional distance between two points, D^2 indexes the degree of agreement concerning the location of a concept. Small values of D^2 indicate a high degree of conceptual congruence or semantic compatibility.

Distances between the judgments of the instructor and the judgments of each group member were averaged to provide a set of data points for each concept.[2]

[2] See table III.

TABLE III.

Summary of Changes in Congruence as Measured by Average Distances (D²)

CONCEPT	T_1	T_2	T_3	T_4	X_r^2*	p**
A. Non-Allness	11.35	14.41	6.63	8.55	3.12	.5 > p > .3
B. Extensional Orientation	7.41	10.91	6.86	8.18	1.46	.7 > p > .5
C. Interpersonal Communication	7.86	4.23	4.14	7.09	2.80	.5 > p > .3
D. Consciousness of Abstracting	7.09	9.77	5.63	9.55	3.86	.3 > p > .2
E. Non-Aristotelian Systems	14.05	17.18	11.77	18.05	7.40	.1 > p > .05

* Result of Friedman two-way analysis of variance by ranks. (Seigel, 1956)
** Probabilities associated with the occurrence, under the null hypothesis, of the observed X_r^2.

A summary of this analysis of changes in conceptual congruence is pictured in figure 1.

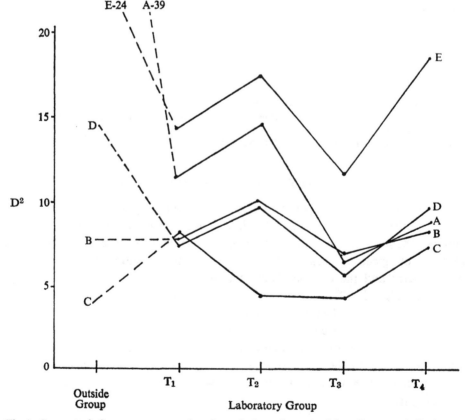

Fig. 1. Conceptual Congruence as a function of time determined by distances (D²) between instructor's locations and group's locations for selected O. G. concepts.

Conceptual congruence between the instructor and the members of the outside group varied substantially depending on the concept. Connotative meanings assigned 'Non-Allness' and 'Non-Aristotelian Systems' were extremely incongruent for the instructor and the outside group but their meanings for 'Interpersonal Communication' were nearly identical. Divergence of meanings for 'Extensional Orientation' and 'Consciousness of Abstracting' was greater than for 'Interpersonal Communication' but less than for 'Non-Allness' and 'Non-Aristotelian Systems'.

Conceptual congruence between the instructor and the laboratory group varied with time. However, during the first seven weekly meetings of the group, changes in the direction of increased harmony were unsteady and slight, though not statistically significant, regression occurred between the seventh and the tenth meetings. For this collection of concepts, congruence between the instructor and the laboratory group was maximal at the beginning of their seventh meeting. At this point, the instructor and the group disagreed most about the meaning of 'Non-Aristotelian Systems' and least about the meaning of 'Interpersonal Communication'. Between these extremes at that time, in order of increasing agreement or congruence, were 'Extensional Orientation', 'Non-Allness' and 'Consciousness of Abstracting'.

Conceptual Similarity as a Function of Time

The foregoing discussion of conceptual congruence focused on the degree of agreement between pairs of individuals regarding a single concept. Here, the focus shifts to pairs of concepts. The generalized distance measure, D^2, indexes the degree of similarity for an individual in the locations of two concepts. Again, small values of D^2 indicate a high degree of conceptual similarity or semantic compatibility.

TABLE IV

Summary of Changes in Conceptual Similarity as Measured by Average Distances (D^2)

CONCEPT	T_1	T_2	T_3	T_4	X_r^{2**}	p^{**}
A. Non-Allness	3.41	9.00	4.73	7.91	7.07	$.1 > p > .05$
B. Extensional Orientation	3.85	6.09	4.59	5.18	4.63	$.3 > p > .2$
C. Interpersonal Communication	1.86	3.14	2.32	5.14	3.73	$.3 > p > .2$
D. Consciousness of Abstracting	3.55	4.77	4.36	6.41	2.34	$.7 > p > .5$
E. Non-Aristotelian Systems	4.77	8.73	10.23	9.27	4.04	$.2 > p > .1$

* Result of Friedman two-way analysis of variance by ranks. (Seigal, 1956)
** Probabilities associated with the occurrence, under the null hypothesis, of the observed X_r^2.

Pairs were formed by matching the concept, 'Professor Elwood Murray', with each of the five general semantics concepts. Distances between concepts were averaged to provide a set of data points for each of the five pairs.[3] This analysis of changes in conceptual similarity is summarized in figure 2.

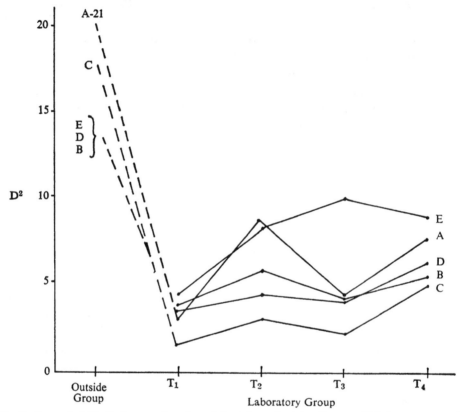

Fig. 2. Conceptual Similarity as a function of time determined by distances (D^2) between group's locations for Professor Elwood Murray and group's locations for selected concepts.

For members of the outside group, connotative meanings of the general semantics concepts differed sharply from the connotative meaning of 'Professor Murray'. Divergence was greatest for the concept 'Non-Allness', almost as great for 'Interpersonal Communication', and only slightly less for the other three concepts — 'Non-Aristotelian Systems', Consciousness of Abstracting', and 'Extensional Orientation'.

Among the members of the laboratory group, however, maximal similarity between 'Professor Murray' and each of the five general semantics concepts occurred at the beginning of the first meeting. With the possible exception of 'Non-Allness', changes in the direction of increasing dissociation between the general semantics concepts

[3] See table IV.

and the concept, 'Professor Elwood Murray', as evidenced by increases in the size of the D^2 values from the first to the tenth meetings, were not statistically reliable. Moreover, meanings of 'Murray' and each of the other concepts displayed consistently greater similarity for participants in the laboratory than for members of the outside group.

Conceptual Structure as a Function of Time

To determine the pattern or structure of this set of concepts, it was necessary to extend the examination of distances between concepts to all possible pairs. Osgood indicates that "the distances between each concept and every other concept can be calculated and entered into an $m \times m$ matrix. This matrix represents the semantic structure of the set of m concepts, giving distances or similarity relations among all concepts" (1957, p. 93).

Conceptual structures for the outside group and for the laboratory group at each time of measurement are presented in tables V through IX. Since each entry in every matrix represents a distance between two concepts in semantic space, the entries in a particular matrix can be examined to determine whether any clusters of

TABLE V

Laboratory Group distances (D) between concepts at T_1

CONCEPTS:	B	C	D	E	F
A. Non-Allness	.33	.42	.21	1.02	.63
B. Ext. Orient.		.68	.14	.77	.87
C. Inpsl. Comm.			.59	1.17	.21
D. Con. of Abstr.				.87	.80
E. Non-A. Systems					1.26
F. Prof. E. M.					

TABLE VI

Laboratory Group distances (D) between concepts at T_2

CONCEPTS:	B	C	D	E	F
A. Non-Allness	.42	1.30	.59	.47	1.59
B. Ext. Orient.		1.07	.55	.55	1.32
C. Inpsl. Comm.			.79	1.57	.32
D. Con. of Abstr.				.87	1.09
E. Non-A. Systems					1.82
F. Prof. E. M.					

KENNETH FRANDSEN

TABLE VII

Laboratory Group distances (D) between concepts at T_3

CONCEPTS:	B	C	D	E	F
A. Non-Allness	.23	.92	.35	1.17	1.24
B. Ext. Orient.		.89	.39	1.12	1.18
C. Inpsl. Comm.			.57	1.96	.32
D. Con. of Abstr.				1.45	.88
E. Non-A. Systems					2.22
F. Prof. E. M.					

TABLE VIII

Laboratory Group distances (D) between concepts at T_4

CONCEPTS:	B	C	D	E	F
A. Non-Allness	.77	1.21	.62	.81	1.45
B. Ext. Orient.		.56	.32	1.48	.76
C. Inpsl. Comm.			.60	1.98	.39
D. Con. of Abstr.				1.39	.86
E. Non-A. Systems					2.15
F. Prof. E. M.					

TABLE IX

Outside Group distances (D) between concepts

CONCEPTS:	B	C	D	E	F
A. Non-Allness	3.62	4.50	2.39	1.77	1.64
B. Ext. Orient.		1.06	1.37	1.86	2.05
C. Inpsl. Comm.			2.31	2.80	2.88
D. Con. of Abstr.				.80	1.09
E. Non-A. Systems					.49
F. Prof. E. M.					

concepts are evident. A cluster is defined as the existence of a subset of concepts such that distances between concepts within the subset are smaller than distances with concepts outside the subset (Osgood, 1957, p. 102).

Although the conceptual structures for the laboratory group are relatively compact when compared with the outside group's conceptual structure, clustering is evident in each.

At the first, seventh and tenth meetings of the laboratory group, concepts were clustered in essentially the same manner. One cluster included the concepts, 'Non-Allness', 'Extensional Orientation' and 'Consciousness of Abstracting'. The other cluster was composed of 'Interpersonal Communication' and 'Professor Elwood Murray'. The remaining concept, 'Non-Aristotelian Systems', was alone. The pattern at the fourth meeting of this group departed from the other patterns. On that occasion, 'Non-Aristotelian Systems' was located within the cluster that contained 'Non-Allness', 'Extensional Orientation' and 'Consciousness of Abstracting', and, again, the other cluster included 'Interpersonal Communication' and 'Professor Elwood Murray'.

The outside group's conceptual structure differs from the other structures in two respects. First, distances between concept pairs were generally greater for the outside group. Second, concepts were clustered in a different manner for this group than for the laboratory group. 'Consciousness of Abstracting', 'Non-Aristotelian Systems' and 'Professor Elwood Murray' constituted one cluster. 'Extensional Orientation' and 'Interpersonal Communication' formed another and the remaining concept, 'Non-Allness', was distant from both clusters.

Finally, by comparing each matrix representing a pattern with every other matrix, relations or similarities among conceptual structures were determined. The correlation coefficients presented in table X provide indexes of these relations. The magnitude of the correlations among conceptual structures for the laboratory group and the strong inverse relation between the outside group's pattern and the laboratory group's initial pattern lend support to earlier observations.

TABLE X

Correlations between Conceptual Structures

TIME:	1	2	3	4
Outside Group	− .446*	− .189	− .385	− .135
Lab. Group T_1		+ .611**	+ .973**	+ .735**
Lab. Group T_2			+ .772**	+ .702**
Lab. Group T_3				+ .892**

* $p < .05$	** $p < .01$

Differences and similarities in clustering of concepts are reflected, for example, in a comparison of the degree of relationship between patterns one and two with the degree of relationship between patterns one and three for the laboratory group. That is, the change in clustering occasioned by movement of the concept, 'Non-Aristotelian Systems', between the first and second and between the first and third times of measurement is reflected in the difference between correlations of +.611 and +.973, respectively. The strong inverse relation (—.442) between the outside group and the laboratory group suggests a pronounced difference in clustering.

V. DISCUSSION

Several differences between the conditions of this study and those of other studies of changes in semantic compatibility may account for discrepancies in the results. For example, changes in the direction of increased harmony between directors and performers in a theater setting were explained, in part, by the fact that "both tended to move TOWARD ONE ANOTHER" (Tannenbaum, Greenberg and Leitner, 1963). In the present study, the instructor's connotative meanings for the concepts remained stable and the group exhibited only slight changes.

The studies involving members of a Readers Theater cast (Rockey, 1964), and participants in a speech training program (Williams, Clark, and Sundene, 1965) focused on compatibility in connection with relatively structured and specific encoding tasks. The experience afforded by participation in the Interpersonal Communication Laboratory is characterized by a considerable amount of freedom in encoding behavior and a wide variety of encoding tasks. What is surprising is the amount of semantic compatibility that was observed under these conditions.

Unexpected and highly tentative findings, exemplified by the trend in the direction of increasing dissociation between the general semantic concepts and the concept, 'Professor Elwood Murray', or by the variations in concept clustering associated with the movement of the concept, 'Non-Aristotellan Systems', might provoke speculative explanations. However, none is offered for the present. Instead, a comment about the implications of semantic differential methodology for theory and research under the rubric of General Semantics seems appropriate.

In contrast to Mowrer's (1960) assertion that "general semantics, despite its name, is concerned with a really quite specific and probably not very important point", Rapoport (1961) has suggested that "general semantics is an attempt to extend language analysis beyond logical syntax and object-referent relations to psychological matters and therefore to the relation between language and human conduct". Although the temptation to embrace Rapoport's view and discard Mowrer's may be great for some, the crux of the conflict for many was sharpened by Barnlund's (1963) observation that "general semantics is not a set of findings, a body of data, or a department of knowledge but is, rather, an orientation, an attitude, a methodology". If Barnlund was merely describing a condition to be changed, perhaps the conflict can be resolved.

Much contemporary theorizing and attendant psychological research is concerned with something called mediation (Staats and Staats, 1964). Indeed, the semantic differential was developed for the purpose of indexing what Osgood calls representational mediation processes. Judging by their descriptions and theoretical under-plannings, the parallel between Osgood's representational mediation process and Korzybski's *semantic reaction* is striking. While the name given to what an instrument measures is not important, the predictions that it can test may be. In the context of Rapoport's injunction, the semantic differential carries significant implications.

PENNSYLVANIA STATE UNIVERSITY

REFERENCES

Allen, R. R., "The Effects of Interpersonal and Concept Compatibility on Encoding Behavior and Achievement of Debate Tames", *Central States Speech Journal*, XIV (1963), pp. 23-26.

Barnlund, D. C., "Is There Any New Business?" *ETC.*, XX (1963), pp. 75-83.

Barrow, L. C., "The Effects of Cognitive Incongruity Upon Encoding Behavior", unpubl. diss. (Wisconsin University, 1961).

Coleman, C. J., "Courses in General Semantics in American Higher Education", *ETC.*, XIX (1963), pp. 457-479.

Croft, W. F., "General Semantics and the Teaching of Science", *ETC.*, XVII (1960), pp. 440-448.

Goldberg, Alvin, "The Effects of a Laboratory Course in General Semantics", *ETC.*, XXII (1965), pp. 19-24.

Greenberg, B. S., "The Effects of Communicator Incompatibility on Children's Judgments of Television Programs", *Journal of Broadcasting*, VIII (1964), pp. 157-171.

Greenberg, B. S., and P. H. Tannenbaum, "Communicator Performance Under Cognitive Stress", *Journalism Quarterly*, XXXIX (1962). pp. 169-178.

Hansen, H. M., "A Study of Applications of General Semantics Made by Students During a Course in Interpersonal Communication", unpubl. thesis (University of Denver, 1962).

Hartman, F. R., "A Behavioristic Approach to Communication", *Audio-Visual Communication Review*, XI (1963), pp. 155-190.

Johnson, Wondell, "Some Effects of a Course in General Semantics", *ETC.*, XVIII (1961), 315-346.

Kumata, H., and W. Schramm, "A Pilot Study of Cross-Cultural Methodology", *Public Opinion Quarterly*, XX (1956), pp. 222-237.

Low, J. H., Jr., "Some Effects of Various Group Communication Networks on Concept Meaning as Measured by Osgood's Semantic Differential Technique", unpubl. paper (SAA Conv., Denver, 1963).

Minor, Gene, "The Relationship of Various Characteristics to intensional-extensional Orientation as Measured by the Stroop Color-Word Test", unpubl. thesis (University of Denver, 1964).

Mowrer, O. Hobart, *Learning Theory and the Symbolic Processes* (New York, Wiley, 1960).

Osgood, C. E., "An Exploration into Semantic Space", in *The Science of Human Communication* Wilbur Schramm (Ed.) (New York, Basic Books, 1963), pp. 28-40.

Osgood, C. E., "Studies in the Generality of Affective Meaning Systems", *American Psychologist*, XVII (1962), pp. 10-28.

Osgood, C. E., and G. J. Suci, "Factor Analysis of Meaning", *Journal of Experimental Psychology*, L (1955), 325-338.

Osgood, C. E., G. J. Suci, and P. H. Tannenbaum, *The Measurement of Meaning* (Urbana, Univ. of Ill. Press, 1957).

Rapoport, Anatol, "Two Marxist Critiques of General Semantics: A Report and a Reply", *ETC.*, XVIII (1961), pp. 289-314.

Rockey, J. R., "Effects of 'Directive' and 'Nondirective' Criticism on Changes in Semantic Compatibility During Preparation of a Readers Theater Production", unpubl. thesis (Southern Illinois, 1964).

Siegel, Sidney, *Nonparametric Statistics for the Behavioral Sciences* (New York, McGraw-Hill, 1956).

Smith, R. G., "Semantic Differential Bibliography: Developmental and Experimental Studies", *Central States Speech Journal*, XIII (1962), pp. 209-213.

Staats, A. W., and C. K. Staats, *Complex Human Behavior* (New York, Holt, Rinchart & Winston, 1964).

Suci, G. J., "A Comparison of Semantic Structures in American Southeast Culture Groups", *Journal of Abnormal and Social Psychology*, LXI (1960), pp. 25-30.

Tannenbaum, P. H., B. S. Greenberg, and M. A. Leitner, "Changes is Semantic Compatibility During the Production of a Play", *Speech Monographs*, XXX (1963), pp. 340-344.

Traeiner, J. C., "Experimental Results of Training in General Semantics Upon Intelligence", *Papers from the First American Congress on General Semantics* (New York, 1938).

Triandis, H. C., "Cognitive Similarity and Communication in a Dyad", *Human Relations*, XIII (1960), pp. 175-183. (a)

Triandis, H., "Some Determinants of Interpersonal Communication", *Human Relations*, XII (1960), pp. 279-287.

Triandis, H. C., and C. E. Osgood, "A Comparative Factorial Analysis of Semantic Structures in Monolingual Greek and American College Students", *Journal of Abnormal and Social Psychology*, LVII (1958), pp. 187-196.

Weaver, C. M., "Semantic Distance Between Students and Teachers and its Effect Upon Learning", *Speech Monographs*, XXVI (1959), pp. 273-281.

Williams, Frederick, R. A. Clark, and Barbara Sundene, "Effects of a Speech Training Program Upon Semantic Compatibility", *Speech Monographs*, XXXI (1965), pp. 119-123.

DAN McLACHLAN, JR.

COMMUNICATIONS and CIVILIZATION

INTRODUCTION

Perhaps one of the most outstanding achievements of primitive man was the development of speech. Speech gave man the power to communicate coordinated plans for
action, thus enabling him to achieve great and complex tasks which could not be done
alone. This early advantage of man over the animals of the forests and plains has
grown and is reflected today by the telegraph, telephone, radio, the symbolic language
of mathematics, the logic of computers, robot machinery, and most of all, by the
abstract concepts which tax the brain beyond the level required by the older materi-
alistic scramble for food and shelter.

One of the most fascinating reveries that an old man can indulge in is to look back
over the environment of the various eras through which he has lived and ask "What
did the older and wiser men of each of these periods place the greatest emphasis on?"
As small children, if we were poor, we were taught to save things, material things,
like food, cloth for patching, scraps of wood, buttons, nails, old wheels and money.
Then we became aware, when we were older, that cord-wood, although a material,
was energy for the stove; hay was energy for the horses; coal, energy for the steam
engine, etc. So the world seemed richer because we knew more about it. Maybe some
readers can remember when they felt a little proud that they knew that the cloth in
clothing and iron in the bridges played a different role in our lives than coal or gasoline.
It seems peculiar now to remember the time when we were naive enough to think that
the whole world was just matter and energy.

While we as children were learning the crude meanings of matter and energy and
their value in our economy, we saw our mothers clean house, our fathers arrange
things on the farm, our school teachers begin to get organized two weeks before
school started, until finally the distinction between *order* and *chaos* began to dawn
upon us. Some of us noticed that the older and wiser tend to put more emphasis on
order, and eventually we discovered that 'order' means more than just the systematic
arrangement of static things. It can mean a synchronization of motions of things,
such as the movements of dancers in a Virginia reel, the coordinated actions of players

on a basketball team, the maneuvers of the parts of an army during battle, or the conduct of a nation during crises.

An important word that we learned during our childhood is "cooperation". As cooperation begins to extend between more people over larger distances, the need for one to know what others are doing increases and becomes more difficult. This transfer of information, which gets to be an intricate and cumbersome process, is called "communication". In growing up we learned other important concepts too, such as: material, energy, order, cooperation, and information, and we discovered that some of these things can be measured and numbers assigned to the quantity of them. We learned that material can be measured by the weight in pounds, and every home and store had some kinds of scales. We learned about horse-power-hours. To measure order, cooperation, etc., and to put numbers on them, seemed too abstract and intangible to even attempt. But one of the things that makes life so much fun for an individual is the close parallel between his own development and that of civilization, and civilization, in the course of the progress of science, has found numerical measures for many things including such abstractions as chaos, information, and the like. Let us look at our civilization for a moment.

Civilization in general seems to have been capable of organizing fundamental concepts in an understandable form in almost the same sequence that a person does. Primitive man quickly got the concept of material things. He learned to apply numbers to them as soon as he learned to count. He learned to count almost as soon as he found that there were reliable groups of things upon which a basis of counting could be founded (for example, almost every person has ten fingers, there are arrangements of stars in the sky comprising unchanging numbers etc.). But even such a simple process as the measuring of material is too much to develop fully here.[1] Primitive man had a feeling for distance, direction and time and could measure and count them in a fashion. But energy was for hundreds of generations unfathomable although man was subjected unmercifully to fatigue when he lacked energy and to much brutality when the wind, water or animals had more energy than he could combat. It was not until the seventeenth century, in the days of Newton, that energy began to be understood. So it is not surprising that a child is slow in grasping the idea of energy.

The invention of the steam engine by Watt gave a great impetus to a quantitative study of energy, and it was soon shown by actual tests that energy, E, can be broken into two parts, the useful part E called free energy because it can be used for doing work such as a steam engine can be expected to do, and an unavailable part of the energy, TS, from which no useful work can be obtained. In this term TS, T is the temperature measured in degrees Kelvin and S represents a thing called "entropy". This is expressed sympolically:

$$E = F + TS \tag{1}$$

[1] For example, to count apples is one thing, while measuring apple sauce is another. The reader might recall the problem Archimedes had in determining the gold in the king's crown.

This free energy term F can be thought of as *ordered* energy and is subject to being commanded to useful purposes while the TS represents the *chaotic* energy which can be used only for inducing chaos in other materials. These thoughts will be recognized by the reader to have social implications. For example an organized task force can be directed to preassigned purposes while a disorderly mob, in spite of its energy, size or enthusiasm can only spread chaos. A partially organized group has a portion of both F and TS within it.

While the investigation of TS has brought out something beautiful regarding S it has not cleared up temperature T. This is paradoxical. Every child who has burnt his finger thinks he knows *temperature* and is mystified by the word 'entropy', while the educated physical scientist feels that he understands entropy better than temperature. Although we have been focusing on concepts in the area of thermodynamics, we have not forgotten that we ultimately plan to arrive at a discussion of *information* and *communication*.

The meaning of entropy S was suggested through a man who was not fundamentally a thermodynamicist but more of a statistical mechanist. His name was Boltzmann, and he said,

$$S = - - K \quad W \tag{2}$$

In this equation K is a constant which has since been named the Boltzmann constant and W is the number of ways of arranging atoms in energy levels (or energy packets on atoms).

Thus we see that in engineering we found the concepts of order and disorder in places we intuitively did not expect them. Of course in crystallography we expected and did find order just as fully illustrated by mother nature in gems and rocks as in art and wallpaper designs arranged deliberately. In all these cases we find W of equation (2) to be smaller than expected in disordered things.

In the meantime civilization encountered a thing which Shannon called 'Information' (1) which was so much like entropy S that it is sometimes called *negentropy*. It was a product of our times and its discovery was brought about by the increasing importance of communications in a complex society. It might be instructive to enumerate just a few of the subjects which are recent products of our times and which the reader might wish to look into:

1. Information theory
2. Cybernetics
3. Econometrics
4. Game theory
5. Stochastic processes
6. Markoff chains
7. Uncertainty and the "Uncertainty Principle"
8. Convolutions and Correlation functions

9. Linear and other kinds of programing
10. Feedback, noise etc.
11. Mathematical psychology
12. Mathematics of heredity, evolution and the learning process
13. Decision Processes

THE OHIO STATE UNIVERSITY

PART TWO

GROUP COMMUNICATION

Most human communication occurs in small face-to-face groups. Some groups seldom formalize a goal and rarely transact business. They exist primarily because they provide comradeship, tension release, ego enhancement, and other social and psychological rewards and satisfactions. Other groups are more task-oriented. They exist to get a job done and their effectiveness is generally determined on the basis of their productivity. Both task-oriented and 'socio-emotional' groups are the concern of communication scholars.

The more scientifically inclined communication scholar is interested in how groups operate and what makes them 'tick'. He is curious about such things as how members of small face-to-face groups communicate with each other, establish norms, and develop structure. In addition, he wants to know why group members behave the way they do. To answer these questions he constructs theories of group behavior and tests his constructs by studying groups in natural settings as well as under controlled laboratory conditions.

The communication scholar who engages in human relations training or who applies his knowledge in other ways also seeks a thorough understanding of group phenomena. But he does not stop there. Knowledge to the methodologist is more than a way of satisfying curiosity. The communication methodologist looks for the implications of scientific data so he can apply the findings to practical situations. The small group methodologist is not just a technician with a bag full of techniques and gimmicks. He is a scholar, well grounded in small group theory and research, who knows how to put social scientific insight to use.

In the small group area communication methodologists have a host of interests and perform a variety of tasks. Since the middle thirties those with a traditional rhetorical background in speech have focused on problem-solving phenomena and their effort has generated many principles for effective problem-solving behavior in small task-oriented discussion groups. They have concentrated on the use in discussion of logic and rational thought and on the refinement of such problem-solving procedures as reflective-thinking, brain storming, and more recently, PERT, a procedure based on the management system first used to develop the atomic submarine. From a methodological point of view the traditionalists have been concerned with the implementation of these procedures in classroom situations, business conferences, legislative committees, and the like, and with such related matters as discussion leadership.

Communication scholars with more of a social scientific orientation and those who have been influenced by developments in the clinical areas have studied the small group as a setting for individual and interpersonal change and adjustment. They have been concerned with group atmosphere or climate, defensive behavior, dependency relationships, and other matters related to the emotional or psychological aspects of human interaction. Methodologically, those with a process orientation have applied their knowledge in human relations courses and workshops, leadership training conferences, programs devoted to community and inter-group relations, and other activities generally associated with adult education.

Although scholars have speculated about groups for centuries, the systematic study of group communication is a relatively recent phenomenon. Most of the research in the small group area has been conducted since World War II and many of the small group methodologies such as T-group training and brainstorming were invented during the past few decades. In addition, small group research has been conducted by scholars representing a wide variety of disciplines, and group methods have been used by academicians and professionals in many specialties. When an area of study is young and of interest to diverse groups, there is likely to develop jealousy, rivalry, and competition among groups committed to different theories, approaches, and points of view. Although conflict can encourage greater productivity on the part of some and may be helpful in stimulating interest in the specialty, it can also stifle and distort growth by discouraging the openness to new ideas and the cooperating so essential to any academic pursuit.

The student of group communication may find research more exciting than methodology, he may be more attracted to the psychological aspects of group behavior than the task aspects, or he may have any other combination of interests and preferences. His inclinations in this regard may determine the group phenomena he studies most thoroughly or the methodologies he understands best or handles most skillfully. Personal preferences should not, however, cause him to ignore, distort, or deny the value of findings and activities in areas that he finds less attractive. The fact that not all group research is equally valid and not all methodologies are equally appropriate does not make it less vital that his evaluations of any piece of research or methodology be based on legitimate criteria rather than his individual preferences or inclinations. The group communication scholar is free to specialize, but if he seeks a well balanced understanding of group behavior he is not likely to obtain one by ignoring the small group literature outside his area of concentration. As a methodologist, he cannot afford to snub the techniques and inventions of any of the professionals in the small group area. Therapists, trainers, discussion teachers, social workers, adult educators, conference planners, industrial consultants, general semanticists, and scores of others have developed worthwhile group methodologies.

The authors of the chapters in this section on group communication represent a wide range of scholarly and methodological interests. Mr. Rupert Cortright, Mr. Gene Rebstock, Mr. Seth Fessenden, Mr. Louis Glorfeld, and Mr. Kim Giffin are identified primarily with the discipline of speech; Mr. Jack Gibb and Mrs. Lorraine Gibb are more closely associated with the fields of psychology and social psychology. Giffin has been primarily interested in group communication as an area of study whereas the others have concentrated largely on the use of group methods in practical situations. As methodologists, Fessenden has become identified with sociometric techniques, Giffin and Cortright have focused on discussion as problem-solving, Jack and Lorraine Gibb have studied group approaches to human relations training, and Gene Rebstock has been interested in the use of the case method and other discussion methodologies in management training.

Trained as a traditionalist, Kim Giffin's scholarly output can best be characterized as broad and eclectic. He has authored scores of articles in such communication specialties as rhetoric, public address, debate, discussion, human relations and management training, and persuasion. His contributions have ranged from the experimental to the critical and historical, and his focus has been on both theory and application. In the area of group process, Giffin has been interested in theoretical and applied research and in the methodological implications of small group investigations.

Giffin is very much aware of the traditional distinction that has been made between 'speech' and small group phenomena, a distinction that is becoming less and less meaningful to serious students of group or interpersonal communication. Giffin begins his contribution to this section on group communication with the warning that "any student of speech communication... neglects small-group research only at his peril". He points out that the small group research literature provides insight into the discussion and conference situations that have so long been the concern of the speech scholar, and, he suggests that the research methods of small group investigators are appropriate for the study of communication in a variety of other settings. In his comprehensive review, Giffin systematically discusses small group research findings and approaches that have implications for the communication specialists.

During the past three decades members of the speech discipline have produced a large body of literature dealing with public and private discussion. Their concern has been with more than an analysis and description of the discussion process. Viewing discussion as an art and as an important methodology for dealing with human affairs, much of their writing has been prescriptive and inspirational in nature. They have focused not only on what happens in a face-to-face discussion but on how discussions OUGHT to happen and on ways to make them happen better.

Rupert Cortright identifies some of the less obvious advantages and limitations of group communication in his philosophic inquiry into the uses and abuses of discussion. His approach is typical of the speech scholar. In good inspirational style he asserts: "...he who engages in free discussion is twice blest; ...as minds work together... we... bring a world closer together;... it is entirely possible that in training for effective discussion we are as directly training for effective thinking...". On a prescriptive level, Cortright recommends discussion as a means of forestalling problems, warns discussants to establish a favorable environment before "plunging into the problem at hand", and not always to consider consensus desirable. Obviously, then, to Cortright and many of his colleagues discussion is more than an area of investigation. It is an essential part of democratic living and through his teaching, writing, and research the group communication scholar can contribute significantly to the common good.

Like Cortright, Jack and Lorraine Gibb are methodologists. They too are concerned with how groups can be helped to operate more effectively. Unlike Cortright, however, the Gibbs have been less interested in discussion as a method of democracy or as a problem-solving technique than they have been in group approaches to human relations training. Their emphasis has been on individual and group health rather than on task effectiveness or efficiency.

In their contribution to this section Jack and Lorraine Gibb draw upon the extensive research they have conducted on longitudinal changes in small groups to identify those personal and group behaviors that seem to be closely related to group growth and productivity. They identify fear, lack of trust, inadequate systems of communication, overaspiration, and a variety of other individual and interpersonal factors that interfere with group development. The obstacles to group actualization identified by the Gibbs would clearly interfere with progress in a training group where the emphasis is on self insight and interpersonal sensitivity. It is also easy to see how these same factors would inhibit growth and productivity in the classroom, the family, the committee, or in any other group situation.

The communication methodologist, it has been pointed out, keeps abreast of and contributes to the growing body of theory, research — and speculation — in the communication arts and sciences. In addition to this, the methodologist concentrates on the methodological implications of communication theory, research, and scholarship. In a sense, he is a social engineer who is interested not only in understanding but in implementation. Sociometry is one of the few social scientific "schools of thought" that has deliberately developed a methodology based upon its own theory and research findings. It provides the communication methodologist with a theory of interpersonal relations, a research approach, and a methodology for working more effectively with groups.

As a communication scholar Seth Fessenden has long been interested in sociometry. In his contribution to this section he summarizes some of his sociometric research and considers some of its methodological significance. Although his discussion deals with the implications of his findings for the classroom, his insights have relevance for other communication situations as well.

The communication scholar has an obvious responsibility to conduct and report his research in an unbiased manner. Eugene Rebstock points out in this section that if he is to be effective, it is vital that the communication specialist be equally objective and open-minded in his pedagogy. Rebstock describes the dramatic changes in teaching methods and philosophy he and his colleagues underwent during a four-year period of communication training for a large private corporation. Initially, Rebstock and his staff planned to cover small group theory and general semantics in their course. They soon discovered that such communication processes as reflection, argumentation, persuasion, and group leadership were needed to make the training relevant to the particular needs of their clients.

Rebstock warns the methodologist that training methods which have "popular support and even theoretical validity" may be totally unrelated to the requirements of specific groups or organizations. An educational program for an organization, Rebstock advises, should be based at least in part upon a careful investigation of the activities and personnel of that organization and not entirely on standard or routine approaches.

The essay by Louis Glorfeld underscores the humanistic and aesthetic language used by many scientists and suggests such a rhetoric as an objective approach to allaying world fears and solving organizational, intracultural and intercultural problems.

Collectively, the readings in this section provide the beginning student with an introduction to some of the interests, activities, and thoughts of group communication specialists. The more advanced reader will obtain additional insight into group processes and methods.

KIM GIFFIN

THE STUDY OF SPEECH COMMUNICATION IN SMALL-GROUP RESEARCH

I. INTRODUCTION

The increasing amount of research which analyzes behavior in small groups is so great that it cannot be overlooked by any careful student of the ways in which people talk with people. Any student of speech communication, in fact, neglects small-group research only at his peril.

Small-group analysis plays a fairly unique role as a model which can be followed in a number of areas of the study of speech communication. First, the results of small-group analysis are applicable to many situations of a larger nature, e.g., conferences, meetings, symposia, etc. Second, the method of small-group analysis provides guidelines for the study of communication behavior in almost all other communication settings.

Small-group research shows the value of analysis of communication behavior upon a 'level of abstraction' which permits rigorous study. While the various levels of study of human interaction are probably of equal importance, some are more amenable to research than others. Here are the special values of small-group analysis: (1) the researcher can look 'all the way around' the parts of a small group, i.e., each member can be observed, questioned and interviewed; (2) the small group is a social unit, a content-filled system, and communication systems need to be studied as systems; and (3) the small group is amenable to experimentation, with analysis in depth of the results of experimental treatments.

Small-group analysis is microscopic in comparison to the usual approaches to the study of communication in human organizations, industrial settings, political milieus, etc. The study of such larger communication settings has usually been macroscopic. The inadequacies of the traditional approach indicate a certain value for small-group research in explaining communication behavior; it cannot, however, substitute for the macro-analytic task. The traditional approach and the small-group approach, then, must complement each other.

In a very real sense this review attempts to be critical as well as expository; thus, at times, it will present philosophical or methodological bases as criteria for evaluation and may seem to stray from the narrow path of descriptive review of research findings. In addition, it will take a very careful look at the type and quality of research completed before summaries are made of the contributions to our knowledge of speech communication. No conclusion can be better than the quality of fact and inference which produces it. Our purposes are not simply to summarize and criticize, but to indicate the nature of the problems confronting researchers in this area and to stimulate further research on those problems.

II. DEFINITIONS

The term SPEECH COMMUNICATION is taken to mean the oral-aural-visual communicative act in its entirety, including meaning conveyed by words and by means other than words. It does not ordinarily include the use of written messages unless they are incidental or complementary to the oral-aural-visual message, as in the case of 'visual aids'.

Having made an exception of written communication, the student of speech communication still has a very broad horizon. It involves the entire individual as he talks or listens, his social environment, and the ways in which he relates to it through communication. Scholars in this area are interested in the motivations, perceptions, cognitions and personalities of both the speaker and the listener as they exchange ideas, along with the changes in both persons which are thus produced. They ask this question: WHAT KIND OF PERSON SAYS WHAT TO WHOM, FOR WHAT REASON, IN WHAT WAY, UNDER WHAT CONDITIONS, WITH WHAT EFFECTS IN BOTH DIRECTIONS?

The definition of the term GROUP is not easy; that of SMALL-GROUP RESEARCH is both easier and at the same time more difficult. As in all research, precise identification of pertinent behaviors is very important in the on-going small-group research effort. Important contributions are made occasionally.

The history of the study of 'groups' could be written in terms of a series of concepts: society, primary group, reference group, membership group, and small-group — from a higher-to-lower level of abstraction. As this process was occurring Newcomb (1951, pp. 37-38) noted: "The term 'group' … has achieved no standard meaning…".

The concept of boundary early became crucial in the definition of 'a group'. And 'membership' became the criterion of boundary. Thus, the boundary was defined frequently in an obvious, sometimes elegant, tautology. In discussing this problem Golembiewski (1962, p. 35) recently concluded: "The point is simply that the empirical determination of such 'boundaries' and 'membership roles' for different types of collectivities has been almost untouched."

The most common working definition of SMALL GROUP today involves two factors: (1) a small number of individuals in interdependent role relations who (2) have a set of values (norms) which regulate behavior of members in matters of concern to the group. This definition relates to the size of the group and to the individual's behavior as it affects the behavior of other individuals in the group.

A large number of experimental or laboratory studies employ the definition developed by Robert F. Bales (1950, p. 33): a "group (is) any number of persons engaged in a single face-to-face meeting or series of meetings in which each member receives some impression of each other member ... as an individual person, even though it be only to recall that the other was present". This definition seems to imply a limited number of persons but says little about their behavior.

A third definition frequently used by researchers who work with natural 'real life' groups implies almost any collection of people. This usage neither specifies size nor behavior. For example, a study by Venable (1954) dealt with 'a relatively stable group' of college students; this 'group' consisted of forty-two girls taking the same academic course. George Homans (1950) not only used the term 'group' to refer to a primitive tribe, a street gang, a roomful of factory workers, and a New England village, but produced inferences from the study of these 'groups' IN COMBINATION. Such a treatment seems to imply that "a group is a group", regardless of size or interpersonal relationships. The studies using this loose definition frequently are very valuable — typically they deal with 'real' (not laboratory-created) data; but research results thus obtained must be carefully handled when comparisons are made with results from studies of other 'groups'.

III. CURRENT STATUS OF SMALL-GROUP RESEARCH

Regardless of the difficulty of achieving careful definitions of GROUP and SMALL GROUP, the research efforts multiply and the literature grows. Two collections of research reports, one edited by Cartwright and Zander (1953, revised 1960) which early became a 'scientific' best seller, and another edited by Hare, Borgatta and Bales (1955) together make convenient starting points for becoming acquainted with this literature. Three massive bibliographies are also very helpful, one by Strodtbeck and Hare (1954), an annotated one in the source-book edited by Hare, Borgatta and Bales (1955), and a very recent one by Raven (1965) consisting of over 3,000 items. In addition, three excellent treatments of current theory are available, one by Thibaut and Kelley (1959), another by Stogdill (1959), and a third by Golembiewski (1962).

Investigation of small-group behavior once again affirms the fact that any major research effort faces a dual problem. The researcher must identify certain parts of his world in order to understand relationships between those parts; this process can be called CONCEPTUALIZATION. Also, he must develop ways of measuring these various parts of his world; this process can be called OPERATIONALIZATION. Inquiries into the behavior of small groups have been plagued by the fact that the parts of reality to be studied and the ways in which they should be measured are neither obvious nor static; quite the contrary. Efforts have been made and are being made to find the most useful concept and measurement combinations at any given time, and to willingly adopt new, more useful combinations as they are discovered.

The problem of conceptualization has an immediate bearing upon the work required in preparation of this paper — the analysis of results of small-group studies in terms of their relationship to the study of speech communication. Such analysis depends upon classification, and the dangers of misclassification of the results of these studies are great. These difficulties underline the tentative nature of the inferences to be drawn. The overriding criterion for such analysis is the degree to which any one study leads to the development of concepts and operations which provide more comprehensive explanation and more accurate prediction of people's behavior in small groups. A healthy skepticism must prevail where this criterion is not met.

The research techniques employed in small-group analysis are extremely varied. Poor agreement on a working definition of 'small group' has contributed to this variety. A critical problem has been confusion between 'formal' membership in a group and 'psychological' membership. This problem has been receiving some attention, notably by Jay Jackson (1959), but more work needs to be done.

A profitable pattern of research development always faces the challenge of reducing the large number of vaguely identifiable variables to a set which are measurable, mutually exclusive, and clearly related to valued outcomes. This law of parsimony demands a search for a set of variables which are conceptually clear and operationally measurable.

Such comprehensive approaches have been very small currents running against the flood of small-group research. The vast majority of such research efforts typically focus on two or three variables, make an assumption of homogeneity of the population regarding other (possible) variables, and determine statistically significant relations between the two or three selected variables. Such statistical inferences must be provisional at best when other known variables are unmeasured or uncontrolled.

The ambitious use of statistical techniques seems to encourage neglect of careful conceptualization and measurement of other possible variables. The ultimate objective of research is not to obtain statistical significance. The ultimate objective is to find all the variables which make a difference and then to determine a synthesis of their relationships. Statistical significance between two variables can be a powerful tool in research, but it cannot substitute for the analytical identification of variables. It has been said before: one must control one's machinery or it will control him.

A few comprehensive attacks upon the problem of isolation of variables in small-group behavior have been made. On a theoretical level Cattell (1951) outlined three panels of variables under the headings of POPULATION, STRUCTURE, and SYNTALITY (complementary to the PERSONALITY of an individual). More recently Bjerstedt (1961) produced another theoretical formulation under three headings, PREPARATION, PROCESS, and PRODUCT.

On an operational (but microscopic) level, following an approach of, "Let's observe groups in action and work out categories of behavior observed", Bales (1950) developed his categories of 'interaction process analysis'.

A somewhat different approach was adopted by Hemphill (1956), i. e., sorting variables from research reports, most of which dealt with only two or three variables at a time. Hemphill directed a series of studies which culled fourteen variables from the available research literature. According to Hemphill's system, a group's behavior may be described by choices made by an observer on scales of 'Definitely True' to 'Definitely False' for 150 statements classified into fourteen dimensions: Autonomy, Control, Flexibility, Hedonic Tone, Homogeneity, Intimacy, Participation, Permeability, Polarization, Potency, Stability, Stratification, Viscidity, and Size. These scales were used recently by this writer in an attempt to identify dimensions of behavior in experimentally-derived groups (Giffin and Rhea, 1963). The experience was somewhat like the sightless leading the blind.

Three problems were not handled adequately by the Hemphill approach. First, the dimensions were not orthogonal (independent). Two independent factor analyses, one by Hemphill (1956) and one by Borgatta, Cottrell and Meyer (1956) failed to establish such independence. Second, observers' ratings were not highly in agreement (reliable); some of the studies reported by Hemphill (1956) reveal striking differences between observers' ratings for even small groups. Third, OBVIOUS differences between groups are not always revealed by use of Hemphill's scales. The evidence here is meager, although face-validity is suggested by findings of Hemphill (1956) in a brief experiment with two small groups containing stooges. Further work on validity is indicated.

Factor analysis provides a fairly sophisticated approach to the problem of sorting out variables. Technically it provides a parsimonious model of the independent factors necessary to account for variation in a set of related data. It assumes that a problem area has related parts (factors) and that their relationships can be determined (analyzed). The application of factor analysis to small-group behavior has been reported in three studies, one by Cattell and Wispe (1948), another by Cattell, Saunders and Stice (1953), and one by Borgatta and Cottrell (1955).

Evaluation of such work may be based upon criteria summarized by Guilford (1952) or McNemar (1951), both of whom evaluated the process as it applies to problems of research on human behavior. First, are all possible variables included? The literature currently contains reports on variables which are not included in any of the three studies of factor analysis. Second, are the factor-analyzed variables free from spurious intercorrelations? Each of the reports of the three studies internally contains suggestions or admissions of the possibility of such spurious influences. Third, are the variables factorially simple? Many of the variables in each study seem to be factorially complex. A number of them seem to have both physiological and social aspects.

In general, factor analysis places a heavy premium on the interpretation and naming of factors, as well as the choice of a particular factorial method. Giving a complex factor a handy title (e. g., 'Potency') may confuse more than clarify. A further criticism may be based upon the questionable homogeneity of 'group' populations on which the factorial studies were made (a sorority in the Cattell and Wispe study, and previously unacquainted subjects in the other two), but one cannot be harsh in this criticism because evidences of such homogeneity are precisely what factor-analysis is designed to search out. Another way of saying this is that factor-analysis presupposes the existence of a set of dimensions which characterize a population, and the 'factoring out' of this set of dimensions is the objective. If and when successful, we may be able to tell the difference between a 'collectivity' and a 'group', or varying degrees of 'groupness' in collectivities of people.

IV. SPEECH COMMUNICATION AS A VARIABLE IN SMALL-GROUP RESEARCH

We have acknowledged the very large amount of research on small-group interaction; also, we have been searchingly critical of the quality of that research. We may now review its findings as they relate to speech communication. At this point once again we must raise the question of definition or classification.

The objective of small-group research is to study interpersonal behavior, popularly called group 'interaction'. What is meant by the term, 'interaction'? In a masterful effort to present "an inventory of scientific findings" on all human behavior Berelson and Steiner (1964) give this definition (p. 326):

INTERACTION: This is a generic term for the exchange of meanings between people. Usually interaction is direct communication — mainly talking and listening, often writing and reading — but it can also include gestures, glances, nods or shakes of the head, pats on the back, frowns, caresses or slaps, and any other way in which meanings can be transmitted from one person to another and back again... 'interaction' refers to communication in its broadest sense.

Thus it might appear that the student of speech communication should not neglect ANY of the reported research on group interaction. But let's put this idea together with another one: there is a very great tendency for small-group researchers to use the term 'communication' to refer to only a part of the entire interaction process, i. e., to refer to the amount of verbal message-sending and types of messages sent, and to treat the other broad communication dimensions (e. g., perception of speaker or listener, cognitions, attitudes, personality, etc.) as variables separate from message-sending. Because of this particular usage of the term 'communication' in the small-group research literature, it seems appropriate to employ this usage in our analysis of this literature. We will comment again upon this conceptualization of communication in our concluding section of this paper.

The quantity of the reported research is, of course, a very great problem. It can best be reviewed under a series of subheadings: (1) variables which influence communication in groups; (2) variables which are influenced by communication in groups; and (3) the study of communication patterns in groups.

1. *Variables which Influence Communication in Groups*

Eight variables have been identified which have direct influence upon communication in small groups: (1) member status, (2) group size, (3) norms, (4) power structure, (5) cohesiveness, (6) role-functions, (7) member personality, and (8) group tasks or goals.

GROUP-MEMBER STATUS has been of interest to a very large number of researchers. The concept usually (not always) has been understood to refer to the relative position of a member determined by the degree to which he possesses or embodies some socially approved or generally desired attribute or characteristic. Beyond this point, which is not very specific, the study of status has been characterized by Pfautz (1953, p. 394) as having a "minimum of concensus and a maximum of confusion". This rather large body of literature must be viewed with caution. However, there is little question that status distinctions are potent factors for group communication.

Investigations indicate that high-status members communicate more than low-status members, that highs communicate more with highs than with lows, and that lows communicate more with highs than with other lows. The experimental work of Hurwitz, Zander and Hymovitch (1953) is illustrative. There is some evidence reported by A. R. Cohen (1958) that the type of communication presented by low-status members may be very unfriendly when such lows have strong hopes of rising in status. Although these findings are dependable, two major problems have not been solved in research on status: (1) clarification of the bases for status ranking, and (2) determination of the significance of three status dimensions. These status dimensions are: (1) status concensus — member agreement on status ranks of other members (see Slater, 1955); (2) status congruency — agreement among an individual's status rankings by other members (see Adams, 1953); and (3) status stability — the tendency for any status rank to persist over time (see Berkowitz and Macauley, 1961).

Status concensus, congruency and stability have all seemed to be related to communication, but those relationships are not clear. For example, Bales (1953) and Bales and Slater (1955) determined that when group members were highly agreed upon the status of a member as a 'talker', they also showed high agreement on the status of that member as a 'receiver', a provider of 'best ideas' and 'guidance' (aiding in attainment of group goal). Benne and Sheats (1948) had found similar results in an earlier study. These findings suggest the usefulness of the study of status dimensions, but much work remains to be done.

GROUP SIZE has long interested researchers in two ways: efficiency of groups of various sizes, and processes characterizing small groups of various sizes. A number of researchers, e. g., Bass and Norton (1951), Hare (1952), and Bales (1953) have found group size related to communication behavior. As size increases, the most active participator becomes more and more identifiable as both a communication initiator and receiver, and other less participative group members become less differentiated in communication amounts. Leavitt and Mueller (1951) also found that, as size increased, the degree of feedback decreased, producing loss of communication accuracy and increased hostility.

These findings, of course, are not surprising, and tend to verify inferences based upon casual observation. However, more sophisticated efforts have produced more specific inferences. In an early study Bossard (1945) developed a formula for the number of meaningful relations (R) possible between number (N) of members of various sized groups, $R = N^2 = N/2$, with a sharp curve ascending beyond $N = 4$. Later studies support this work. Carter and his associates (1951) found similar trends in participation patterns with groups numbering between four and eight members. Bales and his associates (1951) found similar results with groups of three to eight members, and Bass and Norton (1951) revealed a general increase in the participation 'gap' between the most participative and the least participative members as group size was increased from eight to twelve. Thus, there is evidence that increased size (above eight) produces a communicating clique of a few members (two to six) while the remaining members participate infrequently.

Feelings of satisfaction of members regarding size of group reflect these findings. Slater (1958) found highest member satisfaction with groups of four to six in dealing with intellectual tasks. Groups larger than six were said to encourage too much aggressiveness, hostility and factionalism; groups smaller than four produced too much psychological 'exposure', tension and constraint.

The inferences listed above must be limited to mental, decision-making tasks; however, additional work by Bales and Borgatta (1955) with "opinion" tasks tend to confirm these results; they also show communication behaviors different for odd-numbered versus even-numbered groups in degree of disagreement and antagonism. An even-numbered opinion split in a small group of two, four or six members may produce, impasse, frustration and unwarranted hostility. This difficulty was most marked in groups of two members. In sum, studies of the relationships between group size and communication behavior have not gone very deep, but the results so far seem reasonable and promising.

GROUP NORMS and conformity have received much attention in the literature. There is fairly convincing evidence summarized well by Stanley Paulson (1958) that people in groups tend to require conformity of behavior among the members. This conformity-requiring tendency was analyzed in an early work by Sherif (1936). The concept of group norms was derived from long usage in socio-psychological studies. It identifies (1) the ways in which members of a group behave, and (2) ways which are thought by them to be proper. Refinement of this very general (if important) conceptualization have been made by Festinger, Schachter and Back (1950), Rommetveit (1955), Bates and Cloyd (1956) and Morris (1956) with a clearer focus upon generally accepted and sanctioned prescriptions for, or proscriptions against, behaviors, beliefs, or feelings, reinforced by threat of withdrawal of membership (see Morris, 1956, p. 610). This definition lacks the operational specificity required for careful measurement, and research on group norms has consequently suffered.

A more useful definition of norms is that developed by Naess (1948) and more recently given attention: a set of directions sent by the group to all its members concerning their behavior. This approach exposes the idea of 'norm-senders' and 'norm-receivers', the exertion of social pressures, and shared opinions individually applied. Work employing this approach has been more fruitful.

The relationship between norms (or conformity) and communication has received considerable attention, notably by Back (1951), Schachter (1951), and by Festinger and Thibaut (1951). Members who do not conform initially are the targets of greater amounts of communication, usually of an instructional nature; if they continue as non-conformists, the tendency is to give them rejecting communication and eventually little or none of any kind. The degree of rejection, according to results found by Schachter (1951) is a direct function of the cohesiveness of the group and the degree to which the non-conformist is deviant. These results do not hold for just any collection of people, but for groups where belonging to the group is fairly attractive to its members. In some tightly knit, highly cohesive groups a non-conformist is almost immediately rejected upon detection, in which case communication is both minimal and rejective. Further consideration of this factor will be given in our discussion of cohesiveness and its influence upon communication.

COHESIVENESS in groups occupies a prominent place in the small-group literature. Theoretically it is the primary characteristic of a small-group, the factor which defines its psychological boundaries and differentiates it from other, perhaps larger or inclusive, social units.

It has taken much work on the part of Festinger, Back, Schachter, Kelley and Thibaut (1950), Festinger, Schachter and Back (1950), and Israel (1956) to clarify the conceptualization of cohesiveness from that of "co-ordinated efforts and task zeal" of group members to that of a unified, operationalizable concept of the members' RESULTANT attraction-to-group, i. e., a consideration of the combined (net) influence of two sets of forces, (1) those exerted on members to stay in the group, and (2) those exerted on members to leave the group.

Operational definition of this conceptualization did not come easily. Early operational definitions produced mixed results which have been summarized and criticized by Gross and Martin (1952). Schachter (1951) early produced a valuable operational definition involving degree of cohesiveness; the value of his work was not generally recognized until much later. Further refinements by Eisman (1959), and Dittes (1959) indicated that cohesiveness is related to a large number of the other dimensions of group behavior, including personality, leadership, communication and group size.

Schachter (1951), Back (1951), Emerson (1954), and Berkowitz (1954) have shown that in groups with high cohesiveness, communication is more equal in amount, more intense, and more valued by members than in groups with low cohesiveness. Festinger, Schachter and Back (1951), and Back (1951) showed that communication between members of groups with high cohesiveness is more effective than between members in less cohesive groups. High cohesiveness groups show greater rejection of deviates, with communication directed toward them more frequently at first and less frequently later, when conversion does not take place.

A rather lonely research effort by Back (1951) attacked the question of varying consequences on communication when the sources of group attractiveness differ. He used three treatment groups with these three cohesiveness sources: (1) attraction of members to members, (2) task attraction, and (3) anticipated prestige gain. Task attraction produced a limited quantity of communication, whereas member attraction produced a much larger amount of longish, pleasant conversation.

Much further work needs to be done to identify ways in which cohesiveness serves as an intervening variable between various other group variables, e. g., leadership, and types and amounts of communication produced.

POWER STRUCTURE or influence structure has received considerable attention by students of group interaction, notably by Grosser, Polansky and Lippitt (1951), March (1951), Lippitt, Polansky and Rosen (1952), Mills (1953), Hurwitz, Zander and Hymovitch (1953), Taylor (1954), and Dahl (1957). A creditable summary of methods of measuring influence in groups has been made by March (1956); measures have been made of general and specific (to a situation) influence of members, of shifts of opinion caused by influential members during group discussions, and of behaviors taken as indicators of influence. Of course, these measures may be tapping other different dimensions; but it does seem that members of small groups can identify and agree upon a rank order of powerful members in a group. Taylor (1954) and also Gellert (1961) found that such powerful members are generally aware of their power in the group and are willing to use it.

The most consistently observed relationship between power of a group member and his communication behavior is a tendency toward a greater amount of communication; findings which are typical are those reported by Hurwitz, Zander and Hymovitch (1953). The direction and content of communication flow are also influenced by the power structure in a group; Kelley (1951), and Thibaut (1950) found that orders seldom flow up a power hierarchy, while other types of communication, notably compliments, frequently do. The study by Hurwitz, Zander and Hymovitch (1953), as well as those of Kelley (1951), and Jackson (1952) indicate that upward communication may substitute for upward locomotion in a power structure, that communication may be used to minimize danger of hostile acts from power superiors, and that such a power superior may use communication to justify his position to his subordinates.

Several studies show that other variables influence the relationships between power and communication; for example, March (1956) found that in a group of mutually well-known members, communication from influential members was more frequent and intense as the task confronting the group was more relevant to their interests; but in groups of less-known members, communication from influential members did not vary with task relevancy. Such findings tend to indicate a real need for further study of relationships between the power structure, other dimensions of group behavior, and communication. An interesting approach to this problem is presented by Cartwright (1959) in which he develops a field-theoretical conceptualization of power and its relationships.

ROLES or role-functions have received much attention in the literature on small groups; the concept is described by Rommetveit (1955) as the theoretical junction between the main lines of psychology and sociology. In a summary of the literature to 1950 Nieman and Hughes (1951) employed a three-element paradigm to review the conceptualizations of role: (1) dynamic process of personality development pertinent to behaviors in a specific situation, (2) patterns of behavior required by a specified social unit, or (3) an individual's 'part' in a definite situation as a member of a group. The common conceptualization in the literature on small groups is a set of behaviors which are functionally related to the goals of the group.

Research on experimental groups has demonstrated that roles tend to appear even in a relatively short time, are functionally related to group goals, require different but specifiable sets of behaviors, and have performance criteria set by the group members. That only a limited number of roles can thus be distinguished was demonstrated by Carter (1954). Factor analysis of a large number of alleged role-functions has done by Clark (1951), Sakoda (1952), Carter (1953), and Wispe (1955). The amount of agreement of the results of these studies is unusual; three factors reappear: (1) INDIVIDUAL PROMINENCE, i.e., a high amount of communication given and received; (2) AIDING GROUP GOAL ATTAINMENT, i. e., presentation of 'best ideas' and general suggestions for guidance of group thinking, and (3) SOCIABILITY, i. e., the characteristics of being well liked by members and emotional stability.

The relationships of roles to communication are quite clear. The role of 'prominent individual' correlates with amount of talking and being talked to by other group members; studies by Benne and Sheats (1948), Bales (1950), and by Bales and Slater (1955) generally support this point. The amount of communication is well correlated with best ideas and guidance; however, individuals who achieve the sociability role, i. e., are well liked, generally do not give nor receive as much communication and ordinarily do not present the best ideas for guidance of the thinking of the group. Philp and Dunphy (1959) found less convincing results for groups of students working for academic grades, but in general their results agreed with earlier studies.

The role-function studies are consistent with results of the group-member status studies described earlier in this paper. There still remains somewhat of a problem of separation of the concepts of status and role. This conceptual problem and the continuation of the study of status-concensus developed by Slater (1955) suggest important work yet to be completed. Slater found high intercorrelation of rank order of roles involving (1) talking, (2) receiving communication, (3) presenting best ideas, and (4) guidance of group toward its goal (pp. 302-4). This was particularly true of persons with high status when performing these roles. These results seem to point toward the possibility of a role for at least one member of a group as an active 'task specialist' who is not particularly well liked, but quite communicative; and at the same time the possibility of a role for at least one other member of the group as 'best liked' man, emotionally stable, a group pacifier, and much less communicative (see Slater, 1955, p. 303). Future work on stability of emotions, group-task role differentiation, and status-concensus should have complementary effects on each other and on our knowledge of communication in groups.

A certain cross-relationship between the variable, ROLE-FUNCTION, and another variable which we have previously discussed, POWER STRUCTURE, requires explanation. The literature crossing these two variables frequently appears under the label of LEADERSHIP studies, and involves a somewhat molar or macroscopic concept. In some studies this concept is identified as group ATMOSPHERE, with special consideration of the degree of permissiveness present in the social climate. The early exploration and conceptualizations were made by Lewin and Lippitt (1938), Lippitt (1939), Lippitt and White (1943), and White and Lippitt (1953), working with groups of small children. These early studies show lack of precise conceptualization, but a developing interest in 'autocratic' versus "democratic" group climate. Schneider (1955) produced a less global cocneptualization of group atmosphere with a more nearly operational definition emphasizing participation: (1) amount and distribution of communication among group members, (2) permissiveness of leader (or supervisor), and (3) extent of group-members' participation in decision-making and goal setting.

Early studies by Preston and Heintz (1949), by Hare (1953), and those reported by Kahn and Katz (1953) showed that group decision-making by employees instead of decisions by management alone produced attractively successful output and employee satisfaction, so much so that "the participation hypothesis" has been in vogue in recent literature on personnel administration. Further work by Baumgartel (1957) supported the hypothesis and studies by Berkowitz (1953) and by Kipnis (1958) began to qualify and sharpen it. At the present time this much can be said: a group with a more permissive atmosphere and with greater opportunities for members to help in setting goals and arriving at decisions will produce a greater quantity and a wider distribution of communication of a type which will likely demonstrate increased flexibility, reduced tension, and better understanding of goals set and decisions reached; however, this question still remains: how much permissiveness should be allowed at what time in the group problem-solving process for what kinds of groups with what types of goals. The conflicting evidence reported early by Berkowitz (1953) and by Riecken and Homans (1954) has not been satisfactorily explained. Berkowitz attempted to explain this conflict, in part, by suggesting that some groups have a NORM which requires their chairman to be quite authoritative; this explanation seems both to say too much and too little. Further attention to group norms as they relate to role-functions may provide useful answers.

The PERSONALITY of a group member obviously can have significant effects upon group behavior, or so it seems. Even if 'obvious' this relationship has been difficult to measure. The concept is basically that group processes will correlate with relevant personality characteristics of members. A major problem, as Cartwright and Zander (1953, p. 337) noted, is that personality as a variable is poorly conceived and unreliably measured.

Early work on personality dimensions centered upon 'traits' of group leaders, i. e., members having high status. Bird (1940) combed the personality literature and found seventy-nine traits cited in twenty studies having some semblance of controlled investigation; he reported, however, that only five per cent of these alleged traits were common to at least twenty per cent of the studies. Gouldner (1950, pp. 21-25) rejected the assumption of simplistic solidity concerning such traits and suggested that a 'trait' (e. g., intelligence) might affect one person's behavior differently from that of another, depending upon the number and strength of his other 'traits'.

Leadership study was being turned by Jenkins (1947) and Stogdill (1948) to SITUATIONS as they related to leadership behavior. Leadership situations quite reasonably came to be defined in terms of leadership FUNCTIONS as analyzed by Dunkerly (1940), Benne and Sheats (1948), Carter, Haythorn, Shriver and Lanzetta (1950), and by Stogdill (1951). Study of leadership functions quite naturally exposed the need to study other functional roles previously discussed in this paper. But the problem of determining relationships between 'personality' and group behavior remained. One approach was focused during World War II on "authoritarianism" by Adorno and his associates (1950). The early center of interest was the potentially fascistic individual (thus, the F-scale) but the scope of interest was soon enlarged.

Flowerman (1950), summarizing a great deal of work done in California, conceptualized the authoritarian personality as (1) a supreme conformist who (2) sees the world as menacing, (3) is rigid, showing little imagination, and (4) puts neat — often false — labels on people. Haythorn (1956a) and his associates found that the authoritarian is less cooperative, more individually striving, and less sensitive to others, and that his communication behavior reflects those characteristics; sixty-one t-tests were computed to determine that almost all data obtained supported these general inferences. Further study by Haythorn (1956b) and his group generally verified these results. Authoritarian types do not communicate as easily nor meaningfully in a group as do non-authoritarians; on the other hand, equalitarian types were found by Shaw (1959) to fit comfortably into a group and to communicate more easily and more effectively. Similarly Schiedel, Crowell and Shepherd (1958) found the personal characteristics of self-confidence, independence and dominance closely related to communication behavior designed to achieve individual prominence in the group, i. e., the role-function of 'individual prominence' isolated by Carter (1954).

A promising approach to the larger picture of personality as it relates directly to group interaction was started by Schutz (1952). His interest at first was in identifying factors leading to group compatibility; later Schutz (1955) turned to the development of a basic personality measure giving special consideration to interpersonal relations in groups. He isolated three factors of compatibility, (1) a 'dependence upon authority' (power) orientation, (2) a personal consideration a (liking and being liked) orientation, and (3) an assertiveness of one's views orientation. To Schutz, compatibility meant that group-members mutually adhered to the same one of these orientations. He experimentally verified the hypothesis that compatibility of this type produced optimal communication behavior in groups and contributed to group task performance.

A promising approach to the general problem of personality in group relations was taken by Cattell and Stice (1954) to compare a comprehensive set of personality dimensions isolated by factor analysis to variables of group behavior. Sixteen personality factors previously had been isolated and questionnaire items developed for them by Cattell, Saunders and Stice (1959); these items relate rather well to the eight characteristics of group behavior earlier identified by Haythorn (1953).

In somewhat similar fashion Berkowitz (1956) viewed personality dimensions as responses to interpersonal stimuli in identifiable group situations, rather than the common stereotyped approach to personality, i. e., self-contained, stabilized personal traits. He developed a 'response-heirarchy' of behaviors ranked in terms of probability of occurrence in changing situations involving different demands (group expectations) of the individual. He determined experimentally that changing situations produced different sets of responses from the individual, including varying degrees of amount of communication, rate of communication, and type of communication with respect to aggressivity-passivity. Berkowitz's work points up the importance of the organization of personality characteristics in terms of probability of interpersonal response behavior, but the full flowering of the developmental work of Haythorn, Schutz, Cattell and Berkowitz is still in the future.

Perhaps the greatest benefit of further work on personality characteristics may be clarification of the 'participation hypothesis'. For example, increased participation in decision-making by 'authoritarian' types of personality may produce quite different types or quantities of communication with quite different effects than that produced by increased participation by a 'non-authoritarian' type. Vroom (1959) and Borg (1960) have started to explore these possibilities.

The TASK dimensions confronting the group, or the types of group goals to which they are committed, involves a concept which developed out of dissatisfaction with the 'trait' approach to the study of leadership and the resulting emphasis on 'situation' instead of 'trait'. But, as Sanford (1952) pointed out, the term 'situation' is sterile unless dimensions are identified. At first, identification of task differences seemed to provide a convenient approach. Work by Cecil Gibb (1949), Carter and Nixon (1949), Carter, Haythorn and Howell (1950), Katz, Blau, Brown and Strodtbeck (1957) and Mann and Mann (1959) have demonstrated that different tasks produce different effects on group behavior and its outcomes.

The isolation of task dimensions has barely begun. Heise and Miller (1951) differentiated degree of task difficulty; this is one approach. Degree to which a task requires interpersonal co-operation, as studied by Deutsch (1949), is another. Degree of manual skill or dexterity is a task dimension employed by Carter, Haythorn and Howell (1950) and many other studies. Different 'constellations of skills required' to perform a task is another approach to task dimensions employed by Barnlund (1962) in a study of emergent leadership. Barnlund's 'constellations of skills' seems to be a very useful approach to the problem.

Factor analysis has been employed in attacks on this problem, mostly in industrial or productive organizations. Melton (1947) reported that a few factors can adequately describe simple manual tasks; however, McQuitty, Wrigley and Gaier (1954) isolated twenty-three factors necessary to differentiate more complex tasks. Further work is needed on this problem, although work completed is highly suggestive that the type of task influences communication in groups.

2. *Group Variables Influenced by Communication*

There are dependable studies which individually report the influence of speech communication upon one or another of six variables of group behavior: (1) status achievement by individuals, (2) group norms (attitudes), (3) group power-structure, (4) group cohesiveness, (5) group role-functions, and (6) achievement of group task.

The concepts listed above have been described and evaluated in the previous section of this paper; further definition and criticism of them as concepts will not be given in this section. Our primary interest here will be acknowledgement of scholarship which has developed information concerning the influence of speech communication upon these variables and the way such influences operate.

STATUS achievement by individuals is influenced by communication. An increase in individual prominence is correlated with increased amounts of giving and receiving, communication according to studies by Bales (1953), and by Bales and Slater (1955). However, the degree to which a person is liked is inversely correlated with amount of talking (as well as degree of individual prominence) according to findings of Benne and Sheats (1948). Similar results were reported by Hurwitz, Zander and Hymovitch (1953), and this same study indicated that low status members used an increase in the amount of communication with high status members as a means of raising their status level in the group. Studies of emergent leadership tend to support this point; for example, Crockett (1955) found that emergent leaders were (1) significantly higher than the other members in amount of communication, (2) significantly higher in amount of communication designed to facilitate group discussion, and (3) contributed information and suggestions significantly more often than other members in the group.

Group NORMS are significantly influenced by communication; the attitudes of the group and degree of attitude-change via group communication have been objectives of considerable research. The classic study on conformity of group judgment was made by Asch (1951). Other studies by Back (1951), Bovard (1951), Festinger and Thibaut (1951), Schachter (1951), and Deutsch and Girard (1955) clarified the hypothesis and confirmed this principle: communication influences deviant individual attitudes, opinions or beliefs to the extent that such communication is specific and can make group membership (belonging) attractive to the deviant individual; instructional communication is usually supported by threat of psychological rejection by the group, depending, of course, upon degree of group cohesiveness present.

The POWER-STRUCTURE of a group is influenced by communication. Mills (1953) found that the 'state of influence' in groups is changed according to the amount of individual verbal contribution to problem-solving and frequency of supporting communication given to individual members. Mills' results were somewhat inconclusive, but were generally supported by results of a later study by Strodtbeck (1954).

Changes in group COHESIVENESS have been shown to be produced by types of messages exchanged: Dittes (1959) artificially induced differences in group cohesiveness by controlling communication (instructions) concerning personal attractiveness of group members, prestige of group membership, and individual role-function assignments. Insufficient evidence is available on these points; more work is needed.

Changes in ROLE-FUNCTIONS in groups are clearly related to communication behavior, particularly role-functions of a leadership nature. In the first place, the AMOUNT of communication by an individual will influence the role or roles the group will expect and allow him to play. The work of Kahn and Katz (1953) has shown less communication from persons in leadership roles will be viewed as more permissiveness and less directive, and ordinarily will encourage an increase in other members' participation in decision-making. In the second place, the CONTENT of communication by an individual will influence the role or roles he will be allowed to play in a group. Analysis of types of communication content has been explored by Bales (1950) in his 'interaction process analysis' approach, and by Heyns and Lippitt (1954). Bales produced the following list of types of communication content: (1) shows solidarity, (2) shows tension release, (3) agrees, (4) gives suggestions, (5) gives opinion, (6) gives orientation, (7) asks for orientation, (8) asks for opinion, (9) asks for suggestions, (10) disagrees, (11) shows tension, and (12) shows antagonism. Bales' procedure is generally well-known; the major problem is that the degree of effect of these various content types upon other variables of group behavior, including role-functions, is not clear. In a limited way Bales has started working in this direction; this work will be discussed further in the next section of this paper.

Heyns and Lippitt (1954, pp. 378-9) developed the following system for analysis of types of content of communication in groups: (1) goal setting, (2) problem proposals, (3) information seeking, (4) information giving, (5) solution proposals, (6) development seeking, (7) development giving, (8) opposing, (9) supporting, (10) summary seeking, (11) summary giving, and (12) non-problem directed. This system follows a problem-oriented pattern closely related to well-known patterns of reflective thinking, and could be especially useful in studying role-functions in problem-solving groups and the ways in which types of communication content influences these role-functions. These relationships have not been carefully explored, although preliminary work has seemed promising.

TASK ACHIEVEMENT, i. e., goal achievement by groups, has been shown to be related to communication. Bales and Slater (1955) showed that the amount of giving and receiving messages, suggestion of "best" ideas, and communication designed to guide the thinking of the group are all positively related to group achievement when the task is fairly complex.

Bales (1954) and Bales and Strodtbeck (1951) have shown that, in general, communication involving certain 'phases' of the problem-solving process contribute to problem-solving. These 'phases' are somewhat similar to the content analysis of communication approach of Heyns and Lippitt (1954) described above and are: (1) problems of orientation, (2) problems of evaluation, (3) problems of control, (4) negative reactions, and (5) positive reactions.

Bales 'phases' in problem-solving in groups are somewhat similar to the problem-solving 'steps' usually attributed to John Dewey (1910), and familiar to speech communication scholars through early writings of Baird (1937), McBurney and Hance (1939) and others.

At this point we have seen that all major variables in group behavior influence communication, and that communication influences each of these variables except size (and could likely influence that) and members' personalities (and it might influence those). It seems quite clear that speech communication is an intervening variable between most (if not all) of the other measurable group variables. The thought may occur, is it the 'crossroads', the point at which all group study should focus? No, not really; remember that we are here using the term 'communication' in the narrow sense it is used in small-group research literature, meaning primarily message sending and receiving, and that in that literature the term "interaction" is usually used to include consideration of all of the variables involved in type of person sending (or receiving) messages as well as his total social environment. The thought that the variable identified by the narrow definition of communication might be the center of focus of small-group research neglects a very important consideration: it appears that EACH of these major dimensions or variables of group interaction, e. g., status, size, norms, power-structure, etc., is an intervening variable between each one and another of the entire set. Thus it seems that the emphasis for the future should be upon the study of all of them at once AS A SYSTEM, with changes in any one of them likely to influence more than one, perhaps all, of the others.

3. *The Study of Communication Patterns in Groups*

A major problem in the future development of small-group research is directly related to the study of communication patterns: the measurement of all known variables at once whenever a group is studied, rather than the consideration of only two or three variables at a time — in effect, the systems-research approach,

Earlier we suggested that one significance of small-group research was that a single study could hope to "get all the way around" an entire social unit, i. e., investigate in depth all important variables in the system. We didn't say it would be easy; knowing all one needs to know about a group which is interacting is a tall order — in fact, it is monumental.

Study of communication patterns in groups is a very real step in the direction of systems-research in group behavior. Apparently very few scholars in small-group research have noted this point; consequently, exploratory efforts at systems-research have not taken full advantage of existing knowledge of all identifiable variables. But the approach employed is a significant start.

Study of communication content via the technique developed by Bales (1950) focused upon observer records; it produces a general picture of a group in terms of volume and type of content of communication. However, work has been started by Bales to determine relationships between variations of communication behavior identified by his analysis process and variations in the major dimensions of group behavior noted above.

Preliminary findings have been summarized by Bales (1954) as follows: (1) members do not seem strongly bound by a group decision unless they have participated in making it; (2) an 'optimum' balance between number of positive reactions to negative ones is about two to one; (3) a high rate of disagreement and antagonism leads to difficulty in decision-making; (4) there can be too many agreements and too few disagreements; (5) successful groups seem to follow the sequence of 'phases' in problem-solving discussed above; and (6) successful groups seem to have two leaders, one who contributes 'best ideas' and another who is 'best liked' — a task leader and a social leader. These findings seem to suggest possible relationships between types of communication content and such variables as norms, cohesiveness, status, task achievement, role-functions and power-structure.

A quite different approach, but one which also employs a systems-research orientation, is that of Bavelas (1950) in his study of group communication 'nets'. Bavelas was clearly interested in relationships between communication patterns and other variables of group behavior. However, the communication patterns were highly constricted for experimental purposes, being limited to either-or, some-or-none communication opportunities between selected individuals in a group. For example, one type of 'net' would allow person A to communicate with person B, and B with C, but A could not communicate with C. Extensions were made of such "chain" patterns, along with development of 'circular' patterns and 'wheel' patterns (with one person at the 'hub').

A further experimental condition imposed, apparently for careful control of message content, was the limitation of communication to written messages. Such experimental conditions severely limit the value of inferences which can be drawn from data thus collected.

The primary concept developed from the group communication 'net' studies is that of 'centrality'. This concept was operationally defined as the number of the group members with which an individual can communicate (either directly or indirectly) divided by the sum of the intervening persons through whom such communications must be sent. Thus, in an A-B-C-D-E chain, C has highest centrality. Studies have typically determined the relationship between centrality and one or more of the major variables of group behavior. Gilchrist, Shaw and Walker (1954) determined that a position of high centrality in a group produced recognizable leadership role-functions and higher status. Shaw (1954a and 1954c) found that the degree of centrality was directly correlated with the amount of messages initiated and received. Leavitt (1951) found centrality directly associated with job satisfaction and satisfaction with role-function. Although these findings may be true for the single individual enjoying high centrality, Leavitt (1951) also found that the group in general shows more satisfaction with nets with less total centrality. Heise and Miller (1951) and Shaw (1954b) found greater speed and accuracy of communications with nets having a greater degree of centrality if the problem confronting the group was simple; however, with complex problems Shaw (1954b) found that nets with low centrality were faster and more accurate, probably because a complex problem more quickly taxes the ability limits of the person in the central position, creating a saturation point or 'bottle-neck'.

The studies on communication patterns and nets which we have cited are illustrative; many more have been completed with results essentially in agreement. The results obtained, however, must be viewed as mainly suggestive because of limitations imposed by experimental conditions. Even so, the approaches made are very important because of their proximity to a systems-research orientation. This orientation holds the key to future definitive research on small-group behavior.

V. CONCLUSION

It seems appropriate to conclude this analysis of study of speech communication in small-group research by underscoring the major problems which must be handled in future research in this area.

The first problem is clarification of the concept of communication. Bales' 'types' may be observed and recorded in terms of QUANTITY in each content-type, but no determination is made of the QUALITY of the content-unit; for example, one intense statement coded as 'disagrees' may have much greater impact or effect than a statement of mild disagreement coded in the same way. Furthermore, Bavelas' some-or-none approach seems to neglect the same problem. The broad definition of communication, i. e., what kind of person, with what perceptions, cognitions, attitudes, purposes and personality, sends what kind of message under what environmental and social conditions to what kind of person(s) with what perceptions, cognitions, attitudes, purposes and personality (personalities) seems to be reflected in the nine major variables (including communication narrowly defined) which we have reviewed. But some clarification of the total concept of communication is still necessary.

A second problem is clarification of the concept of small group. The horses-apples approach frequently found in the literature where, for example, results of a 'group' behavior study in a girls' dormitory are compared with results taken from a 'group' study of the executives of an industrial corporation lead to contradictory inferences and theoretical confusion.

A third problem is produced by the neglect of known variables. Studies dealing with two or three variables, with the other variables unobserved (as well as uncontrolled) may yield results which are 'statistically significant' and meaningfully insignificant. Existing studies involving any one of the known major variables tend to indicate that such a variable is not ordinarily 'randomly spread' in any one small group, even if it is randomly drawn from a large population. To measure two or three variables and assume that the others are 'randomly spread' is not warranted.

A fourth problem is the relative lack of studies of 'natural-state' field groups. Too many studies (relatively) are being made with experimenter-contrived laboratory groups. These are satisfactory for exploratory work; such work, if never subjected to tests in the field, yields a theory of group behavior of college sophomores.

These problems can and will be whipped. The information now available is such that definitive findings are not far away. Speech communication students should be encouraged to join this effort. Speech scholars everywhere should watch for these results.

UNIVERSITY OF KANSAS

REFERENCES

Adams, Stuart (1953), "Status Congruency as a Variable in Small Group Performance", *Social Forces*, 32, 16-22.

Adorno, T. W., Else Frenkel-Brunswik, D. J. Levinson, and R. N. Sanford (1950), *The Authoritarian Personality* (New York, Harper).

Asch, S. E. (1951), "Effects of Group Pressure upon the Modification and Distortion of Judgments", in Harold Guetzkow, *Groups, Leadership and Men* (Pittsburgh, Pa., Carnegie Press).

Back, Kurt W. (1951), "Influence through Social Communication", *Journal of Abnormal and Social Psychology*, 46, 9-23.

Baird, A. Craig (1937), *Public Discussion and Debate* (rev. ed.) (Boston, Mass., Ginn).

Bales, Robert F. (1950), *Interaction Process Analysis: A Method for the Study of Small Social Groups* (Cambridge, Mass., Addison-Wesley).

Bales, Robert F., and F. L. Strodtbeck (1951), "Phases in Group Problem-solving", *Journal of Abnormal and Social Psychology*, 46, 485-95.

Bales, Robert F., F. L. Strodtbeck, T. M. Mills, and Mary E. Roseborough (1951), "Channels of Communication in Small Groups", *American Sociological Review*, 16, 461-68.

Bales, Robert F. (1953), "The Equilibrium Problem in Small Groups", in T. Parsons, R. F. Bales, and E. A. Shils, *Working Papers in the Theory of Action* (Glencoe, Ill., Free Press).

Bales, Robert F. (1954), "In Conference", *Harvard Business Review*, 32, 44-50.

Bales, Robert F., and Edgar F. Borgatta (1955), "Size of Group as a Factor in the Interaction Profile", in Hare, A. Paul, Edgar F. Borgatta, and Robert F. Bales (Eds.) (1955), *Small Groups: Studies in Social Interaction* (New York, Knop).

Bales, Robert F., and Philip E. Slater (1955), "Role Differentiation in Small Decision-Making Groups", in Robert F. Bales, Talcott Parsons, *et. al.*, *Family, Socialization, and Interaction Process* (Glencoe, Ill., Free Press), 259-306.

Barnlund, Dean C. (1962), "Consistency of Emergent Leadership in Groups with Changing Tasks and Members", *Speech Monographs*, 29, 47-52.

Bass, Bernard M., and M. Fay-Tyler Norton (1951), "Group Size and Leaderless Discussion", *Journal of Applied Psychology*, 35, 397-400.

Bates, Alan P., and Jerry S. Cloyd (1956), "Toward the Development of Operations for Defining Group Norms and Member Roles", *Sociometry*, 19, 26-39.

Baumgartel, Howard (1950), "Leadership Style as a Variable in Research Administration", *Administrative Science Quarterly*, 2, 350-59.

Bavelas, Alex (1950), "Communication Patterns in Task-Oriented Groups", *Journal of the Acoustical Society of America*, 22, 725-30.

Benne, Kenneth D., and Paul Sheats (1948), "Functional Roles of Group Members", *Journal of Social Issues*, 4, 41-49.

Berelson, Bernard, and Gary A. Steiner (1964), *Human Behavior: An Inventory of Scientific Findings* (New York, Harcourt, Brace and World).

Berkowitz, Leonard (1953), "Sharing Leadership in Small, Decision-making Groups", *Journal of Abnormal and Social Psychology*, 48, 231-38.

Berkowitz, Leonard (1954), "Group Standards, Cohesiveness, and Productivity", *Human Relations*, 7, 409-19.

Berkowitz, Leonard (1956), "Personality and Group Position", *Sociometry*, 19, 210-22.

Berkowitz, Leonard, and Jacqueline R. Macauley (1961), "Some Effects of Differences in Status Level and Status Stability", *Human Relations*, 14, 135-48.

Bird, Charles (1940), *Social Psychology* (New York, Appleton-Century).

Bjerstedt, Ake (1961), "Preparation, Process, and Product", *Human Relations*, 14, 183-89.

Borg, Walter R. (1960), "Prediction of Small Group Role Behavior from Personality Variables", *Journal of Abnormal and Social Psychology*, 60, 112-16.

Borgatta, E. F. and L. S. Cottrell (1955), "On the Classification of Groups", *Sociometry*, 18, 409-22, 665-78.

Borgatta, E. F., L. S. Cotrell, Jr., and Henry J. Meyer (1956), "On the Dimensions of Group Behavior", *Sociometry*, 19, 238.

Bossard, J. J. S. (1945), "The Law of Family Interaction", *American Journal of Sociology*, 50, 292-94.

Bovard, Everett W., Jr. (1951), "Group Structure and Perception", *Journal of Abnormal and Social Psychology*, 46, 398-405.

Carter, Launor F. (1953), "Leadership and Small-Group Behavior", in Muzafer Sherif and M. O. Wilson Eds.), *Group Relations at the Crossroads* (New York, Harper).

Carter, Launor F., and Mary Nixon (1949), "An Investigation of the Relationship between Four Criteria of Leadership Ability for Three Different Tasks", *Journal of Psychology*, 27, 245-61.

Carter, Launor F., William Haythorn, and Margaret Howell (1950), "Further Investigation of the Criteria of Leadership", *Journal of Abnormal and Social Psychology*, 45, 350-58.

Carter, Launor, William Haythorn, Beatrice Shriver, and John Lanzetta (1950), "The Behavior of Leaders and Other Group Members", *Journal of Abnormal and Social Psychology*, 44, 589-94.

Carter, Launor, William Haythorn, Beatrice Meirowitz, and John Lanzetta (1951), "The Relation of Categorizations and Ratings in the Observation of Group Behavior", *Human Relations*, 3, 239-54.

Carter, Launor F. (1954), "Recording and Evaluating the Performance of Individuals as Members of Small Groups", *Personnnel Psychology*, 7, 477-84.

Cartwright, Dorwin (Ed.) (1959), *Studies in Social Power* (Ann Arbor, Mich., Research Center for Group Dynamics, University of Michigan).

Cartwright, Dorwin, and Alvin Zander (Eds.) (1953), *Group Dynamics: Research and Theory* (Evanston, Ill., Row, Peterson; Second Edition, 1960).

Cattell, Raymond B., and L. G. Wispe (1948), "The Dimensions of Syntality in Small Groups", *Journal of Social Psychology*, 28, 57-78.

Cattell, Raymond B. (1951), "New Concepts for Measuring Leadership in Terms of Group Syntality", *Human Relations*, 4, 161-84.

Cattell, Raymond B., David R. Saunders, and Glen F. Stice (1953), "The Dimensions of Syntality in Small Groups: I. The Neonate Groups", *Human Relations*, 6, 331.

Cattell, Raymond B., and Glen F. Stice (1954), "Four Formulae for Selecting Leaders on the Basis of Personality", *Human Relations*, 7, 493.

Cattell, Raymond B., David R. Saunders and Glen F. Stice (1959), *Handbook for the Sixteen Personality Factor Questionnaire* (Champaign, Ill., Institute for Personality and Ability Testing, University of Illinois).

Clark, Rodney A. (1951), "Analyzing the Group Structure of Combat Rifle Squads", *American Psychologist*, 8, 333.

Cohen, Arthur R. (1958), "Upward Communication in Experimentally Created Hierarchies", *Human Relations*, 11, 41-53.

Crockett, Walter H. (1955), "Emergent Leadership in Small, Decision-making Groups", *Journal of Abnormal and Social Psychology*, 51, 378-83.

Dahl, Robert A. (1957), "The Concept of Power", *Behavioral Science*, 21, 205-7.

Deutsch, Morton (1949), "An Experimental Study of the Effects of Co-operation and Competition upon Group Process", *Human Relations*, 2, 199-231.

Deutsch, Morton and Harold B. Gerard (1955), "A Study of Normative and Informational Social Influences upon Individual Judgement", *Journal of Abnormal and Social Psychology*, 51, 629-36.

Dewey, John (1910), *How We Think* (Boston, Mass., Heath).

Dittes, James E. (1959), "Attractiveness of Group as Function of Self-Esteem and Acceptance by Group", *Journal of Abnormal and Social Psychology*, 59, 77-82.

Dunkerly, M. D. (1940), "A Statistical Study of Leadership among College Women", *Studies in Psychology and Psychiatry*, 4 (Washington, D. C., Catholic University of America).

Eisman, Bernice (1959), "Some Operational Measures of Cohesiveness and Their Interrelations", *Human Relations*, 12, 183-89.

Emerson, Richard (1954), "Deviation and Rejection: An Experimental Replication", *American Sociological Review*, 19, 688-93.

Festinger, Leon, Kurt Back, Stanley Schachter, Harold H. Kelley, and John Thibaut (1950), *Theory and Experiment in Social Communication* (Ann Arbor, Mich., Research Center for Group Dynamics, University of Michigan).

Festinger, Leon, Stanley Schachter, and Kurt Back (1950), *Social Pressures in Informal Groups* (New York, Harper).

Festinger, Leon, and John Thibaut (1951), "Interpersonal Communication in Small Groups", *Journal of Abnormal and Social Psychology*, 46, 92-99.

Flowerman, S. H. (1950), "Portrait of the Authoritarian Man", *New York Times Magazine*, April 23, 9, 28.

Gellert, Elizabeth (1961), "Stability and Fluctuation in Power Relationships of Young Children", *Journal of Abnormal and Social Psychology*, 58, 8-15.

Gibb, Cecil A. (1949), "The Emergence of Leadership in Small Temporary Groups of Men", unpublished Ph. D. dissertation (University of Illinois).

Giffin, Kim, and Joseph Rhea (1963), "An Analysis of Participant Attitudes and Relationships in The University of Kansas Group-Action Tournament", *The Gavel*, 45, 34-39.

Gilchrist, J. C., M. E. Shaw, and L. C. Walker (1954), "Some Effects of Unequal Distribution of Information in a Wheel Group Structure", *Journal of Abnormal and Social Psychology*, 49, 554-56.

Golembiewski, Robert T. (1962), *The Small Group* (Chicago, University of Chicago Press).

Gouldner, Alvin W. (1950), *Studies in Leadership* (New York, Harper).

Gross, N., and W. E. Martin (1952), "On Group Cohesiveness", *American Journal of Sociology*, 57, 546-54.

Grosser, D., N. Polansky and R. Lippitt (1951), "A Laboratory Study of Behavioral Contagion", *Human Relations*, 4, 115-42.

Guttman, Louis (1954), "A New Approach to Factor Analysis: Radex", in P. F. Lazersfeld (Ed.), *Mathematical Thinking in the Social Sciences* (Glencoe, Ill., Free Press), 258-348.

Hare, A. Paul (1952), "Interaction and Consensus in Different Sized Groups", *American Sociological Review*, 17, 261-67.

Hare, A. Paul, Edgar F. Borgatta, and Robert F. Bales (Eds.) (1955), *Small Groups: Studies in Social Interaction* (New York, Knopf).

Haythorn, William (1953), "The Influence of Individual Members on the Characteristics of Small Groups", *Journal of Abnormal and Social Psychology*, 48, 276-84.

Haythorn, William Arthur Couch, Donald Haefner, Peter Langham, and Launor F. Carter (1956a), "The Behavior of Authoritarian and Equalitarian Personalities in Groups", *Human Relations*, 9, 57-74.

Haythorn, William, Donald Haefner, Peter Langham, Arthur Couch and Launor F. Carter (1956b), "The Effects of Varying Combinations of Authoritarian and Equalitarian Leaders and Followers", *Journal of Abnormal and Social Psychology*, 53, 210-19.

Heise, George A., and George A. Miller (1951), "Problem Solving by Small Groups Using Various Communications Nets", *Journal of Abnormal and Social Psychology*, 46, 327-35.

Hemphill, John K., and Charles M. Westie (1950), "The Measurement of Group Dimensions", *Journal of Psychology*, 29, 325-42.

Hemphill, John K. (1956), *Group Dimensions: A Manual for Their Measurement* (= *Ohio Studies in Personnel*, Bureau of Business Research, Monograph No. 87) (Columbus, Ohio State University).

Heyns, Roger W., and Ronald Lippitt (1954), "Systematic Observational Techniques", in Gardner Lindzey (Ed.), *Handbook of Social Psychology: Theory and Method* (Reading, Mass., Addison-Wesley) 370-404.

Homans, George C. (1950), *The Human Group* (New York, Harcourt).

Hurwitz, Jacob I., Alvin F. Zander, and Bernard Hymovitch (1953), "Some Effects of Power on the Relations among Group Members", in Cartwright, Dorwin, and Alvin Zander, *Group Dynamics* (White Plains, New York, Row, Peterson and Company), 483-92.

Israel, Joachim (1956), *Self-Evaluation and Rejection in Groups: Three Experimental Studies and a Conceptual Outline* (Uppsala, Almquist and Wiksells).

Jackson, Jay M. (1952), "Analysis of Interpersonal Relations in a Formal Organization", unpublished doctor's dissertation (University of Michigan).

Jackson, Jay M. (1959), "A Space for Conceptualizing Person-Group Relationships", *Human Relations*, 12, 3-15.

Jenkins, William O. (1947), "Review of Leadership Studies with Particular Reference to Military Problems", *Psychological Bulletin*, 44, 54-79.

Kahn, Robert L., and Daniel Katz (1953), "Leadership Practices in Relation to Productivity and Morale", in Dorwin Cartwright and Alvin Zander (Eds.), *Group Dynamics: Research and Theory* (Evanston, Ill., Row, Peterson), 612-28.

Katz, Elihu, Peter M. Blau, Morton L. Brown, and F. L. Strodtbeck (1957), "Leadership Stability and Social Change: An Experiment with Small Groups", *Sociometry*, 20, 36-50.

Kelley, Harold H. (1951), "Communication in Experimentally Created Hierarchies", *Human Relations*, 4, 39-56.

Kipnis, David (1958), "The Effects of Leadership Style and Leadership Power upon the Inducement of an Attitude Change", *Journal of Abnormal and Social Psychology*, 57, 173-80.

Leavitt, Harold J. (1951), "Some Effects of Certain Communication Patterns on Group Performance", *Journal of Abnormal and Social Psychology*, 46, 38-50.

Leavitt, Harold J., and Ronald A. H. Mueller (1951), "Some Effects of Feedback on Communication", *Human Relations*, 4, 401-10.

Lewin, Kurt, and Ronald Lippitt (1938), "An Experimental Approach to the Study of Autocracy and Democracy: A Preliminary Note", *Sociometry*, 1, 292-300.

Lippitt, Ronald (1939), "Field Theory and Experiment in Social Psychology: Autocratic and Democratic Group Atmospheres", *American Journal of Sociology*, 45, 26-49.

Lippitt, Ronald, and Ralph K. White (1943), "The 'Social Climate' of Children's Groups", in Roger G. Barker, Jacob S. Kounin, and Herbert F. Wright (Eds.), *Child Behavior and Development: A Course of Representative Studies* (New York, McGraw-Hill).

Lippitt, Ronald, Norman Polansky, and Sidney Rosen (1952), "The Dynamics of Power", *Human Relations*, 5, 37-64.

McBurney, James H., and Kenneth G. Hance (1939), *Discussion in Human Affairs* (New York, Harper).

McQuitty, L. L., C. Wrigley, and E. L. Gaier (1954), "An Approach to Isolating Dimensions of Job Success", *Journal of Applied Psychology*, 38, 227-32.

Mann, John H., and Carola H. Mann (1959), "The Importance of a Group Task in Producing Group-Member Personal and Behavioral Changes", *Human Relations*, 12, 65-74.

March, James G. (1951), "An Introduction to the Theory and Measurement of Influence", *American Political Science Review*, 49, 431-51.

March, James G. (1956), "Influence Measurement in Experimental and Semi-Experimental Groups", *Sociometry*, 19, 260-71.

Melton, A. W. (1947), *Apparatus Tests* (= *AAF Aviation Psychological Program*, Research Report No. 4) (Washington D. C., U. S. Governmental Printing Office).

Mills, Theodore M. (1953), "Power Relations in Three Person Groups", *American Sociological Review*, 18, 351-7.

Morris, Richard T. (1956), "A Typology of Norms", *American Sociological Review*, 21, 610.

Naess, A. (1948), *Objectivity of Norms* (Oslo, Universitets Student-Kontor).

Newcomb, Theodore N. (1951), "Social Psychological Theory: Integrating Individual and Social Approaches", in John H. Rohrer and Muzapher Sherif (Eds.), *Social Psychology at the Crossroads* (New York, Harper).

Nieman, Lionel J., and James W. Hughes (1951), "The Problem of the Concept of Role: A Resurvey of the Literature", *Social Forces*, 30, 141-49.

Paulson, Stanley F. (1958), "Pressures Toward Conformity in Group Discussion", *Quarterly Journal of Speech*, 44, 50-55.

Pfautz, Harold W. (1953), "The Current Literature on Social Stratification", *American Journal of Sociology*, 58, 394.

Philp, Hugh, and Dexter Dunphy (1959), "Developmental Trends in Small Groups", *Sociometry*, 22, 162-74.

Raven, Bertram H. (Ed.), (1965), *A Bibliography of Publications Relating to the Small Group* (Third Edition) (= *Technical Report* No. 15, Contract Nonr. 253 [54], Group Psychology Branch, Office of Naval Research, Washington, D. C.).

Riecken, Henry W., and George C. Homans (1954), "Psychological Aspects of Social Structure", in Gardner Lindzey (Ed.), *Handbook of Social Psychology* (Cambridge, Mass., Addison-Wesley) 786-829.

Rommetvelt, Ragner (1955), *Social Norms and Roles: Explorations in the Psychology of Enduring Social Pressures* (Oslo, Akademisk Forlag).

Sakoda, James I. (1952), "Factor Analysis of OSS Situational Tests", *Journal of Abnormal and Social Psychology*, 47, 843-52.

Sanford, F. H. (1952), "Research on Military Leadership", in J. C. Flanagan (Ed.), *Psychology in the World Emergency* (Pittsburgh, Pa., University of Pittsburgh Press).

Schachter, Stanley (1951), "Deviation, Rejection, and Communication", *Journal of Abnormal and Social Psychology*, 46, 190-207.

Scheidel, Thomas M., Laura Crowell and John R. Shepherd (1958), "Personality and Discussion Behavior: A Study of Possible Relationships", *Speech Monographs*, 25, 261-67.

Schneider, Leonard I. (1955), "A Proposed Conceptual Integration of Group Dynamics and Group Therapy", *Journal of Social Psychology*, 42, 174.

Schutz, William C. (1952), "Some Theoretical Considerations for Group Behavior", in Research and Development Board, *Symposium on Techniques for the Measurement of Group Performance* (Washington, D. C., Committee on Human Resources, U. S. Department of Defense).

Schutz, William C. (1955), "What Makes Groups Productive?", *Human Relations*, 8, 429-66.

Shaw, Marvin E. (1954a), "Group Structure and the Behavior of Individuals in Small Groups", *Journal of Psychology*, 38, 139-49.

Shaw, Marvin E. (1954b), "Some Effects of Problem Complexity upon Problem Solution Efficiency in Different Communication Nets", *Journal of Experimental Psychology*, 48, 211-17.

Shaw, Marvin E. (1954c), "Some Effects of Unequal Distribution of Information upon Group Performance in Various Communication Nets", *Journal of Abnormal and Social Psychology*, 49, 547-53.

Shaw, Marvin E. (1959), "Acceptance of Authority, Group Structure, and the Effectiveness of Small Groups", *Journal of Personality*, 27, 196-210.

Sherif, Muzafer (1936), *The Psychology of Social Norms* (New York, Harper).

Slater, Philip E. (1955), "Role Differentiation in Small Groups", *American Sociological Review*, 20, 303.

Slater, Philip E. (1958), "Contrasting Correlates of Group Size", *Sociometry*, 21, 129-39.

Stogdill, Ralph M. (1948), "Personal Factors Associated with Leadership: A Survey of the Literature", *Journal of Psychology*, 25, 35-71.

Stogdill, Ralph M. (1951), "Studies in Naval Leadership, Part II", in Harold Guetzkow (Ed.), *Groups, Leadership and Men* (Pittsburgh, Pa., Carnegie Press).

Stogdill, Ralph M. (1959), *Individual Behavior and Group Achievement* (New York, Oxford University Press).

Strodtbeck, F. L. (1954), "The Family as a Three-Person Group", *American Sociological Review*, 19, 23-29.

Strodtbeck, F. L., and A. Paul Hare (1954), "Bibliography of Small Group Research", *Sociometry*, 17, 107-178.

Taylor, F. Kraupl (1954), "The Three-Dimensional Basis of Emotional Interactions in Small Groups", *Human Relations*, 7, 446-55.

Thibaut, John W. (1950), "An Experimental Study of The Cohesiveness of Underprivileged Groups", *Human Relations*, 3, 251-78.

Thibaut, John W., and Harold H. Kelley (1959), *The Social Psychology of Groups* (New York, Wiley).

Venable, Tom C. (1954), "The Relationship of Selected Factors to the Social Structure of a Stable Group", *Sociometry*, 17, 355-57.

Vroom, Victor H. (1959), "Some Personality Determinants of the Effects of Participation", *Journal of Abnormal and Social Psychology*, 59, 322-27.

White, Ralph, and Ronald Lippitt (1953), "Leader Behavior and Member Reaction in Three Social Climates", in Dorwin Cartwright and Alvin Zander (Eds.), *Group Dynamics: Research and Theory* (Evanston, Ill., Row, Peterson).

Wispe, Lauren G. (1955), "A Sociometric Analysis of Conflicting Role-Expectations", *American Journal of Sociology*, 61, 134-37.

RUPERT L. CORTRIGHT

THE USES AND ABUSES OF DISCUSSION

> "The mutual confidence on which all else depends can be maintained
> only by an open mind and a brave reliance upon free discussion.
> Judge Learned Hand

An open mind is one ever alert and receptive to new ideas. It is in the fullest and truest sense a learning mind; and it becomes a greater mind as it engages in discussion with other open minds. This but emphasizes that the highest and finest use to which discussion may be put in our time is in aiding and furthering the learning process. Since there is an added dividend here of 'mutual confidence on which all else depends', he who engages in free discussion is twice blest; for both learning and understanding are top priority needs. Perhaps it follows as an inevitable corollary that the worst abuse of discussion is to allow it to fall short of its finest potential.

If man is to escape obsolescence he must keep abreast of knowledge. This race is no easy one. We are today in the presence of such tremendous quantities of knowledge as have never before been available to man. Yet the pace of new discovery, new thought, new research seems ever accelerating. In 1965 before the twentieth annual National Conference on Higher Education Dr. Randall M. Whaley, then Vice President for Graduate Studies and Research at Wayne State University, spoke of these "Exponential Increases in Knowledge":

In three centuries, 1600 to 1900, application of science and technology produced more changes in how men lived and worked than were produced in the previous 6,000 years. More changes... will occur during the next 30 or 35 years than... in all previous history. There is about 100 times as much to know now as was available in 1900. By the year 2000 there will be over a thousand times as much knowledge of all kinds to record, to sift, to store, to search out, to teach about and, hopefully, to use with some discrimination and effectiveness... It has been estimated that between 80 and 90 percent of all of the scientists who ever lived are alive and working today. Accompanying this increase in knowledge production has been a comparable development of ancillary enterprises grouped together and characterized as the Knowledge Industry. It has been growing more than twice as fast as the economy itself and increased 43 percent in five years.

Obviously this knowledge explosion presents new challenges to the human mind. It should be reassuring to note the estimate that man possesses 12 billion brain cells. Yet, when told this, Bob Hope asked with discernment, "How's that for unemployment?" Must not all of us ask whether our most urgent task may not be to put more of those cells more efficiently to work for us? Wondrous as is the capacity of the individual human mind, it is in danger of being overwhelmed by the task merely of becoming aware, let alone understanding organizing and applying even a tiny percentage of the whole of available knowledge. Fortunately, however, as Dr. Whaley went on to point out to the leaders of higher education:

We have grossly underestimated the potential ability of human beings to learn. It is becoming increasingly clear that we must provide a more varied repertoire of instructional techniques to develop the full range of human abilities. In essence, what we see ahead is involvement of a wide variety of behavioral scientists, natural scientists, professional educators and other scholars in studying human learning in its various settings.

FACILITATING LEARNING

I would add that we must achieve new means of THINKING COOPERATIVELY, of harnessing minds into teamwork. We have achieved the greater effectiveness of team teaching; now we need to achieve the far-more-important effectiveness of team learning. Really now, how can we hope to comprehend the unity of the universe, the oneness of truth of a veritable infinity of bits of knowledge with anything less than a unity of minds in a common learning endeavor? We know that learning is an active process. May it not take on even increased efficiency as a co-active process? It is becoming increasingly evident that individually and separately no man alone can know all. Only as minds work together in team projects are we learning how to bring a world closer together OR how to blow it apart; how to benefit one's fellow man OR how to destroy him. It is precisely because the consequences of learning or not learning are so desperately vital that we must be about the business of improving the process of learning. This process of learning must, above all, embody making the best possible use of knowledge.

These are the impelling reasons for considering the most important use to which the art and science of discussion can be ever more broadly applied for the greater wisdom of man. Research conclusions seem largely to substantiate the general observations of educators that, comparatively, discussion has advantages over the lecture method in the classroom in terms not only of motivation but also of both immediate and delayed recall. Also there is increasing evidence that the quality of individual decisions usually is improved by group discussion. Government departments of agriculture, agricultural colleges and farm organizations generally were experiencing nearly a half century ago the fact that farmers were less resistive and quicker to learn and adopt new practices such as rotation of crops, use of improved fertilizers and better selection of seeds when these were presented in demonstrations and discussions rather than wholly by lecture. By the mid-thirties John W. Studebaker was directing, with foundation support, a statewide experiment in Iowa seeking to train a better informed electorate through discussions of crucial issues. The encouragingly favorable results were published under the title of *The Inquiry*.

When John W. Studebaker later became U. S. Commissioner of Education it was only natural that his high enthusiasm for the success in Iowa in using discussion as a means of adult education led him to encourage extensive experimentation with the use of discussion as a tool of learning in the public schools. Currently, those who have advanced our limited knowledge of how the mind develops, and how closely the processes of speaking and thinking may be interrelated, have given us new insights into the ways in which discussion so effectively facilities learning. For discussion gives experience simultaneously to the interrelated (and perhaps more interdependent than many have realized) processes of thinking and speaking. It is entirely possible (if not, indeed, probable) that in training for effective discussion we are as directly training for effective thinking as by any known way. Discussion is thus in the fullest and truest sense a means of LEARNING.

FORESTALLING PROBLEMS

A quick overview of history reveals the vital role which discussion has played throughout the centuries of man's progress — from the democracy enjoyed by freemen in the golden age of Greece on through the New England Town Meeting to contemporary religion, education, government, business and industry. The danger on the contemporary scene is that many, perhaps most, of its users have seen its true function only in part, and that the lesser part. Discussion as a means of solving problems always has been, and apparently always will be, a cumbersome, a disappointingly slow and a discouragingly ineffectual tool. This is not to say that we humans have discovered any better means of solving problems once problems have been permitted to grow and fester. That's just the point: incipient difficulties, beginnings of misunderstandings, causes of disharmony need never be allowed to develop into full-blown problems. This is where discussion finds another great usefulness: in dissolving and dispersing the potentialities of problems. The perfect analogy is in the field of health where it was learned long ago that prevention of infection is in all ways preferable to attempted cure after infection has been permitted to set in and spread. Discussion as a means of solving problems all too often has been called upon too late. This, even at best, is to misuse it. Its finest use, its more rewarding use, is for the prevention or FORESTALLING OF PROBLEMS. There are many industries in my home metropolis which have never suffered a strike, or even a work stoppage, because prompt discussion of grievances has dissipated the potential causes of disruption. Obviously in many facets of our society we have yet to learn the opportunities discussion offers for the prevention of such problems as divorce, school drop-outs, delinquency, rehabilitation and all types of resort to violence. This preventive capability — this capacity of discussion to eliminate, or certainly greatly to lessen, many of the divisive and destructive forces in our society certainly is splendidly complementary to its primary use: to motivate, facilitate and activate the process of human learning.

ACHIEVING AND RESTORING MENTAL HEALTH

One of the highest purposes of learning is to free man from ignorance and from all other forms of tyranny — even, if need be, from the tyranny of his own disturbed mind. It remained for rehabilitation centers to discover the great usefulness of the discussion process in the restoration of mental health. Service men from World War II who had suffered enormous shock learned the therapeutic values of discussion in the reattainment of expressional ability and the re-ordering of disoriented mental processes through the rewarding verbal experience of sharing despair and hope, defeat and faith, until wordless loneliness gave way to the understanding companioning made possible by verbalization. As Emerson expressed it:

> The music that can deepest reach,
> And cure all ill, is cordial speech. — (in *Merlin's Wisdom*)

The usefulness of discussion in the achievement and restoration of mental health is no mere incidental matter. In many academic courses in discussion too much is made of pat forms, formulas and methods; while too little attention is given to the far more numerous personal and informal adaptations. Consider but briefly such problems as divorce, juvenile delinquency and school drop-outs. Then think how fuller and freer discussion in home and school might have helped the individuals involved to happier, wiser and more rewarding courses of action. It becomes evident that the use of discussion to contribute to happier living, quicker learning and fuller wisdom, as well as to dissipate conflict and emotionalized problems, is as near and vital to each of us as is our family, as everyday for us as our work, our education, our religion and our citizenship responsibility.

PREDISPOSING RIGHT ATTITUDES

Measured by consequences, one of the more serious misuses of discussion lies in the failure to establish a favorable 'environment' before plunging into the question at hand. It is a mistake to assume: (1) that specific discussants are in a mood either to communicate or to listen, in the meaningful sense of those terms; or (2) that they wish to discuss with any others, let alone with the persons involved; or (3) that they hold their present attitudes TENTATIVELY, subject to change; or (4) that they have any faith in the discussion process as likely to produce helpful outcomes. There are necessary steps of preparation if a discussion is to have a good chance for success, and these go far beyond the availability of pertinent information upon the question to be discussed. Users of discussion seem to learn readily that mere pooling of ignorance is unfruitful; but there seems to be far less awareness that psychologically unready discussants are as unpromising as those who are unknowing.

DISCOVERING THE WHOLE TRUTH

The abuses of discussion are not avoided by good intentions, nor by well-meaning friends and users in all cases. It is, for instance, an abuse of discussion, no matter how well-intentioned, to assume that CONSENSUS is always the most desirable of outcomes for a discussion. In reality, no amount of discussion will result in everyone preferring spinach, or strawberry shortcake, or blonds, or Americans, or work, or even peace. There is good reason to question whether anyone's likes, dislikes or attitudes are much changed by anything less than experience. In the area of likes and dislikes it may be fortunate that everyone's favorite color isn't orchid, even though most women may pretend so for a style season. Consensus may all too often be a cause for concern rather than a reassuring happening. Most alarming of all is the possibility — or even probability — that unless thorough debate follows, or parallels discussion, some vital facts, evidence, opinion or experience will be overlooked. Yet there are those who advocate that discussion ought to discourage argument within it. Perhaps only in argument (debate) is the WHOLE TRUTH most certain to emerge. There is research evidence to indicate that group opinion is more likely to influence individual agreement than is expert opinion.[1] Is it not a dangerous possibility, then, that even the encouragement of consensus as a desirable outcome of discussion may act as a deterrent, if not actual impediment, to the full and free expression of ideas, attitudes and experiences? More than a century ago John Stuart Mill, in his brilliant essay *On Liberty*, set forth the danger of failing to listen to a minority, even a minority of one:

If all mankind minus one, were of one opinion, and only one person were of the contrary opinion, mankind would be no more justified in silencing that one person, than he, if he had the power, would be justified in silencing mankind... But the peculiar evil of silencing the expression of an opinion is, that it is robbing the human race; posterity as well as the existing generation; those who dissent from the opinion, still more than those who hold it. If the opinion is right, they are deprived of the opportunity of exchanging error for truth: if wrong, they lose, what is almost as great a benefit, the clearer perception and livelier impression of truth, produced by its collision with error.[2]

Perhaps there is something more important in discussion than reaching consensus. The goal which should have priority may well be that of discovering the WHOLE TRUTH. Those of us who have undertaken the use of discussion in business, industry, religion, education, government or family know that there is no more difficult task than to get the whole truth — the full truth — expressed by each and every participant. When vital facts, attitudes or opinions are withheld any appearance of con-

[1] H. E. Burtt, and D. R. Falkenberg, "The Influence of Majority and Expert Opinion on Religious Attitudes", *J. of Social Psychol.* (1941), 14:269-78, and D. Wheeler, and H. Jordan, "Change of Individual Opinion to Accord With Group Opinion", *J. of Abnorm. Soc. Psychol.* (1929), 24:203-6.
[2] John Stuart Mill, *On Liberty*, first written in 1859. This quotation from p. 35 of the 1895 edition published by Henry Holt & Co.

sensus is appearance only. May it not be, then, that those who strive most for consensus as an outcome abuse discussion by endangering its more fragile objective:
the complete discovery of truth — truth, whether from majority or minority position,
whether advanced by friend or stranger?

RECOGNIZING THAT NOT ALL THINGS ARE POSSIBLE

When we discussed the relative ineffectuality of discussion as a tool for problem
solving one aspect of this was left for later mention. Human nature being as it is,
discussion frequently is called upon to solve that which is not solvable. This is an
additional misuse of discussion. Of course we like to believe that every problem has
a solution. We come reluctantly to learn that some problems may outlive us and
that the most we are able to do is to modify them a bit and learn to live with them.
Healthy, happy living has elements of patience in it as well as of impatience. Discussion can be useful in helping us to distinguish the utterly impossible from the
merely difficult.

BETTER DECISIONS, BETTER UNDERSTOOD AND BETTER SUPPORTED

If I have been suggesting it too indirectly, I here emphasize with all possible direct-
ness: the use of discussion is basic to the superiority of democracy as the way to
freedom and progress. As discussion remains prevalent wherever decision-making is
in progress the survival and strengthening of democracy are made more sure. The
alternative to democracy: authoritarian action, cannot long survive in a competitive
industry nor in a world in conflict. Obviously, if the authoritative decision is the
wrong one all will be the better off for its avoidance; but no less certainly, even were
the authoritative decision the right one, democratic participation (discussion) in its
making would have added broader understanding with resultant unreserved support
in its execution. We have noted previously, of course, that a decision made following
discussion by competent persons is likely to be a better decision than any one of the
competent persons might be likely to make in solitary analysis.

THE BEST FROM EVERY INDIVIDUAL ADDS UP TO THE GREATNESS OF ALL

There is another attribute of democracy which is at the very heart of any confidence
we place in the discussion process. This is the enthroning of each individual and his
high potential for contribution. The value of the individual is at the center of man's
deepest religious faith. A student of the world's great religions, Paul Hutchinson,
concluded "Man is a religious being."[3] The historian, Arnold Toynbee, has observed:

---

[3]   Paul Hutchinson was for many years editor of *The Christian Century*. Before his untimely death
he had completed the Introduction to *The World's Great Religions* published by Life in 1957.

"The four higher religions (now alive are) four variations on a single theme." At its best man's religious quest is to find and achieve his better self. As one reads Emerson's or Thoreau's or Whitman's powerful phrasings of evolving American ideals one is enthused to make his own life a thrilling and triumphant search for his best self.

A study of genetics reveals that each individual is unique — there never before has been and in all future time never will be another individual of exactly alike physical heritage. The Vienna psychiatrist, Frankl, suggests that the finest mental health results as each individual strives to attain the full potential of his own uniqueness of talents. Perhaps herein lies the reason for the true greatness of the dream of freedom and the democratic way of life. William Penn had written of one of the colonial experiments in democracy as early as 1676: "We put the power in the people." By 1903 those already descriptive, yet still prophetic, words of Emma Lazarus were on the base of the Statue of Liberty: "I lift my lamp beside the golden door." "Those yearning to breathe free", immigrants from lands where only the nobility and the wealthy could find opportunity, builded well our nation. Their names are legion who like Einstein had been denied opportunity in their homelands but found here the chance to give of their talents to their and our everlasting enrichment. Our United States may well owe its role of greatness in today's world to that simple basic religious faith in the worth of each individual translated into the economic, governmental and educational goals of giving opportunity to each person to achieve the fullest possible realization of his talents. So does discussion, as an instrument of democracy, put its trust in the people. Surely this is one of the most rewarding outcomes of discussion, that when you begin you never know and seldom guess correctly which member will make the most valuable contribution. Often it will not be the most learned, the best educated, the most culturally advantaged or the highest paid. Experience with discussion soon teaches, if you have not learned it before, that each, when given a chance, has something of value to contribute. Each individual merits the respect and confidence of every other. Every church, every unit of government, every industry needs to benefit from the best ideas of every individual member involved. We have discovered no better way than that of discussion thus to tap into the talents and ideas of all persons involved. One of discussion's most rewarding uses is that it places high value upon the judgment of each man — no matter what his IQ, or education, or wealth, or social status, or position, or liking for you.

THE FUTURE IS A WORLD LIMITED ONLY BY OURSELVES

Since CHANGE seems to be the only constant, we need to make wise use of discussion as an effective instrument of change.

Since leisure time is rapidly becoming a sharp test of man's ability to be civilized, we will be well advised to use discussion as a means to learning and to the attainment of a healthy mind in a healthy body caught up and lifted to new highs of self-realization.

Since hate and conflict persist as imminent dangers even to man's survival, we will do well to make of discussion a most hopeful way to understanding and respect and love of others and of causes greater than our selfish selves.

Since one man alone seems all too impotent amidst the immensity of human knowledge, we need to resort more confidently and more efficiently to team learning, to learning cooperatively that we may better understand ourselves and live more harmoniously with others.

All this is a vital part of the ever ongoing search for the more abundant life.

The preceding words have not, of course, undertaken to set forth the usually listed uses and abuses of discussion. These are readily available in one of the many fine textbooks on the subject. The purpose has been, rather, to stimulate reflection upon less examined aspects of both the promise and the perfidy of discussion. How and what you think on these things become a part of you.[4]

WAYNE STATE UNIVERSITY

---

[4] "If you make people think they're thinking, they'll love you. If you really make them think they'll hate you". — Donald Robert Perry Marquis in *The Sun Dial*

JACK R. GIBB and LORRAINE M. GIBB

THE PROCESS OF GROUP ACTUALIZATION

People grow. This is a familiar but dramatic fact of life. Change does occur. Both change and growth are often less than they might be. The potential of personal growth is greater than we had earlier imagined. Life can become much more than it may seem to be. Life can be richer, more exciting, more creative, and more productive than it is. Recent research in the behavioral sciences has given us some leads as to how growth may be accelerated and how higher human potential may be reached.

So it is with groups. Groups have great potential for growth. A group can change, learn, and grow.

It takes little perspicacity to note that not all groups grow — perhaps that most groups don't grow. Some seem to stagnate. Members come to group meetings from a sense of duty. The product of the group thinking may be quite pedestrian. Decisions may not be implemented. Attendance drops off. Group meetings become occupied with trivia. Members may speak defensively about belonging.

Families, crews, committees, classes, clinics, clubs, teams, and staffs — groups of all kinds form the fabric of the society in which we live. Although the number of formal memberships that individuals hold varies greatly, it is probably true that all healthy persons are members to some extent in many relevant groups. In fact, it seems valid to say that group membership in itself is health producing. People need to belong, to hold membership. Growth and health are social processes. People must have significant relationships in depth.

What makes growth? When are groups sick and should be discontinued? When do groups have potential for growth and should be fostered?

These questions are of concern both to the individual person who makes decisions about the organizations to which he will belong and to community engineers who use group constructions as a social engineering device.

Social practitioners are exploring group formation in many situations. Residence hall advisers and managers in university communities are experimenting with the composition, physical housing, and size of the residential groups. YMCA youth directors are trying out various ways of building healthy Hi-Y clubs, experimenting with format, presence or absence of advisers, size, leadership, training, and other variables. Housing developers are confronted with the problem of composition and selection in forming geographical residential units, particularly when retired people or large families are concerned. School administrators have long been interested in size of groups and relatively static population variables. The more imaginative ones are now examining the problem of building groups as classroom media for effective teaching-learning.[1]

Military commanders have the significant problem of forming platoons and regiments, which have high morale and are maximally effective, operating groups for military action. Looked at from the standpoint of group formation, squad composition is a significant problem in group dynamics.

Coaches of such non-team effort sports as tennis, swimming, and golf have the problem of using group variables to produce relationships that lead to the effectiveness of swimming teams as teams. The vast difference in results between various athletic clubs is due, not only to training method and coach recruiting, but also to significant variables of team growth.

Staff, line, assembly crew, and other units of industrial and manufacturing operations should be observed from the standpoint of group performance and health. These observations are often camouflaged in such pseudo-questions as span of control, but are increasingly looked on by modern management as problems of group growth. There is clear evidence that healthy groups with appropriate development, effective decision making, and team formation require very little of the classical functions of management such as supervision, delegation, and motivation. Effective groups solve their problems much more easily than ineffective groups. Managing as such becomes decreasingly necessary as we learn more about health in groups.

Parents are faced with the group health problem in planning family size, instituting family councils, and encouraging or discouraging total family activities. The father can look at the family as a series of relationships between him and each of the other members in turn, or he can look at the family as a group. This perceptual stance makes a great deal of difference in family growth and child rearing. For example, when the father sees himself as the manager of the family, he will call in each child and individually praise or correct him. But when he sees the members as a group, there is a possibility of forming a family council where members discuss issues, build an agenda, form a roster for doing chores, make vital decisions together, and the process itself becomes intrinsically rewarding or punishing depending upon its effectiveness.

All managers and people with special responsibilities have the option of looking at their systems as groups or as clusters of dyads. Our knowledge of system effectiveness is relevant to the building of management theory — in the home, church ort factory.

---

[1] N. B. Henry, (Ed.), "The dynamics of instructional groups", *The Fifty-ninth Yearbook of the National Society for the Study of Education* (Chicago, The University of Chicago Press, 1960).

During the past 16 years the authors, largely financed by grants from the Office of Naval Research, have been engaged in a program of research to determine the nature of the group experience and how it may be made more creative, more satisfying, more productive and more growth-enhancing. We have analyzed over 600 groups in various settings — therapy groups, training groups, laboratory research groups, classes, teams, families, committees, clubs, and staffs.[2] We will make an effort in this chapter to summarize some of our findings as they relate to the differential growth of sick and healthy groups in our society, and to what we as parents, teachers, and managers — group 'engineers' — can do about it.

THE TORI PROCESSES

One significant finding is that there are four central modal concerns that recur continuously as themes in the lives of persons and groups. These basic life concerns are represented in the columns of Table 1. The process of growth and of becoming seems to involve continuous, sometimes cyclic, processing of these concerns. The four processes are interrelated in the sense that there seems to be a priority sequence that occurs when optimum growth occurs.

TABLE 1

Basic Life Concerns of the Person and the Group

Basic Concerns in Personal Growth	Basic Concerns in Group Growth
TRUST: (How do I learn to love and trust myself? How do I learn to give love and trust?)	MEMBERSHIP: (How do we create a genuine feeling of membership in all persons in the group?)
OPENNESS: (How do I get in touch with the real me? How do I communicate in depth and intimacy with others?)	DECISION-MAKING: (How do we process feelings and perceptions into significant decisions about things that matter to us?)
REALIZATION: (How can I find out what I want out of life, get personal fulfillment, and give fulfillment to others?)	PRODUCTIVITY: (How do we determine and achieve meaningful goals and purposes for our group?)
INTERDEPENDENCE: (How do I develop an inner control system that gives me freedom and allows me to give freedom to others?)	ORGANIZATION: (How do we develop satisfying and genuine interdependence and with-relations?)

[2]   J. R., Gibb, *Factors producing defensive behavior within groups*, (= *Final Technical Report VII*), Office of Naval Research, Contract Nonr-3088(00) (1963).

The ACCEPTANCE-MEMBERSHIP-TRUST concern relates to acceptance of self, acceptance of others, reduction of fears, increase of trust, reduction of defensive behavior,
and attainment of membership in significant groups. Every person seems to be
concerned at some level with how he can give and get love, and how he can build
a relationship of trust and acceptance with other persons. This concern has first
priority. Only as a person and as a group work through this concern can growth be
attained on the other concerns.

The OPENNESS-INTIMACY-DECISION-MAKING concern relates to communication with
self and others, with role and personness, with authenticity, with understanding and
being understood, and with the process of building decisions out of these data.
Only as some progress has been achieved in working through the acceptance concern
can meaningful growth occur on this data flow concern. Every person seems to be
concerned with giving and getting understanding and the reduction of ambiguity.

The REALIZATION-GOAL-PRODUCTIVITY concern has to do with finding an identity,
building immediate and life goals, finding common goals with relevant others, and
influencing the goals of others. Only as progress has been achieved on the acceptance
and data flow concerns can meaningful growth occur in setting goals in depth. Every
person seems to be concerned with giving and getting personal fulfillment.

The CONTROL-INTERDEPENDENCE-ORGANIZATION concern has to do with freedom
and control, relations with authority, and the development of interdependence. These
problems seem to be generated and exacerbated when concerns about acceptance,
data flow, and goal formation have been inadequately dealt with by the person or
by the group. Everyone apparently has concerns about freedom and influence. These
concerns apparently disappear as persons learn to work on a common emergent goal
in intimacy and trust.

For communicative ease we have called the basic growth processes in persons
and in groups the TORI processes — of growth toward trust, openness, realization,
and interdependence and away from fear, facade, imposition and dependency. These
processes seem inevitable in healthy social relationships. The significant question for
us is how these TORI processes can be accelerated and continued beyond the familiar
habit levels in our present organizational and community life.

THE FORMATION OF TRUST

In Tables 2 and 3 are schematic presentations of the changes that take place
during group development. The pace maker variable in personal and group growth
is the formation of trust and the accompanying reduction of fear. From this movement
from fear toward trust stems each of the other processes. In one sense the other
three variables define trust. One who trusts is able to communicate in depth and
intimacy, to explore the goals of himself and of others in sufficient authenticity to be
able to arrive at satisfying common goals, and to develop a with-relation of true
interdependence with others.

Fear and trust are antonyms representing polar ends of a central process. In the early stages of all groups fears are prevalent. The latent fears are represented in a variety of ways in the group. Fearful people are cautious, inhibited, formal, ambiguous, resistant, controlling, anxious, defensive, punitive, closed, and concerned with image, status and power. That is, latent fear is associated with the other aspects of early group life: facade, imposition, and dependency.

Fearful group members and leaders try to maintain structure in order to reduce uncertainty. A person is fearful when he feels his predicted response repertoire may not be adequate to meet an ambiguous situation. He therefore makes every effort to increase the predictability of his world. He thus becomes conserving of the world that is familiar to him, particularly of structures in which he has learned to act properly (i.e. in a fear-reductive way). Members in fear make and preserve rules. They have formal agenda, seating regulations, attendance rules, parliamentary rules, many titles, bylaws, formal clothing and seating, clear role expectations, elaborate ceremonials, and a variety of ways of keeping things orderly, predictable, safe, and less frightening. Procedures which were conceived or born in fear tend to preserve themselves, become functionally autonomous, and members may be only partially conscious of the underlying dynamics of emergence.

Another way of handling fear and distrust is to be cautious. People can be self-protective and cautious in many ways. Some chatter about familiar and safe topics. Some stay within protective and familiar roles. All have masks and walls of varying degrees of opacity and durability. Some talk a great deal about familiar topics. Others talk little or not at all, perhaps smiling politely and cautiously in a non-commital way.

A person is also being self-protective if he engages in a variety of unconscious and partially conscious delaying tactics: semantic quibbles, legalistic arguments, displaced discussions of minor issues, and overelaborateness of plans. All are ways of keeping the group from making direct movements toward unknown and feared vistas.

In order to feed and care for one's fears one keeps them from coming to awareness and attention. In order to do this a group member may use various distancing and camouflaging methods. Being polite keeps people at a safe distance, discourages frankness, prevents retaliation, covers negative feelings, and meets many needs of the fearful person. Humor serves the same ends. By using humor a person can avoid embarrassing or painful exposure of his emotions, can deny hostile intent if the listener accuses him of being unfriendly, and send up a trial balloon to see what people's reactions will be before feelings are expressed directly.

Fear is related to distrust. People who are afraid distrust the motivations of other members, particularly those who are in authority or status. Distrusting the motivations of others, the fearful person suspects with some justification that his own motives will be derogated, and thus becomes very much aware of his image and his public relations.

Fearful people often have concerns about inclusion. They want to be sure to be in an appropriate group, to be paired with someone safe, strong or of high status, and to be in the 'in' portion of the group. Belonging to the most 'popular' church in town, joining only clubs or organizations that are considered acceptable, and choosing socially acceptable friends in the group are all methods used by the fearful person.

People who are insecure tend to evaluate and judge others, sort of beat them to the punch. Remarks are placed in a moral frame of reference. This stance toward others is communicated in many ways and tends to reenforce the defensive cycle.

Only as fear of others is reduced can people show genuine affection for others, concern for them as persons, and care for their well being. Early in all groups there are latent hostilities and alienation feelings. Until people establish a relation of trust they tend to feel apart, anxious, suspicious, cynical or impersonal. The world of the group is often undifferentiated. Only as one trusts and accepts himself can he become genuinely PERSONAL, in the sense of establishing a relation between his person and the person of the other. With a personal relation comes affection, caring, concern, and love for the other person. Our research has led us to the conviction that people are basically loving when one gets to the deep core of the being. The closer group members get to the 'persons' of each other the more caring they become.

With increasing trust many things tend to happen in the group. Structure tends to be unnecessary. Controls diminish. Hostile humor drops down and most humor disappears. Formalities are reduced. People tend to use first names or pet names. People no longer use formal titles. Clothing, seating, chair arrangements, furniture, and other physical arrangements become more informal. Behavior becomes more congruent — motivations are accepted for what they seem and people are not suspected of devious or strategic motivations. Members tend to give emotional support to each other. Members feel safe in the group, feel they can be late or absent without motives being called into question, feel they can leave or be deviant in behavior with impunity.

Increasing trust and reduced fear makes possible movement of the other TORI processes.

FROM FACADE TO INTIMACY

Tables 2 and 3 indicate another of the TORI processes of growth — the development from facade and psychological distance to intimacy and openness. All groups start with some protective and defensive masking, maintain a safe privacy of person, and start with a polite appearance of honesty and candor.[3]

So habitual is this protective screen that people are usually not aware of its existence. People have often not even experienced anything else at any greater depth of

---

[3] J. R., Gibb, "Defensive communication", *The Journal of Communication* (1961), 11(3), 141-148.

relationship or degree of intimacy. Being 'social' is a process of being polite. We have developed an elaborate posture and language to maintain the face of candor. Nowhere is the facade more apparent or caricatured than in the middle class board or club meeting. The rules of 'society' seem devised for the purpose of maintaining superficial and safe psychological distance.

One gets an accurate image of the communicative distortion in the early stages of group formation by thinking of the disparity between what people say about each other in the committee meeting and what they say about each other when discussing other members in the intimacy of bathroom or boudoir. A good measure of communicative validity is the congruency between openness in the total committee and openness in one of the intimate subgroups.

The lack of openness of communication in early stages of the group is related to the development of skills of concealment, gamesmanship, strategy, or politeness. Much energy is spent in maintaining a surface calm, an atmosphere of sweetness,

TABLE 2

Directions of Personal and Group Actualization

Directions of Personal Growth and Actualization		Directions of Group Growth and Actualization	
From	Toward	From	Toward
FEAR: (latent and manifest fears, distrusts, evaluation, high defense)	TRUST: (trust and love of self and others: less fear and defense)	FEAR: (climate of latent fear, distrust, alienation)	TRUST: (Climate of trust and support, low defense and low fear)
FACADE: (inner dissonance, masking, withdrawal, distancing)	OPENNESS: (inner consonance, serenity, ability and need to be intimate)	FACADE: (climate of strategy, ambiguity, formality, closed behavior)	OPENNESS: (an open feedback and data processing system, intimacy)
IMPOSITION: (goals coming from duty, others, outside forces, persuasion)	REALIZATION: (self-determined goals and activities; goal integration; self-assessment)	IMPOSITION: (goals coming from authority, leaders, image concern, or history)	REALIZATION: (integration of goals from group consensus and shared concerns)
DEPENDENCY: (controls from outside person, from authority, status or rebellion)	INTERDEPENDENCY: (controls from inside and from emergent concern for others; withrelations)	DEPENDENCY: (controls come from power, status, leaders, duty)	INTERDEPENDENCY: (emergent controls within norms of the group, participative cooperation)

TABLE 3

Change in Behavior and Feelings With Group Growth

Early Behavior and Attitudes	Early Feelings	Later Behavior and Attitudes	Later Feelings
DISTRUST-PUNISHMENT: (evaluation, distrust, judgment, moralizing, advice giving)	ALIENATION: (hostility, lack of concern, fear, cynicism, envy)	TRUST-ACCEPTANCE: (confidence, non-role and personal relations, acceptance)	WARMTH: (affection, love, esteem, sympathy, caring)
STRATEGY-DISTANCING: (circumvention, distortion, superficial and formal communication, masking)	LONELINESS: (estrangement, sadness, depression, neutrality, aloneness)	EMPATHY-LISTENING: (spontaneity, rapport, impulsive and free behavior, communion)	INTIMACY: (serenity, warmth, comfort, coziness, freedom, safety)
PERSUASION-COMPETITION: (coercion, guidance, passivity, resistance, competition, polemic)	INDIFFERENCE: (apathy, disinterest, resentment, latent hostility)	SEARCHING-QUESTING: (exploration, search, fulfillment, shared problem solving)	ZEST: (eagerness, exhilaration, fervency, satisfaction, well being)
DOMINANCE-CONTROL: (management, dependency, rebellion, submission, counterdependency, resentment)	IMPOTENCE: (inadequacy, tension, latent or manifest hostility, fear)	EMERGENCE-COOPERATION: (interaction, freedom, working with, participation, spontaneity)	FREEDOM: (power, importance, worth, adequacy, potency, sense of being needed)

the appearance of friendliness, the facade of heartiness, and the pretense that we are in better communication than we are.

Perhaps because of guilts induced by the vague awareness of this elaborate deceit, members often use protective phrases to cover up their intentions to themselves and to others. Thus, one who is intending to interrupt might say "I don't want to interrupt but...". One who is going to be critical could say "I don't want to criticize, but...". Or one who is offering a debatable point might precede it by "obviously...".

As a person grows he gets more closely in touch with himself. As the group grows persons struggle to express genuine feelings, honest perceptions, real attitudes, and controversial opinions. As persons grow in ability to communicate with themselves they make efforts to develop a group communication system. The inadequacy of the formal communication system is commonly revealed when members try to make simple decisions in open discussion. In early groups one can, with equal and indeterminate validity, accept the assumption that 'silence means dissent' or that "silence means assent". Reducing the formal structure by permitting open discussion quickly reveals to group members the often depressing fact that much disagreement and conflict has gone unrecognized.

The ambiguity that inevitably accompanies closed behavior increases and feeds the fears and distrusts. In training and therapy groups it becomes quickly apparent that the silent members are usually feared. Most everyone enters the group with latent fears and it is easy to project these fears upon the silent members. Lacking disconfirming data, fearful group members assume that silent members are disinterested, ignorant, bored, resistant, frightened, timid or disdainful.

In interviews with persons who are members of low growth groups we find feelings of loneliness, neutrality, estrangement, and withdrawal. This is not always the case. Group members sometimes report feelings of comfort, and deny feelings of distance. After depth experiences with groups attaining more intimacy members report that their natural groups are less satisfying. They become sensitized to the social distance in the natural groups.

As groups grow they develop greater depth in genuine communication. Members become more spontaneous, impulsive, uninhibited and in greater rapport. As fears diminish members become less protective and cautious and more open. Openness is accompanied by greater comfort, freedom, safety and warmth. With preliminary efforts to be open, prior to sufficient fear reduction, members report anxiety about what other members might do with the feelings and opinions they have revealed.

As the group develops members learn that it is possible to deal with many deep-seated feelings and concerns without undue fear and anxiety about being hurt. The participants discover that release of feelings may be disturbing to many but that the alternative of withholding pent up feelings has even more detrimental effects upon the group. It becomes clear to group members that feelings and attitudes can be genuinely integrated into productive and creative problem solving. The group can become a more effective decision making organism.[4]

FROM IMPOSITION TO REALIZATION

As Indicated in Tables 2 and 3, group growth is partly a process of movement from imposed and arbitrary goals to group-determined goals and activities. The healthy person is one who is self-determined and who is able to assess his own development toward goals he has chosen. Groups often start with inherited goals which come from organizers, leaders, central headquarters, status members, or tradition and history. Growth is a process of developing enough trust and openness to enable the group to determine what it most deeply wants to do and to create meaningful group con-

---

[4] J. R. Gibb, Fear and facade; defensive management. In R. E. Farson, (Ed.), *Science and Human Affairs* (Palo Alto: Science and Behavioral Books, Inc., 1966) 197-214.

sensual goals out of some kind of integration of the goals of the members. The goal of an effective group, however, is something more than the sum total of the goals of individual members, and something more than the goal of the majority of members. The emergent goal of an effective group is not a compromise but a creative product of interaction sufficient for a novel product to emerge.

In low growth groups members may not know what they as individuals want to do and particularly what they want to do in the group. If the goals are specified by organizers or leaders or by the central organization there may be vague — or perhaps explicit — resistance to the goals. People resist imposition, but with embryonic mechanisms for making decisions find it difficult to come up with group-determined goals. In setting goals immature groups fall into many traps. They may set over-aspirational goals and then not be able to meet them in any reasonable time, thus causing member dissatisfactions and possible resentments of the group and its presumed inefficiency. They may set goals that are so abstract as to be meaningless in providing the energizing and directing functions that adequate group goals must perform.

Polarization of segments of the group may occur when subgroups form clusters which have different goals. Impatience over the necessary time that goal creation takes may cause premature decision making, voting, or hurried statements of compromise statements. Goal setting is a creative process and a difficult one. It is a necessary process because groups do not work at optimal levels of performance or with high satisfaction until they have satisfying common goals.

Unless groups have adequately worked through to a degree of trust and intimacy that permits direct goal formation there is guilt and anxiety about the disparity between the 'real' goals as implicit in the activities that go on and the formal stated goals. Thus bridge groups may meet to gossip, scientific conferences may meet to relieve boredom and get travel pay, and poker groups may meet to escape baby sitting. As groups grow there is a developmental congruence among public goals, functional goals, and verbalizations by members of why they come to meetings.

Because of the difficulties of the goal setting processes members engage in a variety of persuasive-coercive behaviors designed to get others to accept goals. Imposition, whether in the guise of guidance or in the form of direct control, results in various forms of resistance. Undigested and partially emergent goals produce apathy, indifference, fragmentation, counter-persuasion, and hostility.

One problem is that there are many varieties of 'goals'. Thus a group may be working at a fairly well organized task which may be seen by most members as their goal, and at the same time doing many other highly motivated subterranean 'tasks', such as punishing another group, winning a competition, demonstrating its worth to itself or to others, or avoiding a less desirable task. In order for a group to work most productively and satisfyingly there must be a high degree of integration of the verbalized task goals, the subliminal group efforts, and the individual needs and aspirations of members.

Motivation of group members is of course related to the goal structure. As groups grow the original apathy and indifference of group members is gradually replaced by more eagerness, satisfaction, zest and positive forces toward the goal. A healthy group is a searching, exploring, curious effort to solve problems, accomplish work, have fun, or move toward a goal.

One frequent attitude of undeveloped groups is a general feeling that goals are not necessary, that good things will just happen, that whatever we do will be meaningful, that goals will somehow naturally emerge in the process of interaction. This attitude is usually the product of many frustrating experiences at creating a meaningful goal. It may also result from customary abdication of the less articulate or strong members in favor of the more verbal, powerful, or visible members. It may result from premature goal efforts attempted prior to appropriate development of trust and openness.

When a group is growing goals become explicit, there is a functional relationship between goals and activities, and a commitment to the goal and the goal-directed activities. An emergent goal energizes, integrates, and directs the activities of the group.

FROM DEPENDENCE TO INTERDEPENDENCE

As indicated in Tables 2 and 3, one of the TORI growth processes is a development from external controls to emergent freedom and interdependence. With the growth of trust, intimacy, and emergent goals the need for external control systems diminishes or disappears. The need for control systems arises from fear and distrust of the members of the group system. As trust grows, as data processing becomes more efficient and habitual, and as goals become emergent from the conscious interactions of members then controls emerge and function as norms of the group. Special rules, arbitrary controls, and assigned authority roles become decreasingly necessary as the group grows.

In early stages of development, distrust, distorted communication, and impositional goals make necessary some kind of control system. In order to overcome initial feelings of powerlessness and fears of ambiguity, the group or the leaders develop a variety of structures. Structures differ in form: seating patterns, rules of parliamentary debate, formal agenda, voting procedures, rules for clothing and speech, gimmicks to stimulate attendance, elaborate sub-committee structures, penalties for rule violations, use of a variety of formal titles, written role prescriptions, formal work assignments, rotating chairmanships, and seating procedures.

Controls breed resistance — in either latent forms of apathy or more manifest forms of rebellion. Group members may spend much time and energy testing boundaries, finding out what the limits are, determining how powerful the chairman is, and perhaps quibbling about the rules. Another reaction to tight control is abdication of responsibility. Members let the leaders do the work, assume responsibility, devise methods of motivating members, appoint sub-committees, and lead the group. The resultant — and perhaps inevitable — hostility is often displaced and focussed upon passive members, other groups, natural processes, or other targets.

Another reaction to controls is circumvention. Rules are made to be broken. Members may spend a great amount of energy trying to get around the rules, re-interpret the regulations, get away with infractions without being caught, and perhaps pretend that they are obeying the rules.

Perhaps the most detrimental result of tight controls, however, is the dependent state of living complacently by the rules, becoming habituated to a life of regulations, and building up elaborate theories to rationalize the necessity of tight controls. Groups get in habits of rule making and rule keeping. Obedience becomes a virtue. Quality of membership is judged on a criteria of compliance with regulations. People get security from form and arbitrary regulations and develop fears of freedom and fluidity. The constitution becomes an end or a good in itself. Preservation of order becomes a goal. The purpose of the group becomes the goal to preserve itself. We once were observing a small religious group in which one of the members opened the session with a prayer which asked among other things that 'the group be able to finish its lesson on time!'

As members develop some awareness of the dynamics of authority and freedom they become increasingly resistant to imposed order. The resistance is usually camouflaged and takes the form of passivity, excessive politeness, denial, humor, and counter-strategy. Of diagnostic significance is an increasing development of feelings of impotence, indifference, and inadequacy. Groups, *qua* groups, cannot become strong with tight controls. Emergent freedom is characteristic of strong individuals and powerful groups.

As groups grow, trust increases and fear decreases. Increased openness and emergent goals make controls less necessary. Group members gradually abolish the various controls listed above. Life becomes considerably more informal and spon-taneous. Groups form their own agenda in interaction. Communication meshes without rules for speaking. Members, aware of goals and obligations that grew out of group interaction, assume feelings of responsibility and do not require penalty and sanction systems to induce responsible behavior. Responsibility comes from within and from a sense of dedication to group goals.

Group members learn to feel powerful, adequate, and of high worth from a sense of participation and influence. Group members begin to feel that they are important as persons and that they can control themselves and the processes they participate in.

Interdependent cooperation is the ultimate behavioral mark of the high growth and high productivity group. In interdependent groups members develop feelings of freedom and power. There is freedom from contraints. The group develops a tolera-tion for and acceptance of deviations in form and content. Deviation and diversity is the visible characteristic of interdependence. Conformity occurs in dominance and in dependency.

The feeling theme of interdependence is one of permissiveness. The permissiveness is accompanied by trust, communication in depth, and common goals. The group is 'managed', in a sense, but is managed not by persons but by task requirements, goal directions, and common perceptions of reality data. There is an optimal distribution of roles in the sense that problems get solved, roles are taken, duties are assumed, assignments are made — but these things happen at the initiation of various members of the group. Duties, roles and assignments are not concentrated in one person or in one power subgroup. Key members are not essential to the success of the group. There are no indispensable members. In true interdependence, members rise to the occasion and respond to challenge. The interdependence is not gained by 'bringing everyone down to the level of the group'. In every group there is so much untapped potential that the freedom of emergence seems to create new powers and release unrealized potential in all members. Members rise to unrealized and indeterminate levels of potential and performance.

THE TORI ACTUALIZING EXPERIENCES

Up to now we have described processes that occur in groups with which most readers are familiar. From our past experience we find that most people are far more familiar with defensive and fearful groups than with emergent and consensual groups. Only rarely do the healthy groups described at the end of each of the foregoing sections appear in our experiences with committees, teams, clubs and families. These healthy groups do exist, however, and in increasing numbers, in our corporations, school systems, communities, and volunteer agencies. A transition is occurring in our culture. As the cultural revolution advances, our institutions are creating more freedoms, more trust, greater commitment, and greater participation. Our young people are more aware of what a free society might be and more impatient with the restraints, fears, and distrusts of our quasi-authoritarian way of life. New developments in behavioral science, particularly in the studies of group behavior, have had their mark. New developments in the technologies of training and education have created new experiences in group creativity and potential.

It is in our studies of training and therapy groups that we have seen new frontiers in group development. In Table 4 are presented what we have called the four TORI ACTUALIZING EXPERIENCES which we have seen occur in advanced stages of training groups.[5] We have seen each of the experiences develop in advanced stages of T groups which have been in existence for 140 hours or more, and have seen the experiences occur in marathon training groups which have been in role-free contact

[5] J. R. Gibb, "Climate for trust formation", in L. P. Bradford, J. R. Gibb, and K. D. Benne (Eds.), *T-group Theory & Laboratory Method* (New York, John Wiley & Sons, 1964), 279-309.

TABLE 4

The TORI Actualizing Experiences

The TORI Personal Actualization Experiences	The TORI Group Actualization Experiences
TRUST-LOVE: (I feel loved and trusted now and am a lovable person, fully deserving of love and trust)	CARING: (All group members have a deep feeling of trust and love for all members of the group)
INTIMACY: (I feel at this moment completely understood at all levels and feel that I can be again; am relating as a role-free person)	CONSENSUS: (Complete group understanding and agreement on a course of action after full exploration of all relevant alternatives in personal, role-free interaction)
ZEST: (I have found a goal that is deeply mine and gives full meaning and becoming to my life at this moment)	COMMITMENT: (Sustained and genuinely zestful search by all members for an enduring, consensual goal)
FREEDOM-POWER: (I feel exhilaratingly free and powerful and am not anxious about anyone abridging either my freedom or my power)	EMERGENCE: (The emergence of a true constraint-free group interdependence with no rules or status-role hierarchy)

for 80 hours. The experiences do not necessarily occur in all T groups or in all marathon groups. They occur inevitably in leaderless groups of this duration, and less often with trainers present, depending upon the style of the trainer. The occurrence of the experiences seems to be a function of the ability of the trainer to take a personal, intimate, and interdependent presence in the group. If the trainer can BE A PERSON, and not a 'trainer', the experiences are likely to occur.

The TORI experiences are an extension of the TORI processes of trust, openness, realization, and interdependence.

The CARING EXPERIENCE is an experience of trust and love at a depth not previously experienced by members in a group situation. Members often have a new feeling of trust. The member feels with a deep sense of reality and validity that he is loved and trusted, and that he is a deservedly lovable person. All growing persons have experienced this feeling at some time in their growth. This feeling of being lovable makes it possible for the person to love others, care for others, and trust group members in a way that would be impossible without such a personal experience. What we have called the 'caring experience' is a special depth experience that takes on great significance for those who are participants. The people in the group become special and significant, but people in general seem worthy of new levels of trust and new levels of worth. Members get a new concept or image of what group life can be like.

The CONSENSUS EXPERIENCE occurs when there is complete understanding and agreement on the part of all group members on a course of action after full exploration of all creative and relevant alternatives in personal, role-free interaction. This experience is particularly revealing to members who have not heretofore experienced the possibilities of group action. Members have often experienced false consensus on other occasions, but now are able to discriminate between a genuine, achieved consensus and an apparent agreement. Especially significant to members is a personal experience that some members have of being completely understood at all levels. Full consensus can only come when persons become role-free in intimate communication. People abandon roles and enter the group as persons. For many persons this freedom from role is a new experience, and important in personal growth.

The COMMITMENT EXPERIENCE occurs only after the group has felt deeply the caring and consensus experiences and is able to achieve a creative and enduring group goal that is perceived as worthy of sustained and zestful commitment by all members. This involves creating a goal that is truly superordinate and genuinely a unique property of this group at this particular time. This experience is exceedingly rare in our research. When this occurs the needs for constraints and other impositions disappear. The group is truly EMERGENT and seeking. Management comes from within the group resources. Often group members find anew an experience of ZEST, of finding something to which the person can give full commitment and full mobilization of personal resources and potential. This experience in the training group sometimes gives new directions to the life of the person, causing him to change his occupation, his basic work organization, or his central way of life.

The EMERGENCE EXPERIENCE occurs when the group has experienced caring, consensus, commitment and a true feeling of genuine interdependence. The significant element of this group experience is that members come to feel exhilaratingly free from all restraint but at the same time powerful and of great worth and significance. This blending of power and freedom is also rare in our observations and is an impressive experience to undergo as a person and even to observe. This experience is the culmination of the TORI growth processes as we have observed them in natural and training groups. It seems to mark the essence of growth as we now visualize the growth process. Those members who have experienced genuine emergence for a sustained period develop a new conception of what group behavior can be and often change basic attitudes towards the social processes.

The TORI experiences are reported by members to be special and often unique. Members feel a sense of experiential validity which is characteristic of deep trust. They are interrelated and sequential. They are essentially GROUP experiences and are seen as such by the members — as having special group qualities that transcend individual differences and seem to give members, perhaps for the first time, a sense of what a group may mean. They seem to be ACHIEVED and not accidental and represent a creative group effort. They don't 'just happen', as one member put it. They are deeply satisfying to group members. Members report such things as: "I have never before felt so serene in my life"; "It is the first time that I have ever had a truly religious experience"; or "It is the most significant experience in my entire life."

Participating in a number of TORI actualizing experiences and observing a number of others has contributed to some new theorizing about human potential.[6] Central to what we are calling an 'emergence theory of growth' is a concept of contrapuntal, dyadic need systems in the person, sketched in Table 5.

In early stages of group life, when the themes of development are fear, facade, imposition, and dependency (Table 2), members act as if their basic needs were to give and receive punishment, distance, imposition, and control. When persons feel defensive and fearful these high defense need systems are mobilized and triggered. These mechanisms are functional and adaptive in the sense that they meet immediate

TABLE 5

Contrapuntal, Dyadic Need Systems in the Person

Parallel TORI Process	Defense Needs (Those ascendent during low trust, high fear)	Growth Needs (Those ascendent during high trust, low fear)
TRUST	PUNISHMENT: (To give and receive punishment, to manage warmth and affection)	LOVE: (To give and receive love and trust)
OPENNESS	DISTANCE: (To give and receive social distance, to withdraw, need privacy, to manage intimacy)	INTIMACY: (To give and receive communication in depth, to be intimate)
REALIZATION	PERSUASION: (To give and receive persuasion-imposition, to manage goals)	REALIZATION: (To give and receive personal fulfillment)
INTERDEPENDENCE	CONTROL: (To give and receive controls, to be dominant or dependent)	FREEDOM: (To give and receive freedom)

[6] J.R. Gibb, & Lorraine M., Gibb, "Emergence therapy: the TORI processes in the emergent group", in G. M. Gazda, (Ed.), *Theories and Methods of Group Psychotherapy and Counseling* (New York, Charles C. Thomas, in press).

demands of the organism. The mechanisms (punishing, distancing, persuading, and controlling) are neurotic and dysfunctional in the sense that they do not meet the long term needs of the organism, and probably are detrimental to these enduring needs.

During later stages of growth, in supportive and growth-inducing climates, group members act as if the basic needs of the organism were to give and receive love, intimacy, fulfillment, and freedom. These need-mechanism sequences are deeply functional to the sustaining and enduring needs of the organism.

Growth in persons and in groups is a polyphonic process of counterbalancing within the organism the needs to love and to punish, to be intimate and to withdraw, to fulfill others and to manipulate them, to interdepend and to control. There is a high degree of interrelationship in the cluster of high-trust motivations and behaviors, and also in the cluster of high-fear motivations and behaviors. An angry, hostile person is likely to attempt to control and to manipulate. Punishment and control are especially often correlated, both in manifestation and in motivation. We are assuming that the need system is triggered in a genotypically unitary way. This is true of both the fear system and the trust system. Phenotypical diversity masks the underlying unity of the two need systems.

The relevance to this discussion is that we seem to find evidence that the basic, fundamental, and intrinsic nature of organism is such that the person is predisposed to trust, to open, to realize, and to interdepend. The actualizing group, as we have pictured it here, is the fitting climate for such a person. The actualizing group is an organism in which a growing person can achieve human potentials which we are only now beginning to dimly recognize.

LA JOLLA, CALIFORNIA

SETH A. FESSENDEN

USING SOCIOMETRY TO DISCOVER INTRA-GROUP
RELATIONSHIPS

Dr. J. L. Moreno is generally credited with the discovery of the sociometric method of measuring degrees and types of social relationships. He writes in the 1953 edition of *Who Shall Survive?*:

The closest approximation to an official start of the sociometric movement occurred on April 3-5, 1933, when the Medical Society of the State of New York exhibited a few dozen sociometric charts during its convention... Since then sociometry and its derivatives and extensions, social microscopy and—group dynamics, group psychotherapy, roleplaying an interaction research, psychodrama and sociodrama, have maintained their fascination for the general public and have matured to a widely known and respected school of thought.

SOCIOMETRY, broadly defined as 'social measurement', has found application in sociology, military, community affairs, religion, education, and many other fields than medicine. The application of sociometry to the classroom is made most evident by Dr. Helen Hall Jennings in the 1959 edition of *Sociometry in Group Relations*, a publication of the American Council on Education:

Findings indicate that it is appropriate and central to the educative process that the teacher take more than a passing interest in sociometric method. They show that the way an individual feels about himself depends to a large extent upon the way others feel about him and he toward others. The kind of use an individual may or can make of being literate or capable in other learnings may depend on his self-esteem. Indeed, the view of himself he has developed in the course of growing up may affect the direction and the quality of his future mental and emotional growth and to what purposes he is able to put any of his learnings.

...the systematic use of sociometric procedures enables the faculty to cultivate the role of social relationships for a more fortunate development of everyone. This is made possible because sociometric method tends to widen the faculty's awareness of the needs of all pupils and, thus, to prevent exclusive attention to those who have marked emotional difficulties.

The broad field of sociometrics needs to be greatly limited for discussion. The segment chosen for this occasion is largely the gathering and recording of data, primarily the latter, in the classroom setting. Obviously, some consideration must be given to the purpose for which the data are gathered and ways that are commonly used for interpretation.

Some experimental approaches that have been used by the writer are mentioned here to suggest varied possibilities. These are followed with discussion in greater detail of methods of recording and interpretating data for classroom use by the teacher.

An investigation into the pattern of sociometric choices and the extent to which the consistency of choices was retained over a period of time when the manner in which class conduct changed or did not change was reported in an article titled "Perseveration of Group Status" (*Sociometry*, November, 1949). This type of analysis was then applied to examine the character of inter-personal relationships according to the intra-class distribution of *tele* or the attractiveness that elements of a unit have for each other.

Based on three assumptions, (1) there should be no isolates or even unchosen members, (2) there should be many mutual choices, and (3) there should be no extreme stars, an effort was made to devise a procedure of recording and interpreting data that would be sensitive enough to note minor shifts in class status. The conclusions were reported in "An Index of Cohesiveness -- Morale Based on the Analysis of Sociometric Choice Distribution" (*Sociometry*, November, 1953).

Another approach was to compare the sociometric status of students in several classes with the manner in which the class was conducted. Students in freshman classes at the University of Denver and Montana State University were administered a sociometric questionnaire asking for choices concerning committee work. The indexes of cohesiveness were computed and related to the degree of open or free discussion allowed by the several instructors. In each instance the class freedom allowed in discussion in class was judged by the instructor and his colleages.

These data indicated a high correlation between class openness and sociometric status using all groups, that a rank coefficient of .90 was obtained between index and freedom of class discussion.

This result seemed to indicate a possible relationship between a type of teaching and its effect on group status. About thirty years ago a series of five experiments were made of the actual teaching of a college subject by the two methods of (1) the teacher doing all of the talking, and (2) discussion within the class led by the teacher. On immediate recall, only two of the five gave any superiority to the discussion groups, but on delayed recall all five of the experiments gave the discussion process the superior ranking.

More recently Paul Richard ran at Northwestern University "An experimental study of the effectiveness of group discussion in the teaching of factual content". He reported in part that only a few class sessions were necessary for the students to get into the swing of things. His most significant findings for our present consideration were these: (1) by the end of the semester the superior student learns 17% more factual content through discussion, while the inferior student learns 25% more; and (2) in six months the average student will be able to recall 56% more factual content than he would have under the lecture. The study was reported at the National Convention of the Speech Association of America in 1955.

A final study, "A Clique in the Class" (*Central Speech Journal*, Autumn, 1958) using sociometric data to examine the class structure was based on the assumption that within every group there is a tendency for cliques to form. The more autocratic the leadership, the more firmly the clique is established and the more permanent its nature. But whether democratic or autocratic, the wise leader should seek to identify these and measure their internal strength and degree of influence on others in the group. This can be done sociometrically.

There are several uses for which this type of analysis can be valuable. One is to enable the instructor to check on the cohesiveness and influence of certain possible cliques which he believes to exist from his observation of class activity. By means of this approach both the reality of the clique can be determined and the potential spread of influence examined.

A second use is the opportunity to search among the interpersonal relationships in a class for possible clique situations which may be having an effect on class morale or activity. The sociometric examination of class relationships can be a revealing activity. The instructor who uses a permissive approach in his teaching will find in this method new information to strengthen the learning opportunities. Even he who lectures only or is autocratic in his hold on the classroom conduct may find centers of power among his students that should not remain unexplored.

Many teachers are counseled to observe the behavior of their pupils to discover the ways in which they react in different situations. Continued and careful observation by the teacher is vital. However, sociometry is a method by which the teacher can confirm or challenge his observational judgment as well as provide him with a fairly complete picture of the attitudes of all the class members. Unfortunately as teachers we do not always know our pupils well enough to identify those best adjusted to the class and to their fellows. One study (Norman C. Gnolund, "The accuracy of teachers' judgments Concerning the Sociometric Status of Sixth-Grade Pupils", *Sociometry* Nov. 1950) concludes in part:

1. There is a difference among teachers in the accuracy of their judgments of the sociometric status of sixth grade pupils in the classroom. Correlation coefficients representing the average accuracy of each teacher's judgment ranged from .268 to .838, with a mean of .595.
2. There is no difference in the accuracy of teachers' judgments of the sociometric status of boys and girls in the classroom.

* * *

6. There is a tendency for teachers to over-judge the sociometric status of the three boys and the three girls they most prefer as pupils in class, and to under-judge the sociometric status of the three boys and the three girls they least prefer as pupils in class.

The sociometric method involves asking individuals with whom they would like to be associated in some task or activity; it is asking them to express their degree of acceptance or rejection of their colleagues in terms of a specific situation. The procedure is relatively simple, but the basic conception upon which it is built — that the effective functioning of groups depends upon the spontaneity with which members accept one another — offers a good way for the observer to examine the interaction among the members and to select those who need special help.

As has been implied, the sociometric method of inquiries of members of a group about their intra-group relationships has been examined most fully in educational settings. For this reason, because the writer has worked more consistently with the application of sociometry in the classroom, and inasmuch as the same BASIC principles become adaptable to other settings, much of the following discussion will use the teaching situation for illustration.

The use of sociometry should always be preceded with considerable planning for the use of the data to be obtained. The researcher who seeks inter-personal choice information from the members of a group needs to have in mind both what kind of data he wants, how he will record the data, and how he will translate the data into an action report to those who supply the data. In general, for example, the value of sociometry in the classroom might be considered to be:

(1) To help the teacher to discover isolated or rejected children who may need anything from special counseling to such a simple outlet as the opportunity to exhibit skills that will gain for them colleague acceptance;

(2) To help the teacher to discover the secure, popular children around whom some of the isolates can be grouped;

(3) To help the teacher to discover cliques that may remain tightly knit units unless provided with new outlets in a friendly atmosphere. Cliques are often the bane of the teacher's existence, but when such are found and steps are taken to expand the relationships of the members, they can often grow into forceful, valuable units.

When the teacher administers the question he should do two things: (1) He should try to make the pupils want to answer. (2) He should be sure that they know why they are making their choices. The prime requisite for the sociometric question is that it asks the individual to consider himself in relation to others in respect to some given situation. To ask, "Whom do you like best?" is not a sociometric approach, for it establishes no limited criterion by which the person can determine his answer. To ask, "Whom would you like to have sit next to you in this class?" places the individual in a realistic choice-making situation, and by means of his own values he can establish criteria for his answers. To ask, "Whom would you like to have represent you on the steering committee?" is little more than any voting procedure; it is hardly sociometric in nature. "Assume that you are to be a member of a steering committee to meet with me on class problems. Which members of this class would you like most to work with you?" becomes more truly sociometric because it asks the individual to consider the others in relation to himself in the performance of a specified task.

Occasionally it is desirable to ask the students to make their choices in order of first, second, and third, but this procedure tends to create some resentment when the student feels favorable toward each of those whom he chooses. The same may be said for asking students to identify their colleagues with whom they would prefer not to work. This, it is said, too often points up the negative side of inter-personal relations. Whether choices are to be ranked and whether rejections are to be asked for should be largely a decision determined by what one plans to do with the collected data.

In the administration of the sociometric question, special cards may be used, together with a mimeographed page for recording responses to the questions, or the entire process may be oral and apparently extemporaneous. Often it is desirable to be very informal and to avoid any implication that a 'test' is being given or that the members are rating or scoring their colleagues in any way that will affect their standing with the teacher or leader.

There is some disagreement as to whether the question used must be real, must involve a situation that can and will be put into practice; but it would seem that if the situation used is not to become real, it should be made known to the group in advance. There is considerable evidence to indicate that the quasi-sociometric question provides data that are dependable if the administration of the questionnaire is done in a way to elicit the full cooperation of the persons involved.

RECORDING SOCIOMETRIC DATA FOR STUDY

When the data from the members of the group have been collected, some procedure is necessary if they are to be in a form for use and interpretation. The simplest procedure would probably be merely to list the names of the pupils and to follow each name with the names of the persons chosen by that particular pupil. Adding numbers for reference would be an additional step. This process, however, makes the use of the data more difficult because of the constant need of cross references. Table 1 is of this type. These same data will be used in each of the following tables so that they can be used for comparative reference.

The most common method of recording these data is that of a pictorial graph devised by Moreno called the sociogram (see Table 2). The data are made into a sociogram. This manner of recording has the obvious advantage of the visual presentation of the lines of relationships. It has the disadvantages of not being subject to mathematical analysis and of developing into a rather complex design when the numbers of the group become large or when responses to more than one question are plotted on the same sheet.

In the legend under the sociogram, you will note that boys are represented by

TABLE 1

Choice tabulation

Class Member CHOOSING	Chosen as FIRST choice	Chosen as SECOND choice	Chosen as THIRD choice	Rejected
1. Alberta	Judith (12)	Mary (14)	Helen (13)	Barbara (4)
2. Agnes	Alberta (1)	Barbara (4)	Claude (3)	
3. Claude.....	Agnes (2)	John (10)	Barbara (4)	
4. Barbara	John (10)	Agnes (2)	Claude (3)	Ruth (17)
5. Celia.......	David (6)	John (10)	Agnes (2)	
6. David	James (9)	Ralph (8)	Celia (5)	
7. Edwin	Ralph (8)	James (9)	Janet (11)	
8. Ralph	Janet (11)	Thomas (18)	Judith (12)	Helen (13
9. James	Thomas (18)	Edwin (7)	Ralph (8)	
10. John	Ralph (8)	Janet (11)	Agnes (2)	Margaret (15)
11. Janet	James (9)	Ralph (8)	Samuel (16)	
12. Judith......	Alberta (1)	Helen (13)	Mary (14)	
13. Helen	Mary (14)	Judith (12)	Alberta (1)	Samuel (16)
14. Mary (absent on this day)				
15. Margaret ..	Thomas (18)	Judith (12)	Barbara (4)	
16. Samuel	Janet (11)	Agnes (2)	Barbara (4)	
17. Ruth.......	Ralph (8)	James (9)	Thomas (18)	Samuel (16)
18. Thomas	Edwin (7)	James (9)	Judith (12)	Ruth (17)

triangles and girls by circles, that one-way choices are indicated by arrows to the person chosen, that mutual choices are indicated by lines without arrow heads but with a small cross line near the middle, that first, second, and third choices are noted by the number on the chooser's end of the arrows or lines, that rejections are dotted lines, and that those who were chosen but not present at the time of the question-naire are shown in broken symbols. In this instance, pupil number 14 was absent.

In making the sociogram, it is often advisable to start with the highly chosen in the middle and to work around them. One or more trial sociograms are often neces-sary before one can be produced what will not have a confusing array of intermingling lines. As a general rule, lines never cross the symbols of the people; they are straight lines; and, when necessary to avoid symbols, sharp angles (or corners) are used.

The square matrix has the advantages of ease in recording and of simplicity in reading. In many respects it is like the tabulation, but with the matrix the highly chosen and the infrequently chosen can more readily be recognized. It is convenient for many mathematical manipulations and can accomodate responses to more than one question. Among the disadvantages is the difficulty in discovering mutual choices. Usually the matrix takes the simple form of squares in such a way that the persons who choose and the persons who are chosen can easily be noted. Table 3 presents the data in matrix form.

The Sociograph (*Bonney-Fessenden Sociograph*, California Test Bureau) is one of

TABLE 2

Sociogram

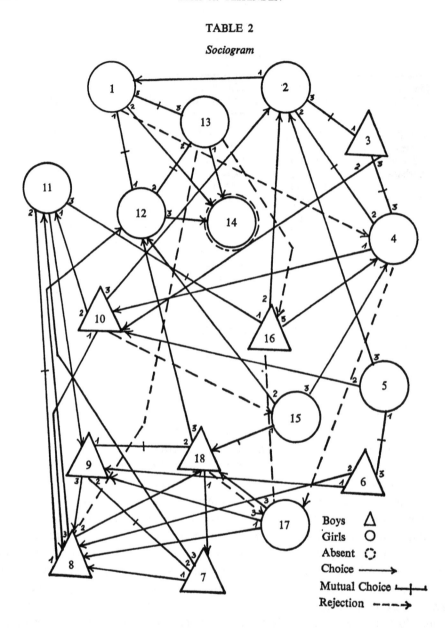

the newer contributions. It is designed to combine the advantages of the sociogram and the matrix, to overcome the major disadvantages of each, and to make more flexible the recording and interpreting of the data. Basically, the Sociograph is a square matrix folded into a triangular shape in such a manner that any information on the matrix is retained and identifiable without distortion (see Table 4).

Sociometric data are collected for many purposes including research, counseling, and grouping. Teachers are primarily concerned with the last two of these three

TABLE 3

Matrix

Chosen

Pupil	1	2	3	4	5	6	7	8	9	10	11	12	13	14	15	16	17	18
1 Alberta				R								1	3	2				
2 Agnes	1		3	2														
3 Claude		1		3						2								
4 Barbara		2	3							1						R		
5 Celia		3			3	1				2								
6 David				3				2	1									
7 Edwin								1	2		3							
8 Ralph											1	3	R					2
9 James						2	3											1
10 John		3						1			2				R			
11 Janet								2	1							3		
12 Judith	1											2	3					
13 Helen	3											2		1	R			
14 Mary (ab)																		
15 Margaret				3								2						1
16 Samuel		2		3							1							
17 Ruth								1	2							R		3
18 Thomas						1			2				3			R		
Ch. Rec.	3	5	2	4	1	1	2	6	5	3	4	5	2	3	0	1	0	4
Rej. Rec.	0	0	0	1	0	0	0	0	0	0	0	0	1	0	1	2	2	0

major purposes, and probably most teachers are chiefly concerned with the third, namely, grouping.

The writer is indebted to the California Test Bureau, Del Monte Research Park, Monterey, California, for permission to use in this article much of the following discussion taken from the manual for the *Bonney-Fessenden Sociograph*. In fact, if it were not that several thousand of the *Sociographs* continue to be bought every year for the past ten years since its initial publication, he might not be so firm in his belief that the sociometric method of observation of intra-group relationships is valid and vital.

TABLE 4

The Bonney-Fessenden Sociograph

INSTRUCTIONS

SAMPLE

A. RECORDING CHOICES GIVEN: Choices given are recorded in the left half of each square on the line a student's name is on and in the right side of the squares in his vertical column. The appropriate half of each square in student No. 3's line and column is shaded to show where his choices are recorded.

B. READING CHOICES RECEIVED: Choices received are read in the right half of each square in the line the student's name is on and in the left half of the squares in his vertical column. These are the unshaded sides in No. 3's line and column.

NOTE: A √, an X, a number or any suitable symbol may be used for choices given. A different symbol should be used if rejections are recorded.

Identifies Mutual choice ☐

NAME	No
Alberta	1
Agnes	2
Claude	3
Barbara	4
Celia	5
David	6
Edwin	7
Ralph	8
James	9
John	10
Janet	11
Judith	12
Helen	13
Mary (ab)	14
Margaret	15
Samuel	16
Ruth	17
Thomas	18

	1	2	3	4	5	6	7	8	9	10	11	12	13	14	15	16	17	18	19	20
A. Choices Given	3	3	3	3	3	3	3	3	3	3	3	3	3	.	3	3	3	3		
B. Choices Rec'd	3	5	2	4	1	1	2	6	5	3	4	5	2	3	0	1	0	4		
C. Mutual Choices	2	2	2	2	1	1	1	1	2	0	2	2	9	0	0	9	0	1		
D. Rejec- tions				1									1		1	2	2			

THE FORMATION OF SUBGROUPS FOR WORK OR RECREATIONAL PURPOSES

Recent studies among both children and adults have shown that groups composed very largely of persons who have indicated a preference for each other are more likely to be harmonious and productive than other types of groups. When, therefore, a teacher wishes to use sociometric choices as a basis for forming groups in a class-room, there are several guiding principles which will generally be found useful.

a. When either the teacher or pupils are inexperienced in group work it is best to begin on a small scale, such as by having this type of work only once or twice a week, or for only part of the class period. In beginning this kind of work it is important that the teacher help the class to decide quite definitely what the groups are going to do when they come together. Furthermore, the size of the subgroups should be kept quite small — probably not more than three or four.

b. Separating the members of a strong clique is usually not effective. It is more profitable to place several other pupils with the clique in order to try to widen it. The best ones to put with the clique are the pupils who have chosen some of its members. Cliques should not be retained as closed units.

c. In placing the unchosen pupils it is best not to put more than two of them in any one group of five or more. Usually each group of five or more pupils should be composed of a few highly-chosen individuals, one or two low-choice or unchosen individuals, and the rest of average sociometric status. In cases of infrequently-chosen, unchosen, or re-jected pupils, the teachers' judgment must often be the determining factor in making the placement. If possible, the unchosen or rejected individual should be placed with one of those whom he listed as his first choice. Two or more individuals who reject each other should never be put together.

d. Every pupil should be in a group with at least one whom he has chosen. In doing this it is probably more important to pay attention to reciprocated choices than to the order of choices. This means that whether a choice is a first-, second-, or third-level preference is probably less important than the fact of reciprocation.

e. It is important that each group include more than one representative of each of the major subgroupings in the class. Thus there should be more than one boy in a group composed of mostly girls, or more than one person of a particular race along with others of another race.

The process for the formation of these groups will vary as the experience of the teacher increases. One of the most common procedures is to start with one of the individuals with the fewest choices received and pair him with some moderately-chosen person who has either chosen him or whom he has chosen. Do the same thing with other infrequently-chosen persons until nuclei of as many groups as are to be established are formed. Usually the most highly-chosen members can be most readily placed, so the principle often followed is to place them in the groups last.

Representative questions which are frequently used for sociometric testing in schools are:

Which other pupils would you:
    like to sit near?
    eat lunch with in the school cafeteria?
    go with on a field trip?

have on your side for team play in your physical education class?
like to work with on an oral report to the class or on a unit in social studies?
like to work with in preparing an experiment in your science class, putting
on a one-act play, for vocabulary drill in your Latin class, or for preparing
a meal in your homemaking class?

If a teacher wishes to know more about the interpersonal preferences among his
pupils in out-of-class associations, he may ask such questions as:

Which other pupils would you:
most like to have as your best friends?
most like to go with to a movie?
invite to your home?
participate with in a leisure-time pursuit?

OTHER USES OF THE SOCIOGRAPH

To this point, the use of the sociometric questionnaire as an aid in improving individual interpersonal relationships has been stressed, as well as a device for grouping
children for seating, for club activities, for social events, for classwork, and the like.
In addition, the procedure is valuable in helping the teacher direct the work and
administration of the classroom. For example, if the data showed a strong cleavage
between the boys and girls, the teacher might take steps to encourage more inter-
group socialization. Or, if the results indicated considerable prejudice toward any
minority group, steps could be taken to integrate majority and minority group
members into mutually profitable classroom or school groups.

The Sociograph can also be used to record types of evaluative data other than
sociometric results. It lends itself to any research method in which intra-group
judgments of the individual members can be pooled to obtain a consensus score in
a performance activity. Where the rater is also a rated performer, as would be true
in a glee club, for example, the data will reveal the judgments of the rater's choices,
in regard to the rater's own performance. Such evidence might reveal that ability
or quality are not the only criteria employed in the ratings, but that even here feelings
of friendship and social acceptance are important elements. The Sociograph provides
a convenient table on which a summary and analysis can be made.

ASSESSMENT OF INDIVIDUAL ADJUSTMENT PATTERNS

Frequently guiding questions can help the teacher analyze the reasons behind a
pupil's low sociometric status. These questions are only illustrative. Many others
might be added.

(1) Has the individual been given opportunities to work or to play with others of the group, especially those with whom he seems to have some affinity?

(2) What are the out-of-class contacts of the person like? Is he a 'hanger-on' or is he generally accepted?

(3) Does the individual show talent in any area that might be used to bolster his standing with others?

(4) What is the home situation like? Does he seem to have security there?

(5) Are there any obvious reasons why the person should be unchosen or rejected? Can these causes be removed?

(6) What attitudes does he show toward the other members of the class? Is he defensive? Is he oversolicitous or overeager?

(7) What is the attitude of the pupil toward his teacher? Does he attempt to secure status by seeking teacher approval?

(8) Does he often come to the defense of others or help in any way to develop group or class unity?

(9) Does he voluntarily isolate himself? Does he resist efforts toward friendliness?

(10) Does he seek attention by nonsocial, obstructive action?

Even the highly chosen individual, or 'star', may be a source of concern for the teacher. Because of his influence, the pupil who receives many choices should also be looked upon by the teacher as a potential leader. Probably the central questions which should be asked relative to the highly-chosen are:

(1) Is he worthy?
(2) Why is he a leader?
(3) Are his attitudes constructive?
(4) Is he concerned primarily with group interests or self-interest?
(5) What guidance, if any, does he need?

SUGGESTIONS FOR PROMOTING GREATER SOCIALIZATION IN CLASSROOMS

When a teacher or group leader has studied the sociometric data and has made interpretations relative to the social climate of the group in general and to the socialization needs of specific pupils, he will need to initiate steps to remedy negative situations. The suggestions listed below will prove helpful in remedying many troublesome conditions.

(1) Leadership positions in the class and in all subgroupings should be rotated so that every child has numerous chances every semester to perform in such capacities. It is important, however, that the teacher help the isolated or unchosen child to know exactly what to do and how to do it, so he will do well when his turn comes. Some-

times role-playing can be used to help a child to practice his anticipated duties.

(2) Some way should be found whereby an infrequently-chosen child can help another child in a skill, a game, or a school subject.

(3) A low-choice child should be seated with or near others whom he has chosen.

(4) Grouping a very timid child with others who are known to be much more aggressive and dominating than he is should be avoided. At the same time some training in democratic leadership should be given to the overly aggressive group members.

(5) The teacher might suggest to the mother of a sociometrically low child that she invite one child from the room to her home to play with her child, to go on a car trip with the family, or to go to some point of interest such as a zoo. The teacher might help the mother in choosing the 'most likely' child to invite. He should not, however, inform the mother of the child's low sociometric position.

(6) Health activities, group projects, or a 'cleanup' corner may be used to help all pupils to keep more clean and neat, but with special emphasis on trying to reach a few who are most in need of such aid. A child who is dirty, unkempt, or malodorous cannot be helped until these conditions are removed.

(7) Some legitimate basis for praising an isolated child should be found.

(8) It will prove helpful to provide for the expression of a wide range of different kinds of skills and personal assets. Talent programs, assembly programs, and other events, through which abilities in music, art, drawing, dancing, etc., may be demonstrated, should be encouraged.

(9) Special help in subject-matter skills for those who are low should be provided. A child's status with his peers is affected by how well he can do what is expected in the classroom.

(10) A tolerant and accepting attitude toward an isolated or rejected child so he will know that he is understood, or that he 'belongs', as far as the teacher is concerned, will pay dividends. Favoritism or special help which is obvious to the other pupils should be avoided. However, the aid of other children can sometimes be secured in helping a particular child to make a better adjustment to the classroom group.

(11) The experience background of a poorly-chosen child might be integrated into the classroom work. Such experiences as life on a farm, travels in another state, or participation in recreational pursuits can be exploited to mutual advantage.

(12) Shy, insecure, or 'different' children will feel more free to make contributions in a classroom in which permissive and democratic control is exercised.

A bit of caution should be interjected at this point. Except in newly-formed groups, teachers should not expect to produce large changes in pupils' sociometric positions even though many socializing activities are initiated. Instead, efforts should be centered primarily on developing new mutual attachments, helping the 'isolates' and 'rejects' to gain a social foothold, and in promoting a wider distribution of choices throughout a sociometric structure. If these steps are taken, the members of a group will be more friendly toward each other; new avenues for personal appreciation and for leadership roles will be opened up; and the group will come much closer to a maximum utilization of its personal and technical resources, even though there are not large changes in the relative sociometric ranks of the group members.

As teachers become more familiar with sociometric theory and practice, they will realize that the basic emphasis of sociometry is the securing of the active collaboration of all the members of a group in the management and direction of their collective affairs, as well as the attainment of a maximum degree of interpersonal satisfaction among the participants. These goals are in accord with the principles of democracy, with the objectives of teacher-pupil planning, with the purposes and techniques of action research, and with the recent emphasis on the vital importance of the small-group process. As Moreno has said in one of his publications, "Sociometry is a sociology of the people, by the people, and for the people." As teachers become more imbued with this point of view, they will have more faith in the abilities and good judgment of children and of young people, and will see that one of the major objectives of a teacher should be to promote greater personal-social capacities of all pupils in both leadership roles and in friendly relationships.

The sociometric process includes selecting the choice criterion, gathering data in response to the criterion question, recording them in usable form, and using the data thus available to accomplish some useful purpose.

The teacher needs first to have clearly in mind the reasons why he wishes to gather sociometric data from his class. He will seldom have but one purpose. Even when the immediate need for the data is the establishment of subgroups, he is concerned with individual and class status. Often the reason for using the procedure for grouping is secondary, and the teacher is hopeful of discovering lines of interpersonal relationships and of locating those children who most need help in social adjustment. Yet, as was pointed out earlier, the sociometric question should, whenever possible, relate to real conditions, to an event that can be carried through, and to which the child can give his honest, spontaneous, and full reaction.

Vital to the success of any sociometric process is favorable teacher-student rapport. The teacher should try to motivate the pupils to answer frankly and spontaneously; for if they consider this to be just another test, assignment, or duty, the accuracy of the data may suffer.

The teacher should be somewhat enthusiastic and yet casual enough that any questions can be asked by the members of the class without fear. The introduction should tell of the use to which the choices will be put, that any boy or girl in the class can be chosen, and that they are not evaluating each other but are stating their preferences for associates. Any teacher can administer sociometric questions successfully by keeping in mind the need for clarity, for interest, and for rapport, and by giving assurance that the data will be used in strictest confidence. The teacher prepares for the administration by preplanning in the following ways:

(1) He decides upon the specific activity to be used as the expressed purpose of the question. Usually the groundwork for the activity is laid in previous discussions with the class.

(2) He writes out the question to be used and then examines it to be sure that it will not be misunderstood by the pupils and that it asks them to consider themselves in active relationship with other members of the class whom they might choose.

(3) He determines the method by which the pupils will make their choices and he prepares the materials for this.

Even in relatively small classes there are some who do not know the names of their classmates. In order that all will have an equal chance of being chosen, a procedure should be incorporated in the administration of the sociometric question which will enable each pupil to identify the others by name or number, if numbers are used in the making of the choices. Concurrent with this need is that of using a method which will make the recording of choices easy and rapid. The use of sociometric questions should not place an undue burden on the teacher's time.

There are three common ways for having the pupils make their choices. The simplest in administration but the most difficult in recording for use is that of having each pupil take a piece of paper, put his name in an upper corner, and then list his selections in order of preference on the sheet. A second way is to provide each pupil with a mimeographed class list and have him check the names of those with whom he wishes to work and to indicate his order of preference with 1, 2, 3, etc. The third way and the one which provides for the easiest and fastest recording is to use the answer slips which are furnished with the Sociograph. On these, each pupil merely checks or places his preference-order number above the identifying numbers of the classmates whom he chooses. Providing the pupils with these identifying numbers can be done in several ways:

(1) The teacher can write the names and numbers on the board.

(2) The teacher can mimeograph the names and numbers and hand the sheets out to the pupils. This has the advantage of making the list accessible to the pupils throughout the time they are making their choices.

(3) The teacher can read the names and numbers and ask the members of the class to record them on a piece of paper. This is time-consuming for class members and there are possibilities of error in that the pupil copying the list may not copy the numbers correctly.

(4) The teacher can read names and numbers and ask each pupil to record his own number. Then choices can be made as the pupils repeat the numbers assigned to them. This recount has both the advantage of a check for the teacher and of enabling the pupils to identify each other. This procedure is given in greater detail in the second sample administration given below. It has been found to be generally satisfactory and saves considerable time and detail of preparation.

The use of answer slips is recommended for most classes. However, there may be times when teachers of the lower grades will feel that answer slips are impractical. It is possible that below the fourth grade the two most effective procedures are to have the pupils list their choices on a sheet of paper or to have them check the names on a list from which they then choose. Even then these names might be spaced on a mimeographed sheet in such a way that the pupil could place an answer slip along side of the mimeographed list and check his choice. If the pupil is unable to do that, it might be that the teacher could carry out this procedure. The slips do conserve considerable time in recording the data.

In many instances pupils may be given an opportunity to suggest people with whom they would prefer not to be associated. In general, it may not be advisable to encourage people to find others with whom they have no common bond. On the other hand, a sense of security often comes to most people when they know they will not have to work with those whom they do not like. The usual practice is to provide the opportunity to reject others but not to require that such be done.

Sociometry even as simply discussed here has a broad and comprehensive meaning. The method provides data, but it takes intelligent and experienced teachers or directors to interpret it adequately and purposefully. The effort in this presentation has been to suggest that the more effective interpretations can be aided by the procedure used in the recording of the answers to the questionnaires.

CALIFORNIA STATE COLLEGE AT FULLERTON

EUGENE E. REBSTOCK

EDUCATION IN ORGANIZATIONS[1]

I

This story is essentially about a course offered to middle-level managers of a large private corporation. The course has been in existence for over four years and almost 300 men have participated in the program. Perhaps it is more accurate to say that this is a story of change — a profound change in the teaching methods and philosophy of those of us who taught in the program. The change came not only from evolving theory, but from the impact of the attitudes and needs of the men who participated in the program.

The Bechtel Corporation is a large international engineering management and construction company. Many of the middle-level managers as well as top management are engineers who, having worked in many areas of engineering, are now called upon to negotiate various aspects of engineering development with other companies. The Bechtel Corporation must deal with a wide variety of clients representing such diverse organizations as public utilities, city councils and private companies. Negotiations may take place before a particular contract is signed and at any stage during the ongoing process of construction. Since much of the time of the engineer-manager is spent in conferences, both within the company as well as client meetings, it was felt that a course considering the various aspects of conference participation would be useful. The impetus for the course grew from the realization that many of the engineers who worked for Bechtel had very little, if any, training in the skills of group communication.

About four years and fifteen courses ago we began such a program, meeting once a week for two hours for a period of eight weeks. As the course was initially conceived there would be eight sessions consisting of small group theory, general semantics and, as a practical matter some typical conference problems and relevant case

[1] My profound thanks to Mr. George Wood, Director of Training and Development of the Bechtel Corporation for the use of his role-playing case. My thanks to Dr. Henry McGuckin, who as my partner in these courses has contributed more than his share to the development of new phases of the course. My debt to the 300 participants in the course is beyond measure.

situations. Initially, we began to probe into the realities of conference life in Bechtel by asking our class participants questions about the conferences in which they participated. Slowly there emerged an awareness of group situations which eventually came to change the direction of the course. We learned, for example, that much of the engineer's time was spent in conferences, not within his own particular work group. Rather, much conference time was spent within the company negotiating with representatives of company groups that were going to assist or provide services for the particular project underway. The Bechtel Corporation has a modified project organization supplied from standing divisions such as Power and Industrial, International, and Pipe-line. When a new contract is negotiated, a project team of engineers and supervisors is drawn from the necessary divisions and service areas. A supervising project engineer is selected and, in effect, becomes the field commander for the duration of the project. Because of this kind of organization, there is much shifting of personnel with the resulting dislocation of command patterns. We found, as a result, that one possible frustrating circumstance for beginning engineers as well as senior ones was a constant shifting of leadership styles with which they worked. When projects were relatively short an engineer could work for a number of supervisors during the course of a year. Many of our group members seemed to accept and even like the shifting patterns because the variety allowed for a change of pace of the pattern of leadership and authority.

However, this form of organization raised some issues for a course considering effective participation and effective leadership in work groups. We first considered the nature of informative functions of communication in which organization, conciseness and clarity were demanded. Partly because of the project organization there were engineers who, almost literally, had difficulty in speaking the same language as other project groups. Yet, it was necessary to share information of a highly technical nature with other project groups quickly and many times without elaborate preparation. We included from the outset a section devoted to the development of complex material into quickly understood organizational patterns. Lecture-discussions were followed by a two-hour session with teams of two or three men communicating complex information. The rest of the class would listen as the speaker set up specific work situations and presented his material. They would then ask questions drawn from the specific material using their combined experience as background. These sessions have remained the crucial foundation for other work which follows in the course.

Knowing we were dealing with professional engineers who had to communicate significant information to audiences for whom the language was not always clear, we decided to introduce general semantics and basic communcation theory. This decision was an important step in developing the course for it allowed us to analyze some of the restrictive assumptions about communication which professional engineers seemingly share with others in our society. Our perspective is a blend of transactional psychology and general semantics. From transitional psychology we drew upon the Ames perception experiments and the theoretical position of Hadley Cantril, John Dewey and others. We argued in these early sessions that perception is a unique experience governed by the total past experience and the present private world of each of us. We, nevertheless, hold our perceptions to be absolute rather than relative to our personal past history. General semantics gives us the perspective that language, far from being merely a useful means of interpersonal communication, actually shapes our thoughts and symbolizes categories of experience thus providing us with significance. Such a relativistic perspective sometimes is difficult for an engineer to accept because during much of his professional life he has had to be concerned with specific factual material about which there is substantial agreement. Transactional psychology and general semantics brings a tone of tentativeness, a respect for positions different from ones own and a general tolerance of the ambiguous and the relative.

A second and equally important insight emerged during our third class of engineers. We increasingly became impressed with the fact that there were some unique characteristics to the client meetings which were not so in evidence during conferences within the company. Many of the client meetings consisted of preliminary hearings concerning the needs of prospective clients for engineering. The engineers then confronted a host of meetings designed to deal with problems occurring at every conceivable stage of the project. Such problems as delays of schedules, addition of new work to the job and unexpected difficulties with men, terrain and materials all consume considerable meeting time. These conferences are characterized by the give-and-take of negotiation and bargaining infused with the communication patterns of persuasion and argument. Client conferences differ significantly from company conferences in at least one major aspect: the goals, strategy and tactics of client conferences are often much more in conflict because of the differing perceptions of what is necessary to complete the job. On the other hand, in company conferences agreed upon general policy, goals and even large strategy govern the communication style. Not necessarily so in client conferences. Since our concern was to prepare the engineers for client contact we incorporated a two-fold program into the course. One directional line underscored the necessity that in client meetings the leadership and responsibility for the rational approaches to problem examination and ultimate decision-making ought to be assumed by Bechtel representatives. Too often client representatives had assumed the initiative to the detriment of the position of the Bechtel representatives. We decided to include a number of sessions on the processes of reflective-thinking and its applications to group conferences. We used a modified version of the Dewey pattern of reflective thinking. This pattern emphasized the examination of the details of a problem situation as a prelude to the elimination of alternative solutions leading to the selection of one final solution.

We also spent a session on the various approaches to leadership, taking the position that while group-centered leadership might be more appropriate for the developmental aspects of company conferences, in client meetings leadership patterns will tend to emerge as the result of such forces as the membership of the group, the general nature of the problem, the character of the decision-makers in the group and the relative status position of the parties in the discussion. After months of working with men who participated in a variety of conferences we came to the position that you cannot impose a particular theoretical approach on an organization. The forces within the organization must be closely examined. Then a theoretical approach can be built empirically and inductively. Practical exercises will emerge as a natural evolution of experience. The theoretical approach may not evolve from a particular school or system but will be eclectic, drawing upon what is relevant for the complexities of the particular organization. We were now moving to a different conception of leadership. But, we had to have another push before we could conceptualize what was needed.

We decided to include discussion on the nature of organizational leadership. The class was arbitrarily broken into several small groups of six to eight class members. An organizational subject was selected by a consensus of the group members and in the next session they attempted to arrive at a solution which reflected the best thinking of the members. We analyzed the quality of the solutions and the various styles of leadership which invariably emerged in the discussions. We wanted each man to assume some meaningful leadership functions, especially those which would test his capabilities and potentialities. It was during these particular sessions that we received that push. Many of our class members suggested persuasion was the most important communication function they engaged in at client meetings. We responded by including material on persuasion and, a bit later, we developed sessions on argumentation. "In each of these segments of the course we stress that argumentation and persuasion are both ethically motivated and absolutely necessary if a group is to explore many alternative proposals fully and with the best critical faculties." Not only did these sessions become an integral part of the course, but the psychological basis of the course actually shifted to account for perceived realities of organizational group life and the resulting patterns of communication. When the course began our psychological position was that of group-centered leadership. With the inclusion of the material on persuasion and argumentation our position became in the words of Chris Argyris, 'reality centered' leadership. Such leadership emerges in response to the inner logic of the situation and of course is dependent upon the sensitivities of the leader in perceiving that logic.

II

The total impact of the course as it now stands comes from a mixture of the communication processes of information, reflection, argumentation, persuasion, general semantics and group leadership. For professional engineers in their negotiations there are uses for each of these processes. These processes are all within the speech discipline and are generally accepted now as traditional instructional material. We do not have to go beyond the speech discipline for such work. When we can develop role situations which focus the various aspects of speech in a context we can establish a base for significant learning. The role situation that follows was developed at Bechtel for our program. It is based on an actual problem with the names and places changed. Notice that each of the conflicting parties must represent a specific level within the respective organizations. Thus, the parties have positions to maintain. The communication is drawn from rather clear-cut positions each with its own legitimate defense. If the Bechtel men do not offer a conciliatory position there emerges a mutual rigidity of positions accompanied by resulting breakdown of communication and negotiations. If, however, the Bechtel men think of the needs of the client and communicate in terms of those needs the client representatives usually reciprocate. All of the theory and skills discussed in the course come into sharp focus with this role situation. It represents the extension of our thinking that any course taught to professionals or business people must be specific to their experience.

Situation Background

After several years of effort to add International Petrotergent, Inc. to our list of clients, a contract was executed calling for the design and construction of a complete new manufacturing complex to manufacture a revolutionary new soft detergent. To get the advantage of optimum market conditions for the new product, a completion date of May 1 was essential, production starting on that date being tied to an intensive advertising campaign, dealer promotion, etc.

International Petrotergent, Inc. awarded the contract to Bechtel because of its willingness to take the job on a lump sum basis with bonus-penalty clause for early or late completion. The schedule for the job was tight but there appeared to be no unusual risks, and with favorable conditions possibly resulting in early completion, the job offered a reasonable prospect of high profit in addition to securing a highly desirable client. No unusual factors in the labor market, materials, or climate were foreseen when the schedule was established other than noting that the plant was to be located close to but just outside an area subject to occasional devastating tornadoes. A careful investigation of the location for the past fifty years showed the area free of such disturbances for that period. The trend of these seasonal storms for the past twenty years indicated their general pattern to be moving in the opposite direction, away from the location of the new plant. However, the possibility of such storms did influence the structural design of the plant.

International Petrotergent was confident that product availability by May 1 would enable it to capture the major market for soft detergents. However, the increasing pressure of public opinion for soft detergents to eliminate massive water pollution problems spurred other chemical and petrochemical manufacturers to increase their efforts to develop a similar product.

Shortly after construction on the International Petrotergent plant was started, it become a matter of public knowledge that at least two other major competitors were racing to have a similar product on the market at an earlier date and one major competitor was actively planning to get the advantage of being first on the market by introducing a similar product already in production in Europe. As a result of these competitive activities, International Petrotergent revised the bonus provision for early completion to provide an even greater incentive. At the same time, however, their representatives at the jobsite kept a close watch on the quality of the job.

The major manufacturing equipment, that is, the towers and vessels necessary for the manufacturing process, were ordered from Hooten Manufacturing Company. Their manufacturing schedule normally required ten to twelve months' advance ordering and the order for International Petrotergent's equipment had been placed with this production schedule in mind. An unexpected cancellation, however, enabled Hooten to offer delivery of the International Petrotergent equipment earlier than scheduled. At the time Hooten offered early delivery the over-all progress on the job was running approximately ten days ahead of schedule. Although enclosed storage space would not be available at the jobsite until approximately one week after the early delivery date, the construction superintendent felt that because of the client's pressure for early completion, the fact that construction was running ahead of schedule, and the advantages of having the major equipment at the jobsite cut down on possible future loss of lead time, it would be to the advantage of both Bechtel and the client to accept early delivery. The matter was discussed at the weekly construction meeting in the presence of International Petrotergent's representatives at the jobsite and the consensus of the meeting was that the early delivery date should be accepted. International Petrotergent's men entered into the discussion, not directly opposing the action, but not voting in the consensus decision.

The manufacturing equipment arrived at the jobsite ten days before the date called for in the original schedule. It was stored on a concrete pad with temporary canvas covering, while extra crews were assigned to stripping the forms from the reinforced concrete warehouse for inside storage of this equipment until it could be set in permanent location. At 11:14 p.m., January 5, the second day following arrival of the equipment, an unseasonal tornado of devastating proportions hit the area. While the plant site was not in the direct path of the cataclysm, it was close enough to suffer major damage from both wind and rain. The yard-stored manufacturing equipment was especially hard hit. Approximately one-quarter of it was damaged beyond salvage and required replacement. This alone would delay completion of the plant by at least one month.

The major cost of the loss and damage was adequately covered by insurance but an acrimonious dispute arose between Bechtel and International Petrotergent regarding the completion date and application of the bonus-penalty clause. The International Petrotergent representatives took the position that the original completion date of May 1 should stand with no change in the bonus-penalty provision. They rejected any invoicement of the 'Act of God' clause in the contract to provide for extension of the completion date, supporting their position by pointing out that the possibility of such storms had been recognized at the time of negotiations, that the structural provisions for the installation had been designed to provide protection from such storms, and that had the equipment been delivered on the scheduled date or only when inside protective storage space was available, the major loss and delay would not have occurred. They took the position that the contractor was fully aware of the possibility of such storms and gambled for his advantage in accepting early delivery of the vital equipment without proper protective housing being available.

Bechtel, on the other hand, is eager to recapture and retain the good will of the client but will suffer a substantial loss if the client's stand is not modified. Bechtel feels acceptance of the early delivery of the equipment served the best interests of both parties under the circumstances prevailing at the time and that there should be reasonable modification of the contract which would not place the full weight of the loss on Bechtel. The client's pressure for early completion, as evidenced by the increase of the bonus provision, and the fact that International Petrotergent representatives had been present at the meeting in which the decision to accept early delivery had been made and had taken no definite stand against this action were interpreted as tacit agreement on their part.

These are some of the factors that the Bechtel organization feels argue in favor of revising the completion date to May 15 and allowing the original bonus penalty clause to stand. Such a revision would make it possible for Bechtel to break even or make a small profit on the job. The International Petrotergent representatives are agreeable to the point of being willing to listen and a meeting has been arranged at the request of Bechtel to try to reach an amicable settlement along these lines. However, International Petrotergent is concerned with minimizing any loss it may suffer as the result of the delay in marketing its product and, as a publicly-owned corporation, its actions must be justified to the stockholders and its financial backers. It is now January 15, some ten days since the tornado caused such damage.

Two or three men from each organization will attend this decisive conference. Choose your team from the following titles:

BECHTEL CORPORATION

Division Senior Vice President
Division Manager of Business Development
Executive Vice President
Legal Counsel
Project Manager
Project Construction Superintendent
Manager of Purchasing
Chief Estimator
Treasurer

INTERNATIONAL PETROTERGENT, INC.

Vice President in Charge of Marketing
Vice President in Charge of Manufacturing
Chairman of the Board
Vice President in Charge of Engineering
Project Engineer
Legal Counsel
District Vice President
Treasurer
Contracts Administrator
Manager of Advertising and Sales Promotion

III

What are some implications for organizational education which can be drawn from our experience? In recent years there has been an increasing emphasis on the notion that organizational change is dependent upon the development of new technology and work processes within the organization.[2] If organizational styles are related so closely to the specific work functions of the enterprise, any program of training must be relevant to the particular circumstances of the organization. Education and training which may have popular support and even theoretical validity can, nevertheless, be completely irrelevant to the needs of the organization. Our experience and the growing accumulation of case studies of organizations suggests that a program of management education must be preceded by a careful analysis of the work conditions of that organization. Personal observations and interviews by the prospective instructors is a condition precedent to any classroom work. If possible, case and role-playing studies using company related materials should be developed at least concurrently with the classroom instruction. When these kinds of materials are presented to groups within the organization the quality of the class discussion becomes enriched with realistic and relevant examples.

Organizational education draws its instructional materials from two major sources. The first source emerges from the ever-increasing theory of the various behavioral sciences. This source is extremely important because it calls upon different disciplines with alternate perspectives. The second source is even more more important for a specific educational program. This source emerges from the accumulated experience of the organization, experience which is in many respects absolutely unique. The program which recognizes and uses this uniqueness will not only make an important contribution to the particular organization but will also provide rich material from which our understanding of the processes of management can mature.

[2] See for example: Joan Woodward, *Industrial Organization: Theory and Practice* (London, Oxford University Press, 1965); E. L. Trist, G. W. Higgins, H. Murray and A. B. Pollock, *Organizational Choice* (London, Tavistock Publications, 1963).

SELECTED BIBLIOGRAPHY

Books

Wilfred Brown, *Exploration in Management* (New York, John Wiley and Sons, 1960).
Elliot Jacques, *The Changing Culture of a Factory* (New York, The Dryden Press, 1952).
Paul Lawrence and John A. Seiler, *Organizational Behavior and Administration* (Homewood, Illinois, Richard D. Irwin and The Dorsey Press, Revised Edition, 1965).
A. K. Rice, *The Enterprise and its Environment : A System Theory of Theory of Management Organization* (London, Tavistock Publications, 1963).
A. K. Rice, *Learning for Leadership* (London, Tavistock Publications, 1965).
Leonard W. Sayles, *Managerial Behavior* (New York, McGraw Hill, 1964).
Muzafer Sherif, editor, *Intergroup Relations and Leadership* (New York, John Wiley and Sons, 1962).
Cyril Sofer, *The Organization from Within* (London, Tavistock Publications, 1961).

Articles

Alvin Goldner, "The Role of the Norm of Reciprocity in Social Stabilization", *American Sociological Review*, Vol 25, No. 2 April, 1960.
Gurth Higgins and Harold Bridger, "The Psychodynamics of and Inter-group Experience", *Human Relations*, Vol. 17, No. 4, 1964.
Muzafer Sherif, "Superordinate Goals in the Reduction of Inter-group Conflict", *American Journal of Sociology*, Vol. 63, No. 4, Jan. 1958.
George Strauss, "Tactics of Lateral Relationships", *Administrative Science Quarterly*, Vol. 12, No. 3, 1959.

LOUIS E. GLORFELD

THE RHETORIC OF SCIENCE

I. INTRODUCTION

A topic "Rhetoric of Science as Group Therapy" could encompass a discussion that would fill several volumes. It would seem practical, therefore, to limit the discussion to what might be its most potentially fruitful area. RHETORIC is generally defined as the power of discovering the available means of persuasion in a particular case. Therapy, on the other hand, means 'the nursing or curing of an ailment'. The use of rhetoric as group therapy has a history running parallel to the history of man. From the most primitive chant to bring rain or chase out evil demons to today's most persuasive orator or most sophisticated psychiatrist, rhetoric has indeed occupied an important position in cultural change and adjustment. It is the intent in this paper to confine comments and questions to the rhetoric of scientists and a suggestion for the establishment of a framework for a world culture which should tend to bring about an equilibrium for thinking individuals within a world culture group.

The rhetoric of scientists is that rhetoric which avoids false inferences and attempts through empirical evidence to give a reliable picture of the world as it is. This rhetoric relies on the principle that if words are used incorrectly there is no hope for ideas being either right or understood. The information output is both reliable and valid and is generally descriptive rather than prescriptive. This rhetoric allows not only for the accuracy of scientific statement but for an objective appraisal of the human condition as well. Quotes from scientists using such rhetoric are adequately represented throughout this paper. It is precisely because scientific rhetoric can so readily be extensionalized that it offers a therapy for a world in which time for settling major problems may be extremely limited.

Robert T. Oliver explains in his book *Culture and Communication* that there are a variety of rhetorics. These varied rhetorics are as numerous as are cultures. He points out logically that "what seems important to us is not necessarily important to everyone else".[1] The divergence of rhetorics as well as the divergence of cultures

[1] Robert T. Oliver, *Culture and Communication* (Springfield, Charles C. Thomas, 1962), p. 155.

would seem to indicate the need for a cultural rhetoric that would transcend this diversity. Can we, however, think of scientists as having a culture? If we use what Oliver calls an 'arbitrary definition of culture' it would seem that a culture of scientists definitely exists. Oliver defines a culture group "as a population having a common tradition sufficiently cohesive so that its manners and habits of thinking tend to be similar and, conversely, tend to be different from other cultural groups".[2] It is the rhetoric of science that regards all behavior as lawful and that makes it possible to bring order out of chaos and, in this sense, offers a therapy for the sickness now menacing the world we live in.

The findings of science are not always compatible with our own cultural outlook but most of us live with them, perhaps because we do not wish to be at odds with the physical comforts they offer us. The rest of the world seems willing to embrace the results of science as well. The differences of cultures in India or Egypt or China do not prevent these countries from producing Indian scientists, Egyptian scientists or Chinese scientists.

II. PROBLEM

The ailment suggested here for which the rhetoric of the scientific community might offer therapy is caused by the holistic cultural patterns that work negatively against man making progress toward a better life for all of the billions occupying the planet.

Perhaps there are those who say that the rhetoric of science covers only statistics, mathematical formulas, and test tubes. Work in the empirical world is largely concerned with this. The results, however, have to be communicated, and it is then that the scientist becomes the rhetorician. The best of them extensionalize the results not only with graphs and figures but with words and deeds that exalt the human spirit as well.

This paper attempts to adequately demonstrate that the language of science (language embracing the whole continuum of the meaning of the word *language*) offers to a world culture a therapy long overdue in helping to solve the world's problems.

The culmination of such a rhetoric could result, broadly speaking, in a world community of ideals and ideas. The satellites that circle the globe extensionalize the language of science to its remotest outposts, and the atomic explosion adds a period to the scientific sentence. Ivan Supek, Professor of Theoretical Physics at Zagreb University, as a guest editorialist for the *Bulletin of the Atomic Scientist* obviously poses some rhetorical questions when he writes:

> After contemplating the starry sky for five hundred years, man's hand has reached out
> for the architecture of the universe. The new artifical planet is the messenger of a new era
> of the triumphant stepping of science out into infinity; but while the rocket circles the sun

[2] *Ibid.*, p. 76.

our planet is rushing toward an atomic hell because of political inertia. Will it prove easier to reach distant islands of the universe, to adapt to breathing strange atmospheres, and to establish airconditioned colonies than to settle our disputes here? Will a grain of wheat come out of Mars' sod sooner than an olive branch from the thousand-year-old culture of mankind?[3]

C.P. Snow expands the idea of a scientific culture by clearly emphasizing action and rhetoric that have the problems of the world in focus:

...the greatest achievement the scientific culture could give us is — though it does not originate like that — a moral one. Among scientists, deep natured men know, as starkly as any men have known, that the individual human condition is tragic; for all its triumphs and joys, the essence of it is a loneliness and the end death. But what they will not admit is that, because the individual condition is tragic, therefore the social condition must be tragic too. Because a man must die, that is no excuse for his dying before his time and after a servile life. The impulse behind the scientists drives them to limit the area of tragedy, to take nothing as tragic that can conceivably lie within men's will.[4]

These remarks are not, of course, directed toward separate cultures. They do perhaps stem in part from an Aristotelian background of Western rhetoric combined with what Oliver defines as a new rhetoric "advocated by such men as Ogden, and Richards, and Kenneth Burke, and Benjamin Lee Whorf".[5] One is quick to understand what Oliver means by the futility of 'One World' political oratory.[6] But rhetoric in the scientific area is reinforced by goals that have meaning even to the most remote cultural organizations. This is not to discard entirely, however, a political rhetoric that could become an addend to the scientific rhetoric if the scientist is both scientist and politician. If the scientist can be accepted in the light of earlier comments, then the discussion can continue. Even Russian institutions have the flavor if not the spirit of the West.

III. PRINCIPLES OF APPLICATION

In cultural relationships at almost any level the people most likely to impede progress in terms of human relations suffer from the following attitues: (1) ignorance and complacency; (2) extremism of the 'right' or of the 'left'; (3) rigid, dogmatic, absolutistic views; (4) attitudes of allness.[7] No rhetoric works against attitudes such as these unless it refers to a fact-territory so understandable that these postures are modified or changed. Leaders in science today for the most part are of one world, and their abilities for making evaluations in a pragmatic sense are being heightened daily. Changes in tradition cannot keep pace with the rapid development of scientific achievement but scientific rhetoric can bridge, through the voices of its leaders,

[3] Ivan Supek, "Guest Editorial from Yugoslavia", *Bulletin of the Atomic Scientists*, XVII (December, 1961), p. 402.
[4] C. P. Snow, "The Two Cultures", *New Statesman and Nation*, III (October 6, 1956), p. 414.
[5] Oliver, p. 77.
[6] *Ibid.*, p. 77.
[7] Elwood Murray, Raymond H. Barnard, T. V. Garland, *Integrative Speech* (New York, The Dryden Press, 1953), p. 72.

both the old and the new. Compromise, in many instances is the key to progress. in human relations. The compromise allows tradition, bias, and ignorance a chance to slowly modernize while science takes a substantial lead in reducing the world's most pressing problems — hunger, disease, and poverty.

One might well ask what the rhetoric of science has had to say about human organization, if we are going to agree that it may possess both a structure and rhetoric that could loosely hold so many cultures together. It has been pointed out that "the ethical systems of other professions, such as business or the military, have become models for whole societies. Why should not the practice of science become such a model?"[8] The substance of an article by Warren G. Bennis from which the above quotation is taken runs something like this: The criteria used to measure organizations to the present time has been woefully inadequate, subjective, and limited to measuring the satisfaction of the workers and the efficiency of the production. This criteria has failed to take any account of the very large element of problem-solving which necessarily is a foremost concern of any organization due to constant change brought about by both internal and external stress. Up to this time, criteria for measurement of organizations has failed to apply the scientific attitude and has usually viewed the organization as a machine — i.e., a vending machine, wherein one puts in a given amount of money and a standard product comes out repetitively.[9] Unless some technological or human variable is introduced, the machine continues to operate repetitively. The organization, unlike the machine, cannot habitually spew forth the same product at the same rate perpetually and reflect changes in its environment (the market and personnel and applied science); consequently, new criteria which measure the ability of an organization to solve its problems, and to evaluate its position in its own field and environment must be developed. This element of problem-solving is closely related to the field of mental health. Organizational health (efficiency) and mental health have experienced some parallel developments, such as terms and a search for better, more scientific measurements. Just as a person who has been successfully treated for mental health should see himself as others see him, so should an organization. As a result of many prominent scientists, psychologists, and other theorists wrestling with the problem of developing more accurate criteria for measuring organizational efficiency, Bennis has taken a definition for good mental health by Jahoda and by elaborating upon her three points, has postulated them as being equally adequate for measuring the health of any organization.[12]

[8]   Warren G. Bennis, "Towards a 'Truly' Scientific Management: The Concept of Organization Health", Ludwig von Bertalanffy and Anatol Rapoport, *General Systems*, (= *Yearbook of the Society for General Systems Research*, 1962) (Mental Health Center, Univ. of Mich., Ann Arbor, 1962), p. 269.

[9]   For a further discussion of the human organism viewed as a simple machine in, traditional organization theory, see James G. March and Hubert A. Simon, " 'Classical' Organization Theory", *Organizations* (New York, John Wiley & Sons, 1959), pp. 12-23.

[10]   Bennis discusses the points of a healthy personality as set down by M. Jahoda in *Current Concepts of Positive Mental Health* (New York, Basic Books, 1958).

It is the points made by Jahoda that particularly emphasize any confidence placed in the science community as possessing within its discipline the factors needed for a sufficiently strong cultural organization; desirable factors leading to the health of any other organization can be seen as well.

Jahoda points to the healthy individual as one who has actively mastered his environment. In other words, he has what is known as adaptibility. Second, the healthy individual has a clearly defined identity. The goals are understood and accepted. Third, Jahoda makes clear that the individual is able to see the world and himself correctly. This requires REALITY TESTING for determining the 'real properties' of the field in which he finds himself — an essential prerequisite for any successful mastery over the relevant environment.[11] So, says Jahoda, should it be with the healthy organization. This idea is further supported by G.T. Ghilbaud in his book on cybernetics. He states: "The automatic tendency towards a stable organization is suggestively similar to the processes of adaptation to the environment."[12] Hope and understanding for the health of all organizations is made clear by further postulates of the cyberneticians:

...dynamic systems cease to be liable to breakage, when, and only when, they reach equilibrium. And since a breakage is a change of organization this principle may also be expressed in the equivalent form: A dynamic system will change its organization until it reaches a state of equilibrium.[13]

Concerning the health of any organization, it is interesting to note that people in the scientific culture proceed rather carefully and, in a sense, give what could be compared to a thorough health check or examination before proceeding with either advice or action to a new state or a different culture. Their philosophy for underdeveloped areas is stated like this: " 'Learn before you try to teach', and 'Know what you are trying to change before you start to change it.' "[14]

Ritchie Calder, formerly science editor of the *London News Chronicle*, reports that at the International Conference on Science in the Advancement of New States, Asians made a proposal that orientation centers for foreign experts going in to the new countries (today's Peace Corps) be established. According to Calder this proposal was based on the following:

...for a long, long time, the new countries will be dependent on experts from the advanced countries while their own cadres are being trained. At these centers the incoming experts would be given an insight into the cultures and traditions of the people among whom they were going to work. They might also learn that when the ancestors of the scientific West were running around in woad, there were advanced civilizations in many of the countries which we now call 'underdeveloped'; and that science should add to cultures and not replace them.[15]

[11] Bennis, pp. 276-278.
[12] G. T. Ghilbaud, *What Is Cybernetics?*, trans. by Valerie McKay (New York, Criterion Books, 1958), p. 11.
[13] *Ibid.*, 33.
[14] Ritchie Calder, "New Magic for Old", *Bulletin of the Atomic Scientists*, XVIII (February, 1961), p. 55.
[15] *Ibid.*, p. 77.

It seems certain from the above statements that the rhetoric of science could be applied as therapy to the most pressing problems, and this could in effect bring about both an understanding and the cure for potential misunderstanding. As Oliver points out, "Where we have fallen short in our adaptation to them (all cultures foreign to the West) has been our failure to see that Aristotelianism, Lockianism and own religio-ethical beliefs are OURS, not THEIRS."[16]

There is yet another basis for understanding already clear to the scientist that could be therapeutic in either the health of the individual and the health of a culture or organization, when couched in terms of sufficient clarity. This extensionalizing has been done by P.B. Medawar, Jadrell Professor of Zoology and Comparative Anatomy at University College, London. He points out that philosophers of the nineteenth century and many of their followers in the twentieth century thought that great lessons were to be learned from the similarities drawn between Darwinian and social evolution. According to Medawar, a few 'astute' biologists and hardly any philosophers recognized "a profound truth that nature does not know best; that genetical evolution, if we choose to look at it liverishly instead of with fatuous good humor, is a story of waste, makeshiftness, compromise and blunder".[17]

Medawar explains how, frequently, by the body defending itself the remedy becomes the disease and "that natural devices and dispositions are highly fallible". He clarifies this by stating:

> The immunological defenses are dedicated to the proposition that anything foreign must be harmful; and this formula is ground out in a totally undiscriminating fashion with results that are sometimes irritating, sometimes harmful, and sometimes mortally harmful. It is far better to have immunological defenses than not to have them; but this does not mean that we are to marvel at them as evidences of a high and wise design.[18]

Medawar's point is that we can often better the work of nature but to do this we must continue to 'explore' and 'extend' our knowledge. He warns us against people who brandish us with 'naturalistic principles'. He asks us to think of how much "we have suffered from a belief in the existence and overriding authority of a fighting instinct; from the doctrines of racial superiority and metaphysics of blood and soil; from the belief that warfare between men or classes of men or nations represents a fulfillment of historical laws". Finally Medawar adds this:

> These are all excuses of one kind or another, and pretty thin excuses. The inference we can draw from an analytical study of the differences between ourselves and other animals is surely this: that the bells that toll for mankind are — most of them, anyway, like the bells on Alpine cattle; they are attached to our own necks, and it must be our fault if they do not make a cheerful and harmonious sound.[19]

---

[16]   Oliver, p. 154.
[17]   P. B. Medawar, "The Future of Man", *The Saturday Evening Post* (October 1, 1960), p. 92.
[18]   *Ibid.* p. 93.
[19]   *Ibid.* p. 93.

IV. RESULTS OF DISCUSSION

What are the results to be expected from a rhetoric of science? First, it can be observed that the very nature of the therapy it offers has succeeded in building a culture of its own. The culture has, as Oliver states, a tradition in common that is cohesive and has, as well, habits of similar thinking. The culture itself assumes that its subject matter has been sufficiently tested to be labeled that which Arthur Combs and Donald Snygg call 'regular and lawful'; and that "if this assumption could not be made, there could, of course, be no science".[20] Second, science and the scientific method have themselves become a model for human organization. Third, science and its culture provide a means for REALITY TESTING which can determine not only the health of an individual but the health of an organization. Fourth, the rhetoric of the scientific culture offers a form of extensionalized therapy that works in such a way as to make rational sense in an irrational world. It allows breathing time for cultures and cultural institutions, giving hope that some of our oldest and most cherished traditions can survive and in some cases adjust and progress toward a future filled with hope.

V. CONCLUSIONS

In the final analysis, what must we give up to let a scientific culture and a model of scientific organization work on the peripheral boundaries of all the world's organizations and cultures? Does this seeking for a therapy to bind us closer together destroy our separate institutions that harbor our religions, our philosophies, our politics, our education, our economics, and our families? If this culture of dedicated leaders is willing and able to assist man in somewhat painlessly discarding some of his old views for the new, can we ask more? Oliver explains that "what we need most of all is re-education — not just an enlarged, or more systematic, or more thorough education, but an actual substitution of a world view for the parochial view within which we have been nurtured".[21]

No one works to save the lives of all mankind unless he LOVES. In a sense we are finally forced to choose between love and annihilation, for we have extensionalized Mephistopheles into reality, and should we make the wrong choice the hideous thunder of his laughter would echo across the cinders of a burned out planet whose sun star still shines on.

VI. ISSUES AND UNSOLVED QUESTIONS

The issues discussed in this paper are in relation to science as a culture, the rhetoric of science as group therapy, and science as a model for human organization. Naturally

[20] Arthur W. Combs and Donald Snygg, "The Perceptual View of Behavior", from *Individual Behavior*, quoted in James C. Coleman, *Personality Dynamics and Effective Behavior* (Chicago, Scott Foresman, 1960), p. 466.
[21] Oliver, p. 155.

in a discussion this broad there are unanswered questions. The reality of the scientific culture is yet somewhat of a myth although it certainly performed reality testing during the International Geophysical Year, and its teamwork in space technology has served notice in obvious forms of space achievements. The work of this scientific community in oceanography, medicine, bio-chemistry, physics, the behavioral sciences, and even its impact on human organization has been felt throughout the world. But the world is still divided into two major political camps with those who proclaim to be neutrals looking nervously on. It would seem that the rhetoric of science with its humanitarian work divorced from any political attachment, offers some hope for a better world.

UNIVERSITY OF DENVER

PART THREE

LINGUISTICS

Modern linguistics may be thought of as the science of language. Such a definition is, as Macbeth said, "as broad and general as the 'casing air''. Because linguistics is so extensive in its scope a more specific description of the field will provide greater insight into the discipline.

The linguist today no longer confines himself to the learning and speaking of languages or to the historical-comparative studies so popular during the 19th century. The philologists of that time were concerned with the laws of sound change. These 'laws' were mainly external to the inner nature of language. An understanding of sound changes was a necessary step in the evolution of linguistic thought and did not, for the most part, explain the internal structure of language. Now and then the philologists even broke through toward internal linguistic truth, as in the case of Grimm's law (1822), and later in the century, Werner's law which explained sound changes not discussed in Grimm's statements. In this way philology investigated a field related to and occasionally very near structural linguistics.

Around the early part of the nineteenth century the Sanskrit grammar of the Hindus became known in Europe. The Hindu grammar gave a scientific description of the Sanskrit language. This scientific analysis of Sanskrit was, in time, used as a model by Western scholars to describe a language in terms of its unique structure. Modern linguists work on the premise that each language is unique and must be described in terms of its own patterns rather than by forcing unique patterns into a pre-existing mold. Hence English has been taken out of the Greco-Latin framework by linguists and its own structure is being recognized. The primary emphasis of the linguist today is not on the speaking and translating of many languages but on structures and systems which simplify the learning and understanding of all languages. Although linguists seek to discover the unique characteristics of each language, they also search for language universals.

Linguists recognize the importance of culture and the inter-relationships of cultural influences on communication and on communication breakdowns. As Theodore Clevenger, Jr. said, "... Communication, it is sometimes argued, is not a discipline so much as an interdisciplinary problem area. It is the eternal no man's land where the myriad conflicting ideologies of the life sciences and the arts come into conflict; or if you prefer, the treasury into which they pour their accumulated wealth. In this view, it would be unthinking to (discipline-ize) communication, for then it would lose its value as a meeting ground where men of diverse interests can come together to discuss common problems."[1]

The common problems that are of interest to the linguist and to the communication specialist are based on MAN as a communicator. This section of the book deals with man and his linguistic accomplishments. Language, including its verbal and non-verbal aspects, is viewed by the linguist as man's primary form of communication. Consequently, the linguist feels that he cannot overlook any phase or branch of language study.

Linguistics to many has come to mean the advocacy of a new method of teaching grammar. Great controversies are raging today over the 'linguistic approach to the teaching of English'. Linguists have brought about a revolution in the teaching of grammar because of the new concepts of structure. These new concepts attempt to describe language in terms of its own internal structure.

The various linguistics schools approach the study of grammar objectively. However, tools and terminology often differ. They deal with phonemes, morphemes and syntax as a basis. These principles apply equally to the study of unwritten languages being investigated as well as to languages whose literature is well known. The new approaches to the teaching of English grammar represent one of the most revolutionary and interesting methodological developments in contemporary linguistics.

Language has both structure and process.. The linguist begins his study of structure with the smallest unit in the hierarchy of grammar, the phoneme. The study of phonology is an objective study of the classification of sounds. The sounds group themselves into a larger structure to form morphemes which are the smallest meaningful units of the language. The morphemes are words or parts of words. The grouping is invariant. The groupings then arrange themselves into larger groups which form utterances or grammar. The linguist's next step is concerned with semology or meaning. The study of grammar relates phonology with semology, thus allowing a better understanding of encoding and decoding which represents the primary process of language.

The following articles are considered to be representative rather than exhaustive studies in the field of linguistics. Each also deals with a special communicative problem.

Mr. Samuel Stone in his article "Toward a Psycholinguistic Theory of Teaching" is motivated by the belief that a coherent theory of pedagogical linguistics might greatly improve educational practice. He restricts his argument "to the beginnings of a model for linguistic perception and a brief discussion of pedagogical applica-

---

[1] Theodore Clevenger, Jr., "Some characteristics of the Study of Communication in 1960", *The Journal of Communication*, Vol. X, No. 4, Dec., 1960.

tion." Stone postulates eleven assumptions that help to understand his model. They are based on the work of serious students of linguistics, psychology, and education. He theorizes that we should "find a way of using linguistic resources within a child as a basis for making him literate".

Stone believes that "to make explicit both the relationship between linguistic perception and generative grammar and between linguistic and sensory perception, it will be necessary to develop some algebraic notations including a few lines of a generative grammar." The simplified generative transformational grammar he advocates is an explanation of how sentences are understood. Stone does not believe that pedagogical theory must be derived from practical situations. His simple and straightforward application of the fragmentary psycholinguistic system is an excellent beginning for those who are interested in learning theory as well as an introduction to generative grammar.

Mrs. Zell SoRelle's "Segmental Phonology of Texas Panhandle Speech" is a study in linguistic geography which is the branch of linguistics that deals with regional distribution of language forms and their variants. Work was begun on the Linguistic Atlas of the United States and Canada in the late twenties. The aim of atlas work is to discover differences in pronunciation, grammar and vocabulary, to learn the social and regional distributions of the differences and to learn the historical and cultural explanations of the differences. The evidence is gathered by trained field workers who interview three generations of native residents. The first or older generation is usually the less well educated, the middle or second generation usually has some formal education and the third generation is usually in college or is a college graduate. The field workers transcribe the responses at the time of the interview, or record the responses on tape for later transcription. The data are secured by use of a standard questionnaire designed to provide comparable data throughout the country. When necessary, the questionnaire is modified slightly to suit the area being investigated.

Mrs. SoRelle's study of the phonology of the Panhandle speech is a continuation of the Atlas work. The questionnaire was modified for use in the Panhandle. Ten first generation informants were interviewed instead of the usual three generations. One of SoRelle's aims was to determine through the questionnaire which dialect area of the eastern United States had the greatest influence on the speech of the Panhandle. She also traced the early migration of the settlers through this method. Evidence indicates that the South Midland dialect was more prevalent in this area than the others. South Midland extends south along the Appalachians, into southern Illinois, Missouri, Arkansas, eastern Oklahoma and eastern Texas, thence to the Panhandle. The other large dialect areas had less influence.

Linguistic geography is the study of regional distributions of language. It is sometimes called dialectology. Although linguistic geography and dialectology are not different, they have different emphases. The dialectologist places a heavier emphasis on the study of social dialects. Mr. Raven I. McDavid, Jr. in his essay "On the

Hierarchy of Values: The Clinician and the Dialectologist" gives insight into the often unsuspected relationships between the varieties of American English and social status in a community. McDavid approaches his subject from the point of view of what the speech clinician and the teacher need to know regarding social and cultural influences in different language areas. He points out that the structural linguist can be of assistance to the clinician regarding foreign language problems through a comparison of linguistic systems relating to phonology and grammar. The linguist who is a specialist in dialectology can identify the socially significant variations in language which result from wide varieties of cultural experiences. The teacher should be aware of socially preferred usage in a community. Exotic pronunciations should not be forced on the student because of personal preference of the clinician.

Man's ability to use language is his most complicated attribute. His natural language can be divided into the spoken and written. The structural approach of linguistics is one of the methods of providing insight into the natural language. The two important problems involved in structural linguistics are to construct theories which can be applied to all languages and to give a description of specific languages. Gordon E. Peterson in "Toward a Theory of Symbolization" selects the division of phonology or orthography for his discussion of the symbolic processes of natural languages.

Peterson's manuscript contains a theory of symbolization. The theory consists of a set of interdependent definitions and axioms and it is presented in a form which fits most aspects of human communication. Peterson assumes that a relationship exists between what he calls 'denotes', in which a finite set of objects, properties, relationships, and/or events is associated with another (finite or infinite) set of objects, properties, relationships, and/or events. He elaborates upon this basic axiom to construct a complex theoretical system that students of communication will find quite profound.

To stretch the linguistic scholar beyond the confines of phonology and structures, we have included a provocative essay on the important communicative dimension of the non-verbal. Mr. Ray Birdwhistell, an anthropologist, is widely recognized for his work in the area of kinesics. Kinesics, according to Birdwhistell, is the study of the visual, non-verbal aspects of communication. In his contribution to this section, Birdwhistell goes beyond kinesics and explores common themes and assumptions which run through the communication literature. After outlining some of the fundamental issues that underlie much of the theorizing and research in communication, Birdwhistell discusses ways in which these controversies may be resolved. It is conceivable, he suggests, that interaction becomes more comprehensible when larger rather than smaller groupings are studied. Birdwhistell believes that most of the issues in communication which he identifies will be resolved within the next twenty-five years.

Mr. Albert Upton in his essay on muddled metaphors and ambiguities in the language discusses in depth certain words as used by Shakespeare in specific contexts. His specific intention was an explication of the line "That monster custom, who all sense doth eat." His thesis is that the terms SENSE and CUSTOM involve the entire conversation between Queen Gertrude and Hamlet. He proceeds with his argument upon the semantic principles which apply to any and all communication by means of symbols. The most basic of these he takes to be the following:

(1) The law of matrix — the meaning of a symbol is relevant to its matrix.

(2) Polysemia is essential to symbolic economy. A relatively small number of terms must have a relatively large number of senses if a symbol is to be manageable.

(3) The older a familiar term is, the greater the difficulty in semantic control.

(4) And finally, facility with metaphor (implicit analogy) is essential to sophiticated communication.

Robert Lees discusses a complicated and interesting feature of the pronunciation of modern standard urban Turkish, for which there are two competing analyses which illuminate the historical process of a morphophonemic problem. He cites examples in the literature which show that an ordinary phonemic analysis is often forced to represent predictable features of pronunciation in the form of irreducible elements. Other examples that have been given to show the underlying, least redundant, phonological representations to which the most general rules of an analysis would apply often resemble etymologically prior stages in the language. Still others show that in large part languages change slowly by the addition of low-level phonetic rules and only seldom by radical reorganization of the grammar.

In conclusion he speculates that the Turkish dialect which he describes is in transition with the gradual loss of Altaic*/g/ and the importation of Arabic words with long vowels under partial Turkification. Also that as simplicity of the new $\overline{V}$-/g/-description, gains on that of the old /ğ/-description, there will come a generation of speakers for which an entirely different phonological description becomes correct — this would be a distinct discontinuity in analysis rather than a gradual shift of the pronunciations involved. The new analysis appears to restore Proto-Turkic */g/ (and also Altaic long vowels, though only before /g/).

Sol Saporta and Heles Contreras studied the phonological development of the speech of a bilingual child from the age of twelve months to nineteen months. The two languages were New York City English and a variety of Spanish spoken in Southern Chile. During the period of observation, there is no evidence that the child is dealing with two linguistic systems. There is, however, evidence of the existance of equivalent pairs such as *coffee*, Spanish /kafi/ and English /kófi/ with different phonological features, e.g., the lack of aspiration in the Spanish /k/. The nineteen month period of study is limited to the time when the child had just one system.

The conclusions show acquisition of segmental phonemes and distinctive features. The results are compared with studies made by Velten (1943), Leopold (1947) and Jakobson (1949).

SAMUEL B. STONE

TOWARD A PSYCHOLINGUISTIC THEORY
OF TEACHING

I

Teaching has been described as an art that attempts to apply several sciences in the aid of learning. To the extent that this description refers to training for literacy, however, it is unduly optimistic; for it implies a close connection between what the child does as he learns to read, to write and to think about language and how his teacher tells him to go about these tasks. Such a relationship, unfortunately, is not always easy to see, and at least a few instances can be found where instruction is clearly irrelevant to its own purposes and quite possibly at odds with them. Only rarely do methods and materials for the teaching of phonics reflect up-to-date knowledge of phonology. Many teachers still spend large spans of time on traditional grammar as a basis for writing, even though no one has ever been able to show that it helps at all. And pupils are punished, mildly of course, for labeling *John* and *help* as the subject and predicate of the sentence *I wanted John to help me*, even though the identification follows quite logically from the usual classroom actor-action 'definition'. These are but examples.

All this, despite its sound, is not a 'warm-up' for a denunciation of everything that has ever happened in the language arts curriculum. Obviously, most American children do learn to read and write. Granted, some do not learn well enough to satisfy parents or prospective employers — or even the teacher, whose standards are supposedly getting lower every year; but the spread of literacy during the twentieth century is an accomplishment our schools can be proud of. Perhaps things are as good as they are because the teacher's artistry transcends his scientific knowledge; he is like the poet, who in the estimation of some critics creates great art without really knowing what he is doing.

The motivation for this paper springs from the belief that things would be better if teachers really knew what they were doing. To put it differently, a coherent theory of pedagogical linguistics might greatly improve educational practice. This theory should consist of a body of logically organized facts telling us what language is, how it works, how it is perceived, how it is learned, how language learning can be measured, and how teachers can use linguistic resources already present in the child as a basis for making him literate. Present knowledge does not permit the complete construction of such a theory, but ideas borrowed from generative grammar can be combined with some older notions from Gestalt psychology to suggest a direction that might be taken. This paper, ambitiously enough, will restrict itself to the beginnings of a model for linguistic perception and a brief discussion of pedagogical application.

II

Before proceeding to the model it is necessary to make explicit the assumptions underlying it and its pedagogical application. Some of these may be questioned on prior theoretical or philosophical grounds, but all of them are derived from the work of serious students of linguistics, psychology, and education. To defend them here would simply be to review in watered-down form arguments developed by Leonard Bloomfield, Noam Chomsky, Wolfgang Koehler, John Dewey and others.

(1) Ideally, a pedagogical theory must meet both internal and external conditions. Internally, it must be logically consistent. Externally, it must correspond to empirical data and predict results.

(2) Language is an aspect of human behavior. Adequate grammar rules are simply statements that describe cognitive mechanisms underlying speech.

(3) Language is systematic. The structure of every spoken or written sentence is determined by a complex set of rules shared by a community of native speakers. To equate these rules with the formulations of them found in grammar books, however, is to confuse the word with the thing.

(4) The language system, with slight but important differences from person to person, is assimilated into the nervous system of every native speaker. The terms *intuition* and *intuitive grammatical knowledge* will be used to refer to this assumption. These terms do not imply any kind of mysticism; they simply mean, for example, that the native speaker knows that a verb is a verb in the sense that he can use it in certain word order positions and with certain endings. Moreover, he recognizes what other people say as consistent or inconsistent with his own speech habits. None of this implies that a given speaker is able to verbalize grammatical definitions or that his usage conforms to a preconceived standard.

(5) Simple perception has both environmental and organic bases. Environmentally, it is based upon physical similarities such as phonetic similarity, rhythmic and melodic patterns and so forth. Organically, the inherited structure of the nervous system conditions the manner — and perhaps even the fact — of grouping.

(6) Simple learning is based on simple perception.

(7) Perception and learning form a patterned chain reaction feeding on externally imposed experience. That is, once something has been learned it will strongly influence new perceptions which in turn influence new learning.

(8) Tasks extending or complementing this pattern chain will be easy to learn. Conflicts and contradictions will cause difficulty.

(9) Speech is psychologically prior to writing.

(10) Initial training for literacy will be most economical and effective if based on the child's 'intuitive knowledge' of his language as manifested in his speech.

(11) Extended training must also be based on this intuitive knowledge but can — and must — be modified to allow for the influence of experiences with written language.

III

There is a striking resemblance between the dynamics of visual perception, as developed by *Gestalt* psychology, and the dynamics of linguistic perception. In each, the value of specific elements depends upon both their own properties and their contexts. The raw physical similarities between the vowels of let [l ɛ t] and led [l ɛ : d] (short and long respectively) give rise to a simple sensory classification of sounds, much as randomly mixed white and light gray tiles in a mosaic will form a class, and hence a figure, against a black background. But even at the level of phonology, the organization of the context is fundamental in determining whether differences are relevant or irrelevant to the native speaker. A problem familiar to anyone who has been properly introduced to phonemics will serve to illustrate. If, as in most dialects of American English, short vowels can occur only before voiceless stops [p], [t], and [k], and long vowels occur only before voiced sounds, so that [l ɛ t] and [l ɛ: d] occur but [l ɛ: t] and [l ɛ d] do not, then the difference is not significant to the native speaker.[1] On the other hand, if a language contains sets of words like [l ɛ t], [l ɛ : d], [l ɛ : t] and [l ɛ d] (that is long and short vowels can precede both voiced and voiceless stops) the native speaker, or a foreigner learning the language must learn to attend and respond to the difference in length automatically. If the white and gray tiles of our mosaic are arranged to create an illusion of light and shadow, they constitute ONE class; but if the whites form a bunch of flowers and the grays a vase, they constitute TWO classes. Likewise, in American English the long and short vowels [ɛ :] and [ɛ] belong to the SAME class, but in our hypothetical language they belong to DIFFERENT classes.

At the level of syntax, organization seems even more important. Elements with gross physical differences often assume similar roles. For example, in particular contexts either the -*s* or -*ed* ending of a verb will tell us that a string of words is a complete sentence, and the absence of an ending will produce some kind of fragment. Moreover, certain contextually determined syntactic elements signal contrasts of meaning.

A generative-transformational grammar can be extremely useful as part of an

---

[1] This is an oversimplification. A discussion of vowel length before nasals and sibilants would go far beyond the scope of this paper but would contain several ramifications important to the complete development of a perceptual theory.

explanation of how sentences are understood, but some important restrictions need to be observed. As Chomsky put it:

[A generative grammar is] quite neutral as between speaker and hearer, between synthesis and analysis of given utterances... In fact, these two tasks which the speaker and hearer must perform are essentially the same, and are both outside the scope of [generative] grammars... Each such grammar is simply a description of a certain set of utterances, namely, those which it generates... [But] one might rely on a grammar in the investigation of such special problems as analysis and synthesis of particular utterances.[2]

This statement points toward a sound basis for a psycholinguistic theory, but some extensions and modifications are necessary. The speaker and the hearer must share a certain set of rules in order to communicate; a neutral grammar would be the central part. On one side of the grammar would be a semantic system — a way of organizing experience into meanings — and a system for 'mapping' semantics into the grammar. On the other side would be a set of rules for analyzing utterances (or their written equivalents); analysis would consist of tracing speech sounds (or graphic symbols) back into the same grammar used by the speaker. Presumably, the mutual possession of rules would allow the hearer ultimately to reconstruct as much of the speaker's experience as was organized and mapped into the grammar. Viewed this way, the neutrality of grammar between synthesis and analysis is a necessity.

To say that the tasks of synthesizing and analyzing sentences are essentially the same, however, may blur an important issue. In logic, it is not always possible to discover premises simply by knowing conclusions. In mathematics, it is not always possible to discover factors from a given product; without additional information the expression $xy = 50$ cannot be solved for x and y.

The understanding of phrases and sentences involves similar problems. If a man says "I don't like the hamburger", the sentence is grammatically and semantically ambiguous. That is, *hamburger* may be either a mass or a count noun, grammatically, and may refer to either an unspecified amount of ground beef or to a sandwich. The speaker knows what he meant, but without further information the hearer does not. The speaker may produce a grammatical structure, which he can analyze himself, but the hearer may need further signals in order to perform his own analysis, just as we could quantify x and y if we knew not only $x \cdot y = 10$ but that $x \div y = 2$ or if we knew the value of either to begin with.

A natural language, of course, does not permit all of the possible combinations of its elements as does a system of natural numbers. If the words of *The rat ate the cheese* are scrambled to yield *The ate cheese rat the* the result is not an English sentence. The set of rules for ordering the elements of language — the grammar existing in the nervous system of the native speaker — contains the main features of a signalling system that makes most sentences unambiguous. Nevertheless, a theory that explains how the hearer perceives, or analyzes, sentences must explain how he resolves ambiguities. Moreover, the possibility that the hearer needs a special way of analyzing ambiguous

[2]   Noam Chomsky, *Syntactic Structures* ('s-Gravenhage, Mouton & Co., 1957), p. 48.

components suggests that the analysis of unambiguous phrases may not be a simple inversion of synthesis. At least, he seemingly needs something outside the sentence itself in order to relate, for example, the phrase *the hamburger* either to *a hamburger* or to *some hamburger*. The solution of this problem lies beyond the scope of the present paper, but its existence is part of the reason for the formulation of some of the examples used in the following paragraphs.

To make explicit both the relationship between linguistic perception and generative grammar and between linguistic and sensory perception, it will be necessary to develop some algebraic notations including a few lines of a generative grammar. A description of noun phrases in English should distinguish several subclasses of nouns:

1. $SENT \rightarrow NOM + PRED$
2. $NOM \rightarrow NP + N^o$
3. $NP \rightarrow T + N$
4. $N \rightarrow N_{ct}, N_{mass}, N_{ns}$
5. $N_{ct} \rightarrow N_m, N_f, N_n$
6. $T + N_{mass} + N^o \rightarrow T + N_{mass} + \emptyset_n$
7. $T + N_{ns} + N^o \rightarrow T + N_{ns} + S_n$
8. $N^o \rightarrow \begin{Bmatrix} S_n \\ \emptyset_n \end{Bmatrix}$
9. $T \rightarrow the, T_1$
10. $T_1 + N_{ct} + \emptyset_n \rightarrow a + N_{ct} + \emptyset_n$
11. $T_1 \rightarrow \emptyset_t$

These rules should be read as follows:

1. A sentence consists of a nominal and a predicate.[3]

2. A nominal consists of a noun phrase and its grammatical number. (A complete grammar would also include pronouns, first, second, and third person, and would distinguish common nouns from proper nouns. Here, however, only common nouns are considered.)[4]

3. A noun phrase consists of a noun and a preceding determiner.

4. Nouns are either count nouns, mass nouns, or nonsingular nouns.

5. Count nouns are either masculine, feminine, or neuter.

6. The number of a mass noun (e.g. *gravel, mush, music*) is always singular. (Many nouns can occur as either mass or count nouns: *hamburger, iron, glass*. The symbol $\emptyset_n$ refers to the absence of an ending for number.)

7. The number of a nonsingular noun (e.g. *scissors, pajamas*) is always plural. (Nouns of this class are not preceded by 'numerals' as are the plurals of count nouns; that is, *Two pairs of pajamas* is grammatical but **two pajamas* is not, except perhaps in special kinds of jargon.)

---

[3] Most linguists prefer the reading "Sentence is rewritten as nominal plus predicate".
[4] The parenthetical information is intended primarily to aid the reader who is not familiar with linguistic grammars.

8. The number of any other noun may be either singular or plural.

9. The determiner is either the definite article (*the*) or the indefinite article (T_1). (A complete grammar would need to account for the demonstratives, the possessive pronouns, and words such as *some, any, each, no,* and *many,* all of which are often included in the class of determiners. These are not included here because they have certain formal properties not shared by the articles.)

10. In the context of a count noun whose number is singular, the indefinite article is *a.*

11. Elsewhere — that is, in the context of a mass noun or of any noun whose number is plural — the indefinite article is empty or null. (The sentences *He was digging a sand* and *She was reading a books* are ungrammatical, but if the indefinite articles are eliminated (nullified) the sentences become acceptable.)

Rules like 6, 7, 8, 10, and 11 are CONTEXT SENSITIVE. That is, each one states the form to be taken by a particular component given a specific context of occurrence. Thus, in Rule 7 the component N^o takes the form S_n in the context of a nonsingular noun, and in Rule 10 the component T_1 takes the form a in the context of N_{ct} (a count noun) and $\emptyset_n$ (singular number.) Rules 10 and 11 could have been stated in the form:[5]

$$T_i \begin{bmatrix} N_{ct} + \emptyset_n \\ N_{mass} + \emptyset_n \\ N + S_n \end{bmatrix} \rightarrow \begin{bmatrix} a + N_{ct} + \emptyset_n \\ \emptyset_t + N_{mass} + \emptyset_n \\ \emptyset_t + N + S_n \end{bmatrix}$$

Here the square brackets mean that each of the sequences of noun and number is a member of an ordered set and that each interacts only with the directly corresponding members in other brackets or with unbracketed items. Hence T_1 interacts with the three items to the left of the arrow to form the three directly corresponding strings to the right.

The same symbolic device can be used to explain how linguistic contexts give cues to the hearer, enabling him to trace received utterances back to the neutral grammar and ultimately into the semantic system. The word *hamburger,* because it can be either a mass noun or a count noun, can be used to illustrate. Consider the sentences

The man wants a hamburger.
The man wants hamburgers.
The man wants hamburger.

In the first two sentences it is a count noun, but in the last it is a mass noun. We might represent this symbollically as:

$$\begin{bmatrix} \begin{bmatrix} a \\ \emptyset_t \end{bmatrix} \\ \emptyset_t \end{bmatrix} N \begin{bmatrix} \begin{bmatrix} \emptyset_n \\ S_n \end{bmatrix} \\ \emptyset_n \end{bmatrix} \rightarrow \begin{bmatrix} \begin{bmatrix} a \\ \emptyset_t \end{bmatrix} N_{ct} \\ \emptyset_t + N_{mass} + \end{bmatrix} \begin{bmatrix} \emptyset_m \\ S_n \\ \emptyset_n \end{bmatrix}$$

---

5 Cf. Robert B. Lees, *The Grammar of English Nominalizations* (= *Indiana University Research Center in Anthropology, Folklore, and Linguistics, Publication 12)* (Bloomington, Indiana, 1960)·

The context supplied by the indefinite article and the plural ending, or by the lack of either or both, tells the hearer which subclass the word belongs to and the class distinction becomes the cue for the meaning.[6]

Before raising the question of how the hearer knows the word is a noun of ANY kind, we can profitably examine an example of visual perception which will be used to illustrate the compatibility between linguistic and psychological theory. Practically speaking the height of an image cast on the retina is inversely proportional to the distance between the eye and the object being viewed. Thus, if a man is standing twenty feet from a door and he walks ten feet toward it, the image on his retina doubles in size. Despite the facts of physical sensation, however, he perceives the door as having the same size at both distances.[7]

The dependency of this perception upon its entire visual context can be illustrated by describing a simple optical illusion experiment. A closed chamber one foot high, one foot wide, and thirty inches long has two peep holes in the middle of one end. Three sticks four inches long are suspended vertically eight, sixteen, and twenty-four inches from the peep holes so that their lower ends are in one plane with the holes and so that a viewer can see all three simultaneously as he peeps in. No light is admitted to the chamber, but the sticks are made visible with luminous paint. The viewer is instructed to close one eye, to look into the box, and to tell which stick is longest and by how much. He reports that the second one is half and the last one a third the size of the first. His verbal report, then, corresponds to the sizes of the images on the retina but not to the actual length of the sticks. But if a light is turned on in the chamber and the subject looks in with both eyes at once, his report will fit, or at least approximate, the external facts of size and distance.

The difference between the illusion and the 'normal' situation can be formalized in a pair of formulas like the one used to represent the hearer's perceptual classification of nouns. Let l represent the length of each of the three sticks, d the distance from the peep hole to the first stick, and x the fact that there is no way for the viewer to perceive distance or depth of field. The size of the image cast on the retina by the first stick can then be represented as l/d. The symbols l/d, $l/2d$, and $l/3d$, to the left of the arrow, thus represent an ordered set of retinal images. The symbols in the bracket at the right represent a directly corresponding set of verbal reports:

$$\begin{bmatrix} \dfrac{l}{d} \\[2ex] \dfrac{l}{2d} \\[2ex] \dfrac{l}{3d} \end{bmatrix} dx \rightarrow lx \begin{bmatrix} 1 \\[2ex] \dfrac{1}{2} \\[2ex] \dfrac{1}{3} \end{bmatrix}$$

[6] The hearer 'knows' the word is a noun in the sense that he cannot use it as a conjunction or a preposition, not in the same sense that the grammarian does.

[7] Cf. Wolfgang Koehler, *Gestalt Psychology* (New York, Liveright Publishing Company, 1947).

The difference between the two sides of the equation, obviously, is that d has been cancelled and that l has been factored out. This means that, although the viewer does not know the true size of the sticks, he reports in terms of their length, assumed or unknown. The numerals 1, 1/2 and 1/3 indicate, of course, that the relative sizes of the retinal images are reflected in the verbal report. So long as the original images occur in the context of dx, unperceived distance, there is no way to get rid of this quantified relative difference in perceived size.

To represent the 'normal' perception, we simply replace dx on the left side of the equation with an ordered set of perceived distances, pd, $2pd$, and $3pd$. That is, with the light in the chamber the viewer can perceive relative distances. The right side of the equation now shows no quantities and a constant perceived length for all three sticks.

$$
\begin{bmatrix} \dfrac{l}{d} \\[2mm] \dfrac{l}{2d} \\[2mm] \dfrac{l}{3d} \end{bmatrix}
\begin{bmatrix} pd \\[2mm] 2\,pd \\[2mm] 3\,pd \end{bmatrix}
\rightarrow pl
\begin{bmatrix} 1 \\[2mm] 1 \\[2mm] 1 \end{bmatrix}
$$

Just as our earlier formula raised the question of how the hearer classifies the word *hamburger* as a noun, this formula raises the question of how the viewer perceives distances. A specific answer to the latter is irrelevant to our main issue, but it is important to note that the two questions are quite similar. Neither the linguistic perception nor the visual one can be explained as given in simple sensory experience; both involve previous learning. Just as the psychologist interested in general perception would be obliged to explain the pd and ultimately the p itself by explaining the structural interplay of visual, tactile, and kinesthetic experience, so we must go further in analyzing linguistic contexts to answer our question.

In acquiring speech, the child must learn to associate words not only with referents but with each other and with various word endings so that they become classified — become mathematical sets and subsets — in his language. The endings and function words like the determiners, the modal auxiliaries, and the 'qualifiers' such as *very* and *quite* compose sets whose memberships are small and CLOSED whereas the 'lexical' words belong to large, open sets. These closed sets provide the basis for perceiving the lexical words as various parts of speech, for apprehending 'sequence signals' such as pronoun-antecedent relationships, and for distinguishing such syntactic functions as subjects, predicates and complements; the psychological use of these closed sets, which are deeply stamped into the nervous systems of both speaker and hearer, is analogous to the use of 'given' elements in a theorem. Moreover, some sequences of sets (e.g. $T + N + N^o$) are so basic to the grammatical system of English that it seems highly plausible to assume that the native speaker perceives the potential occurrence of certain sets (e.g. T and N^o) even in specific phrases where no member of the set is physically present. Thus, the null set $\emptyset$, which is used in generative grammars as an economical representation of contrasts between occurrence and nonoccurrence, becomes a symbol for the psychologically 'felt' emptiness of a place holder or a slot in a perceptual system. From the standpoint of the hearer, a noun might be defined as $\{x/T + x + N^o\}$, that is as any element occurring between a determiner and the element of number; either T or N^o or both, of course, could be empty.[8]

The word associate is used here in the sense given to it by Koffka, and does not, of course, refer to Thorndike's laws of frequency, recency, and contiguity. Koffka says, in effect, that if phenomena a, b and c appear once or oftener as members of a structure or a configuration, thereafter one of them occurring alone tends to recall the others.[9] Perhaps at the higher levels of cognition, the term relevant relationship would be a bit better than configuration. In any case, a relational or contextual conception of association is necessary to explain why the word *fights* is in one instance preceived as a verb and in another as a noun or why its -*s* ending is sometimes associated with singularity and sometimes with plurality. The notions of sequences of sets, of open and closed classes, and of place holders or slots seems thoroughly consistent with such a conception.

A generative grammar can be interpreted as implying a slot within slot arrangement. The formula SENT → NOM + PRED, for example, provides slots for a nominal and a predicate and the nominal in turn contains three slots for T, N and N^o. The predicate also contains several slots, which are filled by members of sets essential to sentences. A continuation of the simple generative grammar begun earlier will make several elements explicit.[10]

12. PRED → AUX + V
13. AUX → TNS (M) (*have* + EN) (*be* + ING)
14. M → *can, may, shall, will, must*
15. TNS → PRES, ED
16. $T + N + \emptyset_n + PRES + V → T + N + \emptyset_n + S_v + V$
17. $T + N + S_n + PRES + V → T + N + S_n + \emptyset_v + V$
18. $Af_v + V' → V' + Af\#$

These rules should be read as follows:

12. The predicate consists of an auxiliary and a verb. (This is, of course, a gross oversimplification. V could be expanded and subclassified greatly.)

13. The auxiliary MUST contain a tense marker and it MAY contain a modal auxiliary, *have* and a past participle marker, or *be* and a present participle marker, or any

[8] A complete generative grammar would introduce number words as extensions of the determiner and place adjectives between the determiner and the noun by transformation. Such additions would demand some amendments to the perceptual definition of nouns $\{x / T + x + N^o\}$ but would not repeal it.
[9] Kurt Koffka, *The Growth of the Mind* (New York, Harcourt, Brace and Company, 1924), p. 246.
[10] These rules are adapted from Chomsky, *op. cit.* p. 39.

combination of these so long as they occur in the sequence stated. (The parentheses mean 'This element is optional'.)

14. A modal auxiliary is any member of the closed set consisting of *can, may, shall, will*, and *must*. (*Could, might, should* and *would* are tense forms of these.)

15. Verb tense is either present or past.

16. In the context of a noun phrase whose number is singular, the present tense marker of the verb is an *s* ending.

14. In the context of a noun phrase whose number is plural, the present tense marker is the absence of an ending. (Rules 16 and 17 could have been combined to read

$$T + N \begin{bmatrix} \varnothing_n \\ S_n \end{bmatrix} \quad \text{PRES} + V \rightarrow T + N \begin{bmatrix} \varnothing_n \\ S_n \end{bmatrix} \begin{bmatrix} S_v \\ \varnothing_v \end{bmatrix} V$$

Together these rules, of course, provide for agreement between subject and predicate, except that the five forms of *be* cannot be generated. Adding these forms would introduce a complexity beyond the necessities of this paper.)

18. Verbal suffixes must be shifted to follow the verbal word elements they precede and a word boundary marker # must be inserted to terminate the shifting. (Verbal word elements are verbs, modals, *have*, and *be*; verbal suffixes are S_v, $\varnothing_v$, ED, EN, and ING. Thus a string developed by rules 1-16 would transform by Rule 18 as

(1-16) The + boy + $\varnothing_n$ + S_v + have + EN + go
(18) The + boy + $\varnothing_n$ + have + S_v # go + EN #

This then, by morphophonemic rules, would yield the sentence *The boy has gone.*)

The idea that the hearer perceives a noun as either mass or count on the basis of its determiner and grammatical number presupposes that he has already recognized the 'noun-ness' of the word in question. In utterances where either *a* or *the* is present, the definition N = { x/T + x + N°} can be invoked as an explanation. But where both T and N° are $\varnothing$, and even where only T is $\varnothing$, a difficulty appears. Words like *dust, plaster, iron, paper* and *fire* can quite readily occur as either nouns or as verbs. How does the hearer know which is which?

The set of tense signals (TNS), which includes S_v, $\varnothing_v$, and ED, is a crucial cue for grasping the grammatical structure of sentences. Its primary function is to signal predication; that is, it distinguishes predicates from other verbal structures. Once the hearer has perceived the predicate signal, he has a basis for identifying other sentence components. However, the physical identify of $\varnothing_n$ and S_n with $\varnothing_v$ and S_v, as well as the identity of ED with EN for regular verbs, poses a serious problem.[11]

---

[11] This refers to likeness and difference of past tense and past participle forms. Morphophonemically:
walk + ED →/wakt/ (walked), walk + EN →/wakt/ (walked)
freeze + ED → /frowz/ (froze), freeze + EN →/frowzən/ (frozen)
sing + ED →/sæŋ/ (sang) sing, + EN →/ sɔŋ/sung

Our which-is-which question is still here; some way must be found to account for the perception of tense.

Some of the variants of the tense signals are unambiguous and 'self-sufficient', but others seem to depend partly on other signals. The self-sufficient are irregular forms that cannot be 'something else'. These include the finite forms of be (*am, is, are, was,* and *were*), past tense forms that differ from past participles (like *hid, froze,* and *sang*), a small handful of present tense verbs (*says, does, has*), and the modal auxiliaries. All of these have the signalling value of function words because they are members of closed sets or of closed subsets of open sets. Obviously, be and the modals belong to sets that admit no new members, and although the class of verbs is open, the subclass of IRREGULAR verbs is rigidly closed.

Association of members of closed sets with each other also appears important in the perception of tense (TNS) and hence of predication. Apparently S_v and $\varnothing_v$ tend to call up ED. Thus the strings

> \# The + place + $\varnothing_n$ + bore + S_v \# the + man + $\varnothing_n$ \#
> \# The + place + S_n + bore + $\varnothing_n$ \# the + man + $\varnothing_n$ \#

suggest the strings

> \# The + place + $\varnothing_n$ + bore + ED \# the + man + $\varnothing_n$ \#
> \# The + place + S_n + bore + ED \# the + man + $\varnothing_n$ \#

But the strings

> *\# The + place + ED \# bore + S_v \# the + man + $\varnothing_n$ \#
> *\# The + place + ED \# bore + $\varnothing_v$ \# the + man + $\varnothing_n$ \#

are *not* suggested because ED is not a member of the set N^o. Set membership, then helps to classify the words *place* and *bore*, either of which could be either a noun or a verb given different contexts.

Once the hearer has grasped the tense signal in an utterance like either of the following test frames, such elements as *mush gold, junk,* and *plaster* — or even nonsense syllables like *zoosh* and *brife* — are perceived as nominals because of their proximity to the signal and its carrier.

> _____ is useful
> _____ froze on the fingers

That is, Rule 1 and rules 12-18 of our simplified generative grammar would give us the strings:

> NOM + be + S\# useful[12]
> NOM + freeze + ED\# on + the + finger + S_n

---

[12]   Be + S_v →/iz/ (*is*)

If the hearer shares such a grammar with the speaker, as assumed earlier, then elements actually present in the utterance tell him this much about its structure, but he must deduce the specific content of the nominal. There are several things it *cannot* be: a pronoun, a count noun, or a plural noun. It *could* be either a proper noun or a mass noun; but to know which it actually is the hearer must refer to his intuitive grammar. If NOM → ∅ + N_{mass} + ∅$_n$, then the following strings are possible:

the   + N_{mass} + ∅$_n$ (the *junk*)
some + N_{mass} + ∅$_n$ (some *junk*)
some + of + the + N_{mass} + ∅$_n$ (some of the *junk*)

But if the word in question is a proper noun, none of these structures are admissible. He may use previous experience with the word: is it more likely to occur as a member of this class or of that? But *Gold* is a surname and any of the others COULD be nicknames. He simply selects the most probable, without completely rejecting the other, and awaits confirming evidence in ensuing linguistic structures.

Generative grammar suggests a perceptual definition of verb similar to the definition of noun given earlier: V = {x|AUX + x}.[13] This formulation has several interesting properties. Since the auxiliary (AUX) includes the affixes S_v, ED, EN, and ING, the formula includes the morphological criteria used to define verb by Trager and Smith.[14] But it also includes the modal auxiliaries and *have* and *be* as function words signalling verbal structures. In addition, it excludes the modals from the class of verbs, because of their syntactic position which in turn makes participial endings impossible for them. The dependence of EN and ING upon *have* and *be* in basic, simple sentences also gives insight (which cannot be exploited here) into how participles not in predications are perceived and understood.

The definition has some striking empirical correlates. Not even the most literate adult knows all of the verbs in the English language. Yet if he hears one he has never heard before — say in the present tense with a singular subject — he is automatically able to use it with a plural subject, as a base form, or as a present or a past participle and in appropriate sequence with the auxiliary words. To do this, he does not even have to know what the word means. The adult, of course, simply adds the regular endings, for he has already learned all of the irregular forms of his dialect.

Preschool children exhibit similar behavior, but with one important difference. Because they have not mastered all of the irregular forms, they make false analogies extending regular endings to verbs that are irregular in adult speech: *eated* instead of *ate*. Or they use previously learned irregularities in the wrong places: *brang* instead of

---

[13]   Such 'definitions' have, properly speaking, no place in a generative grammar. Chomsky and his co-workers do not appear to be interested in definitions of this kind, but these formulations do appear useful as part of a system for explaining how sentences are understood.
[14]   George L. Trager and Henry Lee Smith Jr., *An Outline of English Structure* (Norman, Okla., Battenburg Press, 1951), pp. 60-65.

brought. The very existence of these false analogies has long been recognized as evidence that the child has made a valid intuitive inference about the structure of his language and that he is able to use it deductively in framing new sentences.

One further theoretical idea will be useful as a basis for pedagogical application. Some sentences might quite appropriately be called *pro-sentences* because they relate to antecedent sentences much as pronouns relate to nouns. The second sentence of this paragraph, for example, might be antecedent to *Some might*. Notice the relationship of *b* and *c* to *a*:

1. (a) The boy plays well.   (b) He does.   (c) Does he?
2. (a) The boy can play well.   (b) He can.   (c) Can he?
3. (a) The boy has played well. (b) He has.   (c) Has he?
4. (a) The boy is playing well. (b) He is.   (c) Is he?

A nominative case pronoun replaces the nominal and a *pro-verb* replaces the predicate in each instance; that is, both the subject and the predicate of the pro-sentence have antecedents, the subject and the predicate of the original sentence.[15] It is not necessary, of course, that both a pronoun and a pro-verb be used. Certain elliptical sentences are part of the same relationship:

1. (d) He plays well   (e) The boy does.
2. (d) He can play well.   (e) The boy can.
3. (d) He has played well.   (e) The boy has.
4. (d) He is playing well.   (e) The boy is.

The relation of the basic sentence to pro-sentences like *b*, *d*, and *e* can be expressed by a context sensitive rule:

$$NOM_1 \begin{bmatrix} TNS + V_1 + X_1 \\ TNS + M + X_2 \\ TNS + have + X_2 \\ TNS + be + X_2 \end{bmatrix}, \quad NOM_1 \begin{bmatrix} TNS + V_1 + X_1 \\ TNS + M + X_2 \\ TNS + have + X_2 \\ TNS + be + X_2 \end{bmatrix}$$

$$NOM_1 \begin{bmatrix} TNS + V_1 + X_1 \\ TNS + M + X_2 \\ TNS + have + X_2 \\ TNS + be + X_2 \end{bmatrix}, \quad \begin{Bmatrix} NOM_1 \\ PRON \end{Bmatrix} \begin{bmatrix} TNS \begin{Bmatrix} V_1 + X_1 \\ do \end{Bmatrix} \\ TNS + M (X_2) \\ TNS + have + (X_2) \\ TNS + be (X_2) \end{bmatrix}$$

The X's simply stand for 'whatever follows', and the subscripts indicate identity between two elements such that the second in each line of the formula indicates a necessary condition for possible deletion.

---

[15] The elements called pro-verbs here are the same parts of the auxiliary sequence that are manipulated to form interrogatives, negatives and other important predicate variations. See Chomsky, *op. cit.*, pp. 60-72.

The braces {NOM, PRON} and {TNS + V . . . , TNS + DO} indicate a possible choice, but only between the enclosed items. The parentheses, as elsewhere in generative grammars, mean that what is enclosed may be omitted, here providing for the optional dropping of everything but the pro-verb. Notice also the necessity of adding *do* when the verb and its adjuncts are dropped from a pro-sentence based on predicates of the form TNS + V. The rule is stated in this form in an attempt to explain the contextual occurrence of such structures in conversation and in continuing discourse. The fact that the hearer, as he takes the role of the speaker, responds with pro-sentences that may preserve either the complete subject or the complete predicate is evidence that he knows, intuitively, what these structures are; this is as valid for a child as for an adult. Such automatic responses also indicate that the speaker is able to anticipate the same reduced structures when he is simply listening. This, then, makes it appear quite likely that for pro-sentences the process of tracing utterances back to the grammar may approximate a simple inversion of the relevant portions of the synthesis system.

IV

Does the demand that theory and practice be complementary mean that pedagogical theory must be derived from practical situations? Apparently, many educational leaders and researchers wrongheadedly believe so. A theory is an intellectual construct. True, the motivation for creating one may lie in a practical necessity. Granted, one untested in practice may be worthless. But to attempt the construction of a theory primarily from the empirical analysis or experimental comparison of teaching procedures is largely a waste of time. To be sure, observation and experimentation can be extremely useful, but unless they follow a careful theoretical formulation of what to look for or what to test, they are likely to be nothing more than statistical busy-work. To some readers, the points of this sermon may seem too obvious for words, but until sin no longer exists in the world, the pulpit will not be silent. The designs of many statistically sophisticated doctoral dissertations reflect an astounding pedagogical naïveté.

A simple and straightforward application of the fragmentary psycholinguistic system developed here provides an example of a think-first-and-experiment-later approach to educational theory. The theory is not an after-the-fact explanation of what happens in learning but amounts to a way of designing learning tasks with readily predictable responses.

The procedure for teaching parts of speech, which is suitable for either oral or pencil-and-paper exercises, is surprisingly simple. Working orally, the teacher might say "In the sentence *The girls talk about everything*, the word talk is a verb. Now notice that I can use *talk* in two other ways. I can say *Fred talks too fast* and I can say *He isn't talking today*. All right now, what have I done to the word talk in these sentences?"

The pupil gives the obvious answer — that the words have added *s* and *ing* — and the teacher responds by characterizing verbs as words that can add these two endings. Between six and ten more sentences, all with present tense forms or present participles, are then given to make sure that the concept has been grasped. The finite forms of *be* are necessary in some of the sentences and modal auxiliaries may be used in some of them, but none of these should be analyzed in any way. If the teacher leaves them alone, so does the child — which is exactly what the theory would predict.

The next stage starts with a sentence whose verb is a regular verb in the past tense: *The boys waited an hour*. No hint is given — only the question, "What is the verb?" In a few seconds, the answer comes back, "I think it must be *waited* because I can say *wait, waits* and *waiting*." Again a few additional sentences are given.

Next, the past tense forms of irregular verbs are attacked in the same manner. The first sentence, which might be *The worms ate the apple*, usually causes the pupil to pause, but the answer almost invariably comes, "I think it must be *ate*, because *ate* is the same thing as *eated*, only you can't say *eated*, and you can say *eat, eats, eating*." A few more sentences containing irregular past tense forms are given, and then the child is taught an analytic device based on morphophonemics: *walk* + ED is *walked*, *sing* + ED is *sang*, etc. Past participles can then be taught in exactly the same way.

The exercises for verbs and a similar one for nouns were based on Trager and Smith's morphological definitions: verbs are words that add the morphemes S_v, ED, EN, and ING, and nouns are words that add the plural morpheme S_n and a possessive morpheme 'S. So long as only count nouns are used, the pupil moves along smoothly, but mass nouns defy the definition. On first contact with the sentence *The crows ate the corn*, the child identifies *corn* as a noun but then quickly rejects it. Why? Almost certainly, the identification is based on his intuitive recognition that it can occur in contexts identical to those for words he has already learned to call nouns. The rejection is a logical consequence of the definition. The lessons with verbs worked, probably because the set of verb endings is an effective cue for the total verb and auxiliary system, even though the definition was incomplete; intuition and logic were in harmony. The lessons with nouns were only partly successful because the endings supplied cues only to a particular subsystem of the whole; intuition and logic were in discord. The theory, not the child, was wrong.

This practical failure with nouns is in itself an interesting commentary on the relation of theory to practice. The failure was merely a check against continuing with an inadequate theory; it provided little insight into how to construct an adequate one. Intuitively, the teacher might want to include *corn*, *sand* and similar words in the class of nouns, but something went wrong. Or did it? Was the teacher's intuition wrong? If not, what did go wrong? Why? How can the method be corrected? Pure empiricism begets only trial and error. Only a theory — an intellectual construct — will answer these crucial questions.

The relation of sentence to pro-sentence is the basis of a simple method for teaching complete subject and complete predicate. It begins with an exercise consisting of twelve sentences with verbs in either the simple present or simple past tense. The pupil is given directions first to put parentheses around the part of the sentence that can be replaced by *he, she, it, we* or *they* and to write the substitute word above it, and then to put a second set of parentheses around the part of the sentence that can be replaced by *do, does,* or *did* and again to indicate which of the substitute words is appropriate:

She	*did*
(The old woman)	(disappeared yesterday.)
They	*do*
(Green apples)	(always taste sour.)
It	*does*
(The river)	(runs slowly there.)

The next exercise introduces the terms *subject* and *predicate*, which are used in giving all subsequent directions. Two additional exercises bring in *be* as a 'main verb' and *have, be,* and the modals as auxiliaries:

He	*was*
(Mr. Johnson)	(was very fair about it.)
They	*were*
(The trees)	(were singing in the wind.)
They	*can*
(Some people)	(can spend a lot of money.)
It	*had*
(A large boulder)	(had blocked the road.)

All of this thorizing may appear to be like laboring mountainously to bring forth a very small mouse. The sheer efficiency of the method, however, dispells this criticism. In workshop demonstrations, first- and second-grade children need approximately ten minutes to learn the concepts of both noun and verb. It takes about forty-five minutes for subject and predicate.[16] Several of my students have successfully adapted the method for use in their junior high classrooms. And one reports using the parts of speech exercises orally as a bed-time game with her five-year-old daughter — who had not yet been taught to read. This compares favorably with the blood, sweat and busy-work of more conventional approaches.

Teaching a grammatical nomenclature is, of course, a small thing in the perspective of the English teacher who is responsible for teaching pupils to become literate. Despite a lack of supporting evidence, however, many teachers believe that a grammatical vocabulary is useful or even necessary if they are to communicate with their pupils about matters of rhetoric. If there existed a set of terms that referred to the

---

[16] The first guinea pig for these demonstrations was my oldest daughter who was then six years and seven months old.

process of sentence and paragraph building, and if these terms related precisely to the grammatical system built into the pupil's nervous system, perhaps teachers could devise simple, direct, and effective means of teaching writing; perhaps they could dispell the frustrating matter of fact that no one has ever demonstrated a relationship between knowing grammar and being able to write.[17] The relation of sentence to pro-sentence and other known transformational relationships seem to prophesy a time in the near future when linguistics will break the sentence barrier and relate grammar to discourse. The implication for rhetoric is obvious. Educational research must watch these developments closely if we are to realize the ultimate goal of the theory here proposed: to find a way of using the linguistic resources within the child as a basis for making him literate.

WAYNE STATE UNIVERSITY

---

[17] One recent study, Donald R. Bateman and Frank J. Zidonis, *The Effect of a Knowledge of Generative Grammar upon the Growth of Language Complexity* (Columbus, Ohio, The Ohio State University Research Foundation, 1964), is an exception to this pessimistic fact.

ZELL SORELLE

SEGMENTAL PHONOLOGY OF TEXAS
PANHANDLE SPEECH

The designations of General American, Southern and Eastern for the great English speech regions of North America are common to the phonetic literature of the past half-century;[1] however, the tremendous research activity within the framework of the *Linguistic Atlas of the United States and Canada* is subjecting these regions to continuous revision. As the results are added together and compared, the structures are revised from within and on the periphery; there seems to be a reconstruction of the picture of American language areas. Wise states that it is far easier to name speech regions than to define the boundaries that separate them.[2]

The Eastern States occupy a position of great importance for the history of American pronunciation. Evidence from the Atlantic field records compiled by Hans Kurath has led to the recognition of three speech areas located on the eastern seaboard; these speech areas were designated as Northern, Midland and Southern.

It is here that the regional and local types of American English were developed during the Colonial Period. After the Revolution these types of English were carried westward and blended into new regional varieties.[3]

These regional types of American English spread inland as the settlements expanded up the rivers, over the mountains and across the plains, and they were blended anew when settlers from different colonies mingled on the frontier. The speech of these later settlement areas is derived from the speech of the earlier settlements on the Atlantic slope.[4]

New major dialect areas and sub-areas are now being established with a greater degree of specificity. Regional projects are using similar procedures and are collecting the same kinds of evidence; therefore, the results can be added together and compared.

The fact that migrant groups from the three great speech areas, Northern, Midland and Southern as defined by Kurath, have carried dialects along their migratory

[1] Claude Merton Wise, *Applied Phonetics* (Englewood Cliffs, N. J. Prentice-Hall, Inc., 1957), p. 3.
[2] *Ibid.*, p. 172.
[3] Hans Kurath, *A Word Geography of the Eastern United States* (Ann Arbor, Michigan, University of Michigan Press, 1949), p. vi.
[4] *Ibid.* p. 1.

routes has already been verified by research. This westward movement has established a recognized speech area at the eastern edge of Texas. The speech of this area in Texas has been identified as South Midland and is located approximately 500 miles to the southeast of the area which was investigated for this study on Panhandle speech.

In searching for historical explanations for a speech area the general history of the region must be understood. The region's economic and cultural history, the geographical features and the information relevant to the settlement of an area are requisites for depth of understanding. The original settlement, the 'landtaking', is without doubt the most important factor in the genesis of dialect regions.[5]

In physical features, Texas can best be described as the 'meeting place'. Within the boundaries of Texas four great physiographic provinces of the North American Continent come together to give the state a wide variety of surface aspects.

Texas is the "meeting place" of: (1) the Great Coastal Forested Plain; (2) the Great Western Lower Plain; (3) the Rocky Mountain region; (4) the Great Western High Plains.[6]

The Panhandle is located in the Great Western High Plains area. The Panhandle is a large, almost square tract of land appended to the main area of the state at the thirty fourth degree, forty minute parallel. The appended area resembles the 'handle of a pan', and from this analogy came the name Panhandle. This area is often called the Staked Plains or the Spanish equivalent, Llano Estacado. The Spanish explorers penetrated the High Plains; however, historians say that few, if any, crossed the Plains, and that many of them met there "such discouragement and failure as to lead them to retrace their steps the way they came".[7] And it is the relationship of the Coronado Expedition in 1540 that historians have linked with the Spanish name, Llano Estacado. Some think that it came from the fact that the Coronado Expedition while crossing the trackless sea of grass, staked its route so that it would be a guide on the return trip.

Except for the nomadic Indian tribes and the wandering herds of buffalos, the trackless sea of grass remains undisturbed from the time of Coronado until 1870 when the various syndicates came into the area and bought most of the land for their cattle raising empires. These huge cattle empires were instrumental in delaying the settlement of the Panhandle until approximately sixty years ago. To qualify this statement the following two explanations are relevant. The XIT Ranch extended north and south through ten counties of the Panhandle at one time; the Matador Ranch encompassed almost a million acres within its barbed wire fences.

---

[5] Hans Kurath, *Handbook of the Linguistic Geography of New England* (Providence, Rhode Island, Brown University, 1939), p. IX.
[6] Stuart Malcolm McGregor (Ed.), *Texas Almanac* (Dallas, Texas, A. H. Belo Corporation, 1961-1962), p. 24.
[7] Walter Prescott Webb and H. Bailey Carroll, *The Handbook of Texas* (Austin, The Texas State Historical Association of 1952), p. 330.

The report of the United States census in 1880 is pertinent in that it showed that there were only 1,521[8] people in the 20,000 square mile area and one-third of these people lived at an army fort.

The Industrial Revolution was inevitable at the turn of the century. It was the effect of the railroads that brought about a new era. The greatest single decade of railroad building was in 1878-1888, and the bulk of the construction was on the Western Plains.[9] By 1900 four railway companies had built lines over the great, flat, treeless area.

The railway companies were the first boosters of settlement, because the companies had secured large land grants as compensation. Sometimes these companies received as high as forty sections of land for the construction of one mile of railroad.

Through the joint promotion of the railway companies, the land companies and a few individuals, the tide of home seekers was in movement in 1900; by 1906 it was in full swing and by 1910 the Panhandle was settled. One historian reports that the settlement of the Panhandle "gave it an epic growth in the annals of Texas history all its own, and to which no other part of Texas history has had anything to compare".[10] In a brief span of ten years there was a transition from open cattle grazing to farming and ranching. In other parts of the nation a similar transition would require a period of two hundred or even two hundred fifty years.[11] It is evident that this phonological study is concerned with a newly settled area.

Much of Texas was settled by large migrant groups, many of whom came from central and southern mountain areas, many from the central states and many from the 'deep' South.[12] The source of 'landtakers' for the Pandhandle area is in accord with the preceding statement made by Wise. Many of the settlers in the Panhandle came from the already settled parts of south and east Texas, and these particular settlers were originally from the 'deep south'. The Pandhandle was settled in a large measure by people from Denton, Grayson, Jack, Bell, Brown, Mills and Lampasas Counties in Texas.[13]

The questionnaire used in the study of Panhandle speech was the work sheet compiled by Elmer Bagby Atwood. Atwood made modifications, revisions and adaptations of the worksheet of the *Linguistic Atlas of the United States and Canada* in order to allow for regional peculiarities in the West Texas area; thus, it was appropriate and applicable for a phonological study of the Panhandle region.

Ten first generation informants were carefully chosen. These informants were sixty

[8] The Eleventh Census: 1890 (Washington, D. C., Government Printing Office, 1892), pp. 386-402.
[9] Robert E. Riegel, *America Moves West* (New York, Henry Holt and Company, 1947), p. 549.
[10] Carl Frederick Kranzel, *The Great Plains in Transition* (Norman, University of Oklahoma Press, 1955), p. 194.
[11] *Ibid.*, p. 137.
[12] Wise, *op. cit.*, p. 180.
[13] John McCarthy, "Lift Me Up and Let Me Stand by Faith on Heaven's Table Land", *Amarillo News and Globe Times*, August 14, 1938, Volume 13, Number 33, p. 1.

years of age or older, and none had received formal schooling outside of the Panhandle area. Each interview was tape recorded and transcriptions were made at a later date, employing the International Phonetic Alphabet.

In preparing this initial research of the phonology of Panhandle speech the hypothesis was that the differences would be relatively small. This proved to be an accurate assumption. The efficacy of Bloomfield's theory that "in countries over which a speech-community has recently spread and settled, the local differences are relatively small"[14] was consistent.

LINGUISTIC ANALYSIS

In studying a dialect the treatment of /r/ in American speech is recognized as one of the most important criteria in the classification of dialects. The presence or absence of the sound provides one of the most definite means of distinguishing a speech area.

There is a distinct presence of the r-sound in Panhandle speech. The consonantal /r/ is found in all positions. There was one r-less example which was of exceptional interest for it concerned the pronunciation of *barbed wire*, the one commodity which changed the topography of the Panhandle. Nine of the informants pronounced *barbed wire* [bɑ : b wɑ : r].

It was noted that in some words the consonantal /r/ was replaced with a centering diphthong in such words as *barn* [bɑ·ɚn] and *corn* [kɔ·ɚn].

The stressed vocalic /ɚ/ as in *bird*, the unstressed vocalic /ɚ/ as in *father* and the post vocalic /r/ as in *barb* are all features of Panhandle speech showing the pronounced tendency towards the retroflex *r*; this particular feature is characteristic of Midland speech. Gray and Wise state that the "r-sounds are not yet acclimated in the most typical Southern speech".[15]

Midland features which have the same configurations of distinctive phonemic features as the Panhandle are the following:

(1) the use of /ə/ in the unstressed position as in *without* [wəðaʊt], *furniture* [fɚnətʃɚ].

(2) the vowel murmur is used in the suffixes *as, ess, en* as in such words as *Dallas* [dæləs], *careless* [kærləs], *chicken* [tʃɪkən].

(3) the unstressed ending is used in the pronunciation of the days of the week as *Monday* [mʌndɪ], *Tuesday* [tjuzdɪ].

(4) The [ɔ] is used predominantly in stressed syllables spelled with *o* followed by *r* plus a vowel. Examples are: *Florida* [flɔrədə], *orange* [ɔrəndʒ].

(5) the low back vowel /ɑ/ is used in *wash* [wɑʃ], *water* [wɑtɚ], *what* [hwɑt], *watch* [wɑtʃ].

---

[14] Leonard Bloomfield, *Language* (New York, Henry Holt and Company, 1933), p. 47.
[15] Giles Wilkerson Gray and Claude Merton Wise, *The Bases of Speech* (New York, Harper & Row, Publishers, 1959), p. 285.

Southern speech features which have the same configuration of distinctive phonemic features as the Panhandle are the following:

(1) the predominance of /ju/ in *due, new, Tuesday*.[16]

(2) the predominance of /æ/ in *care, chair*.

(3) The near monophthongal variety of /aɪ/ occurring finally and before voiced consonants as in *five, fire, nine*.

(4) the lingua-palatal glide /j/ preceding the diphthong /aʊ/ whose initial sound is raised and fronted as in the word *cow*. Raven I. McDavid states that the "raising and fronting of this /aʊ/ diphthong has a high occurrence in South and South Midland speech."[17]

(5) differentiation of *horse* and *hoarse*; *morning* and *mourning* [hɔrs-hors] [mɔrnɪŋ-mornɪŋ].

(6) the off-glide diphthongal pronunciation of *crib, lid, well*, [krɪᵊb, lɪᵊd, wɛᵊl].

(7) the predominance of /ʌ/ in *soot*.

(8) the predominance of /u/ in *roots, roof*.

Midland speech and Southern speech which have the same configuration of distinctive phonemic features as Panhandle speech are as follows:

(1) /æ/ is used in so-called 'broad - *a*' words as *bath, calf, path*.

(2) /ɔ/ is used in the *og* words as *dog, frog, log*.

(3) /ɛ/ is used in *merry*.

(4) /hw/ the voiceless bilabial glide is strongly aspirated in *what, wheelbarrow, whip, whetrock*.

(5) /u/ is used after /s/ in *suit*.

In conclusion it was found that in Panhandle speech there are (1) five Midland speech features which are the same as distinctive features of the Panhandle; (2) eight Southern speech features which are the same as distinctive features of the Panhandle; (3) five Midland and Southern features in common which are the same as distinctive features of the Panhandle.

The evidence and conclusions from this study indicate that the Texas Panhandle lies in the path of a conjectured movement of South Midland speech. One must be influenced by the weight of evidence which established the South Midland speech area along eastern Texas.[18] The hypothesis has been that there is a South Midland band running westward and northwestward from that established point in east Texas; this band is bounded on the north by the Red River and on the south by the Sabine River.[19]

WEST TEXAS STATE UNIVERSITY

---

[16] Kurath and McDavid, *op. cit.*, p. 257.

[17] Ibid., p. 254.

[18] Allen, *op. cit.*, p. 215.

[19] Albert Donald George, "Some Louisiana Isoglosses, Based on the Workbooks of the Louisiana Dialect Atlas", unpublished master's thesis (Louisiana State University, Baton Rouge, Louisiana, 1951), p. 143.

RAVEN I. McDAVID, JR.

ON A HIERARCHY OF VALUES: THE CLINICIAN
AND THE DIALECTOLOGIST[1]

Of all the feuds currently racking the realm of Academe, few are more ancient, more bitter, or more pointless than the one which pits the member of the speech department against his colleagues in English and linguistics. What he says in his behalf, I do not know; what they say in turn is an old story. The English scholar asserts that the work of the speech teacher is shallow and superficial; the linguist, that it ignores the systematic nature of language and the well-attested variety of standard American English. There is of course some truth in these charges; resorting to anecdote, I can recall my own traumata (1) harassment in my first teaching experience by an ex-four-star-general turned college president, whose prescriptions toward good "ee-nunt-see-ay-shee-awn" derived from classes in elocution given at West Point, in the 1890s, by a broken-down actor; (2) ridicule from the head of a Midwestern speech department because I pronounced the noun *produce* with the vowel /o/, like all cultivated South Carolinians of my own and my father's generation. Even more distressing was the experience of a distinguished anthropologist I know. A native speaker of Cherokee but early acquiring a fluent command of Standard Oklahoma English, on moving to Detroit in his early teens found himself consigned to a class in 'corrective speech'. As eyes met eyes on the first day of classes, it was revealed that everyone enrolled was from Oklahoma, Missouri, Kentucky, West Virginia or Tennessee, and had been enrolled because the speech clinic was definitely hostile to South Midland speech. It became a point of honor among these young maquisards to sabotage the program; twenty years after moving north, my Cherokee friend is more belligerently Oklahoman in his speech habits than he was when he first arrived in Detroit.[2]

But the record of English teachers and even of linguists is far from spotless when it comes to objective evaluation of the evidence. Three years ago, after a long talk

[1] This paper was originally presented at a symposium on linguistics, at the meeting of the American and Hearing Association, Cincinnati, 1957.
[2] My own experience has had a happier ending—or at least a different one. Five years ago my sister, who still lives in South Carolina, informed me, in a telephone conversation, that I talked "just like a Yankee". Though I dare say few Yankees would agree with her, her remark suggests that a degree of assimilation is normal for those whose activities depend on interaction with people form other dialect regions.

and a longer discussion, an active member of the Hammond (Ind.) Council of Teachers of English was not yet convinced that — using inflection, the same criterion by which we establish tenses in Latin and Greek — we can find only two tenses in the English verb. Eight years ago one of the most belligerent hard-scientific linguists displayed his ignorance of American dialects by proclaiming that "nobody says /taˈmætəz/" — a pronunciation very common in the Northern dialect region, and not unknown elsewhere.[3] The four years of 'agonizing deappraisal' of the Merriam *Third New International* (to borrow a dash of Sleddoric) have revealed a distressing ignorance — of linguistics in general, of the history and structure and variety of the English language, and of the tradition of English and American lexicography — both among the illuminati of our English departments and among their disciples who staff our public prints. Yet among the irresponsible and repetitive assaults on the *Third* — and I have read more than my share—I have encountered none emanating from a speech department; the *QJS* symposium (Dec. 1962) presented a generally favorable verdict, from a variety of viewpoints. Even more important is the long tradition of distinguished work by such scholars as Arthur Bronstein, Douglas Chrétien, Lee Hultzén, C. K. Thomas and C. M. Wise. In short, in interdisciplinary communication there is no reason why a linguist or a literary scholar should adopt a patronizing attitude toward his colleagues in speech. That contributions can come from any discipline was particularly clear at the Carmel Conference on the Nomenclature of Communicative Disorders (January 1964), sponsored by the Rehabilitation Codes. Linguists, therapists, anatomists, neurologists, psychologists and others collaborated amicably in the interest of a common objective, and each group learned something from all the others.

A similar common objective we can find in the proper attention to the language problems of the children in a metropolitan school system.[4] Shared by all schoolchildren are needs for fluent and effective use of the spoken idiom, for early and efficient acquisition of the other skills of reading and writing, for broadening and strengthening the command of these skills through a variety of experiences, for opportunity to develop the creative use of these skills in whatever direction a child's abilities and interests may lead him.[5] Perhaps no school system has an adequate supply of good teachers and no publisher an adequate range of texts to satisfy these needs for the child of 'normal intelligence' (whatever that is). For the children below and above that range — and in the American setting, particularly for the latter — the same criticism can be made. But even if we further complicate the problem by adding the differences in temperament and interest that any parent of more than one child is

[3] See Hans Kurath and Raven I. McDavid, Jr., *The Pronunciation of English in the Atlantic States* (Ann Arbor, University of Michigan Press), 1961, §5.8, Map 106.
[4] For a discussion of some of the problems, see the report of the 1964 Conference on Social Dialects and Urban Education (Bloomington, Ind., Aug. 3-5), published by the National Council of Teachers of English.
[5] Creativity, of course, is not restricted to the belletristic disciplines, but may be found in the sciences and in technology as well.

well aware of, these groups do not constitute special problems for linguists or therapists so long as the children have no marked physical or neurological handicaps and come from a relatively homogeneous local background, lower-middle-class or better. Such a background may still prevail in some Middle Western small towns or in some of the more stable suburbs; such a background is apparently that for which most of our school readers have been designed; in such a situation there is now a chance that the physically or psychologically handicapped child will have at least early and intelligent diagnosis and probably some kind of indicated treatment — without the school having to participate overtly.

But our urban schools — as any newspaper can tell us — are different. Stability is less normal than change. People move frequently, even several times in a school year. Despite the tailing off of immigration, there are still large areas where some other language than English is the usual vehicle of communication. Despite our well-publicized notions of democracy, we find stark poverty and social deprivation, as the least skilled find themselves ever less employable in the age of automation. From smaller cities and from rural areas in all parts of the country, newcomers keep arriving, to join those hardly assimilated. The urban classroom is likely to present a bewildering variety of idiolects, with which even the best traditional teacher will have difficulty; since the schools in difficult neighborhoods have a disproportionate number of new and inexperienced teachers, the difficulties are enhanced. The interests of the children, the school program and the community all demand at least some program of diagnosis, and for many a program of treatment.

Here is needed the same kind of cooperation that we found at the Carmel conference, with the realization that no one talent is all-sufficient but that a variety of theoretical disciplines and practical skills must be utilized. The speech therapist and the teacher of remedial English will need to cooperate with the anatomist, the neurologist, the clinical psychologist, the structural linguist, the general dialectologist, the specialist in local dialects, and no doubt others. It is not necessary that every one of these should be present in the clinic all the time; but his findings should be in the hands of the clinicians, and he should be accessible if needed.

Let us sketch a variety of situations, and see what the linguist might have to offer.

In certain situations he would seem to be of little use — in those where the speech problem arises from a clear physical impairment like a cleft palate. He would be of as little service in problems arising from damage to the nervous system, though in marginal cases he might be able to say whether there was any chance of the observed phenomena falling within the probable variations among speakers of the language.

With psychological problems the linguist has more concern, as Pittenger, Hockett and Danehy have already shown.[6] Many apparent personal idiosyncrasies — hesita-

---

[6] R. E. Pittenger, C. F. Hockett and J. J. Danehy, *The First Five Minutes: A Sample of Microscopic Interview Analysis* (Ithaca, N. Y., The Martineau Press, 1960). The more detailed *The Natural History of an Interview*, under the general editorship of Norman A. McQuown, is yet to appear.

tions, stutters, distortions of intonation contours — signal some kind of psychic disturbance. The treatment is often outside the province of linguistics, or that of usual speech therapy. In other situations the gross speech disturbance and its psychological implications may be but outward and visible signs of inner linguistic conflict, between the home language or dialect and that of the neighborhood or of the school. Here the linguist can certainly facilitate the diagnosis, and even suggest directions for the treatment.

With the child of foreign-language background, real or suspected, especially one living in a foreign-language neighborhood, the structural linguist can sort out the problems through a comparison of linguistic systems. English differs from most of its Indo-European contemporaries in having contrasts of *beet* and *bit*, *bait* and *bet*, *pool* and *pull*, *cot* and *cut* and *cat*, as well as in other phonetic details. It differs from Japanese, Korean and many of the Sino-Tibetan languages in having such contrasts as between *red* and *led*, *berry* and *belly*. It differs from Burmese in having a variety of final consonants, let alone complicated clusters. It differs from most other languages in having three pairs of spirants with slight differences in the points of articulation: /f, v; θ, ð; s, z/. In many parts of the grammatical system analogous differences are found: the English use of the articles is troublesome even for speakers of languages that have similar preposed definite and indefinite articles — let alone those where articles are postposed or lacking. Even the most sophisticated Dane or Czech or Lithuanian finds the English articles a problem. The recent research in contrastive linguistics, and the postwar development of new texts for teaching English as a second language provide approaches to these problems, though there is still little material for teaching English in early grades to speakers of other languages. The linguist can help in developing these materials, but he must defer, where necessary, to the pedagogical situation.

In the same way, a structural linguist familiar with American dialects can be useful in both diagnosis and treatment of those students who speak a variety of English markedly different from the local middle-class standard. There is a great deal of evidence in print — though much of it is less accessible than we should like — on the socially significant variations in the pronunciation, grammar and even vocabulary of American English.[7] Research in progress is further specifying these differences, particularly for the larger metropolitan areas, and summaries in a form useful for the classroom teacher should soon be available. Some of the evidence may, at first sight,

---

[7] For bibliography, the most convenient source is H. L. Mencken, *The American Language*, one volume abridged edition (New York, Alfred A. Knopf, 1963). Summaries of evidence are in Kurath and R. I. McDavid, *The Pronunciation of English in the Atlantic States*; E. Bagby Atwood, *A Survey of Verb Forms in The Eastern United States* (Ann Arbor, University of Michigan Press, 1953); Kurath, *A Word Geography of the Eastern United States* (Ann Arbor, University of Michigan Press, 1949); Atwood, *The Regional Vocabulary of Texas* (Austin, The University of Texas Press, 1962); Virginia McDavid, *Verb Forms in the North-Central States and Upper Midwest* (diss., microfilm, University of Minnesota, 1956). A broadgauge summary appears in Chapter 9 of W. N. Francis, *The Structure of American English* (New York, The Ronald Press Co., 1958).

be surprising: for instance, among Caucasians native to the Chicago metropolitan areas there are almost no significant distinctions in pronunciation between educated and uneducated speakers,[8] and even grammatical distinctions are relatively few. On the other hand, there are very sharp social distinctions — both in pronunciation and in grammar — in the Southern states, not only in the plantation area (Southern proper) but in the upland (South Midland) speech area as well. Consequently as Southern Negroes and Appalachian whites crowd into Northern cities in search of better jobs, and congregate — like all new arrivals — in segregated communities, they bring with them social dialects that create serious problems in the school systems. Not only do these dialects have a phonological base sharply different from that of Northern urban middle-class speech; but there is a far wider social gap between these dialects and standard Southern varieties than one finds between educated and un-educated local speech in any Northern community. The conventional programs in English and speech, concentrating on discrete items, are powerless to deal with such major structural problems as the inconsistent use of the -s marker of person and number in the present tense, with the same speaker saying *he do* and *we thinks, it make* and *they tells*. The problem can be treated only by structural analysis, and by the development of structurally organized drills. Without the active cooperation of linguists, any school program concerned with social dialects will have difficulty succeeding. Yet even the best linguistic foundation cannot make such a program succeed if it stigmatizes as inherently inferior the dialect which the student brings to class; whatever the ultimate destiny of any one child, the schools must not alienate him from his own people. The most promising approach seems to be that of functional bi-dialectalism, with the middle-class dialect of the community presented for what it is: the mode of communication with the greatest advantages both in the schools and in clerical, sales and managerial work. In other situations each speaker has the right to judge whether this mode, or some other, will serve him best.

Implicit in this program for social dialects is an appreciation of the nature of dialects, both by the schools and by the middle-class group in the community. Divergences should be understood as reflecting only differences in cultural experience, not differences in intelligence or in moral fiber. Important as this is for approaching social dialects, it is crucial in evaluating regional dialects. Unlike most other Western nations, we do not have one overwhelmingly prestigious variety of standard American English; each cultural focus — Charleston and Chicago, Boston and San Francisco — has its own standard. As people move about, it is possible to find in a single classroom representatives of half a dozen varieties of cultivated speech.[9] Given

[8] See *Communication Barriers for the Culturally Deprived*, an investigation of Chicago social dialects and their implications, under the sponsorship of the University of Chicago and the Illinois Institute of Technology, Cooperative Research Grant 2107, U. S. Office of Education.
[9] This situation has stimulated an interest in dialects among the teachers of the Westport, Conn., school system. One of these, Mrs. Evely Gott, has exchanged tapes of high-school student speech with colleagues in other parts of the United States; out of this project has come a recording, *Our Changing Language* (New York, McGraw-Hill, 1965).

the adaptability of children, it is likely that newcomers will adapt themselves to the local patterns in a short while.[10] The most a teacher should try to do to accelerate the process is to explain, when necessary, but casually and often in private, why a particular utterance is misunderstood, and to utilize the dialect resources in the classroom to enrich the education of all the students. Here the work of traditional dialectologists can be drawn on in many creative ways.

When all is said and done, of course, the purpose of all schoolwork in English and speech is to make each student communicate more freely and effectively with others. However necessary the diagnostic and therapeutic work of the neurologist, the social dialectologist or anyone else, it will not in itself achieve this end. To achieve it we must rely, as ever, on the patience, dedication and skill of the classroom teachers, hoping that we have done a little to make their labors more fruitful.

UNIVERSITY OF CHICAGO

---

[10] As I have indicated, I am a native South Carolinian (the sixth generation in the same county); my wife is a Minnesotan. Our children have noticed differences in our speech, and freely commented on them: "Daddy, why do you say [ɒ-ɔn] when Mamma says [ɑn]?" But their own phonology and grammar are those of their playmates in the Hyde Park area of Chicago.

GORDON E. PETERSON

TOWARD A THEORY OF SYMBOLIZATION*

In man's search for knowledge about the universe in which he lives he has studied almost every aspect of his environment. In this search, however, man has been least able to understand himself. One of the most complicated attributes of man is his ability to use language. To those who study natural language, its great complexity and varied aspects are a continued source of challenge.

The two major divisions of natural language are spoken and written. Each of these two forms has its own complexities and its own problems. The relation between the two, even in languages in which the orthography is considered relatively close to the phonology, is much more complicated than is often assumed.

While there have been numerous approaches to the investigation of natural language, the structural approach of linguistics has predominated. There are two general types of problems in structural linguistics. One is to construct theories which are applicable to all languages but which are essentially independent of any particular language. The primary problem in the construction of such theories is the identification and specification of the basic units of language. The second problem is to provide descriptions of specific languages. Either spoken or written language may serve as the basis for work on each of the above two problems. There are four major areas of linguistic theory and there are four major components of the description of either spoken or written language. These are:

(1). Phonology or orthography
(2). Lexicon
(3). Syntax
(4). Semantics

Linguists have previously attempted to minimize the problems of semantics in structural linguistics, but this attempt is now gnerally recognized as inappropriate and probably futile. It is obviously far beyond the scope of the present paper to examine

* The work on this paper was supported by the Information Sciences Directorate of the Air Force Office of Scientific Research under Grant AF-AFOSR-595-64, and more recently under Grant AF-AFOSR-595-65.

the details of all of the above four components. Rather, it is the objective of the paper to consider the function of the first component in a general way. It is this component which is concerned with the basic symbols used in language. These are the symbols employed in specifying the lexicon. Lexical items, in turn, are the units which are organized by the syntax. In natural language, phonology and orthography are thus at the foundation of linguistic theory and the structural description of languages. Accordingly, it seems appropriate that at this stage of development in linguistic theory the first component of language should receive major attention. The following development is not restricted to the common forms of natural language, however, but is intended to apply to symbolic processes in general.

THE ESSENTIALS OF COMMUNICATION

Communication is normally accomplished by forming various meaningful arrangements of the basic symbols of a language. For example, if [a], [m], and [r] are basic orthographic symbols in English, then [arm], [mar], and [ram] form meaningful arrangements of these symbols.

Each individual has a somewhat different background of experience, however, and the same arrangement of symbols is likely to have a somewhat different meaning to each of us. It is not necessary, of course, that there always be a complete or even a partial correspondence between the meaning of a particular arrangement of symbols to the initiator of a message and to the recipient. Miscommunication is a common experience, though we are typically reluctant to admit that the symbol arrangements which we generate may be interpreted in ways other than we intend. There must usually be something in common between the meaning of a particular arrangement of symbols to one individual and the meaning of that arrangement to other individuals, however, or communication simply could not be carried on successfully.

SYMBOL CONTEXT

No one who has considered the process of symbolization seriously would assume that there is a simple and direct correspondence between individual arrangements of the basic symbols of a language and the external environment. The human interpretation of an environmental condition is highly dependent upon the surrounding conditions. In other words, the human interpretation of a condition depends greatly upon the context in which the condition occurs.

Likewise, the interpretation of any particular arrangement of symbols is highly dependent upon the environment in which the arrangement occurs. Radically different interpretations of an arrangement of symbols may be made, depending upon the sequence within which the arrangement is found. This simply means that the denotation of an arrangement of symbols is not necessarily constant and that the same arrangement of symbols may serve many related functions. Since the denotation of an arrangement of symbols is fundamentally variable, it is not surprising that different observers will make somewhat different interpretations of the same arrangement of symbols, even in the same context.

THE ELEMENTS OF A GENERAL THEORY OF SYMBOLIZATION

The following theory is directed toward all forms of symbolization, not natural language alone or some particular form of natural language. Since the theory is general in nature, it cannot be applied simply and directly to any specified form of communication. Rather, the general concepts and definitions must be reinterpreted for any particular mode of information exchange. The theory is constructed of a set of basic assumptions, here called axioms, and a set of definitions.

AXIOM 1. There exists a relationship, denotes, in which a finite set of objects, properties, relationships, and/or events is associated with another set of objects, properties, relationships, and/or events.

COMMENT: Axiom 1 is the basic axiom of the theory. The first set which is finite denotes the second set which may be finite or infinite. The phrase 'set of objects, properties, relationships, and/or events' is intended to encompass all situations and conditions which may be denoted in the universe. The relation 'denotes' must, of course, be made by some process external to the two sets, such as by a human.

DEFINITION 1. A SYMBOL ARRAY is an individual instance of a finite set of objects, properties, relationships, and/or events which denotes another set of objects, properties, relationships, and/or events.

COMMENT: In the orthographic case, specific symbol arrays may be denoted by subscripts. For example, [arm]$_1$ and [arm]$_2$ are two different symbol arrays. In English: [arm]$_1$, [the arm]$_1$, [The arm of the chair is broken.]$_1$ are all examples of specific symbol arrays. The term array is used in the above definition in the multidimensional sense. In printed language we are accustomed to dealing with symbol strings rather than with symbol arrays. While it is convenient to deal with symbol strings, there is no basic reason why an arrangement of symbols should be restricted to a linear string. 'Symbol array' provides a more specific and concise term than what was previously referred to as a 'meaningful arrangement of basic symbols'. It should be emphasized that the term symbol is used here in a very general sense. For example, a symbol array might consist of a series of facial expressions or of manual gestures.

AXIOM 2. There exist individual elements of a symbol array.

COMMENT: The individual elements are specific instances of the basic symbols of the language. A symbol array may consist of one or more elements. The above axiom obviously does not provide the basis for identifying the individual elements of a symbol array; it simply introduces the assumption that such elements exist. At the operational level, however, it is assumed that a rigorous procedure can be formulated for identifying the elements of symbol arrays. Different types of procedures would doubtless be required for different types of symbols. In the orthographic case, specific elements may be denoted by subscripts. Thus in $[a_2\ r_5\ m_1]_1$ and $[a_4\ r_8\ m_3]_2$ both the occurrence of the elements and the occurrence of the arrays are specified.

DEFINITION 2. A SYMBOL TOKEN is an individual instance of an element of a symbol array.

AXIOM 3. There are different aspects (or properties) of symbol tokens.

COMMENT: These aspects or properties will differ tremendously, of course, depending upon the nature of the symbol tokens. It should be noted that a symbol token is an individual instance, and so the above axiom refers to aspects or properties of a collection of individual instances of symbols. It is certainly not in general an easy task, but it is assumed that it is a manageable task to identify the basic and significant properties of a set of symbol tokens.

AXIOM 4. The different aspects (or properties) of symbol tokens are associated in disjoint classes whose elements are closely related or whose elements are consecutive along a continuum.

COMMENT: Any particular symbolic element has a specific set of properties. Some of these properties are closely related or associated. As a simple example, 'enclosure' might be considered an aspect of certain symbol tokens in English printing. Within the aspect of enclosure, 'closed' is disjoint from 'open'. Thus orthographic [o, b, d] represent closed, whereas orthographic [c, m, u] represent open.

AXIOM 5. The expressions in a language consist of symbol arrays and any given symbol array belongs to one and only one language.

COMMENT: It should be recalled that a symbol array is an individual instance of a finite set of objects, properties, relationships, and/or events. According to the above assumption any such individual instance can be assigned to a single language. Further, the expressions in a language consist only of symbol arrays. Procedures for assigning a particular symbol array to one language rather than to another is a problem of considerable magnitude. For example, certain expressions may be identical in form in more than one natural language. When bilingual speakers use such expressions, it is generally difficult to determine the language to which the expressions should be assigned. Fortunately, however, this type of problem is not central to the following development.

DEFINITION 3. The SYMBOL SYSTEM OF A LANGUAGE specifies the various ways in which the symbol tokens of the language are organized into higher ordered sets and specifies the relationships among these sets.

COMMENT: According to the above definition the symbol system of a language is concerned only with the arrangement of symbol tokens into higher ordered sets. This is a very different matter, of course, from the arrangement of symbol tokens within a symbol array. In effect, the symbol system of a language specifies the way in which the elements of the symbol arrays are combined to form symbolic units. Obviously, languages may differ greatly in the details of their symbol systems.

AXIOM 6. There exist one or more alternative sets of symbol arrays from which the symbol system of a language can be determined.

COMMENT: A language with a fixed corpus is indeed rare. Even for the so-called 'dead' languages, new scripts are sometimes discovered which extend knowledge about the language. It is an essential property of natural language that it does not consist of a closed corpus. In general in natural language it is possible to generate new expressions which have not previously occurred. According to the above axiom, it is not necessary to examine all expressions in a language in order to determine the symbol system of the language. It is assumed that it is possible to select at least one and possibly more than one set of symbol arrays with which the symbol system of the language can be determined. That is, it is assumed that it is possible to select a finite (and presumably manageable) corpus from which the symbol system of the language can be determined. It is implicit in the assumption that the essential properties of the language are fixed at the time the symbol system of the language is specified. Basic changes in the language are thus excluded, since innovations in the essential properties of the language obviously require revisions in the description of the symbol system. The description of a language at one period of time may be important to describing the language at another period, but it hardly seems reasonable to expect one description to specify a language accurately over all periods of time. It would be unrealistic, of course, to attempt in the description to anticipate changes in the language. While there are principles of language change, it is extremely difficult to know which principles will be effective in modifying a particular language as time progresses.

DEFINITION 4. A DISTINGUISHED SET OF SYMBOL ARRAYS is a set of symbol arrays from which the symbol system of a language may be derived.

COMMENT: We are now ready to consider the relationships among symbol tokens within various symbol arrays. These relationships are normally of interest, of course, only when the symbol arrays are from the same language. Thus what follows is of interest only when the arrays referred to are from a distinguished set of symbol arrays.

AXIOM 7. There exists a relation, semantic equivalence, between symbol arrays in which two arrays denote the same set of objects, properties, relationships, and/or events.

COMMENT: In some respects the above axiom is the most fundamental assumption and also the most controversial assumption of the theory. If different arrays of symbol tokens never denote the same set of objects, properties, relationships, and/or events, then it is extremely difficult to see how communication could either be developed or maintained. In effect, axiom 7 simply assumes that different symbol arrays may on occasion serve the same function. The various qualifications regarding meaningful arrangements of symbols mentioned earlier apply, of course, but according to the above axiom there are instances in which different symbol arrays serve precisely the same function. This is very different from assuming that two symbol arrays have precisely the same meaning to two different individuals. It is, indeed, difficult to specify experimental or operational procedures for demonstrating that two different symbol arrays denote the same set of objects, properties, relationships, and/ or events. The lack of an operational procedure, however, does not seem adequate justification for excluding the concept of semantic equivalence from the theory of symbolization. Semantic equivalence is fundamental to the entire concept of language and communication by means of symbols. It seems reasonable, that in the analysis of a specific language a practical procedure for determining semantic equivalence could be implemented.

DEFINITION 5. A SYMBOL PARAMETER is an essential aspect (or property) of a set of symbol tokens.

COMMENT: There are certain essential aspects or properties of symbol tokens. Thus, the 'slope' of the lines in certain symbol tokens of English orthography is an essential aspect or property of those tokens, e.g., in [k, l, f, v, u].

DEFINITION 6. A SYMBOL PARAMETER VALUE is a subdivision (or specific value) of a symbol parameter.

COMMENT: For the example in the discussion of axiom 4, 'enclosure' is a symbol parameter, and 'closed' and 'open' are parameter values within the parameter. In the example of definition 5 immediately above, the 'slope' of the lines is a symbol parameter, and such conditions as 'horizontality', 'diagonality', and 'verticality' are symbol parameter values. Thus 'verticality' is a subdivision of 'slope' which applies to orthographic [b, d, f, k, h, l, p, q, t].

DEFINITION 7. A SYMBOL PARAMETER VALUE IS REPRESENTED if a symbol token has that parameter value.

COMMENT: Numerous symbol tokens will normally have the same value of a particular symbol parameter.

DEFINITION 8. A COMPLETE SET OF SYMBOL PARAMETER VALUES is the set of all symbol parameter values which are represented by a symbol token.

COMMENT: Obviously, when a change is made in the value of any given symbol parameter, there is a change in the complete set of symbol parameter values represented.

DEFINITION 9. SYMBOL DIFFERENCE is the relation in which two symbol tokens are not represented by the same complete set of symbol parameter values.

AXIOM 8. The symbol difference between two complete sets of symbol parameter values may be specified by a non-negative real number.

COMMENT: It would be a major problem, of course, to specify a generalized measure of symbol difference. It seems reasonable, however, to assume that a measure of symbol difference can be specified for a specific set of symbol tokens. The measure would depend very much upon the specific nature of the symbols involved.

DEFINITION 10. SYMBOL EQUIVALENCE is the relation in which two symbol tokens are represented by the same complete set of symbol parameter values.

DEFINITION 11. A SYMBOL TYPE is the set of all symbol tokens which have symbol equivalence.

COMMENT: The concept of symbol token is exceedingly basic in any theory of symbolization. Much confusion in symbol theory has resulted from a failure to maintain a clear distinction between symbol tokens and symbol types. Since considerable theoretical formulation has been necessary before a symbol type could be defined, it is clear that symbol type is not a particularly simple concept.

DEFINITION 12. TWO SYMBOL ARRAYS HAVE SYMBOL EQUIVALENCE if each symbol token in one of the symbol arrays has symbol equivalence to the corresponding symbol token in the other symbol array.

COMMENT: It is implicit in the above definition that two symbol arrays must be isomorphic to have symbol equivalence. Clearly two symbol arrays which contain different numbers of symbol tokens, for example, cannot have symbol equivalence. It is assumed that it is possible to observe the correspondence between symbol tokens in symbol arrays when such a correspondence exists.

DEFINITION 13. TWO SYMBOL TOKENS ARE FUNCTIONALLY EQUIVALENT if they occur in corresponding positions in semantically equivalent arrays which either have symbol equivalence or have symbol equivalence except for the two symbol tokens.

COMMENT: The above definition specifies the conditions under which two symbol tokens function in an equivalent manner. The symbol tokens need not be of the same type, but the other symbol tokens in the two symbol arrays must be of the same symbol types. It is by means of the above definition that symbols of different types can be associated in the environment of specific symbol arrays. It is important to note that tokens from two different symbol types may be functionally equivalent in the environment of certain symbol types and yet may not be functionally equivalent in the environment of other symbol types. For example, if an instance of [grey] and an instance of [gray] have the same meaning, then the orthographic symbol tokens [e] and [a] are functionally equivalent in these two instances. The symbol tokens [e] and [a] are clearly not functionally equivalent, however, in [bet] and [bat]. This variation in functional equivalence among the symbol tokens of different symbol types is a fundamental property of symbolization. It is essentially this property which makes symbolization both flexible and complicated. A failure to recognize the resulting ambiguous nature of symbol types, makes it fundamentally impossible to develop a coherent theory of symbolization. Actually, in a larger context, the situation is even more complex. Two symbol arrays whose symbol tokens are of identical symbol types, that is, two symbol arrays which have symbol equivalence, may not be semantically equivalent. This may occur when two symbol arrays are embedded in different symbol array environments. To illustrate, the [e] in [read] of 'I read the paper yesterday' is not functionally equivalent to the [e] in [read] of 'I hope to read the paper tomorrow'. While it is relatively rare that two symbol arrays which have symbol equivalence do not also have semantic equivalence, this circumstance occurs in most forms of human communication. The circumstances can be understood, however, only if a clear distinction is maintained between symbol tokens and symbol types.

DISCUSSION

The derivation of the sets of functionally equivalent symbol tokens of a language is valid if the symbol tokens from a distinguished set of symbol arrays are consistently and exhaustively assigned to the various sets. If a distinguished set of symbol arrays is employed in determining the sets of functionally equivalent symbol tokens, then the addition of other symbol arrays from the language should not result in the observation of additional symbol types, in additional sets of functionally equivalent symbol tokens, or in the addition of symbol tokens to the established sets of functionally equivalent symbol tokens if the additional tokens are of different symbol types from those already represented in the functionally equivalent sets.

From the above development it should be clear that it is a fundamental property of human communication that symbol tokens of the same symbol type may appear in different sets of functionally equivalent symbol tokens. It is therefore basic that functional equivalence among symbols cannot be established at the level of symbol types.

In the theory presented above a large number of sets of functionally equivalent tokens would normally be derived in any language of versatility. In a complete theory of symbolization there remains the substantial problem of combining certain of the sets of functionally equivalent tokens. This may be done according to a minimum symbol difference. In addition, it may be desirable to remove some symbol tokens from certain sets and to assign them to others. While these problems all appear to be manageable, the present paper is intended only to suggest a foundation for the theory of symbolization; and so additional details will not be considered here.

SUMMARY

This manuscript is directed toward the development of a theory of symbolization. The theory is presented in a general form which should apply to most aspects of human communication, not simply to what is commonly designated natural language. The theory is constructed of a set of axioms and definitions which are highly interdependent. The basic axiom assumes that there exists a relationship, called denotes, in which a finite set of objects, properties, relationships, and/or events is associated with another (finite or infinite set) of objects, properties, relationships, and/or events. A symbol array is defined as an individual instance of a finite set of objects, properties, relationships, and/or events which denotes another set of objects, properties, relationships, and/or events. A symbol token is an individual instance of an element of a symbol array. A symbol type is a set of symbol tokens which have symbol equivalence or zero symbol difference. Essential to the theory is the assumption that there exists a relation, semantic equivalence, between symbol arrays in which two arrays denote the same set of objects, properties, relationships, and/or events. Two symbol tokens are functionally equivalent if they occur in corresponding positions in semantically equivalent arrays which either have symbol equivalence or have symbol equivalence except for the two symbol tokens. A basic result of the theory is that symbol tokens of the same symbol type may appear in different symbol arrays which have symbol equivalence but which are not semantically equivalent.

SPEECH COMMUNICATIONS RESEARCH LABORATORY

SANTA BARBARA, CALIFORNIA

RAY L. BIRDWHISTELL

SOME META-COMMUNICATIONAL THOUGHTS
ABOUT COMMUNICATIONAL STUDIES

Students who would encompass the rapidly expanding literature of communicational studies complain that many of the writings have little more than the term 'communication' in common. Born in the interstices between traditional disciplines, communicational studies have had a variety of shapes and directions. Even if we attend only to the last two decades, review of this literature gives little evidence of agreement among scholars as to the phenomena properly assignable to the communicational rubric. Nor is there any more agreement among them as to the skills, the research designs or the instrumentation required to investigate communication, its component events or its contexts. And, at this writing, there is no clear indication of any general willingness to mediate the overlapping and, often, contradictory definitions which characterize communication terminology.

For all its multiplexity, communicational literature is not without order. If we look beneath the paraphrastics, ignore the specialized argots and are vigilant to underlying assumptions, there are repetitive themes apparent in it. To gain perspective upon these themes it is necessary to avoid the distortions inevitably introduced by concentration upon who said what under which conditions. The literature makes more sense if we concentrate upon thoughts rather than upon thinkers.

In the broadest sense, the heterogeneity of communicational studies reflects an intellectual ANATOMIE occasioned by the impact of new data which is reopening old arguments. Perusal of the more recent literature reveals that it is not merely communicative behavior but human social behavior which is at issue here. And, those who would understand communication behavior as social behavior find that the data they gather, the research designs they construct, and the generalizations they derive are inevitably dependent upon their basic, if seldom manifest, assumptions about the nature of man and of society. The absence of explicitly stated assumptions characteristic of many of these studies cannot be laid to scholarly ineptitude or mischievous technique. The fact of the matter is that many of the most potent assumptions that guide man's thought lie hidden in the common culture, deductible perhaps, but only demonstrable by investigations so structured as to evade such premises as givens.

It seems to me that there are several fundamental issues which underlie divergent

thought about and research into communicational phenomena. The first of these has
to do with whether communication is to be understood as:

(A) An ongoing SYSTEM with its own reality, an aspect of man's social heritage which,
as an individual member of society, he internalizes and modifies to meet the exigencies
of life in an environment of which he is a part. Or, that communication is: (B) A
construct, abstracted from the sum of man's individual adaptations to other men and
to an external environment.

The second fundamental issue is essentially one concerning continuity or discontinuity in the evolution of behavior. On the one hand we have: (A) Those who see
society AND COMMUNICATION as an adaptational imperative for all complex organisms
and, therefore, to be comprehended in an evolutionary, multi-species perspective.
And on the other: (B) Those who see man's invention of spoken language (and, even,
society) as a qualitative developmental leap which renders animal data interesting
but ultimately trivial to the understanding of human, i.e., communicative behavior.

The third fundamental issue is concerned with a monistic versus a dualistic conception of man and his communicative behavior. Here the division is sharp: (A) There
are those who see man as an organismic whole, who emits and receives multi-modal
messages, the shapes of which are determined by the social, that is the communicational system. And in contrast: (B) Those who see communicative behavior as of
two distinct types: (1) The cognitive processes, derived from mental mechanisms and
manifest in spoken and written language. And: (2) The affective or emotive processes
which are derived from the non-mental mechanisms (principally endocrinal or
visceral) and manifest in 'non-verbal communication'.

Related to the third fundamental issue and, perhaps, even more basic are the differences between those:

(A) Who, being unconvinced of the essential duality of humans and their messages,
feel that this is a central subject for research. Without denying the importance of
spoken language in man, these feel that spoken language is an infra-communicational
system, that man and animals are multi-sensory in physiological make-up and are
interconnected multi-modally. Maturation is thus conceived of in multi-modal terms.
The orderliness to be seen in communicative activity derives from a multi-level
regularity in nature. However, communication, *per se*, is restricted to learned behavior.
Yet, that portion of ordered human behavior to be seen as part of the SOCIAL heritage
is a primary subject for research, not an issue to be settled by *a priori* agreement
devices. And those:

(B) Who, having made the assumption of dualisticm essage types, see the cognitive
messages as encapsulated in words and sentences and as the principal, the central or
even the only SIGNIFICANT communicative activity of man. Affective or emotive
communication is seen to be more primitive and of only modificatory significance in
the healthy. Such communicative activity is carried by the other sensory modalities.
Often such theories envisage maturation as the replacement of affective messages by
cognitive messages. The orderliness to be seen in affective, emotive or, at times,

'expressive' messages are seen to be the result of intra-organismic or gene pool regularity.

Like all schemata, this outline is oversimple. The dichotomies are ideally typical; opinion ranges within these heuristic polarities. More cogently, such a delineation as this obscures the overlap and interpenetration of these ideas. There tends to be a basic interdependence between these ideas which makes them exceedingly difficult to sort out for investigation. To compound the sin of over-abstraction with overgeneralization, there is some tendency for the various assumptions included under the A categories to form one rubric of conceptualization, under B to represent a second and distinct focus of preconception. More seriously, such a scheme as this is far from exhaustive and it tends to obscure other influences which shape the conceptualization of communicative phenomena.

A preponderance of the literature does not attempt to discuss communication in terms such as those listed above. Disinterested in the evolutionary implications of research on communication, the problems of ontogenetic development or in the relationship between various kinds of messages sent either by men or animals, many writers tinge their discussions of communication with exhortative phrasing that gives evidence of a preconceptual devotion or aversion, (of which they may or may not be aware). Deeply imbedded in all Western European thought is the imperative that one is or should be responsible for one's communicative behavior. The three monkeys: 'See No Evil', 'Hear No Evil', and 'Speak No Evil' form an ikon expressive of this deep-seated conviction. To suggest to men who are already overburdened with the responsibility for controlling their vocalic activity that their lexical messages compose but part of their communicative activity is to activate a defense system far more effective than any external thought control. It can be dismaying for those who have invested their life to tongue or pen control to realize that they interact with other men by body motion, by emission of odorific and tastable substances and by tactile interchange. It should not be surprising if such complex conceptions as freedom, independence, maturation and education are consciously or unconsciously measured by the extent to which the individual can transform (or reduce) all multi-sensory experience into lexical activity.

Such concepts as Consciousness and Awareness and Will and Responsibility are inseparable for many thoughtful men. To be a 'good' listener, a careful reader, a logical, responsible speaker and a skillful writer can be held as a realistic, if not finally achievable, goal by most scholars. The professional teacher, the psychotherapist, the interviewer or the researcher often realizes that it is his professional responsibility to be aware of his impact upon others and to be sensitive to the structure of his own response system. If he has been fortunate enough in his training period or disciplined enough in his review of his performances, he recognizes that more than 'good will', 'sensitivity' or a 'natural talent' for communication is required to discharge his duty TO INTERACT ON PURPOSE. Unless his sphere and activity is a constant and a limited one, his limited effectivity will soon remind him that 'spontaneity' and 'doing what comes naturally' are insufficient and he finds himself in the ethically uncomfortable position of being a paid amateur. The philosopher, the semanticist, the logician, the grammarian, the lexicologist and the speech instructor tender (or are enticed to proffer) antidotes to malcommunication which will ameliorate lexicative shortcomings. To the extent that the professional interactor can persuade himself that lexication and communication are synonymous he will be able to satisfy himself as to the efficacy of his skills.

Let me hasten to say that there is no intent here to depreciate the meta-communicational advances which have been made possible by the humanist's multi-dimensional and continuous reappraisals of human language utilization. I can think of no achievement in the history of man's search for destiny control comparable to that provided by the recognition that his lexical symbol system is of his own making and thus subject to his own revision. Yet the fruitfulness of his discovery has not been without price. There is a joke in medicine that for the specialist, all other specialists are concerned with a trivial or bothersome surround, the conditioning environment for the area of his central concern. The *post mortem* is a sharp reminder to the physician that over-specialization and denial can be lethal.

If the expert in communication becomes a specialist in lexication to the extent that he denies either the importance or the possibility of control of non-lexical interaction, he becomes captive to his skill. There is an abiding temptation to confuse reality with manipulability. And, even if the specialist does not succumb to this temptation, he may either as researcher or practitioner discharge his duty by pietisms. As a researcher, he can take shelter in an operationalism, heuristic at birth, but which, by successive generations of limited experiment, hides its ancestery in a geneological method of footnotes. As a practitioner, his devotion to the power of words, can lead him to the point that he can feel that if he can control the horse, the wagon will follow. But this tendency to convenient reductionism does not long satisfy the responsible professional. It is all too evident to the observant that the communicational eggs will not fit into the lexical basket. Some scholars sweep the overflow into the purgatory of the statistically non-significant. Others, less confident of their basket-making, re-search their research and the products of that research to find new methods of storage.

There is an appreciable variation to be seen in studies of communication for which none of the above is particularly illuminative. This variation is the result of decisions concerning the spatio-temporal shape of communicative events. It is legitimate and, from any point of view, advisable that scholars investigate universes consistent with their tools and their temperaments. However, confusion results and multidisciplinary cooperation is reduced when particular observational time sequences gain exclusive status as the contexts for the isolation of communicative events. From one point of view, communicative events vary from the size of pitch phonemes (a few thousandths of a second) to that of a piece of kinship behavior (three or four human generations). From other points of view, a word or gesture-shaped event (say, a quarter of a second), a sentence-shaped event (two to four seconds in duration), a question-answer sequence (a three second to a minute long passage of time), a scene (two to four minutes) or an interaction (minutes or hours long) provide the significant data for their investigatory procedures. It should not be surprising, in the absence of some order of unifying theory, if experimental results are contradictory or at least resistant to inter-transformation.

Perhaps even more important as a source of non-agreement are the decisions made or avoided by the scholar and investigator about sequentiality and temporality. One gets one view of communication if one sees time biologically, psychologically, sociologically or culturologically, as moving on a single plane in a posterior-anterior fashion, its component events aligned in sequence. A very different view of communication is occasioned by a theory which sees time as multilaminal, with a variety of velocities and with events influenced at every observational point by not yet completed events on another. The former mono-laminal, uni-directional theory tends to frame conceptions about meaning in terms which encapsulate meaning in particular forms, whether these be morphemes, words, sentences or question-answer, stimulus-response sequences; the latter seeks hierarchies of significance in vari-shaped, multidimensional contexts. 'Meaning', to the latter, requires a statement of context. A communicational event is thus at any level necessarily a statement of an abstracted shape of behavior in its appropriate structural context.

Part of the difficulty of thinking about communicative behavior as continuous, multi-level behavior rests in the kinds of models we derive from introspection shaped by commonsensical experience. As participants in the communicative process, it is difficult to think of this participation as other than discontinuous, episodic and inter-mittent. For those accustomed to thinking about communication in terms of episodes of verbal exchange, in dyadic action and reaction, as carried on by however intricately interconnected transmitter and receiver or coder and decoder, the concept that communication is a continuous process made up of discontinuous elements of over-lapping and differential duration is alien if not nonsensical. It is difficult, if one focuses upon the dialogue between two individual organisms to see that the oscillating dyad is a very special order of social event, statistically relatively rare in incidence, and, even in its purest form, swiftly transitory. And, yet, for many scholars this special form of human interaction is seen as the prototype of communicative sequences.

The intimate moments between focused mother and dependent infant, the ecstatic or painful but fleeting intimacy between lovers, the minutes of negotiation between the merchant and his customer and the passing periods of mutual instruction between teacher and student are among the most memorable and important durations of human experience. But the dramatic intensity, the obvious personal or social impor-tance of these moments do not make them microcosmic of all human experience. We are bound to get a distorted view of human interdependence if we see the whole of human experience as no more than an expansion and/or dilution of these critical moments — if we see communication as comprehensible through the investigation of multiple *pas de deux*.

Clearly, two individual human beings in familiar interaction are communicatively linked. However, it is difficult to believe that even the most exhaustive study of the behavior of these two individuals IN AN ISOLATED SEQUENCE will reveal all that they are communicating, or even, how they are communicating. As one of my students put it, "It's like trying to understand a drainage system from a six inch slice of a river". Some scholars have turned from sequences in despair of ever comprehending interaction. After all, if they can't investigate an interaction between two organisms how can they possibly hope to comprehend a family, a group or a society. Yet, it is possible that they have started with a pseudo-simple task. It may very well be that as we enlarge the personnel of interaction, we increase the visibility of the contextual structure and thus the comprehensibility of the transactions. Except in the most explicitly defined of circumstances, there is the theoretical possibility that a decrease in participants involves an increase in the complexity of the communicative problem. Whatever the relationship between the number of participant organisms and the structure of communicative acts of significance, the fact remains that so long as communicative theory or research does not recognize the hidden assumptions here it will be impossible to test hypothesis against hypothesis — to make information from one kind of research of significance to another.

My own bias that communication is a multi-level, continuous process involving the utilization of structured and learned behavior from man's multi-sensory capacity cannot help but have shaped the foregoing discussion. However, research based upon these assumptions is preliminary and its resultant data tentative. It is my earnest hope that communicational studies will not be too soon captured by any particular scholar or group of scholars and that we will not come to premature closure on the issues at stake here. However, I am convinced that if the scholars involved in communicational research will be more explicit in the assumptions which underlie their investigations the reader will be given readier access to their evidence. It is too much to hope that communicational studies will not become a focus of provincial controversy. Border warfare in *academia* is a tedious and enervating affair, geopolitical and faith-full in shape, and seldom productive. However, it is scholars, not schools, that finally settle intellectual issues. It is my conviction that if they wish to participate in, rather than possess communicational studies, the next twenty-five years will settle most of the issues raised above.

TEMPLE UNIVERSITY MEDICAL CENTER

ROBERT B. LEES

A MORPHOPHONEMIC PROBLEM IN TURKISH

Many examples have been exhibited in the literature to show that an ordinary phonemic analysis is often forced to represent predictable features of pronunciation in the form of irreducible elements. Other examples show that if a phonological description is forced to include a bi-unique and locally determinate transcription, then in some cases otherwise unnecessary rules must be introduced and certain generalizations about pronunciation must be obscured.[1]

Still other examples have been given to show how, in a very striking way, the underlying, least redundant, phonological representations to which the most general rules of an analysis would apply often resemble etymologically prior stages of the language.[2] This is, of course, the feature which permits so-called 'internal reconstruction' in comparative linguistics. While the superficial phonetic character of sentences may long since have changed, some conservative morphophonemic regularities still remain, and the most general description of pronunciation must still be in terms of an underlying representation which reads like a text in the older language, the *Ursprache*, and a set of general rules to derive the regular phonetic facts, the *Lautgesetze*.

This observation shows only that in large part languages change slowly by the addition of low-level phonetic rules and only seldom by radical reorganization of the grammar. Far from being an inadmissible confusion of 'synchronic' with 'diachronic', when we are forced to couch a phonological analysis in terms of underlying representations which strongly resemble Old English or Latin, this fact should be viewed as a powerful confirmation of the description.[3]

---

[1] See, e.g., Morris Halle, "On the Role of Simplicity in Linguistic Descriptions" in Jakobson (ed.): *Structure of Language and its Mathematical Aspects*, Proceedings of the 12th Symposium in Applied Mathematics (Providence, 1961); —, *The Sound Pattern of Russian* (The Hague, 1959); —, "Phonology in a Generative Grammar", *Word*, 18, 54-72 (1962); —and N. A. Chomsky, *The Sound Pattern of English* (New York, 1968); P. M. Postal, "Boas and the Development of Phonology: Comments Based on Iroquoian", *IJAL*, 30, 269-80 (1964).

[2] T. G. Bever, "Theoretical Implications of Bloomfield's Menomini Morphophonemics", *Q.P.R.* 68, R.L.E., M.I.T., 197-203 (1963); also Halle, "Phonology in a Generative Grammar".

[3] Mr. David L. Stampe has remarked that in large part this convergence may reflect merely the extensive overlap in methodology between synchronic description and diachronic reconstruction with

An interesting case in point is the pronunciation of modern standard urban Turkish, for which there are two competing analyses which illuminate this historical process.

A. The 3rd-person possessive suffix for nouns has two regular variants: basically it consists of /s/ plus a harmonic vowel; but after non-vowels, the /s/ is deleted:[4]

boya	'paint'	boya-sı[5]	'its paint'
boy	'stature'	boy-u	'its stature'
ütü	'flatiron'	ütü-sü	'its flatiron'
süt	'milk'	süt-ü	'its milk'

B. When the last consonant of a noun is, however, a velar, then there are certain apparent irregularities. First there are the regular velar-final cases:

kök	'root'	kök-ü	'its root'
oq	'arrow'	oq-u	'its arrow'
ek	'joint'	ek-i	'its joint'

Second, there are some which appear to lose the velar stop before this and other suffixes:

gök	'heaven'	gö-ü	'its heaven'
čilek	'strawberry'	čile-i	'its strawberry'
qašıq	'fork'	qašı-ı	'its fork'

C. These are easy to explain once we note that there is also a regular rule of devoicing of final and pre-consonantal stops before morpheme boundary:

ip	'rope'	ip-i	'its rope'
dip	'bottom'	dib-i	'its bottom'
qap	'cape'	qap-ı	'its cape'
qap	'lid'	qab-ı	'its lid'
bit	'louse'	bit-i	'its louse'
but	'thigh'	bud-u	'its thigh'
at	'horse'	at-ı	'its horse'
at	'name'	ad-ı	'its name'
sač	'hair'	sač-ı	'its hair'
sač	'sheet-iron'	sač-ı	'its sheet-iron'

---

the following analogies: underlying form ~ proto-form, morphoneme ~ proto-phoneme, allomorph ~ cognate, rule ordering ~ relative chronology, and phonological rule ~ sound-law. But circularity in the confirmation of each is avoided by the fact that both a (descriptive) grammar and a historical reconstruction are independently corroborated by linguistically external evidence.

[4] This and the following generalizations are formulated in my now somewhat obsolete *Phonology of Modern Standard Turkish* (Bloomington, 1961).

[5] We use here for the (broad) phonetic transcription a notation adapted somewhat from the standard Turkish orthography, namely: all letters as commonly understood but with γ = voiced back velar g, ı = high mid unrounded V, and ł = velarized l. Moreover, letters between slants are used to transcribe underlying forms, and no claim is thereby intended that these correspond in any particular way to the popular notion 'phonemic'.

Moreover, there are no noun bases with final /g/ except a few loans in final [ŋg] = /ng/:

| reŋk | 'color' | reŋg-i | 'its color' |
| a:heŋk | 'harmony' | a:heŋg-i | 'its harmony' |

D. Thus, it is reasonable to construe the nouns with disappearing consonant to be /g/-final bases which show final devoicing to /k/, and we add a rule to delete /g/ in intervocalic position. Then, the word for 'heaven' would be derived as in:

gög # — devoicing rule → gök #
gög+sü — 3-posses → gög+ü — /g/-loss → gö-ü

Of course, the rule deleting /s/ from the suffix must then precede the rule reducing intervocalic /g/.

E. Incidentally, a rule which adjusts the voicing of initial stops in certain suffixes must follow the devoicing of finals, for we have:

göl	'lake'	göl-de	'in the lake'
göüs	'breast'	göüs-te	'in the breast'
gök	'heaven'	gök-te	'in heaven'

F. Finally, there is another set of correspondences which appear to have vowel-final nouns but no /s/ in the 3rd-possessive; furthermore, the vowel is long in the underived form:

da:	'mountain'	da-i	'its mountain'
či:	'dew'	či-i	'its dew'
bö:	'spider'	bö-ü	'its spider'
čı:	'avalanche'	čı-ı	'its avalanche'

Now, such forms cannot be analyzed simply as vowel-final bases with word-final lengthening, for there are many regular vowel-final cases, both long and short:

ne	'what'	ne-si	'its what'
oda	'room'	oda-sı	'its room'
bina:	'building'	bina:-sı	'its building'
qara	'land'	qara-sı	'its land'
qaza:	'judgment'	qaza:-sı	'its judgment'

These long vowels, incidentally, are all in Arabic and Persian loans, while those of the troublesome alternation cases are native morphemes. The accepted view is that Proto-Turkic long vowels remain distinct only in Türkmen.

There are also some Arabic loans with final long vowel and no /s/ in the possessive:

| mebla: | 'sum' | mebla-ı | 'its sum' |

(Some speakers may mistakenly use the long vowel in the derived form as well:

mebla:-ı)

G. We cannot take any of these cases to contain /h/ or /ʔ/ since there are also regular derivations with these consonants:

| sabah | 'morning' | sabah-ı | 'its morning' |
| ja:mi | 'mosque' | ja:mi ʔ-i | 'its mosque' |

The glottal-stop /ʔ/ disappears regularly before consonants and in final position.

H. It seems, then, that the irregular cases must be analyzed as containing a 'ghost-consonant' in final position; it is voiced, since a following locative suffix has the initial voiced /d/:

| da: | 'mountain' | da:-da | 'on the mountain' |

It need not be distinguished among the stops since it has no voiceless variant in final position.

I. Two rules suffice, then, to yield the observed forms:
Vowels before word-final or pre-consonantal ghost are lengthened.
The ghost is deleted everywhere.
The ghost serves, of course, also to select the post-consonantal variant of the 3rd person possessive suffix.

J. The historical provenience of this ghost consonant is clear, it is always represented in the standard orthography as ğ, and it corresponds exactly to a voiced, velar fricative in Anatolian dialects. It is, of course, the so-called *yumuşak-g*, or 'soft-g', from non-initial Altaic */g/; and in certain Arabic loans it replaces the underlying *ghayn* غ of Arabic.

K. With this analysis it is now also possible to eliminate all vowel sequences in native words and thus to regularize distributions, and there is independent morphophonemic evidence in the verbs that internal vowel sequences are indeed cases of deleted intervocalic 'soft-g':

soan = /soğan/	'onion'
jier = jiğer/	'liver'
düüm = /düğüm/	'knot'
doar = /doğar/	'she bears'
do:du = /doğdu/	'she bore'
doajaq = /doğaẙaq/	'she'll bear'
do:mah = /doğmah/	'she has to bear'

Moreover, certain internal long vowels can also be eliminated as cases of pre-consonantal /ğ/:

ö:le = /öğle/	'noon' (cf. öyle 'thus')
ya:mur = /yağmur/	'rain' (cf. yaar = /yağar/ 'it rains')
do:ru = /doğru/	'straight'

To put the matter briefly, even in the Istanbul pronunciation, where the old */g/ has disappeared entirely after vowels, the standard orthography is still 'phonemic'!

L. Now, this is an interesting result in itself, linguistically speaking, though a Turkological commonplace, for we do not generally think of languages as having zero-phonemes. This one can be analyzed as a voiced, compact glide.

However, as the attentive may by now have noticed, there is another, entirely different, analysis which seems plausible. Since /g/ also disappears intervocalically it may be correct to identify our ghost-consonant with that stop and analyze the vowels differently. The standard orthography also writes the disappearing /g/ as ğ:

gök/göü = gök — göğü

In particular, we would have to construe the examples in section F as containing each an inherent long vowel and a final /g/, and we must reorder the rules, adding two replacement rules, one to shorten vowels before /g/+V, and a following one to delete /g/ intervocalically and after any remaining long vowel (that is, after long-V and before C or final). Let us see, then, what relative advantages or disadvantages these two different analyses have.

M. First, as to the rules used, the two descriptions share several but must also differ in the following way:

where the /ğ/-solution has the three consecutive rules:

a. g ⟶ ∅   if: V_____V

b. V ⟶ V̄   if: _____ğ $\left\{ \begin{matrix} (+)C \\ \# \end{matrix} \right\}$

c. ğ ⟶ ∅

the alternative V̄-/g/ analysis must use the two consecutive rules:

d. V̄ ⟶ V   if: _____g(+)V

e. g ⟶ ∅   if: $\left\{ \begin{matrix} V\text{_____} \\ V\text{_____}V \end{matrix} \right\}$

When these five rules are expressed in terms of distinctive features, and if boundary symbols and the like are each counted as one, then the latter two rules require 24 specifications to the 26 of the former three, a gain of two.

I.e., the first three rules would be:

$$
\text{a.} \quad \begin{bmatrix} +\text{cns} \\ -\text{vcl} \\ +\text{cmp} \\ -\text{cnt} \\ +\text{voi} \end{bmatrix} \longrightarrow \emptyset \qquad \text{if:} \begin{bmatrix} -\text{cns} \\ +\text{vcl} \end{bmatrix} \text{_____} \begin{bmatrix} -\text{cns} \\ +\text{vcl} \end{bmatrix}
$$
$$
\qquad\quad 5 \qquad\qquad 1 \qquad\qquad\qquad 2 \qquad\qquad 2 \qquad = 10
$$

$$
\text{b.} \quad \begin{bmatrix} -\text{cns} \\ +\text{vcl} \end{bmatrix} \longrightarrow [+\text{lng}] \quad \text{if:} \begin{bmatrix} -\text{cns} \\ -\text{vcl} \\ +\text{voi} \\ +\text{cmp} \end{bmatrix} \left\{ (+) \left\{ \begin{matrix} [+\text{cns}] \\ [-\text{vcl}] \\ \# \end{matrix} \right\} \right\}
$$
$$
\qquad\quad 2 \qquad\qquad 1 \qquad\qquad\qquad 4 \qquad\quad 1 \quad 1 \quad 2 \qquad = 11
$$

c.
$$\begin{bmatrix} - \text{cns} \\ - \text{vcl} \\ + \text{voi} \\ + \text{cmp} \end{bmatrix} \longrightarrow \emptyset$$

    4   1   Total $= \dfrac{5}{26}$

where the features are given in the following tree of phonemes for the /ǧ/-analysis:

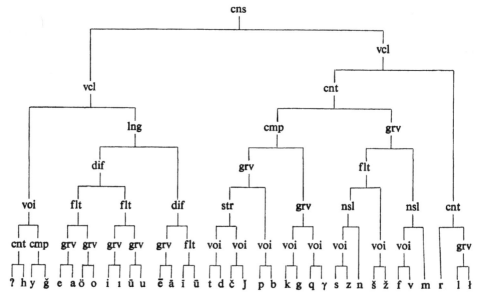

204 decisions/ 37 phonemes = 5.5 dec/phon

$\ln_2 37 = 5.21$ dec/phon   Eff = 0.945 $\left(\text{Efficiency} = \dfrac{\text{decisions/phoneme}}{\log_2 \text{N}^\circ \text{phonemes}} \right)$

The second two rules would be:

d.
$$\begin{bmatrix} - \text{cns} \\ + \text{vcl} \end{bmatrix} \longrightarrow [- \text{lng}] \quad \text{if:} \quad \underline{\hphantom{xx}} \begin{bmatrix} + \text{cns} \\ - \text{vcl} \\ - \text{cnt} \\ + \text{cmp} \\ + \text{voi} \end{bmatrix} (+) \begin{bmatrix} - \text{cns} \\ + \text{vcl} \end{bmatrix}$$

    2   1   5   1   2 = 11

e.
$$\begin{bmatrix} + \text{cns} \\ - \text{vcl} \\ - \text{cnt} \\ + \text{cmp} \\ + \text{voi} \end{bmatrix} \longrightarrow \emptyset \quad \text{if:} \quad \left\{ \begin{matrix} \begin{bmatrix} - \text{cns} \\ + \text{vcl} \\ + \text{lng} \end{bmatrix} \underline{\hphantom{xx}} \\ \begin{bmatrix} - \text{cns} \\ + \text{vcl} \end{bmatrix} \underline{\hphantom{xx}} \begin{bmatrix} - \text{cns} \\ + \text{vcl} \end{bmatrix} \end{matrix} \right\}$$

    5   1   5   2 $= \dfrac{13}{24}$

where the features are chosen from the slightly reformulated tree for the $\bar{V}$-/g/-analysis:

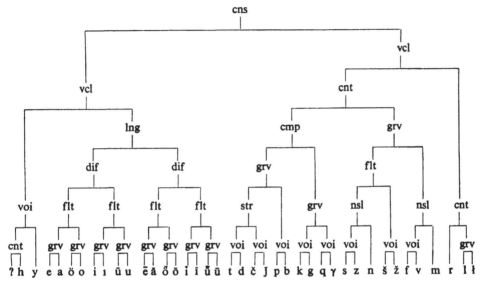

235 dec/40 phon = 5.875 dec/phon
ln₂ 40 = 5.32   Eff = 0.905

N. However, there are a number of other considerations to be evaluated somehow. The most obvious difference is in the underlying phonological system which is presupposed in the two cases. The /ğ/-analysis requires that a new glide be distinguished, say minimally from /y/; this adds one feature to every unpredictable occurrence of /y/ in the lexicon and in the rules.

But the $\bar{V}$-/g/-analysis, on the other hand, requires distinguishing four more long vowels than would otherwise be assumed, namely /ū ī ö and ō/ (/ī e ū and ā/ would be needed for Arabic words in any analysis). These additions increase the specifications for short /ü ı ö and o/ each by one feature per occurrence. This new description uses 40 phonemes with 5.875 decisions per phoneme, or a coding efficiency of 90.5%. The traditionally accepted /ğ/-description, on the other hand, uses only 37 phonemes with 5.51 decisions per phoneme, or a coding efficiency of 94.5%.[6]

---

[6] I certainly do not wish thereby to imply that such a count of features is an entirely satisfactory generality criterion for phonological descriptions, nor did M. Halle make that claim when he suggested this admittedly crude test in his "On the Role of Simplicity in Linguistic Descriptions", *op cit.* Moreover, the information-theoretic characterization of coding efficiency for the phonological trees is given only to point up the difference in utilization of the features in the two cases and the way that difference would affect parsimony in lexical representations, but I do not thereby claim either that the phonological tree is itself a part of a grammatical description, nor that an adequate measure of generality, if we knew of one, would lump together a count of features required in the rules and a count of features required in the lexicon.

O. Another disadvantage of the new $\bar{V}$-/g/-analysis is that one of its rules seems unmotivated, namely the loss of /g/ after long vowels. Of course, there were no cases of -$\bar{V}$g bases in the old analysis since these would have to have been Arabic loans because of the long vowel, but Arabic words certain no /g/, yielding only /k/ and /ǧ/.

P. Finally, the old analysis permits the occurrence of morphemes ending in /-$\bar{V}$ǧ/, while such cases would be fatal for the new analysis; they would be of the form:

dima:	'brain'	dima:-ı	'its brain'
fera:	'renunciation'	fera:-ı	'its renunciation'
diri:	'refusal'	diri:-i	'its refusal'
cf.:			
bina:	'building'	bina:-sı	'its building'
mevzu:	'subject'	mevzu ?-u	'its subject'
mebla:	'sum'	mebla-ı	'its sum'

and would have to be analyzed as bases in -$\bar{V}$g in which the long-V is NOT shortened after /g/ in the derived form.

Now, if we could be quite sure that there would never be any such forms, then the new analysis could be saved. But there ARE Arabic morphemes which should be borrowed with long-vowel plus 'ghayn', and we are concerned with a pronunciation in which such words survive.

The selective reduction of long vowels under Turkification should be in the UN-inflected forms, for there is an independently motivated late rule in Turkish of the form:

$$\text{f.} \quad \bar{V} \longrightarrow V \qquad \text{if:} \quad \dots\dots C \begin{Bmatrix} +C \\ \# \end{Bmatrix}$$

as we see in:

meraq	'attention'	mera:q-ı	'its attention'
zaman	'time'	zama:n-ı	'its time'
huquq	'law(s)'	huqu:q-u	'its law(s)'

In other words, Rule d. of vowel shortening before C+V violates the usual tendency, and does so under the implausible constraint that the C involved is just /g/.

Q. In conclusion, we might speculate that the dialect described is in transition with the gradual loss of Altaic non-initial */g/ and the importation of Arabic words with long vowels under partial Turkification.

But the interesting thing to note is that as simplicity of the new $\bar{V}$-/g/-description gains on that of the old /ǧ/-description, there will come a generation of speakers for which suddenly an entirely different phonological description becomes correct

— this would be a distinct discontinuity in analysis rather than a gradual shift of the pronunciations involved.

Even more weird is the fact that the new analysis appears to restore Proto-Turkic */g/ (and also Altaic long vowels, though only before /g/).

UNIVERSITY OF ILLINOIS
Submitted for Publication 1966

HELES CONTRERAS and SOL SAPORTA

PHONOLOGICAL DEVELOPMENT IN THE SPEECH
OF A BILINGUAL CHILD

1. INTRODUCTION

This study describes the phonological development of a child (David) from the age of 1 year (1;0) to 1 year and 7 months (1;7).[1] The analysis includes the acquisition of phonological distinctions (1.), a summary and comparison of the development presented here with that observed by other authors (2.), followed by a glossary of the items in the corpus which served as a basis for the analysis (3.).

The second author, i.e., the child's father, is a speaker of a variety of the English spoken in New York City; the child's mother is a speaker of a variety of the Spanish of Southern Chile. However, during the period under discussion, there is no evidence that the child is dealing with two linguistic systems. Subsequently, however, there is such evidence, as for example the existence of equivalent pairs like the words for 'coffee', Spanish /kafé/ and English /kófi/, with different phonological features, e.g., the lack of aspiration in the Spanish /k/, etc. In other words, the period of this study in limited to the time when the child has just one system.

1. THE ACQUISITION OF PHONOLOGICAL DISTINCTIONS

In this section the acquisition of phonemes (A) and the distinctive features (B) are presented in terms of seven chronological stages.[2] The stages are divided in an arbitrary manner, although, except for stages 3 and 4, each stage covers one month. (The notation 1;0, for example, indicates the thirteenth month.) For each phoneme,

[1] This research was supported in part by Research Grant M2385 from the National Institutes of Health, Public Health Service; by Research Grants G2502 and G5555 from the National Science Foundation; and by OE-2-14-014 from the Office of Education. The data were collected by the second, author the child's father; the first author made the initial phonemic analysis (see Contreras, 1961). Alta Rosenzweig and Claire Stevens provided considerable help in the subsequent revision, presented here.
[2] Recent studies by Chomsky (1965) and others illustrate the limitations inherent in studies of child language based on a corpus such as the one available for this study. It is not clear what the relation is between an analysis such as the one presented here and a description of the child's underlying competence.

each of the allophones is presented the first time it occurs, and for consonants, according to their distribution initially (I), medially (M) or finally (F).

For each phoneme, presented in slant lines, the phonetic representation is presented in brackets, together with a phonetic transcription of the word in which it occurs, with the relevant sound underlined, followed by a phonemic transcription preceded by Ch, to indicate the phonemic analysis in terms of the child's system. This is followed by the symbol < and the etymon in English or Spanish which served as the model for the child.

For example, /a/ [a] [bab] Ch /pap/ < E *Bob*; illustrates that the phoneme /a/, with the phonetic variant [a], occurred in the utterance [bab], interpreted phonemically in the child's language as /pap/, based on the English model *Bob*. For all Spanish words, the gloss is given in single quotes; when the meaning for the child is different from that of the adult language, it is also indicated.[3]

Stage 1 (Age 1; 0)

The first phonemes are /a/ and /p/, the first distinctive feature acquired being vocalic/non-vocalic.[4]

A. Segmental phonemes

/a/	[a]		[bab]	Ch /pap/ < E *Bob*;
/p/	[p]	F:	[ba*p*]	Ch /pap/ < E *Bob*;
	[b]	I:	[*b*ap]	Ch /pap/ < E *Bob*;
		F:	[ba*b*]	Ch /pap/ < E *Bob*.

Initial [b] and final [b] and [p] are considered members of the same phoneme, arbitrarily transcribed /p/, on the basis of phonetic similarity and free alternation:[5] [bab] alternates with [bap] < E *Bob*.

B. Distinctive features:

	a	p
1. vocalic/non-vocalic	+	—

Stage 2 (Age 1;1)

The inventory of phonemes is increased from two to four with the addition of /u/ and /n/. The distinctive features acquired during this stage are nasal/oral and diffuse/non-diffuse.

---

[3] All items observed during the period of this study were essentially 'one-word utterances'. Stress, but not intonation, was recorded.

[4] At the stage where only one distinction is relevant, the choice of label consonantal/non-consonantal or vocalic/non-vocalic is largely arbitrary. The difficulty is made clear in stage 6 (1;7) where the feature is split into two features, with the appearance of /l/, which requires a realignment of features, rather than a split. (See Fig. 1)

[5] Free alternation and complementary distribution are hardly meaningful terms with such a limited corpus.

Stress is not transcribed phonemically in stages 2 and 3 since disyllabic words are stressed on the last syllable.

A. Segmental phonemes

/a/	[a]		as in stage 1;		
	[ɔ]		[bɔ]	Ch /pa/	< E *ball*;
/u/	[u̯]		[bau̯u̯áu̯]	Ch /pauuau/	< E *bow-wow* or
					Sp *guauguán*;
/p/	[p]	I:	[*p*an]	Ch /pan/ 'food'	< Sp *pan* 'bread';
		F:	as in stage 1;		
	[b]		as in stage 1;		
/n/	[n]	F:	[pa*n*]	Ch /pan/ 'food'	< Sp *pan* 'bread'.

The relationship between [p] and [b] is not clear. Even though both occur in initial position, there is some reason for believing that the contrast is not completely established. [b-] is recorded only for English words (besides the onomatopoetic [bau̯u̯áu̯], which can come from either English or Spanish or both), and [p-] only for a Spanish word. Spanish [p] is unaspirated, so that it is quite possible that this apparent contrast is due to an overdifferentiated notation.[6] [a] and [ɔ] are considered allophones of the phoneme /a/ since there is free variation between [ba] and [bɔ] Ch /pa/ < E *ball*.

B. Distinctive features

	a	u	p	n
1. vocalic/non-vocalic	+	+	—	—
2. nasal/oral			—	+
3. diffuse/non-diffuse	—	+		

The data do not give any evidence as to relative order of appearance of the features of nasality and diffuseness, or, in other words, as to whether a second vowel or a second consonant appears first.

Stage 3 (Age 1;2 - 1;3)

The inventory of phonemes is increased from four to seven with the addition of /i/, /t/, and /m/. The distinctive feature acquired during this stage is grave/acute.

A. Segmental phonemes

/a/ and /u/ as in stage 2;				
/i/	[i]		[tat*i*]	Ch /tati/	< E *tick-tock* or Sp *tic-tac*;
	[i̯]		[bai̯]	Ch /pai/	< E *bye*;

---

[6]   Further evidence in favor of this solution is supplied by the fact that subsequently, at age 1; 8, the child substitutes [b] for a Spanish initial /p/: [bójo] < Sp *pollo* 'chicken', which suggests that even at this later stage the contrast between /p/ and /b/ is not clearly established.

/p/	[p]	I:	as in stage 2;		
		M:	[papá]	Ch /papa/	< Sp papá 'Daddy';
		F:	as in stage 1;		
	[b]		as in stage 1;		
/t/	[t]	I:	[tatí]	Ch /tati/	< E *tick-tock* or Sp *tic-tac*;
		M:	[tatí]	Ch /tati/	< E *tick-tock* or Sp *tic-tac*;
/m/	[m]	I:	[ma]	Ch /ma/ 'food'	< Sp *mas* 'more';
/n/	[n]	I:	[na]	Ch /na/ 'no more'	< Sp *nada* 'nothing';
		F:	as in stage 2.		

B. Distinctive features

	a	u	i	p	t	m	n
1. vocalic/non-vocalic	+	+	+	—	—	—	—
2. nasal/oral				—	—	+	+
3. diffuse/non-diffuse	—	+	+				
4. grave/acute	+	—	+	—	+	—	

Stage 4 (Age 1; 4 - 1; 5)

The inventory of phonemes is increased from seven to eleven with the addition of /o/, /e/, /ə/ and /k/. The distinctive features acquired are compact/non-compact and flat/plain.

Beginning with stage 4, since disyllabic forms may be stressed on either the first or the second syllable: Ch /pépe/ < Sp. *Pepe* 'teddy-bear' vs. Ch /papá/ < Sp. *papá* 'Daddy', stress is marked.

A. Segmental phonemes

/a/		as in stage 2;			
/i/		as in stage 3;			
/o/	[o]		[boi̯]	Ch /poi/	< E *boy*;
/e/	[e]		[pépe]	Ch /pépe/	< Sp *Pepe* 'name of teddy-bear'
	[ɛ̃]		[mɛ̃]	Ch /me/	< E *man*;
/u/	[ʉ]	as in stage 2;			
	[ʊ]		[bʊ]	Ch /pu/	< E *book*;
/ə/	[ə]		[ə́pə]	Ch /ə́pə/	< E *up*;
/p/, /t/	as in stage 3;				
/k/	[k]	I:	[kom]	Ch /kom/	< E *comb*;
		M:	[kóko]	Ch /kóko/	< E *Coke* or Sp *coca*;
		F:	[bʊk]	Ch /puk/	< E *book*;
	[č]	I:	[či]	Ch /ki/ 'urinate'	< Sp *pichí* 'urine';
/m/	[m]	I:	as in stage 3;		
		F:	[kom]	Ch /kom/	< E *comb*;

/n/   [n]   as in stage 3;
        [ŋ]   F: [koŋ]   Ch /kon/   < E *comb*.

[e] and [ẽ] are considered allophones of the phoneme /e/ on the basis of complementary distribution — [ẽ] occurs only preceded by a nasal ([mẽ] < E *man*), while [e] does not occur in that position — and of phonetic similarity.

/o/, /a/ and /ə/ are considered three separate phonemes on the basis of the minimal contrasts [boj] < E *boy* vs. [baj] < E *bye* vs. [bəj] < Sp *buey* 'ox'. [ɔ] continues to be assigned to /a/ rather than to /o/ or /ə/ on the basis of its free alternation with [a]: [bɔ] ⁓ [ba] < E *ball*.

[k] and [č] are considered allophones of the phoneme /k/ on the basis of complementary distribution: [k] occurs only before /a/ or /o/; [č] occurs only before /i/.

The only occurrence of [ŋ] is in final position, alternating with [m] and [n]: [kon] ⁓ [kom] ⁓ [kon] < E *comb*. We assign it arbitrarily to /n/.[7]

B. Distinctive features

	a	o	ə	e	u	i	k	p	t	m	n
1. vocalic/non-vocalic	+	+	+	+	+	+	−	−	−	−	−
2. nasal/oral							−	−	−	+	+
3. diffuse/non-diffuse	−	−	−	−	+	+	−	+	+		
4. compact/non-compact	+	−	−	−							
5. grave/acute		+	+	−	+	−		+	−	+	−
6. flat/plain		+	−								

The most important structural changes observed at this stage are: a) the appearance of a third stop consonant, so that the feature diffuseness now applies to consonants as well as to vowels; b) the doubling of the vowel inventory (from three to six) with the splitting of the non-diffuse vowel into compact and non-compact, and with the splitting of the non-compact, grave vowel into flat and plain.

Stage 5 (Age 1;6)

The inventory of phonemes is increased from eleven to eigtheen with the addition of /æ/, /g/, /b/, /f/, /d/, /s/ and /ñ/. The distinctive features acquired during this stage are tense/lax and interrupted/continuant.

A. Segmental phonemes

/a/   as in stage 2;
/i/   as in stage 3;
/o/, /e/, and /ə/ as in stage 4;
/æ/   [æ]   [bæk]   Ch /bæk/   < E *put it back* (on the shelf)

---

[7] The problem involved in assigning [n] to a particular phoneme is of long standing. See, for example, Saporta (1960), and Fischer-Jørgensen (1958).

/u/	[u]		as in stage 2;		
	[ʊ]		as in stage 4;		
	[u]		[buš]	Ch /bus/	< Sp *bus* 'bus';
/g/	[g]	I:	[gógo]	Ch /gógo/	< Sp *globo* 'balloon';
		M:	[gógo]	Ch /gógo/	< Sp *globo* 'balloon';
/k/	[k]		as in stage 4;		
	[č]	I:	as in stage 4;		
		M:	[čeča][8]	Ch /keka/	< Sp *Chela* (a name);
/b/	[b]	I:	[buš]	Ch /bus/	< Sp *bus* 'bus';
		F:	[bab]	Ch /bab/	< E *Bob*, 1; 0;
/p/	[p]		as in stage 3;		
/f/	[f]	I:	[ʃuf]	Ch /fuf/	< Sp *jugo* 'juice';
		F:	[fuʃ]	Ch /fuf/	< Sp *jugo* 'juice';
/d/	[d]	I:	[dan]	Ch /dan/	< E *down*;
/t/	[t]		as in stage 3;		
	[ʈ]	F:	[buʈ]	Ch /but/	< Sp *bus* 'bus';
/s/	[s]	I:	[si]	Ch /si/	< Sp *si* 'yes';
		M:	[aɪsí]	Ch /aisí/	< Sp *ay si* 'oh yes';
	[š]	F:	[buš]	Ch /bus/	< Sp *bus* /bus/;
	[z]	M:	[téza]	Ch /tésa/	< Sp *Chela* (a name);
	[ž]	M:	[čéža]	Ch /késa/	< Sp *Chela* (a name);
	[x]	F:	[buɪx]	Ch /buis/	< Sp *bus* 'bus';
/m/	[m]	I:	as in stage 3;		
		M:	[mámo]	Ch /mámo/	< Sp *mambo* 'mambo';
		F:	as in stage 4;		
/n/	[n]	I:	as in stage 3;		
		M:	[ána]	Ch /ána/	< Sp *anda* 'go';
		F:	as in stage 2;		
	[ŋ]		as in stage 4;		
/ñ/	[ñ]	I:	[ñáña]	Ch /ñáña/	< Sp *Ignacio* 'Ignatius';
		M:	[ñáña]	Ch /ñáña/	< Sp *Ignacio* 'Ignatius'.

B. Distinctive features

	a	æ	o	ə	e	u	i	g	k	b	p	f	d	t	s	m	n	ñ
1. vocalic/non-vocalic	+	+	+	+	+	+	+	−	−	−	−	−	−	−	−	−	−	−
2. nasal/oral								−	−	−	−	−	−	−	−	+	+	+
3. grave/acute	+	−	+	+	−	+	−	+	+	+	+	+	−	−	−	+	−	−
4. diffuse/non-diffuse	−	−	−	−	−	+	+	−	−	+	+	+					+	−
5. compact/non-compact	+	+	−	−	−													
6. flat/plain				+	−													

---

[8] Although [č] and [k] now both appear before /a/, they are analyzed as members of the same phoneme, the occurrence of [č] in this position being conditioned by the [č] in the previous syllable.

	a	æ	o	ə	e	u	i	g	k	b	p	f	d	t	s	m	n	ñ
7. interrupted/continuant										+	+	−	+	+	−			
8. tense/lax								−	+		−	+		−	+			

The data do not give any evidence as to the relative order of appearance of the features of interruptedness and tenseness. The feature of diffuseness is extended now to the acute nasals: /n/ and /ñ/. The appearance of the vowel /æ/ extends the feature grave/acute to the compact vowels.

The new feature of interruptedness applies to the acute orals: /d/, /t/ and /s/, and to the diffuse orals: /b/, /p/ and /f/. The new feature of tenseness applies to all the stops: /g/ vs. /k/, /b/ vs. /p/ and /d/ vs. /t/.

Stage 6 (Age 1; 7)

The inventory of phonemes is increased from eighteen to twenty-one with the addition of /l/, /č/ and /š/. The distinctive features acquired during this stage are strident/mellow and consonantal/non-consonantal, with the appearance of /l/.

Two new trisyllabic words, which appeared during this stage, Ch /tapáto/ < Sp *zapato* 'shoe', Ch /kabáio/ < Sp *caballo* 'horse', are stressed on the middle syllable, as was the trisyllabic Ch /patúmba/ < E *Mattoon* which appeared at 1; 6.

A. Segmental phonemes

/ə/		as in stage 2;			
/i/		as in stage 3;			
/o/, /e/		as in stage 4;			
/æ/, /u/		as in stage 5;			
/ə/	[ə]	as in stage 4;			
	[ə̰]		[bḛə]	Ch /beə/	< E *bear*;
/p/		as in stage 3;			
/k/		as in stage 4;			
/g/, /t/, /m/, /n/ and /ñ/ as in stage 5;					
/l/	[l]	I:	[lálo]	Ch /lálo/	< Sp *radio* 'radio';
		M:	[lélo]	Ch /lálo/	< Sp *radio* 'radio';
/č/	[č]	I:	[čato]	Ch /čáto/	< Sp *chancho* 'pig';
		M:	[čéče]	Ch /čéče/	< Sp *leche* 'milk';
/š/	[š]	I:	[šei]	Ch /šei/	< E *shave*;
		M:	[čášo]	Ch /čáčo/	< Sp *chancho* 'pig';
		F:	[suš]	Ch /suš/	< Sp *sucio* 'dirty';
	[ž]	M:	[čéza]	Ch /čéča/	< Sp *Chela* (a name)
/b/	[b]	as in stage 5;			
	[v]	M:	[kaváio]	Ch /kabáio/	< Sp *caballo* 'horse';

/f/	[f]	I and F: as in stage 5;			
		M:	[ófo]	Ch /ófo/	< Sp *ojo* 'eye';
	[x]	M:	[óxo]	Ch /ófo/	< Sp *ojo* 'eye';
	[h]	M:	[óho]	Ch /ófo/	< Sp *ojo* 'eye';
	[g]	M:	[ogo]	Ch /ófo/	< Sp *ojo* 'eye';
/d/	[d]	I: as in stage 5;			
		M:	[adú]	Ch /adú/	< Sp *adiós* 'good-bye';
/s/	[s]	I and M: as in stage 5;			
		F:	[dus]	Ch /dus/	< Sp *luz* 'light';
	[z]	as in stage 5.			

B. Distinctive features

	o	a	æ	e	u	ə	i	l	g	k	č	š	b	p	f	d	t	s	m	n	ñ
1. vocalic/ non-vocalic	+	+	+	+	+	+	+	+	−	−	−	−	−	−	−	−	−	−	−	−	−
2. consonantal/ non-conson.	−	−	−	−	−	−	−	+													
3. nasal/oral									−	−	−	−	−	−	−	−	−	−	+	+	+
4. grave/acute	+	+	−	−	+	+	−		+	+	+	+	+	+	+	−	−	−	+	−	−
5. diffuse/ non-diffuse	−	−	−	−	+	−	+		−	−	−	−	+	+	+					+	−
6. compact/ non-compact	−	+	+	−	−																
7. flat/plain	+				−																
8. interrupted/ continuant									+	+	+	−	+	+	−	+	+	−			
9. tense/lax									−	+	+		−	+		−	+				
10. strident/mellow											−	+									

The opposition vocalic/non-vocalic splits into two features (/l/ is both consonantal and vocalic) and the opposition interrupted/continuant, which until now applied to the labials: /b/, /p/ and /f/, and dentals: /d/, /t/ and /s/, is extended to the palato-velars: /g/, /k/ and /š/.

2. SUMMARY AND COMPARISON

In this section we summarize the order of acquisition of segmental phonemes and distinctive features and compare the results of this study with studies by Leopold (1947), Velten (1948) and Jakobson (1949).

By age 1;7, the subject's phonological system shows ten distinctive oppositions. The order of appearance of these oppositions can be enumerated chronologically in a list of the following kind:

1.	vocalic/non-vocalic	Stage 1; age 1;0
2/3.	diffuse/non-diffuse and nasal/oral	Stage 2; age 1;1
4.	grave/acute	Stage 3; age 1;2 - 1;3
5/6.	compact/non-compact and flat/plain	Stage 4; age 1;4 - 1;5
7/8.	tense/lax and interrupted/continuant	Stage 5; age 1;6
9/10.	consonantal/non-consonantal and strident/mellow	Stage 6; age 1;7

However, this list oversimplifies certain relevant facts and obscures others. For instance, the feature of diffuse/non-diffuse, which was acquired in stage 2, applies first only to the vowels (stages 2 and 3), then to the vowels and grave oral consonants (stage 4), and finally to the vowels, grave oral and acute nasal consonants (stage 5).

Figure 1 represents a second type of description which, in addition to their order of acquisition, includes the interrelationships between the distinctive features.

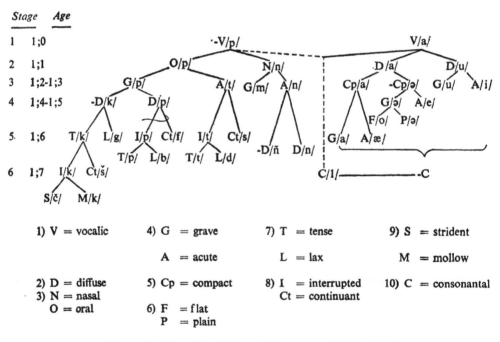

Figure 1. Order of acquisition of phonemes and distinctive features

The following development is shown in Figure 1: At stage 1, age 1;0, only the opposition vocalic (V)/non-vocalic (-V), represented by the phonemes /p/ and /a/, is present. These are the phonemes which occur in the first word, Ch /pap/ < E *Bob*.

At stage 2, age 1;1, the opposition nasal (N)/oral (O) is added in the consonantal system (/n/ vs. /p/ as shown by the word Ch /pan/ < Sp *pan* 'bread'), and the opposition diffuse (D)/non-diffuse (-D) is added to the vocalic system (/u/ vs. /a/, as illustrated by the word Ch /pauuau/ < E *bow-wow* or Sp *guauguáu*).

Stage 3 shows the appearance of the opposition grave (G)/acute (A), which applies to all consonants, both oral (/p/ vs. /t/, as in Ch /pan/ < Sp *pan* vs. Ch /tati/ < E *ticktock* or Sp *tic-tac*) and nasal (/m/ vs. /n/, as in Ch (ma/ < Sp *más* 'more' vs. Ch /pan/), and to the diffuse vowels (/u/ vs. /i/, as in Ch /pauuau/ vs. Ch /tati/).

At stage 4, the opposition diffuse/non-diffuse is extended to the grave orals (/k/ vs. /p/, as in Ch /ko/ < E *Coke* or Sp *coca* vs. Ch /pa/ Sp *papá* 'Daddy'), while in the vowel system the non-diffuse vowels split into compact (Cp)/non-compact (-Cp) (/a/ vs. /ə/ as in Ch /na/ < Sp *nada* 'nothing' vs. Ch /ə́pə/ < E *up*), and the non-compact split into grave and acute (/ə/ vs. /e/, as in Ch /ə́pə/ vs. Ch /me/ < E *man*); and the grave again split into flat (F)/plain (P) (/o/ vs. /ə/ as in Ch /ko/ vs. Ch /ə́pə/).

It is not clear whether the order is precisely as suggested, since the vowels /e/, /o/ and /ə/ all are introduced at approximately the same time.

Stage 5 shows a rich development of the consonantal system: (a) the feature of diffuse/non-diffuse is extended to the acute nasals (/ñ/ vs. /n/, as in Ch /ñáña/ < Sp Ignacio 'Ignatius' vs. Ch /ána/ < Sp *anda* 'go'); (b) a new opposition, interrupted (I)/continuant (Ct), applies to the diffuse grave orals (/p/ vs. /f/, as in Ch /páta/ < Sp *patas* 'feet' vs. Ch /fuf/ < Sp *jugo* 'juice') and to the acute orals (/t/ vs. /s/, as in Ch /tatí/ vs. Ch /si/ < Sp *si* 'yes'); (c) the opposition tense (T)/lax (L) is introduced, applying to the compact orals (/k/ vs. /g/, as in Ch /kóko/ < E *Coke* or Sp *coca* vs. Ch /gógo/ < Sp *globo* 'balloon'), to the interrupted diffuse orals (/p/ vs. /b/, as in Ch /páta/ vs. Ch /bab/ < E *Bob*), and to the interrupted acute orals (/t/ vs. /d/, as in Ch /tatí/ vs. Ch /dan/ < E *down*).

In the vowel system, the compact vowels split into grave and acute (/a/ vs. /æ/, as in Ch /ma/ vs. Ch /bæk/ < E *back*).

At stage 6, the opposition vocalic/non-vocalic splits into two features, consonantal (C)/non-consonantal (-C) and vocalic/non-vocalic, with the appearance of /l/, as in Ch /lálo/ < Sp *radio* /radio/; the opposition interrupted/continuant is extended to the voiceless compact consonants (/k/ vs. /š/, as in Ch /kóko/ vs. Ch /šei/ < E *shave*); and a new opposition, strident (S)/mellow (M) appears, applying to the tense interrupted compact consonants (/č/ vs. /k/, as in Ch /čáto/ < Sp *chancho* 'pig' vs. Ch /káka/ < Sp *casa* 'house').

We now turn to Jakobson's laws of phoneme acquisition and to Leopold's and Velten's studies.

According to Jakobson (p. 373), the first contrast established is that between a labial stop (less often a dental stop) and an open vowel, that is, between phonemes representing the maximum degrees of closure and of opening respectively. This first law of phoneme acquisition is fully confirmed by our data (stage 1, age 1;0). Velten (p. 282) records the same result. Leopold's record (§ 418) shows both a labial and a dental stop, with earlier appearance of the dental but later predominance of the labial.

Jakobson's second step (p. 374) consists of the splitting of the consonant into an oral and a nasal, which our data confirm (stage 2, age 1;1). Leopold (§ 419) observes this contrast only after the contrasts labial/dental and low vowel/high vowel. Our data also show an early appearance of a second vowel. Velten (p. 282) considers the alternative stop/continuant as well as oral/nasal as a possible first consonant split.

Jakobson's third stage (p. 370) is the appearance of a high vowel to contrast with the existing low vowel. We record this step simultaneously with the oral/nasal split for the consonants. Velten's third stage (p. 282) is the appearance of a second stop, which agrees with our data (stage 3, age 1;2 - 1;3) except for the fact that, simultaneously, we record the splitting of the high vowel into front and back, and the appearance of a second nasal. Both Jakobson (p. 370) and Velten (p. 282) posit the priority of a four-consonant system over the appearance of a second vowel. For Jakobson, these four consonants are two stops (labial and dental) and two nasals (labial and dental); for Velten, either two stops and two nasals or two stops and two fricatives (labial and dental). We have already stated that both Leopold's and our data suggest an earlier appearance of a second vowel. However, we cannot argue very strongly for it, since the only example containing a second vowel at stage 2 is the onomatopoetic Ch /pauuau/ < E bow-wow or Sp guauguáu, in which the /u/, moreover, is non-syllabic.

After the acquisition of the vowel, Jakobson (p. 370) considers two alternatives: either a mid vowel appears or the high vowel splits into a high front and a high back vowel. We record the second alternative, simultaneously with the appearance of the second stop and the second nasal (stage 3, age 1;2 - 1;3).

As for the phonemes acquired later, Jakobson's laws of implication (p. 371) are in general confirmed. Thus, /k/ appears only after /p/ and /t/, /š/ only after /f/ and /s/, and /ñ/ after /m/ and /n/; the first two fricatives, /f/ and /s/, appear only after the stop series /p t k/ is complete; and the first affricate /č/ comes after the corresponding stop /t/ and not before the corresponding fricative /š/. Leopold (§ 420) basically agrees with Jakobson as to the nasals: even though both [n] and [ŋ] are recorded, they do not constitute separate phonemes, so that at the end of the second year, the only nasals his subject has are /m/ and /n/. He also agress as to the priority of stops as a category over fricatives (§ 421). He disagrees, though, as to the order of appearance of /š/, which in his records shows up before both /s/ and /f/ (§ 422). Velten (1949) has shown, however, that the early appearance of /š/ "does not contradict any principle established by Jakobson." Thus, "it is true that in the languages of the world, the existence of /š/ presupposes the presence of /s/, but wherever only one sibilant is found the phonetic representation is irrelevant" (p. 219).

In general, and in agreement with Velten and Leopold, we find that Jakobson's theory provides an adequate framework for the order of acquisition of phonemes. In fact, all observations seem to confirm the general thesis that the child proceeds from the grossest to the finest discriminations. However, our data show points where alternative developments appear to be possible.

The consensus of opinion with regard to the order of acquisition of phonemes, then, is as follows:

(1) The first contrast involves an open vowel and a stop, labial or dental.

(2) The second contrast, which according to Leopold may appear simultaneously with the first, may involve one of three pairs of consonants: (a) an oral and a nasal (Jakobson, Contreras-Saporta); (b) a stop and a fricative (Velten); (c) a labial and a dental stop (Leopold).

(3) The third contrast may develop in the consonant or in the vowel system. In the first case, its actual realization depends on the contrasts acquired previously. Thus if (a) oral/nasal occurred in the previous stage, the next contrast involves the feature of gravity, and it may affect either member of the existing pair first, or both at the same time, producing one of these consonantal systems:

$$
\begin{array}{ccccc}
\text{p} - \text{t} & & \text{P} & & \text{p} - \text{t} \\
\diagdown\diagup & \text{or} & \diagup\diagdown & \text{or} & | \quad | \\
\text{N} & & \text{m} - \text{n} & & \text{m} - \text{n}
\end{array}
\qquad \text{(Jakobson, Contreras-Saporta)}
$$

where N represents either /m/ or /n/, and P represents a labial or a dental stop.

If (b) stop/fricative occurred at the previous stage, the next contrast also involves the feature of gravity, giving one of these two systems:

$$
\begin{array}{ccc}
\text{p} - \text{t} & & \text{p} - \text{t} \\
\diagdown\diagup & \text{(Velten, Leopold)} \quad \text{or} & | \quad | \\
\text{S} & & \text{f} - \text{s}
\end{array}
\qquad \text{(Velten)}
$$

where S represents any fricative.

If (c) labial/dental occurred at the previous stage, the next phoneme to appear will be a nasal or a fricative (Leopold) which in turn will split into labial and dental, according to the development outlined above.

If the third contrast develops in the vowel system, it implies the appearance of a high vowel (Leopold, Contreras-Saporta), which contrasts with the already existing low vowel. In this case, the consonantal development sketched above follows.

(4) The next step may adopt either of two forms: (a) the appearance of a third vowel, involving either front-back opposition for the high vowels (Contreras-Saporta) or an intermediate degree of opening for the front vowels (Leopold); or (b) the expansion of the consonantal system to include two stops, two nasals, and two fricatives, labial and dental (Velten).

From here on, Jakobson's laws of implication seem to hold true. Thus, the acquisition of back consonants (palatal or velar) implies the existence of front consonants (labial and dental); the acquisition of affricates implies the existence of homorganic stops and fricatives, etc.

3. GLOSSARY

In this section we present the subject's vocabulary, divided into an English and a Spanish section. Entries are given alphabetically in the model language form, with the child's version in phonetic and phonemic transcription; items whose origin may be either English or Spanish are included in both sections, with cross-references. Each item is included as it appeared in the original corpus; if items illustrate re-phonemicization from a previous stage, such information is recorded. In addition, each entry contains information as to changes in form or meaning.

The indication 'echo' is used to illustrate that the form did not appear spontaneously, but only as a repetition. Such forms are included in the glossary for completeness, since they were not used as a basis for phonemic analysis. (A complete glossary through age 2;0 is found in Contreras, *op. cit.*)

English

1. *apple*: [ə́pə] /ə́pə/ ~ [ə́pəl] /ə́pəl/ 'echo', 1;5
2. *baby*: (or Sp *bebé*): [bébe] /bébe/ ~ [bébi] /bébi/, 1;7
3. *back*: [bæk] /bæk/ 'put it back; shelf', 1;6; [bǽki] /bǽki/ 'back', 1;7
4. *ball*: [bə] ~ [ba] /pa/, 1;1
5. *bear*: [beə̣] /beə/, 1;7
6. *blocks*: [bákə] /bákə/ ~ [báki] /báki/ 'echo', 1; 6
7. *Bob*: [bab] ~ [bap] /pap/, 1; 0; [bab] /bab/, 1; 6
8. *book*: [bu] /pu/ ~ [búkə] /púkə/ ~ [buk] /puk/, 1;4
9. *bow-wow* (or Sp *guauguau*): [baṵ̯ṵ̯áṵ̯] /pauuáu/, 1;1; [baṵ̯ṵ̯áu] /bauuàú/, 1;6
10. *boy*: [boi̯] /poi/, 1;4; [boi̯] /boi/, 1; 6
11. *bye*: [bai̯] /pai/, 1;2
12. *Chicago*: [kao] /kao/ 'echo', 1;6
13. *Coke* (or Sp *coca*): [kóko] /kóko/ ~ [kóka] /kóka/ ~ [ko] /ko/, 1;5
14. *comb*: [koŋ] ~ [kon] /kon/ ~ [kom] /kom/, 1;5
15. *cookie*: [kóki] /kúki/, 1;6
16. *cow*: [kaṵ̯] /kau/, 1;6
17. *down*: [dan] /dan/,. 1;6
18. *fountain pen*: [faṵ̯n] /faun/ ~ [faṵ̯m] /faum/, 1;7
19. *Hi*: [ai̯] /ai/, 1;4
20. *kangaroo*: [kaŋgú] /kangú/, 1;7
21. *man*: [mæ̃] /me/, 1;4; [mɛən] /men/ ~ [man] /man/, 1;5
22. *Mattoon*: [matún] /matún/ ~ [patúmba] /patúmba/ 'echo', 1;6
23. *please*: [pii̯] /pii/ 'echo', 1;6
24. *Ricky*: [kíki] /kíki/ ~ [kíke] /kíke/, 1;6
25. *shave*: [šei̯] /šei/, 1;7
26. *shoes*: [tuṵ̯] /tuu/, 1;6
27. *ticktock*: (or Sp *tic-tac*): [tatí] /tatí/, 1;2
28. *tree*: [ti] ~ [tii̯] /ti/ 'echo', 1;6
29. *up*: [ɔp] ~ [ap] /ap/ 'up; down', 1;1; [ə́pə] /ə́pə/ ~ [ə́pəl] /ə́pəl/, 1;4

Spanish

1. *adiós* 'good-bye': [adú] /adú/, 1;7
2. *anda* 'go': [ána] /ána/ ~ [ánda] /ánda/ 'echo', 1;6
3. *aquí* 'here': [akí] /akí/, 1;6
4. *auto* 'car': [áu̯to] /áuto/, 1;6
5. *ay no* 'oh no': [ai̯nó] /ainó/ 'echo', 1;6
6. *ay sí* 'oh yes': [ai̯sí] /aisí/ 'echo', 1;6
7. *bah* 'oh': [ba] /ba/ 'oops' (when dropping something), 1;6
8. *bebé* (or E *baby*): see E *baby*
9. *boca* 'mouth': [bóga] ~ [bóge] /bóga/, 1;7
10. *bravo* 'bravo': [bábu] /bábu/ ~ [bábo] /bábo/, 1;7
11. *buey* 'ox': [bai̯] /pəi/, 1;5
12. *bus* 'bus': [buš] /bus/ ~ [but̠] /but/, bu̯i̯x] /buis/, 1;6
13. *caballo* 'horse': [kavájo] ~ [kabájo] /kabáio/, 1;7
14. *cacú* 'excrement': [kakú] /kakú/, 1;6
15. *cae* 'he falls': [kai̯] /kai/ 'I'm falling', 1;7
16. *cama* 'bed': [káma] /káma/, 1;7
17. *casa* 'house': [káka] /káka/ ~ [kaša] /káša/, 1;7
18. *chancho* 'pig': [šáčon] /šáčon/ ~ [šatón] /šatón/ ~ [čášo] /čášo/ ~ [čáto] /čáto/, 1;7
19. *Chela* (a name): [čéča] /kéka/ ~ [čéža] /késa/ ~ [téza] /tésa/, 1;6; [čéža] /čéša/, 1;7
20. *chupete* 'pacifier': [péte] /péte/, 1;7
21. *coca* (or E *Coke*): see E *Coke*
22. *ella* 'she': [éi̯a] /éia/ 'echo', 1;6
23. *globo* 'balloon': [gógo] /gógo/, 1;6
24. *grande* 'big': [gan] /gan/, 1;7
25. *guauguáu* (or E *bow-wow*): see E *bow-wow*.
26. *Ignacio* 'Ignatius': [ñáña] /ñáña/, 1;6
27. *jugo* 'juice'; [fuf] /fuf/, 1;6; [fúgo] /fúgo/, 1;7
28. *lámpara* 'lamp': [lámpa] /lámpa/ ~ [lába] /lába/, 1;7
29. *leche* 'milk': [čéče] /čéče/, 1;7
30. *luna* 'moon': [núna] /núna/, 1;7
31. *luz* 'light': [dus] /dus/, 1;7
32. *mambo* 'mambo': [mámbo] /mámbo/ ~ [mámo] /mámo/ ~ [bámbo] /bámbo/ 'echo', 1;6
33. *manos* 'hands': [máno] /máno/, 1;6
34. *mantequilla* 'butter': [kíi̯a] /kíia/, 1;7
35. *más* 'more': [ma] /ma/ 'food', 1;3; 'more', 1;6
36. *nada* 'nothing': [na] /na/ 'no more', 1;3
37. *niau* (onomatopoeia for 'cat'): [ni̯áu̯] /niáu/, 1;6
38. *niña* 'girl': [níña] /níña/ ~ [nína] /nína/ ~ [nía] /nía/ ~ [ní̯a] /níia/ 'echo', 1;6

39. *no* 'no': [no] /no/ 'echo', 1;6; 'no', 1;7
40. *ojo* 'eye': [óho] ~ [ógo] ~ [ófo] ~ [óxo] /ófo/, 1;7
41. *oscuro* 'dark': [ku] /ku/, 1;6; [kúku] /kúku/, 1;7
42. *pajaro* 'bird': [páxo] /páfo/, 1;7
43. *pan* 'bread': [pan] /pan/ 'food', 1;1; 'bread', 1;5
44. *papa* 'Daddy': [pa] /pa/ ~ [papá] /papa/, 1;3 [papá] /papá/, 1;6
45. *patas* 'feet': [pata] /páta/ 'feet; shoes', 1;6
46. *Pepe* 'name of teddy-bear': [pépe] /pépe/ ~ [pépi] /pépi/, 1;5
47. *pichí* 'urine': [či] /ki/ 'urinate', 1;5; [pičí] /pičí/, 1;7
48. *pierna* 'leg': [péna] /péna/, 1;7
49. *plátano* 'banana': [páke] /páke/ ~ [pəká] /pəká/, 1;6
50. *¿qué hay?* 'how is it going?': [kaɪ] /kai/ ~ [kɪáɪ] /kiái/, 1;5
51. *Raca* nickname for 'Raquel': [káka] /káka/ 'echo', 1;6
52. *radio* 'radio': [lálo] /lálo/ 'radio; television', 1;7
53. *sí* 'yes': [si] /si/ 'echo', 1;6
54. *silla* 'chair': [síɹa] /síia/, 1;7
55. *sucio* 'dirty'; [sus] /sus/ ~ [suš] /suš/ ~ [sut] /sut/ 'echo', 1;7
56. *toma* 'take (it)': [tóma] /tóma/ 'take it; give me', 1;7
57. *toni* 'clown': [tóno] /tóno/ ~ [tóna] /tóna/, 1;6
58. *tostada* 'toast': [totá] /totá/ 'toast; toaster', 1;6
59. *tuto* 'sleep': [tútu] /tútu/ ~ [tutú] /tutú/, 1;6
60. *ves* 'see': [be] /be/ (only as a question, e.g., after falling), 1;6
61. *zapato* 'shoe': [tapáto] /tapáto/ ~ [páto] /páto/, 1;7

UNIVERSITY OF WASHINGTON

REFERENCES

Contreras, H. *The Phonological System of a Bilingual Child*, Doctoral dissertation (Indiana University, 1961).
Chomsky, N. (1965), *Aspects of the Theory of Syntax* (Cambridge, M. I. T. Press).
Fischer-Jørgensen, E. (1958), "What can the new techniques of acoustic phonetics contribute to linguistics? *Proceedings of the Eighth International Congress of Linguists* (Oslo), pp. 433-478.
Jakobson, R. (1949), "Les lois phoniques du langage enfantin et leur place dans la phonologie générale", in N. S. Trubetzkoy, *Principes de Phonologie*, translated by J. Cantineau (Paris: Klincksieck).
Leopold, W. (1947), *Speech Development of a Bilingual Child*, Vol. II (Evanston, Illinois, Northwestern University Press).
Saporta, S. (1960), Review of J. Mattoso Camara, Jr., *Princípios de lingüistica geral*, *Language*, 36, pp. 89-97.
Velten, H. (1943), "The growth of phonemic and lexical patterns in infant language", *Language*, 19, pp. 281-292.
Velten, H. (1949), Review of W. Leopold (1947), *Language*, 25, pp. 215-219.

ALBERT UPTON

THAT MONSTER CUSTOM

The poor monsters's my subject and he shall not suffer indignity.

The Tempest

A paper with the oily odor of an old-fashioned *explication de texte* would not appeal to the discriminative nostril as a fitting tribute to the vigorous modern intellect of an Elwood Murray. I therefore hasten to assure the Murray Fellowship that I am not a scholar. Just as electronics engineers are known, upon occasion, to stay home nights and play with short-wave radios in order to communicate with other 'hams' in faraway places, so I am a communications engineer whose hobby is to stay home nights and attempt to tune in on a professional named Shakespeare.

Although the satisfactions are sometimes intense, it is a one-sided enterprise which must substitute the law of parsimony for the pleasant exchange of confirmation cards. One proceeds, nevertheless, upon the same semantic principles which apply to any and all communication by means of symbols. The most basic of these I take to be the following:

(1) The law of matrix — the meaning of a symbol is relevant to its matrix.

(2) Polysemia is essential to symbolic economy. A relatively small number of terms must have a relatively large number of senses if a system is to be manageable.

(3) The older a familiar term is, the greater the difficulty of semantic control.

(4) And finally, facility with metaphor (implicit analogy) is essential to sophisticated communication.

"When I first began editing Shakespeare in 1919", said John Dover Wilson, "I was prepared for fresh tillage in the field of textual exploration and emendation, but in that of commentary I looked to find few stones unturned by editors of the eighteenth and nineteenth centuries. Nothing has surprised me more than the amount of work of this sort still to be done ... . Indeed, the further I went upon my way the more the need for commentary forced itself upon my attention, and in *Hamlet*, the most popular and most frequently edited of them all, the task is heavier than ever" (*H*, p. xxxii).

The probable causes are the traditional acceptance of the Folio as exemplar instead of the Second Quarto, the lack of an Oxford Dictionary and a Bartlett concordance during the eighteenth and nineteenth centuries, and the neglect of their rigorous use during the twentieth. Perhaps one should also add the failure to conduct the interpretation of metaphor with appropriate care and imagination — imagination, that is, in the sense of image-making, not 'creativity'. For "in the quick forge and working-house" of Shakespearean thought metaphors are not mere "flowers of rhetoric" but "conceits" — conceptual models skillfully designed for the communication of abstract ideas and their accompanying emotions.

Let me dwell for a moment upon a case in point. I once set a graduate student, Miss Sheila Dwight, the task of checking the instances of divergence between the Second Quarto and the so-called received text. She soon returned with a gleam in her eye and the following passage.

> Why seemes it so perticuler with thee.
>   Ham. Seemes Maddam nay it is, I know not seemes,
> Tis not alone my incky cloake coold mother
> Nor customary suites of solembe blacke
> Nor windie suspiration of forst breath
> No, nor the fruitfull riuer in the eye,
> Nor the dejected hauier of the visage
> Together with all formes, moodes, chapes of griefe
> That can deuote me truely, these indeede seeme,
> For they are actions that a man might play
> But I haue that within which passes showe
> These but the trapping and the suites of woe. (Ed. Vietor, I, ii, 76 ff p. 23)

Now the Folio reads "shews of Griefe" but modern editors, including Wilson himself, emend *chapes* to *shapes*. Miss Dwight found that the O.E.D. defines *chape* as "A plate of metal with which anything is covered, overlaid, or ornamented", and "The metal plate or mounting of a scabbard or sheath". In other words, what a suit is to a man and a trapping to a horse, a chape is to various other objects including swords and daggers. Just as imaginative Hamlet thinks of a pair of indentures when looking down upon the suture of a skull in Act V, so here he might well have been fingering the sheath of his dagger as he uttered the word *chape*.

While the present paper specifically intends the explication of the line "That monster custom, who all sense doth eat", consideration of the terms *sense* and *custom* involves the entire conversation between Gertrude and Hamlet.

"Leave wringing of your hands ... . And let me wring your hart", says he, "for so I shall/If it be made of penitrable stuffe, If damned custom have not brasd it so. That it be proofe and bulwark against sence." And thus the *chape* of previous reference which hides that within becomes the brass covering which prevents penetration from without. Hamlet's preoccupation with the superficiality of custom has been under-emphasized, if not unnoticed, partly because of the emendation of *chapes* and the misinterpretation of *brasd* (the Folio has *braz'd*) 'as to make hard like brass' instead of 'to cover as with brass'.

The two passages with which we are most concerned are further noteworthy in that more than half the lines occur only in the Second Quarto and were regarded by Wilson and Pollard as possibly 'pruned' from the First Folio copy by Shakespeare himself (*MSH*, p. 167). Here are the passages. (The italics indicate the lines not found in the Folio.)

> You cannot call it loue, for at your age
> The heyday in the blood is tame, it's humble.
> And waits vppon the judgement, and what judgement
> Would step from this to this, *sence sure youe haue*
> *Els could you not haue motion, but sure that sence*
> *Is appoplex, for madnesse would not erre*
> *Nor fence to extacie was nere so thral'd*
> *But it reseru'd some quantity of choise*
> *To serue in such a difference, what deuill wast*
> That thus hath cosund you at hodman blind;
> *Eyes without feeling, feeling without sight,*
> *Eares without hands, or eyes, smelling sance all,*
> *Or but a sickly part of one true sence*
> *Could not do mope:* ....

> Assume a vertue if you haue it not,
> *That monster custome, who all sance doth eate*
> *Of habits deuill, is angell yet in this*
> *That to the vse of actions faire and good,*
> *He likewise giues a frock or Liuery*
> *That aptly is put on* to refraine night,
> And that shall lend a kind of easines
> To the next abstinence, *the next more easie:*
> *For use almost can change the stamp of nature,*
> *And either the deuill, or throwe him out*
> *With wonderous potency:* (Ed. Vietor, p. 197 ff.)

The discussion of Gertrude's sinful conduct seems clearly to be based upon classical psychology. Although Aristotelian *loci* may be found for the entire system of concepts with the exception of the function of the brain, it is more to the present purpose to review it in the language of an Elizabethan contemporary, Robert Burton; I refer, of course, to the essay on the soul in the First Partition, Member 2, of the *Anatomy of Melancholy*. We begin with the heart "which is the seat and fountain of life, of heat, of spirits, of pulse and respiration; the Sun of our body, the King and sole commander of it: the seat and organ of all passions and affections". Then there is the brain "which by his nerves gives sense and motion to the rest" and is "the most noble organ under heaven, the dwellinghouse and seat of the soul, the habitation of wisdom, memory, judgment, reason, and in which man is most like unto God". Shakespeare agrees with Burton in embracing the Alexandrian theory of brain function as opposed to Aristotle's and like Burton clings nevertheless to the Philosopher's conception of the heart as the organ of emotion.

Hamlet proposes to wring his mother's "heart" if "damned custom has not brassed it so that it be proof and bulwark against sense". Wilson glosses *sense* here as 'feeling, perceptive sensibility' and does likewise with *sense* in lines 71 and 72; this scarcely clarifies the meaning. If we seek light from Burton, we learn that "the common division of the SOUL is into three principal faculties, VEGETAL, SENSITIVE, and RATIONAL, which make three distinct kinds of living creatures: *vegetal* plants, SENSIBLE beasts, RATIONAL men. How these three principal faculties are distinguished and connected is beyond human capacity, as Taurellus, Philip, Flavius, and others suppose. The inferior may be alone, but the superior cannot subsist without the other; so SENSIBLE includes VEGETAL, RATIONAL both; which are contained in it (saith Aristotle) as a triangle in a quadrangle" (p. 135, Ed. Dell and Smith). After ana-tomizing the vegetal soul, he continues:

Next in order is the SENSIBLE faculty, which is as far beyond the other in dignity, as a beast is preferred to a plant, having those vegetal powers included in it. 'Tis defined AN ACT OF AN ORGANICAL BODY, BY WHICH IT LIVES, HATH SENSE, APPETITE, JUDGEMENT, BREATH, AND MOTION. His object in general is a sensible or possible quality, because the sense is affected with it. The general organ is the brain, from which principally the sensible operations are derived. This sensible soul is divided into two parts, APPREHENDING OR MOVING. By the APPREHENSIVE power we perceive the species [Shakespeare would have used *image* for *species* here.] of sensible things, present or absent, and retain them as wax doth the print of a seal. By the MOVING the body is outwardly carried from one place to another, or inwardly moved by spirits & pulse. The APPREHENSIVE faculty is subdivided into two parts, INWARD or OUTWARD; OUTWARD, as the five senses, of TOUCHING, HEARING, SEEING, SMELLING, TASTING, to which you may add Scaliger's sixth of TITILLATION, if you please; or that of speech, which is the sixth external sense according to Lullius; inward are three, COMMON SENSE, PHANTASY, MEMORY. These five outward senses have their object in outward things only, and such as are present, as the eye sees no colour except it be at hand, the ear no sound. (p. 137).

And of the rational, he concludes:

This REASONABLE SOUL, which Austin calls a spiritual substance moving itself, is defined by Philosophers to be THE FIRST SUBSTANTIAL ACT OF A NATURAL, HUMAN, ORGANICAL BODY BY WHICH A MAN LIVES, PERCEIVES, AND UNDERSTANDS, FREELY DOING ALL THINGS, AND WITH ELECTION. Out of which definition we may gather, that this RATIONAL SOUL includes the powers, and performs the duties of the two other, which are contained in it, and all three faculties make one SOUL, which is inorganical of itself although it be in all parts, incorporel, using their organs, and working by them. It is divided into two chief parts, differing in office only, not in essence; the UNDERSTANDING, which is the RATIONAL power APPREHENDING; the WILL, which is the RATIONAL power MOVING; to which two all the other *rational* powers are subject and reduced (p. 144).

The understanding is a complex power of some "fourteen species", including "sense, experience, intelligence... and conscience". And, finally, there is the will, a power of the rational soul

...WHICH COVETS OR AVOIDS SUCH THINGS AS HAVE BEEN BEFORE JUDGED AND APPREHENDED BY THE UNDERSTANDING. If good, it approves; if evil, it abhors it: so that his object is either good or evil. Aristotle calls this our RATIONAL APPETITE; for as in the SENSITIVE we are moved to good or bad by our APPETITE, ruled and directed by sense; so in this we are carried by REASON. Besides, the SENSITIVE APPETITE hath a particular object, good or bad: this an universal immaterial; that respects only things delectable and pleasant, this honest. Again, they differ in liberty. The SENSUAL APPETITE seeing an object, if it be a convenient good, cannot but desire it; if evil, avoid it: but this is free in his essence, MUCH NOW DEPRAVED, OBSCURED, AND FALLEN FROM HIS FIRST PERFECTION; YET IN SOME OF HIS OPERATIONS STILL FREE, as to go, walk, move at his pleasure, and to choose whether it will do or not do, steal or not steal. Otherwise in vain were laws, deliberations, exhortations, counsels, precepts, rewards, promises, threats, and punishments: and God should be the author of sin (p. 146).

Thus, just as the general faculties are progressively inclusive, so are the senses of *sense*. The sensible soul experiences through the five (or more) senses; the 'common sense' organizes the sensations into perceptions and makes immediate practical identifications and evaluations. But, as Montaigne observes in Chapter 23 of the *Essays*, "custom dulls the senses" and "blinds the eye of Judgment". Hamlet's first use of *sense* may therefore mean as little as the indicated employment of ears and eyes and as much as that minimum essential comprehension of his point sufficient to cause a change of attitude. He wants Gertrude to 'see' herself as he 'sees' her, but the appeal is to her understanding and thence to her will. Since Gertrude naturally responds defensively, his next "assay" takes the primary form. He asks her, literally, to look at portraits of his tall, blond ("Hyperion's curls") father, and his short, brunet ("this Moore") uncle. He then discusses the appearance of the two kings, but the words "you cannot call it love" show that he is thinking of his mother's appetitive attitude of the sensible order toward her second husband. He then says "Sense sure you have/Else could you not have motion." Wilson glosses *sense* here as 'before' and *motion* as 'impulse, desire'. He may be right, but I am inclined to the opinion that he is at best half right. The most relevant source passages I am acquainted with are two in Aristotle's *De Motu*, 701a.

The living creature is moved and goes forward by reason of desire or purpose, when alteration has been set going on the occasion of SENSATION or imagination... I want a drink, says appetite; this is a drink says SENSE or imagination or mind: straightway I drink. In this way living creatures are impelled TO MOVE and to act, and desire is the last or immediate cause of MOVEMENT, and desire arises after perception or after imagination and conception.

Now Wilson certainly would not have us interpret Hamlet as saying "Feeling sure you have else you would not have DESIRE", but we might read it "Perceptive sensibility sure you have else would you not HAVE desire." That is, Hamlet would be saying "You cannot call it love, but it is the same sort of appetitive behavior (motion), so I know that you must have perceptive sensibility because living creatures do not HAVE motion unless it is occasioned by perceptive sensibility." And *perceptive sensibility* would mean 'sensation', 'imagination', and/or 'conception'. This suggests that Shakespeare has in mind the standard bipartite division of the sensible soul as cited above and that Hamlet may even be saying "an apprehending faculty you must have else you would not have a moving faculty". This would very definitely make sense in the light of Burton's definition and commentary:

This MOVING FACULTY is the other power of the SENSITIVE SOUL, which causeth all those INWARD AND OUTWARD ANIMAL MOTIONS IN THE BODY. It is divided into two faculties, the power of *appetite*, and of MOVING FROM PLACE TO PLACE. This of APPETITE is threefold, so some will have it; natural, as it signifies any such inclination, as of a stone to fall downward, and such actions as RETENTION, EXPULSION, which depend not on sense, but are vegetal, as the appetite of meat and drink, hunger and thirst. SENSITIVE is common to men and brutes. VOLUNTARY, the third, or intellective, which commands the other two in men, and is a curb unto them, or at least should be, but for the most part is captivated and overruled by them: and men are led like beasts by sense, giving reins to their concupiscence and several lusts. For by this appetite the soul is led or inclined to follow that good which the senses shall approve, or avoid that which they hold evil. His object being good or evil, the one he embraceth, the other he rejecteth: according to that Aphorism, all things seek their own good, or at least seeming good. This power is inseparable from sense; for where sense is, there is likewise pleasure and pain (p. 140).

I would finally reemphasize the point that the semantic connection between "it" (this passion of yours) as a species of the genus "motion" should be expressed by emphasis upon the word HAVE before MOTION.

It seems, however, that if we take the motion-as-feeling gambit, we are assuming that Hamlet's "question" here is, What IS this strange passion, seeing that your age precludes its being lust? Now to me this is to miss the flash and impact of a superb Shakespearean hyperbole. Proceeding on the assumption that Hamlet is trying to move his mother to a sense of shame and thence repentance, the logic of his dialectic, as I see it, would go like this:

If I am to move her to a feeling of shame, I must get at her inner being by way of her senses, then her common sense, then her understanding, and finally her will, provided damned custom has not made them all insensible to my attempt. I'll begin with the audio-visual approach. "Mother, look at these portraits. Are you so accustomed to their appearance that you can't 'see' the difference? I admit that emotional disturbance corrupts the vision. If that's the trouble, it can't be because of sexual passion; you're too old for that. You're not blind, are you? I know you have at least one of the five senses in some sort of working order because I can see you move, and as the Philosopher says, we animals can't move without sensation. Certainly your sensible faculty must be paralyzed for no woman ever fell so madly in love or was so overborne with the ecstacy of it that her senses couldn't detect the vast difference between two such men. I guess some devil must have pulled the wool over your eyes. Because if you just had vision with no sense of touch, or just touch and no sight, or just hearing without either touch or sight, or, confound it, the sense of smell with no other sense whatsoever, or just a puny little fraction of any one real sense, you could tell what a stinker this uncle of mine is.

He makes his point successfully, but the arrival of the ghost of husband number one confuses the issue. His position is reestablished, however, with Gertrude's, "O, Hamlet, thou hast cleft my heart in twain."

At this point, Wilson silently shuffles in an emendation from the Folio in spite of his insistence that Q2 "is the text to build on" (*H*, p. XXVIII). For in the Quarto, Hamlet answers:

> O throw away the worser part of it
> And leave the purer with the other half.

The Folio has *live*, but does not *leave* do better with *go*? "When you LEAVE me, do not GO to my uncle's bed! And if you feel half-hearted in your purity, pretend that you are whole." Here Hamlet manifests Shakespeare's partial agreement with the Aristotelian theory of heart function.

And now comes the avowed subject of MY story, the meaning of the two lines:

> That monster custom, who all since doth eate
> Of habits deuill, is angell yet in this

Wilson tells us only that *sense* again means 'feeling, perceptive sensibility' and again honors HIS custom in the breach by emending the Quarto's *habits devil* to *habits evil*. Here are his notes on the passage:

162. Of *habits evil* (Theobald aft. Thirlby) Q2 'of habits deuill.' The misprint would be easy (v. MSH pp. 320-1), especially as the compositor, like all edd, since Johnson, may have been misled by a supposed antithesis between 'devil' and 'angel' whereas SH. intends, I think, to contrast 'monster' with 'angel' and 'habits evil' with 'actions fair and good.'

164. *frock or livery* Two sorts of uniform: 'frock' of a monk, suggesting religion, and 'livery' of a servant, suggesting duty. The image springs from 'assume' (v. G.) and 'habits' (in a quibbling sense) just before.

167-70. *the next...potency* F 1 omits. MSM. pp. 28-9, 167.

169. *And either...the devil* Q2 "And either the deuill." The compositor has prob. as so often elsewhere omitted a word. It is conceivable, on the other hand, that 'either' (sp. 'eyther') may be a misprint or miscorrection of 'exorcise', a word which suits the context and must come near SH's meaning. For want of a better, it may serve to fill the gap in the text. MSH. pp. 302-3.

Hamlet, like Montaigne, with whom he frequently sees eye to eye, took a jaundiced view of custom. To the one it was a "damned custom", a "monster", and a "tyrant"; to the other a "sovereign" thing whose principal effect "is to seize and grip us so firmly, that we are scarce able to escape from its grasp"; and to both it was characteristically superficial. In customary suits it shows us actions that a man might play and in Montaigne's view "hides from us the true aspect of things".

To my way of thinking, the crux is the word ALL and the key sense is 'exclusively'. That monster custom who eats nothing but sense (i.e., is nourished exclusively on appearance as 'apprehended' by the 'outward senses') is a monster not only in respect of his monstrously unbalanced diet but also in the matter of dress. Naturally being a damned thing concerned with the letter and not the spirit, he dresses as a devil; but he is an angel (and thus a monster, part devil and part angel) in that he lends his "countenance" and hence the frock and livery of his house to the practice (i.e., the repeated overt behavior) of actions fair and good. (The "essential" charac-

teristic of an "action" is the inward will and purpose of the agent.) You can well
imagine that he has no trouble getting into HIS habit; and a fair action in custom's
house finds it LIKEWISE easy to don the customary garment of its office, for custom
aptly makes it "a property of easiness". The use of *monster* in connection with
incongruous dress occurs amusingly in *The Taming of the Shrew*.

> O, sir! his lackey, for all the world
> caparisoned like the horse; with a linen stock
> on one leg and a kersey boot-hose on the other,
> gartered with a red and blue list; an old hat,
> and the 'humour of forty fancies' pricked in't
> for a feather: a monster, a very monster in
> apparel, and not like a Christian footboy or a
> gentleman's lackey. (III, ii 67 ff.)

Wilson's remark on line 169 as quoted above also calls for comment. I would supply
shame here after Furness who prints *master* but seems to prefer *shame*. In Shakespeare's idiom the devil is once appalled, cheated, commanded, cozened, curbed,
defied, denied, and scotched; but he is thrice shamed by Hotspur. It is truth that
shames him and truth is manifested when the "outward habit" "truly denotes" the
"inward man", or the outward manifestation truly denotes the inward cause.

As for 'exorcise' coming "near Shakespeare's meaning", one must observe that
Shakespeare's three known uses of the concept (exorciser, exorcism, exorcist) all
seem to imply 'conjuration', a sense which would necessitate the additional emendation of *and* for *or* and result in a possible "And exorcise (conjure up) the devil
and throw him out." When we give *exorcise* its alternate sense of 'cast out', we have
a tautology, exorcise and throw out, without the emphatic Shakespearean ring,
(if we may use the term loosely to designate such expressions as 'gross and scope',
'cheer and comfort', 'thews and bulk', 'food and diet').

In conclusion, I think one must allow that if we are to follow the Cambridge notes
and glosses, then Hamlet has roared us a monstrous muddled metaphor indeed —
an all-devouring chimera who goes about sharking up human decency is transformed
in mid-sentence into a noble lord who provides appropriate raiment for his retinue.[1]
Now I do not aver that the Bard never fumbled a figure, but to charge him with the
rank incongruity of such an enseamed period is a course most incorrect to her-
meneutics.

WHITTIER COLLEGE

---

[1] In Shakespeare's idiom we get monsters when "things change from their ordinance, their natures
and preformed faculties" or "err against all rules of nature". Bottom offers to speak the part of
Thisbe in "a monstrous little voice" and if Quince will but give him the part of the lion also, "I will
roar you", says he, "as gently as any sucking dove; I will roar you an 'twere any nightingale".
(*M N D*, I, ii). My point is that a so-called 'mixed metaphor' is, itself, a semantic monstrosity.

PART FOUR

COMMUNICATION DISORDERS

The academic and professional development of speech pathology and audiology has occurred in less than a half-century. One of the first laboratories established for the purpose of studying defective speech was an outgrowth of the curiosity on the part of a psychologist at the University of Iowa. At almost the same point in time, other clinical facilities were being developed by scholars who had their roots in traditional areas of Speech. It is only recently that many of the disorders of speech and hearing have been seen as co-existing with medical and emotional problems. Today speech and hearing problems are viewed as non-medical although in many respects medically allied. They are also considered non-psychopathological although many communication disorders have an emotional component.

One large group of speech correctionists is interested in primary education where the most predominant problem encountered is that of the child who has not learned proper articulation. Since most articulation problems have no apparent organic cause they are generally considered 'functional' in nature. Other speech clinicians work in hospital settings perhaps as members of a team interested in the problems of the child with a cleft palate. Here the stress is almost completely away from the functional aspects of speech deviation because a clearly observable physical anomaly is assumed to be the primary cause of the defective speech. Speech clinicians working with a condition such as aphasia are also likely to be hospital-based but they may have stronger interests and greater training in the area of linguistics and language since their primary goal is the re-education of a variety of language functions left impaired as a result of cerebral insult or trauma. Delayed speech, voice disorders, and foreign or regional dialects are additional problems the speech correctionist may encounter.

Audiology, a discipline concerned primarily with hearing measurement and the rehabilitation of the acoustically impaired, is the most recent development in the area of communication disorders. Its extremely rapid growth over the past twenty years can be attributed to World War II. Prior to the war, hearing rehabilitation was the domain of the teacher of the deaf. This specialty, devoted to educating the deaf child in academic matters, has been recognized since the 1600's. The existence of large numbers of veterans who had suffered varying degrees of hearing loss in the war generated a need for more facilities for hearing testing and training and better rehabilitation techniques. While the electronic instrumentation required for the accurate measurement of hearing had been developed a number of years before World War II, the problem of hearing loss and rehabilitation had not reached sufficient magnitude to require large numbers of trained academicians and clinicians in audiology. The field of audiology has also been significantly influenced in its growth by the medical specialty of otology and the academic specialty of speech pathology. Research by experimental psychologists, acousticians, and electronic engineers has also had a strong impact on the field.

This section, which deals with communication disorders, parallels in many respects the historical development of the field of speech pathology and audiology. The contribution by Mr. Gerald Phillips represents what is quite probably the point of view that would have developed at this point in time had speech correction never become a separate branch of the speech discipline. It is possible that, had viewpoints such as the one expressed by Phillips been prevalent at the time separation was contemplated, speech pathology might have remained in the general fold for a considerably longer period of time.

Phillips' point of view is illustrative of the area of commonality existing between the parent general speech field and its highly specialized offspring. 'Stage fright' is thought to be outside the area of speech correction by most speech clinicians. At the same time, 'minor' problems of a similar nature are considered by clinicians to be very much within their realm. The determining factor would appear to be the fact that the speaker suffering stage fright is generally not discovered unless he is called upon to speak before a group. As a result, the general speech teacher is usually the first specialist to recognize and treat the problem. The severe stutterer, on the other hand, generally fears any speaking situation to such an extent that his oral communication may be highly restricted and he is more likely to seek the help of a speech clinician. Phillips' contribution is particularly significant in that it provides both the generalist in speech and the speech correctionist with an awareness of the interrelationships between their respective areas of interest.

Much of the early work in speech pathology appears to have been concerned primarily with developing a vocabulary. Any number of systems of diagnostic classification, each with its appropriate armamentarium of Greek and Latin prefixes and suffixes, were proposed. It is to the profession's credit that most of these systems have not survived. To a large extent, however, the concept of diagnosis by classification remains intact. This has resulted far too often in the unfortunate assumption that having named a person's difficulty one has said something about it. Phillip Rosenberg is one of the more recent audiologists in the field to decry this practice. He has pointed out that such labels as 'congenital aphasia', 'auditory scramble', 'central auditory imperception', 'central dysacousis', 'neurological deafness', and 'central deafness' are widely used even though "the proliferation of these diagnoses is out of proportion to the possibility of their occurrence in the general population''.

In this volume, Mr. Paul Ptacek proposes an alternative to this practice. He recommends that diagnostic categories be dispensed with and that they be replaced with behavioral descriptions. Ptacek's contribution also focuses upon one of the most serious problems within the profession of speech pathology and one that, by its very nature, tends largely to be ignored. It is the problem of diagnosis. Ptacek makes a rational and thoughtful case for descriptive evaluation rather than nomenclature in diagnostic evaluation. This article is one which can be profitably studied by the beginning student and the long time practitioner alike for it challenges both the novice and the skilled professional to examine the unconscious assumptions of their discipline.

Mr. Wendell Johnson and co-author Mr. Joseph L. Stewart discuss some of the breakdowns of communication. Before his death in August 1965, Wendell Johnson was one of the most active proponents of looking at human behavior from a communication point of view. Johnson is known in speech pathology circles for his 'semantogenic' theory of stuttering, a theory which suggests the interesting thesis that stuttering does not occur in cultures which have no word for it. The article which appears in this volume will be the last to have come from the hand of Wendell Johnson.

GERALD M. PHILLIPS

A NEW DIRECTION FOR THE SPEECH PROFESSION

SPEECH AND PERSONALITY

The recent separation between departments of speech pathology and departments of speech have not ended the dialogue between the two fields. The proliferation on one hand, of articles on etiology, diagnosis and treatment of organic and functional speech defects marks the fruition of years of patient research. The new emphasis of both fields is now legitimately on the psychological and psychiatric involvement in pathologies of speech. Travis (1957) states:

Speech pathologists have manifested in both practice and research an ever-quickening interest in psychotherapy. To them have come those suffering from troubles in communication without organic impairment of either the sensory or motor speech equipment. Voice and speech drills have not always been too effective with these cases. The recognition of emotional disturbances as etiological factors in these disorders have forced speech therapists to seek the promising help of psychotherapy as developed by psychiatrists and psychologists.

In dealing with abnormalities of speech behavior, some definition of normal appears to be necessary. In the context of the close relationship between speech and personality (Murray; 1937) it appears impossible to construct a definition. Recognition of the connection between psychology and speech disorders led to a search for possible relationships between personality patterns and disorders of speech and communication. Speech disorders and personality disorders are now widely acknowledged to be related malfunctions. This attitude is implicit in such definitions as, "a speech disorder is a disorder of the person as well as a disorder in the reception and transmission of spoken language" (Travis; 1957) or "...speech is a peculiarly HUMAN function and its disorders reflect all the complex troubles of humanity" (Van Riper; 1963). Confirmation from psychiatrists can be found in Becker's (1962) statement that speech is the most prominent projection of human personality so intrinsic that it is only amenable to study in a holistic matrix of personality. The implications here are obvious. If there is any disorder at all in a speaker's personality, it will, in some way, be reflected in his verbal patterns. Scher (1962) refers to "verbal dysrhythmia" as a salient symptom of personality disorder. Thus speech therapist and psychotherapist alike agree on the relationship between speech and personality. Berry and Eisenson (1956) sum up:

Speech may be considered defective if the speaker is excessively self-conscious or apprehensive about objectively small deviations in his manner of speaking. In a broad sense, any speech deviation, however small, becomes a significant defect if it interferes with the speaker's social adjustment.

The awareness expressed by Johnson (1946) of semantogenic involvement in etiology of speech pathologies is confirmed again by psychologists and psychiatrists. It appears that a social definition is made of a 'deviation' and a human becomes involved as a total personality. It is this very admission of the psychological and social context of speech problems that re-opens the dialogue between stuttering, the domain of the speech pathologist, stage fright, the province of the speech teacher, and reticence, which no one works with at all. In addition, there is the growing awareness of a problem which cuts across all lines, the problem of the cultural chasm which separates the communication patterns of various socio-economic levels (Pines; 1965).

All of these can be connected by designating normality as the set of 'neurotic behaviors' accorded positive value by society, as opposed to equally neurotic, but not necessarily more serious behaviors denigrated by society. Thus, the fluent, smooth, quick-witted speaker given high value in both the speech classroom AND middle-class social situation may be suffering from anxieties equivalent to those of the shy, withdrawn person who is often ignored. Speech behavior as a projection of total personality would be one of many responses to threat inducing situations. Variability of response to anxiety might result from perception of situation, previous experience, amount of self at stake and the value accorded success in the threat situation. Some persons would be motivated to take control; others to withdraw. Some would be positively evaluated in their behavior and be reinforced, others would be evaluated negatively and induced to withdraw (Masserman; 1962).

A variety of social and psychological connections have been proposed for deviation in speech communication patterns. Brady (1958) notes that a primary symptom of schizophrenia is reduced or modified verbal output. Freedman, Ebing and Wilson (1962) add that quantity and quality of verbalization and vocalization must be considered in any diagnosis of schizophrenia. Schachter, Meyer and Loomis (1962) generalize that any failure to use speech for conventional purposes of communication may be considered a sign of mental illness to a greater or lesser degree. Rowley and Keller (1962) refer to social approval as the influential factor in verbal effectiveness or failure, while Rogler and Hollingshead (1961) demonstrate a relationship between movement in social classes and disturbances in speech. Speech, as a projection of personality, is evaluated by society against implied standards. Individuals assume a role based largely on the reflection of their personality back from society (Combs and Snygg; 1959). That means that abnormal speech must be considered a function of normal speech in any deviation where a physiopathological diagnosis cannot be made.

Speech behavior is neither separable from personality nor trainable apart from personality as a whole. Any approach to speech training with alteration of behavior as the goal means a revision of total personality is necessary. Any alteration in treatment level or motivation will alter speech behavior. Recent discoveries in neuro-endocrinology indicate that drastic changes in systemic function may come about because of response to social stimuli (Leiderman and Shapiro; 1964). The precise nature of the personality change is not obvious. Masserman (1962) demonstrated that conflict in motivations may produce temporary copying behavior but heighten anxieties in subsequent experiences. For example, the needs motivated by the grading system may induce a student to manage his fears and survive in the speech classroom, but impair his ability to function in future experiences. Attention to compensatory paralinguistic and kinesic behaviors has been noted by Szasz (1962) and Sebeok and Hayes (1964) as they demonstrated that the emotional and physiological state of the person demands one sort of communication or another. If not verbal, some sort of bodily action not excluding hysterical or psychosomatic manifestations is produced. A human may be able to mask a personality disturbance by controlling overt speech behavior, but the necessity to communicate the phenomenal self will produce a variety of other types of communication more indicative of the 'true' personality state. Quantitative and qualitative withdrawal from oral communication, therefore, may be considered as a sign of personality problems, requiring total treatment rather than symptomatic treatment in the form of speech training. The student who displays 'enthusiastic' gesture patterns and who receives an 'A' therefore may also require total treatment rather than reward in a speech class for manifesting neurotic symptoms. The ultimate catastrophe of 'silent man' is exemplified by the alienation of Lee Harvey Oswald. The man whose communicative channels are blocked must either strike back against an evaluating society or withdraw into the grey anonymity which his society forces on him (Holmes; 1965). Society's loss of potentially productive human beings is the price paid for failure to train people in adequate communication.

Reticence is defined as, "avoidance of social, verbal interaction. Unwillingness to communicate unless prodded; disposed to be silent; not inclined to speak freely; reserved" (Barnhart; 1950). Teachers of speech and academic advisers are familiar with people who fit the definition. They are a small, but noticeable, proportion of the total student body. It would require a rather gross stretch of psychiatric nosology to classify these people as 'schizophrenic'. They do not show the symptoms of blocking and tension usually associated with stuttering. However, their behavior assists them to achieve the same ends as the schizophrenic or the stutterer, i.e. avoidance of the communication act. For this reason, their behavior can be considered pathological in terms of Van Riper's definition, "speech is defective when it deviates so far from the speech of people that it calls attention to itself, interferes with communication, or causes its possessor to be maladjusted" (Van Riper; 1963). The fact that we have a definition of reticence generally applied to 'non-verbal' persons would indicate that our society negatively evaluates individuals who withdraw from communication.

Ruesch and Bateson (1957) state, "disturbances in communicative behavior of the speaker occur when he says too much or too little, or when his expressions are unintelligible". Where effective verbal behavior is demanded, inability to perform according to society's expectations would signal a deviation. In this dimension, reticence could be interpreted as existing on a continuum with stuttering and stage fright. To the extent that all people are, to some extent, 'disturbed', each 'verbal problem' would be complicated by whatever 'disturbance' overtones existed. At any event, the problem of failure to perform up to the expectations of society appears more complicated than simply revealing a resistance to the directed learning of the classroom.

It would be naive to declare a manifesto of 'civil rights' for quiet people: to declare that no one need speak unless he wants to. The demands of our modern society preclude this 'easy way out'. Full utilization of the talents of human material, the integration of personalities into connection with 'useful work' demands that each man contribute his share to his society (Goodman; 1960). Allowing an individual to take refuge from the challenges of life by refusing to participate in the communication level of the game would be to deny the whole concept of preventive mental health. Thus speech teacher and clinician alike assume the role of quasi-psychotherapist as they attempt to alter the behavior of the people who come to them, many of whom are not only inadequate in communication behavior but inadequate in total personality as well.

It is generally assumed by teachers and parents that everyone can be trained, to some degree, in communication skills. The existence of problem speakers, readers, writers and listeners which torment today's college administrators, clearly indicates that training is not universally successful. Indeed, some problem speakers testify that they have regressed because of training. While few speech teachers fail to recognize the existence of these 'failures', the phenomenon has not been studied in an organized way. Muir (1964) in a series of interviews with reticent persons, hypothesized a connection between regression of speaking skill and the training given in the conventional communication training. Several of her subjects traced their inability to cope with speech situations back to an unpleasant or intimidating verbal performance sometimes in a speech class, more often in classes where 'speech' was being taught by an untrained teacher.

In general, the therapy of the speech class is based on the classical Greek model (Ruesch, 1961) which holds that 'strength of will' is sufficient to remedy any human defect. This approach may be reasonably effective in traning the speech of those who suffer from no disturbance of personality. For those who are moderately disturbed to begin with, however, formal speech training may do considerable psychological damage, particularly by stimulating iatrogenic disturbances based on awareness of performance criteria (voice, gestures, etc.) over which the subject has no apparent control. The apprehensions thus induced may act in somewhat the same fashion as the etiological factors in stuttering, i.e. setting off hypertonic, apprehensive reactions about the malfeasance in question. Most studies of apprehension use objective evaluations as a validity criterion (Holtzman; 1950). There is no available study based on subjective testimony of students about their own apprehension levels. It has already been noted that the drive to succeed in the broad academic game may temporarily permit masking of anxiety symptoms, but there is no reasonable guarantee that the result of the whole experience has not been a heightening of the desire to avoid communication. Muir's study poses this as a possibility.

Syllabic repetitions do not seem to become problems until a name, 'stuttering', together with a pejorative connotation has been given to them, and anxieties triggered. Denigrating comments about 'eye contact,' 'gesture patterns', 'voice quality', etc. evoke similar apprehensions in some students, which heighten the general anxiety in a public speaking situation. If the pattern were carried to its logical end, a whole complex of avoidance-type symptoms could be set off. A directive mode of criticism of performance criteria makes as much sense as commands to 'be taller' or 'be thinner'. Even if accompanied by methodological suggestions, direct criticism implies threat (Masserman; 1962). Direct criticism and attendant directive therapy has not worked so well in the psychological clinic (Stein; 1960). The emphasis is modally upon a non-directive method to allay rather than heighten anxiety (Rogers; 1951). If a teacher could identify in advance which of his students would profit from a directive approach, there would be little problem. The tendency of the human, however, is to mask personality disruptions, hence, the teacher can really never know that his directive approach is not causing hidden psychological damage. An analysis by the writer of diary reports of 300 subjects with 10 different instructors shows about 15% of the students report having severe physiological and emotional symptoms in response to criticism. The anxiety level expressed may represent a burgeoning core of personality-disturbed individuals whose potential is for regression unless given a very special sort of treatment. When removed for special training in a non-directive, permissive milieu, most anxiety laden speakers tend to lose their symptoms and begin to make communicative contact, though a sizable minority fight against contact and strive to sustain their withdrawal defenses.

Even effective performance in a traditional classroom does not mean that anxieties have been quelled. Masserman (1962) reports that subjects confronted with conflicting goals may use their desire to achieve a greater goal to help them overcome anxieties about a lesser goal. In the speech classroom this could mean that desire for 'survival' in the grading system would enable the student to control anxieties in the classroom. The question is, of course, what happens to anxiety levels in subsequent speech situations? If Masserman's evidence can be believed, we must assume that anxieties would be substantially increased.

RELATIONSHIPS BETWEEN DISORDERED AND NORMAL SPEECH

As a first step in determining the potential for existence of 'problem-speakers' or 'reticents' the relationship between the various types of identified speech disorders and normal speech needs to be investigated. There is virtually no material dealing with the problem of reticence *per se*, nor, indeed is it recognized as a problem. Lillywhite, (1964) however, points out that generally, inability to communicate is a disease; for example, the person who is psychologically incapable of listening is suffering from just as much of a defect as the person who sustains an organic hearing loss. He declares;

> Our very limited concepts of what we call 'speech defect' and disorders of communication have prevented us from seeing the relationship between clinical communicative disorders and disorders of communication in 'normal' speakers. It would be helpful if we could think of disordered communication as a continuum with difficulties arising from many different causes; some pathological, some psychological, and some social — all contributing to the failure to be understood or to understand. Such a point of view would enable us to make use of the techniques employed in the clinics and the laboratories of speech pathologists and audiologists for help in evaluation, diagnosis and treatment of the problems in communication outside as well as inside the clinic.

Lillywhite may be advocating an extended role for the speech pathologist. His statement may also mean that the wide nosological range of identified speech problems requires the combined diagnostic talents of speech pathologists, psychologists, psychiatrists, and teachers of 'normal speech'. If we accept the premise that many speech disorders result from societal evaluation, there would be no lacuna between normal and abnormal. Any 'normal' speaker enrolled in a public speaking class may be considered a potential 'defective'. That is, any identified pattern may develop to the point where it interferes with communication and requires special treatment. The public speaking teacher thus finds himself in a new and unwelcome role, that of clinical diagnostician. He may be called upon to do therapy also, in which case, his whole classroom necessarily takes on the aura of a clinic. Each student would have to be treated as a unique personality with equally unique communication patterns. Diagnosis would reveal those who would benefit from directive training in the form of performance criticism as well as those whose anxiety state would permit only non-directive approaches. Also, such restructuring of the classroom would enable the speech teacher to coordinate his efforts with those of the speech clinician or psychologist to assist rehabilitation of discharged subjects. If properly trained, the teacher of normal speech could play a major role in reinforcing clinical gain, in addition to his own clinical role of improving the speech patterns of 'normals'.

A new approach to training the teacher of speech would be required in order to make him an effective clinician. Many traditional assumptions would have to be abandoned, the pedagogical influence of Quintilian minimized. Training would involve attempting to derive insights into the factors contributing to 'disordered communication' and would require knowledge mastery of many fields now alien to the traditional teacher of speech. Both psychological problems and speech problems can be temporary or permanent, chronic or acute. Insights that apply to both temporary deviations in normal speakers and chronic patterns in diagnosed communication defectives must be sought. Above all, an understanding of verbal behavior in general and its relation to personality in general is necessary. One psychiatrist (Gold; 1965) comments, "the teacher of speech does the work of the psychiatrist. He tries to teach people to think in symbols rather than actions".

Several authorities agree that communication behavior is so direct a function of personality that any maladjustment, temporary or permanent, would be projected in some way through deviant communication. Johnson (1946) speaks of a "language of personality maladjustment", and Barbara (1960) refers to a "neurosis in speaking". Under the general heading of "Language of Maladjustment", Johnson (1946) discusses two kinds of individuals, classified according to verbal output. Admitting the difficulty of arriving at an accurate estimate of what might constitute a normal amount of talking, he says:

Among the definitely maladjusted there would appear to be a disproportionate number of these over-verbalized and under-verbalized individuals. Both appear to have great difficulty in expressing themselves with any considerable degree of satisfaction either to themselves or to their listeners.

He goes on to classify verbose individuals into three categories: (1) "those who talk mainly to avoid silence", (2) "others who use language chiefly to conceal truth", and (3) "those whose incessant talking appears to serve the function of a great nervously twitching proboscis with which they explore unceasingly in search of certainty". Of people who talk very little, Johnson says, "as a broad generalization it can be said that they have progressed more deeply into stages of demoralization". Apparently he feels that the person who is still speaking offers some hope for therapy. Gold (1965) agrees, as he notes that it is far more difficult for a psychiatrist to treat a non-communicative subject who wants only to 'lean' on the therapist. Johnson considers the person who withdraws from speech a more severe case. He says, for example, of the stutterer:

A person's speaking time is a fundamental indicator of the degree to which he is handicapped by the communicative difficulty ... the importance of a particular individual's speech problem is felt by him in a peculiarly basic way in the extent to which he restricts or inhibits his communication with other people.

Stuttering is important not only because it is a verbal deviation accorded low status by society, but also because of its effect on the individual stutterer. The phrase 'syllabic repetition' is not distressing. In most cases, a simple directive, corrective remark remedies the 'defect'. It is clear that directive therapy works for many. In a significant minority of cases, however, the context of the directive reinforces tension and a stuttering syndrome is induced. Stuttering inhibits communication with others. It is one of many ways in which persons whose personality needs impel them to withdraw or avoid the communication meet this need in their communication behavior. The vector is not certain. Sometimes communication disorders result from personality problems. Sometimes the disorder is conditioned or present and a personality disorder results. Once the personality disorder has been rooted, however, treatment solely directed to speech phenomena is generally useless. Unfortunately, there is no infallible method for distinguishing in advance of treatment the subject who will profit from directive therapy from the one who will not.

Szasz (1962) develops a 'game theory' model for understanding personality disorders characterized by avoidance of communication. A human being who seeks to mask his emotions or hide his values and/or suffers threat from the existence of potential responses to his communication may elect to withdraw through stuttering, through manifest stage fright, through monosyllabic responses, through maintenance of a pathic level of communication, through compulsive iteration, etc. Berne (1964) extends the potential of the model by noting how verbal responses tend to become routinized or ritual-like. Regardless of the specific method of verbal avoidance elected, it serves as an explanation to the individual for his failure to cope with the role-demands of society. Reticence thus means more than simply low-quantity verbal output. It may denote a nosologic category for any communicative disorder which results in reducing the effectiveness of the individual in the normative verbal intercourse demanded by his culture. The psychiatrist may conveniently classify these deviations as 'mild schizophrenia' or 'manic-depressiveness'. However, few persons with mild personality disorders will ever see a psychiatrist. Their problem must be treated in the normal routine of their daily existence if it is treated at all. The fortunate ones may perhaps learn to stutter and be referred to a speech clinic for help. Those who deviate in an unclassifiable format will be ignored and rendered permanently unable to contribute their verbal share to society. Even worse, they will be prevented the privilege of self-actualization simply because they are unable to integrate their own personality into a society.

Barbara (1960) also discusses in great detail the relationship between personality traits of 'neurotic' persons and the characteristics of their speech. One classification is 'the man of few words', the resigned speaker, of whom he says:

Unable to face himself most times in a realistic sense, one of the resigned person's active neurotic solutions is to remove himself from the conflicting situation by assuming the attitude of being the on-looker or nonparticipating spectator. He represses or denies many of his real feelings and desires by placing inhibitions and checks in the path of their expression.

Society often reinforces such withdrawn behavior with the classification, 'good listener'. The premium placed on 'good listeners' as sounding boards for the excessively fluent might also be examined in terms of the development of an authoritarian hierarchy in which verbal quantity alone determines the acceptance of ideas. Muir (1964) for example, detected a trend among classified 'reticent' persons toward variance or clash in their basic value structure with those of the modal group of which they were ostensibly members. That a prevailing style of values exists in national cultures has been definitively documented by Charles Morris (1950). Examination of micro-cultures or sub-cultures within the American culture also indicate that sub-styles emerge and those individuals who are members of a sub-culture by propinquity or ascription may avoid threat to his value structure by electing a reticence pattern (Phillips and Erickson; 1964). Thus the total culture is denied the contribution of their ideas, and they are denied the opportunity to release the tensions they feel.

While 'normals' may be reticent on occasion, the chronically reticent may have adopted a permanent game behavior because of inability to cope with felt or projected values in the group around him. Riesman (1953) refers to the ability of the genuinely other-directed individual to detect the basic operant value pattern in his social group with the metaphor of 'internal radar'. If the individual is suitably other-directed, he will also have no trouble altering his behavior and values to suit those of the mode he selects to interact with. On the other hand, the individual who still clings to an inner-directed set may feel values and behaviors hostile to his own and find it necessary to adopt a reticence mechanism to prevent discovery and threat to his value deviation. Stuttering, stage fright, verbal withdrawal and various types of compulsive speaking may be variously elected. Riesman's hypothetical constructs were experimentally confirmed by Williams (1964).

Barbara (1960) also discusses two qualities of deviant speech behavior. The self-effacing speaker, he says:

...is in constant dread of failing in the speaking situation. He is in a perpetual state of self-consciousness, tension apprehension and in fear of suffering stage-fright or freezing at some particular stage of speaking.

His nervous mannerisms call attention to themselves, his voice often lacks control, his speech is full of vocalized or unvocalized pauses. He has a fear of using words which may have connotations of violence, aggressiveness, presumption or arrogance. He avoids direct assertion and carefully selects his vocabulary. The average speech teacher is familiar with this type. His behavior generally leads to the classification of 'lazy' or 'unwilling' and earns him a 'C' or less in the course.

The expansive speaker, Barbara continues, is one who has a compulsive need to talk and whose speech is egocentric, aggressive, onesided and two-valued:

In the speaking situation, the expansive speaker feels he should be and is the LAST WORD. In any discussion he fears mutual exchange of ideas, is usually stubborn, resistant, and highly reluctant to face issues squarely and honestly.

Frequently this type of speaker is rewarded with high grades because of fluency alone or else put on the varsity debating team. Highly developed performance criteria succeed in masking the personality disturbance that enabled him to develop as a 'capable' speaker.

There are apparently two levels of disturbed speech behavior with which the class-room speech teacher might be confronted. These may be classified as (1) restricted verbal output, and (2) excessive verbal output. In either case, the disturbed speech pattern would be indicative of a disturbed personality pattern requiring special treatment. The frequency with which such cases are encountered may imply the non-applicability of a uniform pedagogy and the adoption of a clinical format for the teaching of 'normal' speakers.

CLINICAL IMPLICATIONS FOR THE TEACHER OF SPEECH

If we accept the twin premises that (1) speech problems are related to personality problems, and (2) the bulk of such cases exist in the 'normal' population rather than in the clinic, some drastic revisions must be made in the assumptions underlying speech pedagogy. Currently the speech teacher functions as a diagnostician, but does so in the framework of the classical view of speech as a separable human behavior capable of pedagogical manipulation in isolation through a variety of directive methods. The 'rhetorical canons' are misinterpreted by the rhetorically trained. They become prescriptive, rather than normative or critical categories, interpreted to mean that it is possible to train speech in 'parts' or 'units' in which emphasis may be variably placed on sources of ideas, organizations, language, delivery patterns or use of notes. That is, if we make the diagnosis 'faulty organization', 'poor research', 'soft voice', 'poor eye contact', 'sloppy gestures', and the like, specific directions for improvement are warranted as though each were equally capable of improvement separately. The underlying assumption is that there is a standard, up to which the student must measure.

Improvement, however, is judged by the teacher, not by an objective observer nor by subjective report from the student. Little attempt is made to discover how the student feels about speaking. Observed improvement is attributed to the success of the method; non-improvement is the fault of the student. The relationship between training methods and improvement has not been measured — only hypothesized from the hopes of the instructor. An equally tenable hypothesis would be that the mere opportunity to speak has a salubrious effect and motivates improved performance by desensitizing the speaker to the audience situation in the absence of threat.

Becker (1962) notes that society imposes on man the necessity to speak clearly and fluently. Offering a student a chance to speak in a classroom also provides a mechanism for catharsis. This is the one place in the college environment where the student will receive a little undivided attention, not only from peers but also from an authority figure whose approval is being sought. This opportunity makes his personality more vulnerable to threat, because the rules of the academic game as he understands it do not seem to prevail. His improvement may be analysed in terms of a 'game model'. The student understands what is expected of him generally in the academic game, and is ready to comply, since compliance also serves to fit the rules of his own 'game' of socially motivated self-expression. Society rewards the fluent, coherent speaker for his behavior and so reinforces his desire and ability to play the game. Reticent behavior is not rewarded. The reticent (substitute 'C') speaker is

penalized by both criticism AND a poor grade. This is a shock to a vulnerable personality that may have exposed itself. Negative reinforcement results, particularly when
peers are permitted to join in the criticism. Their insensitivity to threat-cues often
leads them to overcriticize, particularly projections of intrinsic personality mechanisms, heightening the threat to the phenomenal self of the speaker that was exposed,
ostensibly to meet the new rules of the speech class game. The unthreatened students
can learn something of the nature of social response by listening to their peers'
criticism. For the reticent speaker, peer criticism only reinforces negative self-image
and a further penalty is exacted for a failure he has already admitted and expected
would not figure in the game. Up until the time the speech teacher asked him to express
himself he had devised a method of working around the threat he felt from speaking,
but now the classroom situation demands reversal of his internalized behavior in order
to succeed. He may try, or he may withdraw, but his internal tension is heightened,
whatever he elects to do.

When the treatened speaker exposes his personality and his values, he expects to
be reacted to as 'person' rather than 'performer'. He mistakes a neutral suggestion
about performance behavior as a hostile statement about his projected phenomenal
self. One possible response is to withdraw into dullness, to play the game as best he
can and preserve a little self-esteem. The threat of the criticism, however, will affect
his personality and his communication ability for a long time to come. Muir (1964)
has traced several adult speech problems to speech criticisms offered by teachers
(and only rarely speech teachers), parents, significant others in the subject's
ontogenesis. In the light of this, an even more satisfactory framework for evaluations
would be to examine the student's manifest and covert apprehension levels to
determine whether transferable training has come about. Emphasis should be on
problems in communication felt external to the speech class. The speech class is only
a clinic in which real problems can be worked out with a minimum of threat.

Becker (1962) contends that a child develops his verbal patterns in the framework
of a total social setting. The child must learn the arbitrary nature of symbolization and
its effect on his world. He learns that he can manipulate the world to greater or lesser
degrees through the use of his symbolic capacity. He may learn that he is capable of
mature control, or he may learn futility, or something in between. In any case, the
response of his world of peers and superiors will alter his total personality and this
will be reflected in his verbal behavior. The speech teacher can do little short of using
clinical methods to alter verbal patterns so inculcated. The speech teacher may not be
qualified to practice psychiatry, but he cannot be permitted to be an authoritarian
director of performances. For the student who 'succeeds' the class as traditionally
operated may represent a successful directive therapy. For those who do not succeed,
another therapeutic pattern is indicated. There is too little evidence that traditional
directive methods succeed in altering human communication behavior to warrant
continuation with present methods without solid testing.

The 'normal' approach to the problem of reticence is through the designation 'stage fright'. The approach to the compulsive over-talker is often 'get off my back' or 'go out for debate'. In either case, the assumption is that conditioning through training under criticism will improve whatever criteria are diagnosed as deficient. The literature on 'stage fright' is insightful, but it has not as yet been generally translated into an approach to pedagogy in the typical classroom.

Douglass (1948) noted that feelings of personal security are related to effectiveness in public speaking. Those individuals who were rated as 'better speakers' tended to possess the characteristics of mature personal security, self assurance, group identification, and optimism. Poorer speakers gave evidence more typical of chronic insecurity. Penalizing the poorer speaker with a low grade heightens the feeling of insecurity, while the 'A' speaker has his feelings of acceptance heightened. The rift between the two widens and the potentiality for authoritarian domination of the 'better speaker' over the 'poorer' becomes apparent. The poor speaker tends to withdraw even further from participation and plays the game with a little less *elan* than before. He may rationalize his discouragement by verbalizing a need to study for other courses, or complain about the unfairness of the speech requirement. His limited preparation time is spent mostly in generating anxieties and thus his performance potential is even further reduced.

Ainsworth (1949) tended to confirm the connection between stage fright and personality problems by noting tendencies toward shyness, seclusiveness, withdrawal, depression, guilt feelings, and inhibited disposition in stage fright subjects. Several other authorities agree with the findings: Jones (1943), Gilkinson (1943), Wilkinson (1944) and Greenleaf (1948) offer similar conclusions that frightened speakers are threatened people. The logical inference is that maximization of threat will heighten anxiety and reduce the potential for effective speaking.

Apprehension or nervousness does not necessarily mean failure on the platform. In the greater number of cases, anxiety is generalized toward the unfamiliar context. Once the teacher and the class become 'known' automatic desensitization has had its effect and performance improves in a familiar situation. This leads to success in the class and POSSIBLE carryover. In the minority, perhaps a large minority, of cases, however, anxiety deepens. We assume that mastery of tension in the classroom will carry over, but this assumption is not fully tenable. Those students who master the situaton because of the greater fear of failure in the total college context will not necessarily have their anxieties quelled in relation to an unrelated speech performance. Management of anxieties, not necessarily elimination of anxieties is the apparent key to platform success. Mastery imposed by authoritarian threat is temporary, and it has already been noted how, in such circumstances, they may return in a specific situation and interfere even more with performance potential. Thorough measurement of both the long and short term effects of speech training must be made to determine what proportion and what type of student does succeed in making a carryover of performance skill from classroom to more typical public situations. There is enough new evidence about the association of speech problems and personality problems to invalidate the blanket assumption that success in class equals success out of class.

If we accept the idea that there is some connection between reticence, verbal withdrawal, and dysrhythmia with personality disturbance, the need for special treatment is sharply delineated. Gold (1965) reports his view that current thinking in psychiatry classifies any verbal withdrawal as a form of schizophrenia. Goldfarb (1963) shows that schizophrenics are generaly disjointed in conceptual responses, particularly space-time orientations. Guertin (1961) offers evidence that schizophrenic verbal patterns range over a wide field of difficulty, varying by social conditioning. Seth and Beloff (1959) generalize the verbal problem of schizophrenics by showing their inability to handle abstract ideas spontaneously. Fenichel, Freedman, and Klapper (1960) construct a theory of therapy which has as its base the removal of the schizo-phrenic from the offending environment. Recent studies by the Chapmans (1965) underscore this point by showing the differentiation in verbal responses by schizo-phrenics and normals. Connect all these things together and the weight of the evidence supports the contention that the only rational approach to the treatment of per-sonality-associated verbal disorders is through special treatment in a constructed environment preparatory for effectiveness in a normal environment. Speech pathologists have recognized this for a long time. Severe cases usually require institu tionalization. These cases, however, would probably not appear in a typical speech classroom. The mild personality-associated speech disorders commonly seen by the speech teacher demand little more than an alteration of pedagogical approach designed to minimize threat and allow personality to come more in harmony with the social context.

Morse (1958) among others, attacks the overuse of the schizophrenic diagnosis by psychiatrists but does so without minimizing the importance of a verbal disturbance for the person who suffers from it. Certainly specialists in the field of speech are not sufficiently sophisticated in psychiatric nosology to diagnose or treat 'schizophrenia'. However, the field has already assumed the burden of special clinical treatment for one type of verbal disorder, stuttering. It has been demonstrated that stage fright, verbal withdrawal, and excessive compulsiveness in speech, regardless of psychiatric diagnosis, exist on a continuum with stuttering and fit the same dimension of aiding the subject to avoid the normal communicative context. These, therefore, should be considered worthy of special treatment as well.

Research findings for stuttering show a pattern similar to those for verbal problems in general. Goodstein (1958) and Johnson (1959) both demonstrate an association between stuttering and desire for social withdrawal. In this sense, the typical speech problems encountered by the public speaking teacher may be regarded as related to stuttering. Those individuals most intimidated by the classroom situation deserve an essentially similar approach. It cannot be inferred that conditioning a speaker by forcing him to speak will work any better than forcing an acrophobic to go up in an airplane, or locking a claustrophobic in a broom closet, particularly in the light of

Heilbrun's (1960) findings that authoritarian environments heighten personality disintegration and communication disturbance. The broadness of the agreement about stuttering is significant, despite surface disagreements among experts. Barbara (1954) notes that regardless of the approach to THERAPY, there appears to be general agreement that stuttering has an emotional base; Blanton, Fletcher, Gifford, Robbins, and Solomon are offered in evidence.

It is clear that not all fearful people stutter or show manifest stage fright symptoms, nor even display patterns of reticence. Some attempt must be made to connect situation with speech disturbance. Perhaps disturbed oral communication is a function of a specific anxiety in a predetermined social setting. Berry and Eisenson (1956) note that the variation in stuttering pattern depends on social context:

Students of stuttering have long known that stutterers have varying difficulty according to the nature and size of their audience. Almost all stutterers are completely fluent when talking aloud to themselves in the privacy of their own rooms. They can talk with normal or almost normal fluency when addressing animal pets. Adult stutterers usually have little difficulty talking to small children. When we analyse the relatively easy situations for most stutterers, we find that a 'common denominator' of the speaking situations is a relative absence of communicative responsibility.

Johnson (1946) says almost the same thing about stage fright:

Relative particularly to fluency problems are anxiety-tension manifestations commonly termed 'stage fright.' This is, of course, not confined to the stage, and involves a more or less serious disturbance of speech. This is very common and in severe cases, the effects on speech are both disintegrative and restrictive.

Social context appears critical, and this is the peg on which therapy can be hung, for by altering social context as in a clinical environment it is possible to bring about some adjustment to the difficulty, though not necessarily elimination of it. West et, al. (1957) refer to context when they say:

Some persons classify themselves as stutterers and consider their problem serious who have few or no obvious breaks in the fluency pattern. Judged by overt symptoms alone, the latter would frequently not be classified as stutterers at all....

In short, the internal feelings of the individual, conditioned by social cues, result in the self-evaluation difficulty. Many times the depth of feeling-involvement cannot be inferred from overt symptoms. Once an individual has given a name to his feelings, they can become tokens in the game that the individual has elected to play. Blanton (1956) notes:

Stuttering is a blocking of the person's ability to adjust to other people. It is a personality defect due to anxiety in meeting various social situations, rather than a speech defect.

The words 'stage fright', 'reticence', or 'disturbed verbal behavior' could be neatly substituted for 'stuttering'. Further, it is clear that therapies offered for stuttering could not be carried on in the normal speech classroom (Rieber; 1963).

There seems to be sufficient indication that stuttering and stage fright are, in some way related, and further, that they are related to a general category of personality disturbances characterized by inability to function well in situations where oral interaction is necessary. Recent preliminary investigations[1] of subjects classified into the categories of 'stutter', 'stage fright victim', and 'reticent' serve to confirm this connection. Interviews and written projectives of forty subjects tend to indicate a uniform fear of social context, a uniform expression of capability when confronted with inferiors, and most important, a generalized deviation from the value structures of the norm. If these findings are confirmed in a more rigid experimental context, then the significance for the teacher of speech cannot be overestimated. He would cease to be a teacher in the classical sense, imparting knowledge and directing behavior, but would become a non-directive clinician. Each student would have to be approached as an individual clinical subject. Backus (1957) has already stated vigorously that there is no real separation between 'normal' and 'abnormal' behaviors, let alone a separation between the various categories of abnormality. She states:

Speech is viewed in psychological terms for all persons, not just for those judged to have 'maladjustments', or not just for those who have 'speech disorders'. The concept of a dichotomy between normal and disordered speech may have a convience administratively in speech departments, but it is not considered relevant in discovering causal relations in a client's behavior. For instance, available evidence appears to indicate that the same laws... govern phenomena classed 'stage fright' in the classroom and... 'anxiety' in the clinic.

A similar view is expressed by Nelson (1964):

It may be possible now to discern that these people (reticents) have actual communication disorders or 'speech defects', and certainly they experience a concern similar to that of a person with a clinically diagnosed speech or language disorder. These indivicuals may reasonably require diagnosis and clinical type treatment before they can expect to function successfully before an audience.

The precise nature of the clinical approach necessary in the typical public speaking class has not yet been worked out. There is no question but what it is necessary. Imposition of arbitrary threats like grades on speeches, peer criticisms, and the variety of personality-attacks that result from instructor criticism honestly and sincerely given may have some success in improving overt verbal quantity and quality for a majority of students. The incidence of physiological symptoms, emotional fantasies, verbalized threats, etc. in a typical population of speech students, however, is large enough to warrant a broad reevaluation of pedagogical assumptions and methods, leading to the development of a new set of goals and methods for the teaching of speech. One thing is sure. The traditional motif of teaching speech on a recitation-criticism basis now has the burden of proof, and must show it is not harmful or be revised!

THE PENNSYLVANIA STATE UNIVERSITY

[1] Investigations carried on by the writer and his associates, David Butt and Michael Sexson are supported by a grant from the Central Fund for Research, Pennsylvania State University.

REFERENCES

Ainsworth, Stanley H., "A Study of Fear, Nervousness and Anxiety in the Public Speaking Situation", *Speech Monographs* XVIII, 3, 1949.
Backus, Ollie, "Group Structures in Speech Therapy", in Lee Travis (Ed.), *Handbook of Speech Pathology* (New York, Appleton-Century-Crofts, 1957).
Barbara, Dominick, *Stuttering* (New York, The Julian Press, 1954).
Barbara, Dominick (Ed.), *Psychological and Psychiatric Aspects of Speech and Hearing* (Springfield, Illinois, Charles Thomas, 1960).
Barnhart, Clarence L. (Ed.), *American College Encyclopedic Dictionary* (Chicago, The Spencer Press, 1950).
Becker, Ernest, *The Birth and Death of Meaning* (New York, The Free Press, 1962).
Berne, Eric, *Games People Play* (New York, Grove Press, 1964).
Berry, Mildred F. and Jon Eisenson, *Speech Disorders: Principles and Practices of Therapy* (New York, Appleton-Century-Crofts, 1956).
Blanton, Smiley, "Stuttering", *Journal of the American Medical Association* CLX, 17, 1956.
Brady, John Paul, "Language in Schizophrenia", *America Journal of Psychiatry* XII, 1958.
Chapman, Loren J. and Jean P. Chapman, "Interpretations of Words in Schizophrenic", *Journal of Abnormal and Social Psychology* I, 2, February, 1965.
Combs, Arthur W. and Donald Snygg, *Inidvidual Behavior* (New York, Harper and Brothers, 1959).
Douglass, Robert L., "The Relation of Feelings of Personal Security to Effective Public Speaking", *Speech Monographs*, 1948.
Fenichel, Carl, Alfred Freedman and Zelda Klapper, "A Day School for Schizophrenic Children", *American Journal of Orthopsychiatry*, 30, January, 1960.
Freedman, Alfred M., Eva Ebing and Ethel W. Wilson, "Autistic Schizophrenic Children", *Archives of General Psychiatry* VI, 3, 1962.
Gilkinson, Howard, "Social Fears as Reported by Students in College", *Speech Monographs* IX, 1943.
Gold, Frank (M.D., Private Psychiatric Practice), Interview conducted in Cleveland, Ohio, October 18, 1965.
Goldfarb, William, "Self-Awareness in Schizophrenic Children", *Archives of General Psychiatry* VIII, 1, 1963.
Goodman, Paul, *Growing Up Absurd* (New York, Random House, 1960).
Goodstein, Leonard, "Functional Speech Disorders and Personality: A Survey of the Research", *Journal of Speech and Hearing Research*, December, 1958.
Greenleaf, Floyd I., "An Exploratory Study of Social Speech Fright", *Speech Monographs* XII, 1948.
Guertin, Wilson H., "Are Differences in Schizophrenic Symptoms Related to the Mother's Avowed Attitude Toward Child-Rearing?", *Journal of Abnormal and Social Psychology*, 63, 1961.
Heilbrun, Alfred B., Jr., "Perception of Maternal Child-Rearing Attitudes in Schizophrenics", *Journal of Consulting Psychology*, 24, April, 1960.
Holmes, John Clellon, "The Silence of Oswald", *Playboy*, 12, 11, November, 1965.
Holtzman, Paul, *An Experimental Study of Some Relationships Among Several Indices of Stage Fright and Personality*, Unpublished Ph. D. dissertation, (University of Southern California, 1950).
Johnson, Wendell, *People in Quandaries* (New York, Harper and Brothers, 1946).
Johnson, Wendell, "Problems of Impaired Speech", *Journal of the American Medical Association* LXX, 17, 1959.
Jones, Marnetta, "The Relationship of Certain Personality Traits to Stage Fright", *Speech Monographs* IX, 1943.
Leiderman, P. Herbert and David Shapiro, *Psychobiological Approaches to Social Behavior* (Stanford California, Stanford University Press, 1964).
Lillywhite, Herold, "Symposium on 'A Broader Concept of Communication Disorders', An Introduction", *The Journal of Communication* XIV, 1, 1964.
Masserman, Jules, "Ethology Comparative Biodynamics and Psychoanalytic Research", in Jordan Scher, (Ed.), *Theories of the Mind* (New York, The Free Press, 1962)
Morris, Charles, *Varieties of Human Value* (Chicago, University of Chicago Press, 1950).
Morse, Hilde, "The Misuse of the Diagnosis 'Childhood Schizophrenia' ", *American Journal of Psychiatry*, 114, 1958.

Muir, Laura, *Case Studies of Selected Examples of Reticence and Fluency* unpublished M.A. Thesis (Washington State University, Pullman, Washington, 1964).

Murray, Elwood, *The Speech Personality* (Philadelphia, J. B. Lippincott Co., 1937).

Nelson, D. Donald, "Student Speaking Disorders — Beyond the Symptoms", *The Journal of Communication* XIV, 1, 1964.

Phillips, Gerald M. and Eugene Erickson, *Marvis and Melinda Modal in Collegeville: A Preliminary Study of Student Values* (Mimeo) (Washington State University, Pullman, Washington, 1964).

Pines, Maya, "The Coming Upheaval in Psychiatry", *Harper's* Vol. 231, No. 138, October, 1965.

Rieber, Robert W., "Stuttering and Self-Concept", *Journal of Psychology* 55, 1963.

Riesman, David, *The Lonely Crowd* (Garden City, Doubleday, Anchor Books, 1953).

Rogers, Carl, *Client Centered Therapy* (New York, Houghton Mifflin, 1951).

Rogler, Lloyd and August Hollingshead, "Class and Disordered Speech in the Mentally Ill", *Journal of Health and Human Behavior* II, Fall, 1961.

Rowley, Victor and Dwayne Keller, "Changes in Children's Verbal Behavior as a Function of Social Approval and Manifest Anxiety", *Journal of Abnormal and Social Psychology*, 65, July, 1962.

Ruesch, Jurgen, *Therapeutic Communication* (New York, Norton and Co., 1961).

Ruesch, Jurgen and Gregory Bateson, *Disturbed Communication* (New York, Norton and Co., 1957).

Schachter, Francis, Lucie Mayer and Earl Loomis, "Childhood Schizophrenia and Mental Retardation: Differential Diagnosis Before and After One Year of Psychotherapy", *American Journal of Orthopsychiatry* XXXII, 4, 1962.

Scher, Jordan, "Ontoanalysis, the New Psychiatry", unpublished paper for delivery at the Speech Association of America Convention, Denver, 1962.

Sebeok, Thomas A., Alfred S. Hayes and Mary Catherine Bateson, *Approaches to Semiotics* (The Hague, Mouton and Co., 1964).

Seth, George and Halla Beloff, "Language Impairments in a Group of Schizophrenics", *British Journal of Medical Psychology*, 32, 1959.

Stein, W., *Contemporary Psychotherapies* (New York, The Free Press, 1960).

Szasz, Thomas, *The Myth of Mental Illness* (New York, Harper-Hoeber, 1962).

Travis, Lee Edward (ed.) *Handbook of Speech Pathology* (New York, Appleton-Century-Crofts, 1957).

Van Riper, Charles, *Speech Correction: Principles and Methods* (Englewood Cliffs, New Jersey, Prentice-Hall, Inc., 1963).

West, Robert, Merle Ansberry, and Anna Carr, *The Rehabilitation of Speech* (New York, Harper and Brothers, 1957).

Wilkinson, Esther Jenson, "A Study of Disintegrating Background Factors in the Development of Effective Speech Personality", *Speech Monographs* XI, 1944.

Williams, Walter, "Inner-Directedness and Other-Directedness in New Perspective", *The Sociological Quarterly*, V, 3, Summer, 1964.

PAUL H. PTACEK

GENERAL SEMANTICS AND THE EVALUATIVE PROCESS
IN SPEECH PATHOLOGY

The ability to communicate through the use of symbols is a distinctly human characteristic. Not only is this ability unique to man, but it is generally considered to be one of the most complex sensory-motor activities in which he engages. Therefore, it is not surprising that frequently something interferes with this extremely complex process of communicating. In fact, children with communicative problems far outnumber those with other types of handicapping conditions. Conservative estimates indicate that three to five percent of the school-age population suffer from some type of handicapping communication problem. Also, it has been estimated that an additional five percent have a noticeable, but not necessarily handicapping, speech variation. In addition to the complexity of the communicative act itself, we find that both speaking and hearing are influenced directly and indirectly by a multitude of factors both internal and external to the person involved. It is difficult to conceive of a more challenging and imposing task than that of properly evaluating variations in the speaking process.

Only recently has much attention been directed to the actual process of evaluation in the field of speech pathology (Johnson, *et al,* 1963; Darley, 1964). The fact that a bewildering array of over 700 labels has been attached to the various types of speech variations is indicative of a primary preoccupation with classification or labeling rather than with understanding the person and his speech variation with a view to modifying his speech behavior. Examination of these terms reveals that some are descriptive in nature, some have etiological implications or assumptions, some are both descriptive and etiological, and some are primarily idiosyncratic pedantries. Unlike the field of medicine, where a diagnosis frequently implies an etiology and a specific therapy, the field of speech pathology deals with problems which, for the most part, have neither a single cause nor a specific remedy. If we are to modify the speech behavior of a person with a speech problem, the goal should not be a taxonomic category or a diagnostic label, but an understanding of the client and his problem with a view toward prognosis and therapeutic planning. It is this writer's view that taxonomic categories and diagnostic labels have done much mischief in this field. This mischief is in the form of creating the impression for the user that because he has a name for a variation he understands it. This tends to stifle attempts to look deeper into the problem and the factors that may be contributing to the deviant behavior. Also, the fact that the terms used are not consistently descriptive or etiological interferes with communication among professionals in this field as well as with those in allied fields. In addition, the label, being essentially static in nature, does not reveal the dynamics or the on going changes within the person having the problem. It should be remembered that the goal of the process of evaluation is understanding the client and his problem in order to arrive at a prognosis and to formulate, if needed, an appropriate plan of therapy. Speech pathologists have spent and are spending too much time attaching labels and categories to persons and problems, and this activity does not directly contribute to the above stated goal.

Since general semantics has a major concern with the process of evaluation, it would appear to be clearly applicable to what is frequently called the 'diagnostic' process in Speech Pathology. Moreover, general semantics recommends the method of science as the model for problem solving, since it appears to be the most fruitful approach extant for the systematic evaluation of any problem, whether it is a communicative problem involving human beings or one more directly concerned with the physical universe. The purpose of this paper is to discuss how a scientific orientation and the formulations of general semantics apply to the 'diagnostic' process in Speech Pathology.

Before elaborating on the application of general semantics to the 'diagnostic' process, a model of the speech production is presented to serve as framework for the discussion (Figure 1). As with all models, considerable detail is left out; however, it is felt that this model does express important relationships between the environment and the individual and interrelationships among the organs and processes within the individual which are responsible for speech production.

Generally, the first contact the speech pathologist has with a client occurs at Stage 'D' on the diagram. This stage represents the acoustic product, the spoken output of the human being. In other words, this is what we hear as the person speaks and it may be analyzed in at least two ways. One way is to make physical measurements of the frequency, intensity and time factors inherent in the acoustic signal. This is generally done through the aid of instruments such as pitch meters, power level meters and rate meters. Another way is to look at the acoustic product from the standpoint of what may be considered to be the parameters of speech. These parameters include: articulation, which refers to the ability of the individual to form the sounds composing our language; phonation, which refers to the voice-producing mechanism providing the basic acoustic energy for speech; rhythm, which refers to the rate, regularity and inflectional patterns involved in speaking; and symbolization, which refers to the acoustic code which by convention transmits the meaning of what was intended to be communicated. Through training, each of these parameters may be judged and, to a certain extent, measured, either through instrumentation or forms of scaling devices.

Stage 'C' represents the speech-producing mechanism which is composed of a

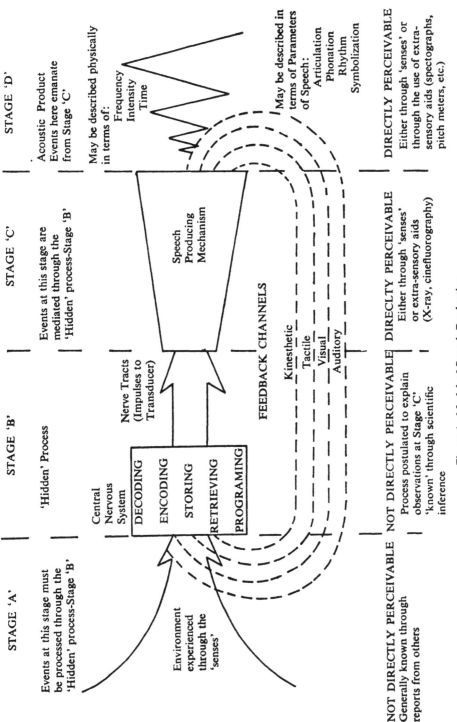

Figure 1. Model of Speech Production

complex of the lips, teeth, jaw, tongue, velum, larynx, etc, and serves as a transducer to convert the impulses sent from the central nervous system into acoustic energy. This mechanism is directly perceivable in a peripheral sense and may be examined by the speech pathologist to make estimates regarding the adequacy of the structure and functioning of the mechanism. Instruments, again, may be used as extra-sensory aids in perceiving both the structure and function of this mechanism. It is important to realize that what we perceive as the acoustic product is generated by this speech-producing mechanism. This does not mean that the mechanism operates in isolation, but any meaningful communicative event emanates from this speech-producing mechanism.

Moving backward to stage 'B' we are confronted with what may be termed a 'hidden' process. For our purposes we will label this the central nervous system. From the speech pathologist's viewpoint the functioning of this system is postulated on the basis of the observations made at Stages 'C' and 'D'. Since it is not directly amenable to observation, this system is known only through scientific inference. Implicit to this model is the fact that all events occuring at Stages 'C' and 'D' are mediated through Stage 'B'.

Stage 'A' on the model represents the impingement of the environment on the individual through his gross 'senses'. Events at this stage must be processed through the 'hidden' process. It should be noted that the impulse to speak may be triggered by events in the environment external to the person or by feelings and attitudes within the person exclusive of the outer environment.

The feedback channels on the model serve the function of monitoring the speech-producing mechanism and the acoustic product so that compensatory signals may be fed into the input. The precise extent to which each channel contributes to this monitoring is not known; however, it is generally assumed that the auditory channel is the most important channel. Kinesthetic and tactile channels are also important contributors to this process. The visual channel usually does not play too active a role unless there are decrements in the auditory channel.

With this brief overview of speech production, we are in a better position to discuss the evaluative process. However, a word is in order regarding the use of the terms 'speech defect', 'speech disorder', and 'speech defective'. The first two terms are sometimes used interchangeably by writers in the field and some authorities make clear distinctions between the terms. More specifically, some writers when speaking of 'speech disorders' include not only the speech variation but the cause of the variation and reserve the term 'speech defect' for referring to the variation only. Regardless of the definitions used by the writers and authorities, the fact that there is not general agreement as to what constitutes a 'speech defect' or a 'speech disorder' reduces the utility of these terms when attempting to communicate within and outside the profession. In addition, the terms are too often used without an awareness that they imply causal relationships. The latter of the three terms, 'speech defective', not only contains the flaws of the first two terms, but also involves a gross overgeneralization from one aspect of a person's behavior to the total person. In a sense, this is personifying the speech variation. It is not uncommon to hear speech pathologists refer to persons as 'stutterers', 'aphasics', etc. As indicated earlier, labeling of this nature can be a very deceptive practice in that it lumps together the similarities and disregards the differences. More distressing is the fact that there is frequently lack of agreement as to when a person is engaging in stuttering behavior, when a person is 'aphasic', or what specific behavior constitutes stuttering or aphasic speech. The prevalent use of these terms reflects how frequently the order of the process of abstracting as recommended by Korzybski is reversed. Korzybski suggested that observations should come first, then description, and then the various levels of inference. Some examiners after a cursory observation of a person's behavior, jump to an inferential level and label either the person or his behavior as defective.

Since the terms 'speech defect', 'speech disorder', and 'speech defective' have the above-mentioned drawbacks, the term speech variation will be used throughout this discussion. It is felt that this term is a more appropriate one because it places greater emphasis on describing the speech, not classifying it. This term places a burden on the speech pathologist to state the norms, if available, around which the speech varies. Since we do not have in all cases relevant normative data for the various parameters of speech at different ages, and under various conditions, this can be a very salutary experience. Without relevant normative data one should be more cautious when labeling speech or aspects of speech as defective or deviant. Newman (1961) after questioning the incidence figures for speech impairment and stressing the need for an empirically derived definition of speech impairment stated:

When it (the empirically derived definition) appears current beliefs, attitudes and practices may undergo substantial modification. These would, no doubt, affect training procedures. research, clinical endeavors, administrative actions, legisiation, etc.

The speech pathologist should be aware of the tendency of labels to influence his observations. Attention should be directed toward observing the person and his speech variation as free from diagnostic labels as possible with a view toward accurately describing what was observed. If quantitative measures can be made of the phenomena under observation, so much the better. If such measures are not available, the language used to describe the variation should be as clearly and factually descriptive as possible.

The arriving at inferences is not to be eschewed but merely delayed until a clear and accurate description of all the observations has been made. Moreover, such inferences should be tested against the observational level whenever possible in order to ascertain whether or not the descriptions were adequate and the inference warranted.

☞ The three basic premises upon which Korzybski based his non-Aristotielian system have important implications for the appraisal process in speech pathology. The first premise, a map is not the territory or words are not the things they represent, when applied rigorously to the evaluative process can have a profound impact on it.

A recent example comes to mind involving a seven-year-old child who was referred to a speech clinic with the classification of mental retardation. The speech pathologist assigned to evaluating the speech of this child accepted without question this label of the child as mentally retarded and proceeded with the appraisal process with this implicit assumption. After gathering case history information from the mother and completing an articulatory inventory of the child's speech, the speech pathologist proceeded to examine the child's peripheral speech mechanism, i.e., lips, tongue, teeth, palate, etc. During this procedure, the speech pathologist in an aside to the mother, said that the child had labored tongue movements. Upon hearing this casual comment, the child spoke up and said, "Ha, I have a hard working tongue." Fortunately for this youngster, the examination was being observed by other specialists and this spontaneous bit of humor from a seven-year-old child raised serious question in the minds of these observers as to the accuracy of the classification of mental retardation. As a result, additional tests assessing intellectual functioning were administered, and the final evaluation eliminated mental retardation as a contributing factor to the child's speech variation. This speech pathologist was blind to the child's spontaneous comment because he was accepting and responding to the child in terms of the label, 'mentally retarded'. In short, he was acting as if the words were the territory.

The second premise, a map does not represent all of the territory or words cannot say all about anything, also has important implications for the speech pathologist. Students frequently ask not to be assigned to a person having an articulation problem because they feel articulation problems are simple and they know all about them. The fact that approximately 75% of all types of speech variations are articulatory seems to indicate to these students that because they are so common they must be simple. Quite likely the reverse is true. The motor coordination required to form the individual speech sounds of our language is probably one of the most complex aspects of the speech act. Hence, that aspect of speech requiring the greatest precision in coordination would be the one most apt to be subject to malfunctioning. Therefore, instead of being a simple variation, it is quite probably one of the more complex variations and subject to more individual differences than the other aspects of speech. The statement that a child has an articulation problem most assuredly does not say all about the person and his problem, even though students and sometimes speech pathologists erroneously act as if it does. There is a failure on their part to realize that words, of necessity, lump together the similarities of persons and processes that they represent and disregard the differences. Also, there is a failure to realize that words can never say all about any event, object, or process. Our descriptions, at best, are incomplete.

The third premise, the map is self-reflexive or that we may make maps of maps or speak words about words etc., is particularly pertinent to the evaluative process. Typically, the speech pathologist depends upon reports from informants and other specialists to round out the picture necessary for an appropriate evaluation.

Examination of the summary statements appearing in case history files reveals the operation of this self-reflexive process. Statements about statements are a frequent occurrence. Unfortunately, not always is there a realization that the statement is a statement about a statement. Too often, also, there is a failure to check back to the observational level to ascertain whether or not what is being said is descriptive of an underlying 'reality'. The fact that we can make statements about statements is of immense value to us, but it is also not without pitfalls. Unless there is checking back at each verbal level to the observational level, we can produce beautiful, grammatically correct constructions which have little relevance to an underlying 'reality'.

With these three basic premises as a base, Korzybski developed several formulations which he felt if applied to human problem solving would yield beneficial results. Only those formulations which apply most directly to the evaluative process in speech pathology will be discussed.

CONSCIOUSNESS OF ABSTRACTION: Perhaps one of the most important formulations of General Semantics is the one referred to as consciousness of abstracting. The significance of this formulation is that the perceiver should be aware of the fact that whatever is perceived is a joint product of the perceiver and the perceived. Moreover, what we perceive is partial and unique, and we are always in the picture whether we like it or not. It is especially important for the speech pathologist not to forget that he is a partner in this perceptual process when evaluating a person with a speech variation. The very process of abstracting, that is, going from observation to description to inference to judgment is a process of leaving out more and more details. As generalizations and inferences move higher and higher, more details are omitted. Being conscious of one's self in this abstracting process not only can serve as a guard against dogmatism and absolutism, but also should yield more valid judgements about the person and his variation.

NON-ELEMENTALISM: This formulation points up the need to recognize and be aware of the fact that events, processes, and objects are not isolated phenomena but are being influenced and acted upon by other factors and forces. In our efforts to categorize, we often compartmentalize our knowledge and information in such a way that we begin reacting to our categories as if they were isolated and unchanging and a valid picture of 'reality'. Failure to take into account the fact that any event, process or person is being acted upon by other forces leads to poor predictability. The speech pathologist conducting his appraisal of the person's variation should be constantly on the alert to recognize the operation of these other variables. An example from this writer's experience points up the need to apply this formulation. After working with a child for weeks with no apparent progress, the father, instead of the mother, brought the child to the clinic for his weekly session. It was only upon hearing the father speak that it was discovered that he had essentially the same variation in his speech that his child had. The child was simply imitating the speech pattern of his father and therapeutic efforts to modify his speech pattern were being sabotaged by the child's exposure to the father's variant speech pattern. Had a more thorough investigation been made of the speech patterns of the parents and close associates, much time and frustration could have been saved.

INNER SILENCE: This formulation reminds us that words, labels and categories often intrude in the observational process. Since much of the terminology and many of the diagnostic labels in speech pathology are permeated with unconscious assumptions and causal relationships, this formulation is an important one for the speech pathologist. Observing in a detached manner, without the 'noisy' intrusion of words, labels, and categories, should increase the probability of observing relationships and aspects of behavior which would not be observed had the screening effect terms and categories been permitted to operate. A clear example of the lack of inner silence in the observational process occurred at one university in the process of screening the speech of incoming students. Prior to the screening process, the examiners had been participants in a lengthy research study devoted to rating the extent of nasality in the speech of experimental subjects. As a result of this extensive exposure to nasality, the examiners judged four times as many incoming students as having nasal speech than had been so judged in previous years. A few weeks later, after the perceptual set had died out, less than a quarter of those judged to have nasal speech originally were found to have it on reevaluation.

NON-ALLNESS: As stated earlier words cannot say all about anything; however, in addition to this limitation of words, people may react as if they perceived all of the facts and characteristics of an event or person. The earlier example of some students not wanting to work with persons having articulation variations because they felt they knew all about articulation is an example of this type of allness reaction. Awareness that we cannot know all about any one thing is important for the speech pathologist to recognize in the evaluative process. He must always be open to new information whether it is in the formal 'diagnostic' phase or the therapeutic phase of his work. There is basically no separation between 'diagnostic' process and therapeutic process from the viewpoint of observing and garnering information about the client and his speech. There may be a difference in emphasis during the two processes but each relates to the other and can and should influence the other.

DELAYED REACTION: This formulation is suggested as a safeguard from habitual conditioned responses. The delay in reaction does not need to be for a great length of time, but should be long enough to afford an opportunity to entertain a greater variety of responses. In other words, a delay in responding permits the person to select from a greater repertoire of responses and should lead to more appropriate reactions to the person and his situation.

NON-IDENTITY: Scientists have demonstrated that no two things are absolutely identical. However, our language with its subject-predicate structure permits us to equate two or more things as equal or identical. Behaving or reacting to non-identical events and persons as though they were identical is called identification. Too often, in the appraisal process, speech pathologists are looking for similarities and disregarding differences. The differences are masked not only by a drive to perceive similarities but also the structure of our language facilitates the equating of non-identical items. Differences can make a difference and an awareness of this fact should lead to a more thorough and appropriate examination of the person and his speech evaluation. Articulation problems are not simply articulation problems. Unique individuals have unique variations under unique conditions even though there are also striking similarities among the people, variations, and conditions.

EXTENSIONAL ORIENTATION: An extensional orientation demands that the person check his verbal maps with the 'reality' under consideration. With such an orientation a person is aware of sub-verbal levels both in the external world and one's own reactions. Without an extensional orientation a person sees no need to check his verbal maps with 'reality'. In the field of speech pathology, with its vast areas of unknown, it is quite easy to fall prey to an intensional orientation. Too often, our theories are reacted to as if they were facts; thereby reducing the probability that the theory will be checked against 'reality'.

In addition to the formulations discussed above, Korzybski suggested five extensional devices as an aid in making our language and our reactions to language more in keeping with our present scientific awareness. These aids are to be used overtly and tacitly to delay reactions and to insure an extensional orientation. The writer has found each of these aids excellent reminders during the evaluative process for achieving an extensional orientation.

(1) INDEXING: Words lump together unique individuals, objects, persons, and/or events under a common name. Hence, they give a false impression of identity to non-identical objects and events; and this impression, when translated into behavior, results in uniform identical reaction to individuals or objects to which the name can be given. Terms such as stuttering, cleft palate speech, aphasia, etc. may and do evoke in some people fixed identical reactions. The little index or superscript is a reminder that there are differences among individuals or processes with the same name. In other words, articulation variation[1] is not articulation variation[2], aphasia[1] is not aphasia[2], etc.

(2) DATING: General semantics accepts as a basic premise that the world and everything in it is in the process of change. By dating statements, beliefs and judgments, the person becomes aware of these changes. In the evaluative process, it is important to be reminded of the fact that the person is changing day to day and minute to minute. Observations made at one time are not necessarily valid for another time. This device of dating reminds us that names and labels alone do not reflect changes going on within the individual and within his environment.

(3) ETC. This little device, to be used either tacitly or overtly, should accompany any statement in order to remind us that maps do not represent all of the territory. By being aware of the fact that all of the evidence is not in, we are more prone to reevaluate our judgments and statements when new evidence is available. The etc. is another way of guarding against premature inferences which frequently lead to misevaluations.

(4) HYPHEN: Our traditional language with its structure permits us to separate many things which cannot be separated in 'reality'. This artificial splitting up of events and processes into independent entities is called elementalism by the general semanticist. The hypthen when used between words such as socio-economic, sensory-motor, etc., is a means of reminding us that although the persons and events may be verbally split into independent, isolated categories, they are still influenced by other events, objects and persons. Speech pathologists need to be aware of the potential inter-relationships between a person's attitudes, general health, environment, motivation and the functioning of his speech-producing structures.

(5) QUOTE: Many times we use terms that tend to be highly multi-ordinal, and, as such, their meanings are dependent upon the level of abstraction and context in which they are used. Such terms as 'intelligence', 'mind', 'objective', 'heredity', 'environment' are multi-ordinal terms. The quotation marks around them reminds us to be aware that these terms may have quite different meanings to different people. Such terms can be trouble-makers as far as communication is concerned, for some persons react to them as if they do have fixed connotations and meanings. The terms 'organic', 'functional', 'psychogenic', 'central', etc. are ones in the area of speech pathology which frequently produce confusion in communication.

In summary, speech pathologists certainly do not know all about the production of speech or variations in it. In fact, the federal government, universities, and private foundations are awarding large sums of money to finance research for the purpose of learning more about this complex process. Thus, the concept of ETC. reminds us that in the area of speech production we do not know all about it. The extensional device of INDEXING reminds us of the many differences among persons with speech variations. By selection, most of the persons speech pathologists encounter have speech that differs; however, speech variation^1 is not speech variation^2. The extensional device of DATING indicates recognition of the fact that the same person's speech patterns are constantly undergoing change. It alerts us to the fact that our speech varies and differs from time to time. A speech pathologist is concerned primarily with the speech of the person; however, he should and must be very much concerned about the rest of the person physiologically and socially. Therefore, the HYPHEN reminds us that other interrelationships exist and that these should be taken into account in his evaluation. The case history includes detailed information regarding the emotional as well as the physical and social environment in which the person is operating. Speech variations are not just the result of a physical condition but reflect the style of living and other forces operating in a person's life. Moreover, the speech variation may influence the adjustment of the person. The extensional device of the QUOTE reminds us that terms such as 'speech defect', 'speech disorders', 'functional', and 'organic' are to be used with an awareness that they may have different meanings to different people, and these meanings vary with the context and level of abstraction. The term 'defective speech', if used, should be used with either an overt or tacit quotation mark because of the variety of conditions that are subsumed under this term.

Referring again to the model of speech production in Figure 1, attention is directed this time to the speech pathologist's activities as he goes about 'diagnosing'. Stage 'D' is where the speech pathologist generally initiates his evaluative process. This is one of the two stages where the speech pathologist is able to make a direct observation, and it is in this area that he is uniquely qualified to observe, describe, and infer. An integral part of the speech pathologist's training involves calibrating his hearing in order to make judgments as to the adequacy of the acoustic product. In addition to his calibrated hearing, the speech pathologist has at his disposal special techniques and instruments which aid him in making more reliable observations and descriptions of these observations. Sound spectographs, pitch meters, oscillographs, volume indicators, rate meters, etc., serve as instrumental aids to the speech pathologist's nervous system. If he is to use these instrumental aids effectively, he needs to know their characteristics, i.e., frequency response, delay time, tolerances, etc. These instruments are extraneural aids to the speech pathologist's nervous system and as such, they have limitations. At this time, correlations between physical measurements of the acoustic product and perceptual judgments of the product are not particularly high. Moreover, a speech pathologist must make the final judgments as to adequacy or extent of variation of the acoustic product, since the instruments are only aids to his observational system. Perhaps, with the development of more sophisticated instrumentation to measure the acoustic product, and with the development of more sophisticated rating scales, a closer correlation between the physical attributes of the acoustic product and the perceptual judgments about it will be found. Since instruments alone are not capable of making these judgments, the speech pathologist must, of course, rely on his internal calibration in some cases, and the combined judgments of additional speech pathologists in other cases. Rating scales requiring the use of additional observers may be used in order to achieve greater agreement as to the extent and quality of a speech variation. When used, it is important for the speech pathologist to recognize the limitations of this technique and take them into account when he collates data from other stages and sources. Unfortunately, this is not always the case and inappropriate evaluations do occur. For example, research has indicated that the stimulus used to evoke an articulatory response may influence the response, and some unsophisticated clinicians are unaware of this factor. When attempting to assess the pitch range of the human voice, care must be exercised to control not only the method of eliciting the range but also the intensity level used during the assessment. Without controlling these factors, reliable estimates of pitch range cannot be made. As indicated on the model, events at Stage 'D' emanate from Stage 'C', the speech producing mechanism, and it is important that the speech pathologist in making judgments about the person and his speech is cautious in inferring causal relationships between Stage 'C' and 'D'. Some of the problems regarding inferring such relationships will be discussed in a later section.

Stage 'C', the speech-producing mechanism, is another stage where the speech pathologist is able to make direct observations. When he examines a speech-producing mechanism, he is doing so with a purpose and manner quite different from that of the physician or a dentist. These other specialists examine the person primarily to determine disease conditions or structural variations which are either endangering or potentially capable of endangering the physical health of the human being involved. Speech pathologists examine the mechanism from the standpoint of determining whether or not the functioning of the structure is adequate for the purposes of producing acceptable speech. In his examination, he may recognize disease conditions, malformed structures, etc., but it is not his function to medically diagnose these conditions. When such conditions are recognized, his function is to refer the person to an appropriate specialist who is qualified to make either a medical or dental diagnosis.

Although the acoustic product emanates from Stage 'C', the speech-producing mechanism, there is not a direct relationship between variations in its structures and the acoustic product. In cases of extreme variations in the structure and functioning, the relationship appears to be more direct; however, even in these cases, compensatory activities by the person may yield an acceptable acoustic product. This does not mean that the speech pathologist is not concerned about the status of the speech-producing mechanism, but, again, must be cautious in inferring a direct relationship between a structural variation or the physiological functioning of this mechanism and its impact on the acoustic product.

At Stage 'B' on the model of speech production, we find that events occurring at this Stage are not directly perceivable by the speech pathologist. This area encompasses the 'hidden' process that is postulated to explain observations at Stage 'C'. It is known only through scientific inference; and, in addition to not being directly perceivable by the speech pathologist, it is also not directly manipulatable. Judgments as to the intactness of the central nervous system are within the province of the neurologist, not the speech pathologist. It may be that the speech pathologist suspects malfunctioning of the central nervous system as seen by the behavior in Stage 'C'; however, he is not trained or in a position to make judgments and inferences relative to the intactness of the system from the standpoint of the physical health of the human being involved. He may postulate how this particular process functions to produce the effects of Stage 'C', but this postulatory activity is aimed at attempting to understand, and hopefully predict, events occurring at Stage 'C' and 'D'. Such activities primarily are in the realm of theory and exploratory research; and, before critical actions are taken on the basis of such constructs, they must be checked out experimentally. It would be redundant to labor the point of the complexity of the central nervous system and our limited understanding of its functioning. It suffices to say that from the standpoint of the 'diagnostic' process the speech pathologist is not in a position to make statements concerning the medical status of this stage. Moreover, as stated earlier, at this time there is little the speech pathologist can do to modify defects within Stage 'B'. Speech pathologists must depend on reports from neurologists and other medical personnel concerned with evaluating the central nervous system. And, even after such reports, there is a great hazard in postulating certain relationships between a malfunctioning central nervous system and its direct impact at Stages 'C' or 'D'. This is not to say that the speech pathologist should not be concerned with the central nervous system, but must be cautious about postulating cause and effect or strong relationships between events there and at Stages 'C' and 'D'.

Stage 'A' on the speech production model relates to the impingements of the environment, that is the total environment of the person, on his sensory apparatus. Obviously, the speech pathologist cannot directly observe all of the experiences the person has had and must depend upon either the reports of the person with the variation or other informants who have known the person. The validity and reliability of all reports of this nature must be estimated. It is at this point where words about words or maps of maps are frequently made. And if made, they should be made with full awareness of the foibles of human recall as well as the distortion, conscious and unconscious, of informants giving information to the examiner. We do know that events occurring at this stage must be processed through the 'hidden' process of Stage 'B'. But again, we can only conjecture as to how this process takes place. However, one of the most important avenues for modifying the speech and speech-associated behavior must be initiated at Stage 'A'. Other than those few instances in which prosthetic devices can be used in the speech producing mechanism or surgical intervention can be employed, most of the work of the speech pathologist is directed toward Stage 'B' through Stage 'A'. It is disturbing to see unsupported statements in case history reports and summaries stating that 'emotional' conflict or 'emotional' trauma is responsible for the speech variation occurring at Stages 'C' or 'D'. Examination of the model reveals that such a relationship is indeed a very tenuous and highly conjectural one. It is one thing to say emotional conflict is the primary cause of the speech variation of Stage 'D', but it is another thing to try to explain how such emotional conflict can pass through the 'hidden' process of Stage 'B' and then to Stage 'C' and yield a variation at Stage 'D'. It is easy to see that if the child is stimulated in his home by defective speech he will probably learn defective speech. Indeed he is quite likely to speak as his parents or other persons in his home speak. We have little doubt that French children speak French because they are exposed to French, and English children speak English because they are exposed to English. However, just how a person learns to speak is not known at this time and statements made about it are largely based on theory and conjecture. To step beyond this obviously gross relationship to more subtle relationships requires postulating constructs in the central nervous system. To date, research based data on such constructs is very minimal.

The feedback channels on the model of speech production refer to the sensory avenues employed during speaking to monitor the acoustic product, and the speech-producing mechanism. As indicated earlier, the auditory channel is generally considered to be the most important one for monitoring the speech. The speech pathologist in conducting his appraisal process needs to know the status of the person's hearing. The audiometer is one of the basic instruments used to assess auditory functioning and it yields a graphic representation of the person's hearing acuity at selected frequencies. The stimulus used in these cases is generally a pure tone. Not in all cases is there a high correlation between pure tone acuity and a person's ability to understand and comprehend speech. This fact should be taken into account during the appraisal process and at times it may be necessary to employ other types of stimuli to test the person's hearing. A statement indicating that hearing is normal should always be accompanied by a description of the type of test used and the conditions under which the testing was done. Recent research indicates the need to explore other types of auditory testing if we are to have a more complete picture of the person's auditory functioning. For example, auditory pattern recognition and temporal ordering ability may be important indicators of variations in the auditory system which are not customarily assessed. Too often, tests are administered simply because they have been administered before. They are employed in a ritual-like fashion without a full awareness of the reasons for administering them or whether the tests have adequate reliability or validity to be useful.

Finally, and of crucial importance, is the fact that the application of the formulations of general semantics as a blind ritual will neither improve the quality of the appraisal process nor improve the effectiveness of the speech pathologist. As Korzybski (1941) repeatedly emphasized in his *Science and Sanity*, general semantics involves a retraining of the nervous system. In other words, it requires a change in the speech pathologist himself, and this change must be an 'under the skin' change and not just a mouthing of a scientific orientation and the formulations of general semantics. This metamorphosis, ideally, would be a fusion of the scientist and the clinician — a blending of the art, responsiveness and intuition of the clinician with the experimental attitude, logic, objectivity, and critical faculty of the scientist. The scientist-clinician would be one who has achieved a balance between an interest in the individual as a person and interest in the individual as a research problem to be investigated with the rigor appropriate to our scientific knowledge today. A scientific orientation provides the clinician with a means for continued growth and evolution. Without such an orientation and the methods of science available to him, the clinician has restricted opportunities for growth and development. Dana W. Atchley, (1954) in his article "The Healer and the Scientist", provides us with not only a clear description of the evolution of the healer and the scientist in the medical profession, but also a graphic example of how a scientific orientation in one field has yielded profound progress.

As the healer has merged with the scientist he has undergone several interesting changes. Exposition has been substituted for pompous authoritarianism. With some real knowledge of what is occurring in his patient, he need no longer discourage questions from his patient or speak *ex cathedra*. He gladly explains those areas which he understands with a self-confidence that permits him to face his ignorance of other areas. An honest simplicity supplants the complicated pseudo-scientific double talk of "catarrhs", "intoxications", "biliousness", and so forth; the "beside manner", where it survives, is frankly salesmanship. Although sectarianism in medicine had begun to decline forty years ago, there was still much orthodoxy, and deviations from a ritual in the examination of a patient were frowned on merely because they were deviations. This attitude is no longer evident in the best circles (exclusive of the psycho-analytic group). The master-disciple relationship, so common in the past, is rarely seen. The oft-repeated aphorisms of the great clinician are supplanted by information quoted from a variety of scientific journals. The atmosphere is experimental, the mood is inquiring, the goal is understanding. Moreover, there is as much concern with the understanding of the total individual as of his chemical processes. The healer is as alert as the scientist.

It is thus apparent that the physician of today, at his best, represents a fusion of the healer and the scientist. In his role he analyzes the multiple components presented by a single human being. As healer his intuitive understanding of the personality and environment is amplified by modern psychology; and scientific studies of the many facets of the structure and functions of the physical machine inform him as to the existing organic status. The appraisal resulting from an integration of these data leads naturally to the special management appropriate to the particular individual. The introduction of the highest possible standards of scientific precision into clinical medicine is no deterrent to the exhibition of compassion or any of the other generous gifts of the healer. Merging the healer and the scientist combines the best capacities of both and loses nothing by the union.

CASE WESTERN RESERVE UNIVERSITY

REFERENCES

Atchley, D.W., "The healer and the scientist", *Saturday Review Reader* No. 3. (Bantam Books, New York, 1954), pp. 5-14.

Darley, F.L., *Diagnosis and Appraisal of Communication Disorders*, (Englewood Cliffs, N.J., Prentice-Hall, Inc., 1964).

Johnson, W., F.L. Darley, D.C. Spriestersbach, *Diagnostic Methods in Speech Pathology* (New York Harper and Row, Publishers, Inc., 1963).

Korzybski, A., *Science and Sanity: An Introduction to Non-Aristotelian Systems and General Semantics*, Second Edition (Lancaster, Pennsylvania, Science Press Printing Co., 1941).

Newman, P.W., "Speech impaired"? *Am. Speech and Hrng Assoc.*, 3, No. 1, (1961), 9-10.

WENDELL JOHNSON[1] and JOSEPH L. STEWART[2]

STUTTERING AND NORTH AMERICAN INDIANS

Of all the disorders of verbal communication, the problem of stuttering probably has been of most interest to anthropologists. A number of observations pertaining to the presence or absence of stutterers among a group have been made but there has yet to be published in the anthropological literature a comprehensive study of cultural factors related to this problem.

Most of the accounts in which the problem of stuttering has been mentioned pertain to the North American Indians. The earliest published observation relating stuttering to the Indian that the authors are aware of is that of Hrdlička (1908:100): "Defects of speech, such as stammering or stuttering, have never been met with by the writer in any of the tribes visited." Hrdlička reported physiological and medical data gathered between 1898 and 1905 from 102 Indian localities in the western United States and northern Mexico. Unfortunately, Hrdlička did not speculate upon the reasons for the absence of such speech difficulties.

More recently, Bullen (1945) investigated cross-cultural influence in the problem of stuttering and cited the Navahos as a group in which the incidence of the problem was quite low. The number of Navaho stutterers existing at the time of the field work is unclear as Bullen did not see most of those reported to exist. Bullen also quoted a Dr. Ekblaw to the effect that, while living among a group of Polar Eskimos for four years, he had observed none who stuttered.

In the field of speech pathology, one of the best known observations of the absence of the problem of stuttering in an Indian society is that pertaining to the Bannock and Shoshone Indians of Idaho as reported by Johnson (1944) and Snidecor (1947).

[1] Shortly before his death, Dr. Johnson expressed his willingness to submit an article as his contribution to this volume. Due to the state of his health at the time, it was not possible for him to complete his contribution. The present article was written shortly before Dr. Johnson's final illness and the responsibility for submitting it in his name is that of the editor. The materials included in footnote 4 have been added since this article was originally completed.

[2] The authors wish to express their gratitude to Professor David B. Stout, then of the Department of Sociology and Anthropology, University of Iowa, for his substantial contribution to the study reported. This investigation was supported by Grant RD-319, administered by Wendell Johnson, and by a fellowship awarded to Joseph L. Stewart by the United States Office of Vocational Rehabilitation.

Johnson appears to be the first to note that in the absence of the problem there was also an absence of a word or words pertaining to the problem.

That the problem of stuttering has existed in some North American Indian groups can be inferred from the Salish vocabularies published by Hill-Tout (1902:355, 1904:20, 1905:120) in which native terms for 'stuttering' and 'stutterer' are given. No other mention of the problem is made by Hill-Tout. Sapir (1915:190, 194), in his treatise on "abnormal speech in Nootka" makes two references to stuttering:

A fifth, not uncommon, speech defect among the Nootka is stuttering. Stutterers, like all other persons who have something abnormal about their speech, are derided by being imitated.

and

The most northern Nootka tribe...are said to be all stutterers and are accordingly imitated in jest.

A more recent report on the existence of stuttering on the Northwest Coast was made by Lemert (1953) who stated that the Nootka, Kwakiutl, Salish, Haida, and Tsimshian societies have stutterers and a well-defined word for stuttering in their languages and that there is evidence of this type of speech impairment existing long before any contact with white society.

The most obvious omission in the foregoing reports is a definition of the term or description of the behavior referred to as 'stuttering'. It is presumed that the accounts reporting the existence of stuttering refer to the relative lack of speech fluency shown by a particular speaker. From the clinical view, however, the problem of stuttering encompasses much more. According to Johnson (1959), the problem of stuttering first arises in the sensitivity of a listener to the disfluency of a speaker, together with the listener's unfavorable evaluation of this disfluency and his classification of it as 'stuttering'. A second variable, according to Johnson, pertains to the kinds of speech hesitations and the relative frequency with which they are performed. A third variable is the degree to which the speaker is sensitive to the evaluations of the listener, and perhaps to his own disfluency. The problem of stuttering then, according to Johnson, involves an interaction between at least two persons, a speaker and a listener. A disfluent speaker who is not aware of or not concerned over his disfluency, and whose speech does not meet with the disapproval of the listeners around him, can hardly be considered as having a problem of stuttering.

Under the terms of this hypothesis, the reports, cited above, of the problem of stuttering are to be evaluated with reference to the general lack of information that would establish the fact that the 'stutterers' were so considered by members of their own group. It is also to be considered that, with the exception of the Lemert publication, the reports contain no mention in any case of the reactions of the 'stutterer' to his own speech and of the evaluations of it by members of the group. Judgments pertaining to the significance of the speech fluency and disfluency of any person must be made according to the standards of the society to which he belongs. Bullen (1945:4-5) noted one of the problems inherent in making such an evaluation:

In collecting cross-cultural data on stuttering, therefore, it is of extreme importance for the validity of the count to allow for whatever 'normal roughness' appears in the particular speech of a particular people. Otherwise, overeager investigators might bring back staggering instances of stuttering in a culture with almost everyone classified as a stutterer.

Another difficulty to be encountered arises from translating a term as abstract in its general usage as 'stuttering'. The term 'stuttering' functions generally, and most clearly, on the abstraction level of classification rather than that of relatively dis-criminative description. This probably accounts for some of the confusion in deter-mining the incidence of the problem. Again, the Navaho are a case in point. Leighton and Kluckhohn (1947:14) have stated that if a parent breaks a pot one of the conse-quences might be that "the child will stutter or stammer or have other speech difficulties". Johnson (1953) subsequently had a former student at the University of Iowa, George Kriehn, investigate the Navaho term for "stuttering" while Kriehn was employed as a teacher on the Navaho Reservation. The Navaho term given Kriehn by Fr. Berard Haile as the one that has been employed on occasion as equivalent to 'stuttering' was defined, by Haile, as "just a waiting." Further, also according to Haile, there is no other descriptive-level meaning for the term and no stigma is attached to the behavior to which the term refers. This Navaho term, at least, does not appear to refer to the behavior that 'stuttering' refers to as used by most North American English-speaking persons.

The most recent publication dealing with the problem of stuttering in North American Indian societies is that of Stewart (1960), which is based upon a doctoral dissertation directed by Johnson and Stout. In this study, two American Indian groups, the Cowichans of Vancouver Island (a 'stuttering group') and the Ute (a 'non-stuttering group')[3], were compared on variables in child training which may accompany the presence or absence of the problem of stuttering. Members of thirty households in each group were interviewed about various aspects of the training and socialization of a particular child in each family. The dimensions investigated were nursing and feeding, toilet training, sexual socialization, dependence, aggression, and speech and language development. From other informants additional information was obtained concerning the cultural patterns and customs which may or may not have been directly related to child training practices.

In order to anticipate some of the difficulty pointed out above pertaining to translation of terms, the following cross-cultural definition of 'stuttering' was established. First, the relevant aspects of the alleged 'stutterer's speech must be regarded, by members of his own group, as deviant and subject to disapproval.

[3] The selection of the Ute as the 'non-stuttering group' followed from a report to Wendell Johnson by two physicians then residing in Vernal, Utah, that the Ute had neither stutterers nor a word for the problem in their language. This report was later substantiated by Francis McKinley, Director of Community Services for the Ute tribe, Fort Duchesne, Utah.

Second, the behavior involved in the act called 'stuttering' must consist, in part, of culturally unacceptable speech hesitation forms and culturally unacceptable reactions to such hesitations. The speaker should show exertions of effort in speaking that are apparently motivated by concern over the apparent difficulty, or conflict, involved in initiating or continuing the act of speaking and apprehension over the failure to proceed smoothly. Finally, the linguistic concept of stuttering, as revealed by the existence of one or more words in the native language which are essentially the equivalent to our word 'stuttering' must be present, since it would appear to be unlikely that a problem would be known or recognized in a society that had no way to talk about it.

Three other Vancouver Island bands in addition to the Cowichan — the Sheshaht Nootka, Campbell River-Cape Mudge Kwakiutl, and Nanaimo Salish were also contacted briefly in order to obtain an estimate of the incidence of the relevant speech problems among them. The results of this inquiry indicate the incidence of stuttering among these societies to be approximately two per thousand, or 0.2 percent as compared to approximately 0.7 percent in the non-Indian population of the United States. No stuttering was found among the Ute.

The items from the interviews which were found to show statistically significant differences between the Cowichans and Ute were as follows: more Cowichan mothers and fathers reported having held a sex preference for the child before its birth; Ute mothers were more indulgent in initial nursing of the infant; Cowichan mothers were more severe in toilet training and in severity and frequency of punishment; Ute parents paid more initial attention to the child, had more body contact with the child for a longer period of time and reduced the amount of body contact more gradually than did the Cowichans; Cowichans had higher standards of speech fluency than the Ute and stressed conformity to these standards.

There were few differences between the groups in the reported ages at which the children attained early-learned motor skills, although there was a tendency for the Cowichan mean age to be lower than the Ute.

All the significant differences indicated that the Ute were less demanding of the child and more tolerant in allowing him to establish his own rate of development.

The language environments and methods of teaching the child to talk were also investigated. The presence or absence of a term equivalent to 'stuttering' was of primary interest in this regard. The Cowichan dialect differed from Ute in providing for verbal expression of such a term. Due consideration must be given to the possibility that Cowichan, unlike Ute, tends in some degree because of the presence of a term equivalent to 'stuttering', to influence its users to be attentive to disfluency and to evaluate it as a deviant characteristic.

The role of reduplication in the child's early speech appears to reflect the extent to which the members of each society are aware of and tolerant of the normal repetitions and hesitations which are characteristic of this development. The Cowichans did not seem to expect the child to reduplicate and repeat sounds, syllables, or words while he was learning to speak. The Ute, in whose language reduplication is highly characteristic of childhood usage, not only recognize this tendency in the child's speech but also encourage it. The Ute language also reflects a recognition of the developmental stages of childhood through a shifting vocabulary of different words applied to the child during the course of his development. The Cowichan dialect does not appear to provide for respresentation of the more subtle changes in childhood. A fundamental difference between the groups, which is presumed to be related to the linguistic differences noted, is seen in the acceptance of the role of the parent as a language teacher. The process nature of language learning was more clearly recognized by the Ute parents than by the Cowichan parents.

It is inferred that these various differences, when related to the evaluation by the Cowichan parent that speech repetition and hesitation are undesirable, might indicate a greater likelihood of the development of the problem of stuttering in the Cowichan society.

The tolerance of the Ute in allowing the child to establish his own rate of development, in both speech and attainment of independence, was more extreme than that of the less tolerant, but by our standards still permissive, Cowichans.

The hypothesis underlying the investigation, that cultural factors may exist which, through an interaction with a combination of variables, tend to foster the development of the problem called stuttering, seems tenable on the basis of the following findings and conclusions:

(1) The incidence of the problem called stuttering appears to have declined on Vancouver Island with the deterioration of the aboriginal culture with its elaborate and highly competitive socio-economic system and social stratification. The use of the native language is also seen to have declined and with it the formal, competitive speech rituals associated with the ceremonial aspects of the social system.

(2) The difficulty experienced in speaking by those Indians who were considered to be stutterers does not seem to have been as severe as that of most clinically diagnosed stutterers in our non-Indian North American society. It is hypothesized that this may be related to the degree to which the child is held responsible for his own disfluency in our society. The Cowichans generally assumed that an outside factor, essentially supernatural, was the cause of the so-called deviance in speech fluency and this appears to have relieved the speaker to some degree of feelings of personal responsibility for the relevant aspects of his speech behavior.

(3) The traditional methods of child training still practiced by the Cowichans reflect the relatively limited extent to which growth is regarded as a dynamic process. The Cowichans seem to be less aware than the Ute that the child's independence training is dependent upon certain levels of maturation and development. It is also hypothesized that the use of terms in the common vocabulary which give recognition to the stage of the child's development might further influence the parent's determination of his readiness for particular dimensions of socialization.

(4) The influence of a term essentially equivalent to 'stuttering' in the language in

determining, in part, the development of the problem seems established on the basis of the reported reactions to the diagnostic or significantly evaluational use of the term. In at least one instance in the Cowichan society, and possibly in others, the usage of the term appears to have exerted a more direct influence upon the mother's reaction to her son's speech than did her own objective observations. Further support of this view is inferred from the apparent reduction of the incidence of the problem on Vancouver Island associated with a substantial decrease in the use of the native term for 'stuttering'.

(5) Since some forms of hesitation, or disfluency, in speech may be considered to be deviant in a given culture while others are not so considered, it is hypothesized that the particular hesitation forms that are evaluated as stuttering or as abnormal or negatively valued may vary among societies. A specific person is more likely to judge a particular type of hesitation form as stuttering if, in his society, that form is unacceptable. If nonfunctional reduplication is an unacceptable hesitation form, for example, it might be expected that repetition would be found to be a dominant part of the speech of any person considered to be a stutterer. Should there be a society in which the problem of stuttering is known in which repetition is considered as an acceptable hesitation form and some other hesitation forms are regarded as unacceptable, repetition forms would not be expected to characterize crucially the speech of those persons considered to be stutterers in that society.[4]

UNIVERSITY OF IOWA

NEUROLOGICAL AND SENSORY DISEASE CONTROL PROGRAM

PUBLIC HEALTH SERVICE

BIBLIOGRAPHY

Bullen, Adelaide (1945), "A cross-cultural approach to the problem of stuttering", *Child Development*, 16:1-88.
Hill-Tout, C. (1902), "Ethnological studies of the mainland HalkomelEm, a division of the Salish of British Columbia", *Brit. Ass. Advance. Sci.*, 72:355-449.
— (1904), "Report on ethnology of the Siciatl... of British Columbia", *J. roy. Anthrop. Inst. G. B. and Ire.*, 34:20-91.

[4] Further instances of existence of the problem of stuttering have been observed among the White-river Apaches in Arizona. While this problem has not been researched in depth, it has been determined that there is a word in the Apache language for the problem of stuttering and an incidence estimated at 9 cases in the population of approximately 5,000 persons. All stutterers reported are adult and most of them live in one of two villages near Fort Apache, Arizona. Three of the men are brothers (ranging in age from 30 to 48 years) whose father was also reported to have stuttered. Another man, about 40 years old, and his niece are also reported as are another man of 58 years and his niece. From informant reports, these people do not seem to be overly concerned about their speech and do not appear to be evasive about the problem, much as the Northwest Coast Indians. Also in common with Northwest Coast Indian languages there is little reduplicative speech in the Apache language and beyond "mama" there is little reduplication tolerated by the Apache parent when the child begins to speak using two or more words and he is cautioned against repeating by being told to keep quiet if he cannot talk without repeating. The reason cited is that the parents do not wish to have these repetitions become a 'habit'.

— (1905), Repott on the ethnology of the Stlatlumtl of British Columbia", *J. roy. Anthrop. Inst. G. B. and Ire.*, 35:126-218.

Hrdlička, Alés (1908), "Physiological and medical observations among the Indians of the southwestern United States", *Bull. Bur. Amer. Ethnol.*, 34:1-427.

Johnson, Wendell (1944), "The Indians have no word for it: I. Stuttering in Children", *Quart. J. Speech*, 30: 330-337. Reprinted in modified form in Chapter 17 of *People in Quandaries*, (New York, Harper & Bros. 1946).

— (1953), Personal correspondence from George Kriehn, Brigham City, Utah, January 9, 1953.

— (1959), *The Onset of Stuttering* (Minneapolis, University of Minnesota Press, 1959).

Leighton, Dorothea and Clyde Kluckhohn (1947), *Children of the People* (Cambridge, Harvard University Press).

Lemert, Edwin (1953), "Some Indians who stutter", *J. Speech Hearing Dis.*, 18: 168-174.

Sapir, Edward (1949), "Abnormal speech in Nootka", In D. B. Mandelbaum (Ed.), *Selected Writings of Edward Sapir* (Berkeley, Los Angeles, University of California Press, 179-196).

Snidecor, John (1947), "Why the Indian does not stutter", *Quart. J. Speech.*, 33:493-495.

Stewart, Joseph (1960), *The problem of stuttering in certain North American Indian societies* (= *J. Speech Hearing Dis., Monog. Suppl.*, 6).

INDEX

Abstracting, 48, 105, 110, 329, 331
Abstraction, 104, 106, 139, 334
   consciousness of, 114, 116-123, 331
Adams, S., 144, 157
Adrain, E.D., 46
Adorno, T.W., 150, 157
Affection, 176
Ainsworth, S.H., 319, 323
Albertini, B. von, 26, 32
Allen, R.R. 133, 125
Allophones, 281, 284
Allport, G., 53
Ambiguity, 179
Ames perception experiments, 206
Analogue, 93
Analogue Laboratory, 19, 74-75, 77
Analogy, 46, 74, 75, 227
Ansberry, M., 324
Anxiety, 312-313, 319, 321
Apprehension, 318-319
Archimedes, 128
Argumentation, 207
Argyris, C., 207
Aristotle, 80, 83, 85, 86, 89-92, 297-299
Arnold, A., 79
Articulation, 320, 330, 332
Asch, S.E., 153, 157
Ashby, W.R., 45
Atchley, D.W., 338-339
Atkins, W.H., 86
Attneave, I., 67-68, 71-72
Atwood, E.B., 247, 253
Audiology, 305-306
Auditory channel, 328, 337

Beck, K.W., 145-147, 153, 157, 159
Backus, O., 322-323
Bahn, E., 83
Baird, A.C., 78, 82, 87-88, 154, 157
Baker, V.L., 80
Bales, R.R., 140, 142, 144-145, 148, 152-153, 156, 158, 160
Barbara, D., 314-316, 321, 323

Barker, R., 161
Barnard, R.H., 215
Barnhart, C.L., 310, 323
Barnlund, D.C., 13, 19, 43, 47, 124-125, 152, 158
Barrow, L.C., 113, 125
Bass, B.M., 144, 158
Barzun, J., 96
Bateman, D.R., 244
Bateson, G., 13, 19, 62, 65, 66, 69, 72, 88, 310, 324
Baumgartel, H., 158
Bavelas, A., 155, 157, 158
Bechtel Corporation, 204, 206, 208-210
Beck, L., 22, 32
Becker, E., 308, 317-318, 323
Beloff, H., 320, 324
Benne, K.D., 144, 148, 152, 158, 183
Bennis, W.G., 216
Berelson, B., 143, 158
Berkowitz. L,, 144, 146, 149, 151, 158
Berne, E., 315, 323
Berry, M., 308, 321, 323
Bertalanffy, L. von, 216
Bever, T.G., 271
Binnie, C.A., 30-31
Bird, C., 150, 158
Birdwhistell, R.L., 14, 226, 265
Bjerstedt, A., 141, 158
Black, E., 80-81
Blake, W., 62, 67
Blanton, S., 321, 323
Blau, P.M., 151, 160
Bloomfield, L., 229, 248
Body motion, 267
Bontrager. O,R., 13, 19, 95, 102
Borg, W.R., 151, 158
Borgatta, E.F., 140, 142, 145, 158, 160
Borrman, E.G., 90
Bossard, J.J.S., 145, 158
Boulding, K., 48-49
Bovard, E.W., Jr., 153, 158
Braden, W., 82
Bradford, L.P., 183

Brady, J.P., 309, 323
Brainstorming, 133-134
Bridger, H., 212
Bridger, W.H., 21, 31
Bridgman, P.W., 110
Bronstein, A., 251
Brooks, R.M., 27, 31
Brown, M.L., 151, 160
Brown, W., 212
Bryde, J.F., 30-31
Bugenthal, J.F.T., 44
Bullen, A., 342, 345
Bullis, G.E., 21-22, 32
Burke, K., 215
Burton, R., 297-298
Burtt, H.E., 167
Butt, D., 322

Calder, A., 49
Calder, R., 217
Cameron, W.B., 39
Cantril, H., 206
Caring experience, 184
Carr, A., 324
Carr, H.A., 22, 31
Carroll, H.B., 245
Carter, L.F., 148, 150-152, 158-160
Cartesian premises, 43-44
Cartwright, D., 148, 150, 159-160
Castle, P., 33
Categories, 332
Cattell, R.B., 142-143, 151, 158-159
Causality, 35
Centrality, 156
Change, 169, 171, 204
Chapanis, A., 46
Chapman, J.P., 320-323
Chapman, L.J., 320, 323
Chicago, University of, 74, 95
Child training, 342, 344
Chretien, D., 251
Chisholm, G.B., 101-102
Chomsky, N., 229, 231, 236, 240, 271, 280, 294
Circumvention, 182
Claparede, E., 27, 31
Clark, R.A., 124, 126, 148, 159
Clarke, A., 49-50
Class discussion, 211
Class structure, 190
Clevenger, T., Jr., 223
Cloyd, J.S., 145, 158
Cognitive messages, 266
Cohen, A.R., 144, 159
Cohesiveness, 146, 147, 152-153, 190
Coleman, C.J., 114, 125
Coleman, J.C., 219

Combs, A., 219
Commitment experience, 185
Communication, 9, 34-36, 43, 47-51, 60-61, 76, 78, 79, 82, 87-88, 91, 93, 129, 157, 226, 256, 265-266, 268, 270, 307, 312, 314-315, 318
  mass, 35
  non-verbal, 53, 104-105, 107, 109, 226, 266
  verbal, 104, 107-108
Communication ability, 318
Communication content, 155
Communication disorders, 12, 18, 305-306, 313-314
Communication flow, 147
Communication methodologist, 18, 136
Communication methodology, 10, 12, 17-19
Communication theory, 18, 20, 78-79, 82-87, 89-92, 94, 205
Communicative problems, 325
Compulsiveness, 320
Computer, 65-66
Conant, J.B., 97-98
Concept-building, 34
Conceptualization, 140
Consensus, 167
Consensus experience, 185
Consonance, 56
Contreras, H., 14, 227, 280, 291-292, 294
Control, 76-77
Control systems, 181
Cooper, L., 86
Cope, E.M., 86
Copleston, E., 85
Cortwright, R., 13, 133-136, 163
Cottrell, L.S., 142, 158
Couch, A., 160
Cousins, N., 75
Coutu, W., 48
Croft, W.F., 114, 125
Cross-disciplinary language, 41
Criticism, 312, 318
Crockett, W.H., 152, 159
Cross-cultural, 340
Crowell, L., 150, 161
Cues, 55-59
  artificial, 54
  competing, 56
  natural, 54
  non-verbal, 57
Cultural patterns, 214, 342
Culture, 315
Culture group, 214
Cybernetics, 18, 53, 87, 129, 217

Dahl, R.A., 147, 159
Danehy, J.J., 252
Darley, F.L., 325, 339

Darwinian theory, 99
Dating, 33-334
Decoding, 224
Delayed reaction, 332
Democracy, 168
Denver, University of, 9, 75
Descriptive evaluation, 307
Deutero-learning, 69
Deutsch, K., 75
Deutsch, M., 152-153, 159
Deviations, 182
Deviant individual, 153
Dewey, J., 74, 154, 159, 206, 229
Diagnosis, 306-307, 317, 326, 332, 335
Dialect areas, 245
Dialectologist, 250, 255
Dialectology, 225
Dialects, 254
Dickens, M., 82
Differentiation, 21
Directive therapy, 312, 314-315
Discussion, 163-170, 179, 189
Disfluency, 343-344
Dissonance, 56
Dittes, J.E., 153, 159
Douglass, R.L., 319, 323
Drucker, P., 43-44
Drum, D., 82
Dunkerly, M.D., 150-159
Dunphy, D., 148-161
Dwight, S., 296
Dysrhythmia, 320

Ebing, E., 309, 323
Education, 95-96, 101, 204
Effective groups, 172
Einstein, A., 169
Eiseley, L., 99, 102
Eisenson, J., 309, 321, 323
Eisman, B., 146, 159
Elementalism, 105, 334
Elkind, D., 13, 18-19, 21, 27, 29, 30-32
Emergence experience, 185
Emergence theory of growth, 186
Emerson, R.W., 166, 169
Emerson, R., 146, 159
Emotive processes, 266
Encoding, 244
Entropy, 110, 128
Epistemology, 75
Erickson, E., 316, 324
Eskimos, 340
Etc., 333-334
Ethics, 89
Etymon, 281
Eubanks, R.T., 80

Evaluation, 330
Evaluative process, 325, 328, 335
Ewert, P.H., 22, 32
Expert opinion, 167
Extensional devices, 333
Extensional orientation, 114, 116, 117-123, 333

F-scale, 150
Face-to-face groups, 133
Factor analysis, 142, 143, 152
Falkenberg, D.R., 167
Fantz, R.L., 21, 32
Farson, R.E., 179
Fear, 182
Fear system, 187
Feedback, 55, 76, 88-89, 93, 130, 328, 337
Feedforward, 82
Fenichel, C., 320, 323
Fessenden, S., 13, 88, 135-136, 188
Festinger, L., 56, 145-147, 153, 159
Fischer-Jørgensen, E., 284-294
Flowerman, S.H., 150, 159
Francis, W.N., 253
Frandsen, K., 13, 19, 112
Frankl, V., 169
Freedman, A., 309, 320, 323
Freeman, G.L., 26, 32
Frenkel-Brunswick, E., 157

Gaier, E.L., 152, 161
Game model, 317
Game theory, 315
Gantenbein, M., 24, 32
Gardner, J.W., 98, 101-102
Garland, T.V., 215
Gazda, G.M., 186
Gellert, E., 147, 159
General semanticist, 334, 338
General semantics, 18, 103, 105-106, 113-114, 118, 124, 205-206, 325, 331
George, A.D., 249
Gesell, A., 21-22, 32
Gestalt, 25-26, 28, 229-230
Gesture, 53
Ghent, L., 27, 32
Ghilbaud, G.T., 217
Gibb, C.A., 151, 159
Gibb, J.R., 13, 135-136, 171, 173, 176, 179, 183, 186
Gibb, L.R., 13, 135-136, 171, 186
Gibson, E., 22, 32
Gibson, J.J., 21, 27, 32
Giffin, K., 13, 135, 138, 159
Gilchrist, J.C., 156, 159
Gilkinson, H., 319, 323
Girard, H.B., 153, 159

Glorfeld, L., 13, 135, 136, 213
Gloss, 281
Gnolund, N.C., 190
Go, E., 29 31
Goal setting, 180
Goffman, I., 57
Gold, F., 314-315, 320, 323
Goldberg, A., 114, 125
Goldfarb, W., 320, 323
Goldner, A., 212
Goldstein, A.G., 27, 31
Golembiewski, R.T., 139-140, 160
Gollin, E., 26, 32
Goodman, P., 311, 323
Goodstein, L., 320, 323
Gott, E., 254
Gouldner, A.W., 150, 160
Grammar, 64, 224-225, 229-232, 239
Grant, A., 85-86
Grave/acute, 282
Gray, G.W., 248
Greenberg, B.S., 113, 117, 121, 125
Greene, P.H., 77
Greenleaf, F.I., 319, 323
Grimm's law, 223
Gross, L., 60
Gross, N., 146, 160
Grosser, D., 147, 160
Group, 139-140, 143, 150, 154, 171
Group communication, 12, 204
Group-centered leadership, 206
Group-determined goals, 179-180
Group experiences, 173, 185
Group formation, 171, 177
Group goal attainment, 148
Group growth, 179
Group interaction, 150
Group-member status, 144
Group norms, 145, 152
Group opinion, 167
Group size, 144
Group task, 152
Group therapy, 213
Guertin, W.A., 320, 323
Guetzkow, H., 157
Guttman, L., 160

Haefner, D., 160
Haile, B., 342
Haiman, F.S., 90
Haley, J., 72
Halle, M. 271, 277
Hance, K.G., 154, 161
Hansen, H.M., 114, 125
Hare, A.P., 140, 144, 149, 160, 162
Harris, H., 60

Hartman, F.R., 113, 125
Harvard University, 80
Hayes, A.S., 310, 324
Haythorn, W., 150, 151, 152, 158-160
Heider, F., 56
Heilbrun, A.S., 321, 323
Heise, G.A., 152, 156, 160
Held, R., 33
Hellman, H.E., 90
Hemphill, J.K., 142, 160
Henry, N.B., 172
Hesitation, 343, 345
Heyns, R.W., 153-154, 160
Higgins, G.W., 211-212
Hill-Tout, C., 341, 346
Hoben, J.B., 79
Hockett, C.F., 252
Hogben, L., 96
Hollingshead, A., 309, 324
Holmes, J.C., 310, 323
Holtzman, P., 82, 322-323
Homans, G.C., 140, 149, 160-161
Homeostasis, 93
Homogeneous set, 67
Hooten Manufacturing Company, 209
Hope, B., 163
Horn, J., 27, 29-31
Howell, M., 151-152, 158
Hrdlička, A., 340, 346
Hughes, J.W., 148, 161
Hultzen, L., 251
Human relations training, 133
Hurwitz, J.I., 144, 147, 152, 160
Hutchins, R.M., 96
Hutchinson, P., 168
Huxley, A., 75
Hymovitch, B., 144, 147, 152, 160
Hyphen, 334

Iatrogenic disturbances, 311
Identification, 332
Identity, 108
Ilg, F.L., 21-22, 32
Imposed order, 182
Inclusion, 176
Indexing, 333-334
Indians, North American, 340-345
Individual prominence, 148
Ineffective groups, 172
Influence, 190
Information, 62-63, 66-67, 76, 82, 129
Information theory, 18, 53, 79, 129
Infra-communicational systems, 266
Inner silence, 332
Instructional material, 208
Instrumental aids, 335

Instrumentation, 335
Interaction, 143, 154
Interaction process analysis, 142, 153
Interdependence, 183
Internal learning, 63
International Petrotergent, Inc., 208-210
Interpersonal choice, 191
Interpersonal communication, 35, 114-123, 206
Interpersonal Communication Laboratory, 19, 112, 114, 124
Interpersonal preferences, 198
Interpersonal relationships, 189
Interpersonal stimuli, 151
Intra-group relationships, 188, 191
Intra-personal communication, 53, 55
Invention, 90
Iowa, University of, 305
Isolates, 191
Isomorphism, 73
Israel, J., 146, 160

Jackson, D., 72
Jackson, J., 141, 147, 160
Jacques, E., 212
Jahoda, M., 216-217
Jakobson, R., 287-291, 294
Jenkins, W.O., 150, 160
Jennings, H.H., 188
Jensen, J.V., 90
Johnson, B., 22, 32
Johnson, W., 14, 107, 114, 125, 307, 309, 314, 320-323, 325, 339-342
Jones, M., 319, 323
Jordan, H., 167

Kahn, R.L., 149, 153, 160
Katz, D., 10
Katz, E., 149, 151 153, 160
Kees, W., 87
Keller, D., 309, 324
Kelley, H.H., 50, 146-147, 159-160
Kennedy, G., 83
Kilpatrick, F., 47
Kinesics, 18, 87, 226, 310
Kinesthetic channel, 328
Kinship behavior, 268
Kipnis, D., 149, 160
Klapper, Z., 320, 323
Kluckhohn, C., 342, 346
Knower, F.H., 82
Knowledge explosion, 163
Koegler, R.R., 29, 31
Koehler, W., 229, 234
Koffka, K., 236
Kohler, I., 22, 25, 32

Koppitz, E.M., 21
Korzybski, A., 45, 73-74, 104-105, 124-125, 329, 331, 333, 338-339
Kounin, J.S., 161
Kranzel, C.F., 247
Kriehn, G., 342, 346
Kruger, A., 90
Kumata, H., 112, 125
Kurath, H., 245-246, 249, 251, 253

Label, 326, 329, 332
Lambercier, M., 24, 32
Langer, S., 49, 75
Langham, P., 160
Language, 103, 205, 214, 229, 231, 256-257, 260, 263, 330
Language disorder, 322
Lanzetta, J., 150, 158-159
Larson, M., 30, 32
Lasswell, H.D., 74
Law of matrix, 295
Law of parsimony, 295
Law of the total situation, 60
Lawrence, P., 212
Lazarus, E., 169
Lazersfeld, P.F., 160
Leaderless groups, 184
Leadership, 148, 150, 190, 205-207
Learning, 62, 164-165, 190, 229
Learning triad, 69-71
Leavitt, H.J., 145, 160-161
Lecture method, 164
Lees, R.B., 14, 227, 233, 271
Leiderman, P.H., 310, 323
Leighton, D., 342, 346
Leitner, M.A., 117, 121, 125
Lemert, E., 341, 346
Leopold, W., 287, 289, 291, 294
Lerner, D., 74
Levinson, D.J., 150, 157
Lewin, K., 45, 149, 161
Lexicon, 256
Lillywhite, H., 313, 323
Lindzey, G., 161
Linear causality, 50
Linguistic Atlas of the United States and Canada, 225, 245, 247
Linguistic geography, 225
Linguistic perception, 229, 232, 235
Linguistics, 12, 18, 85, 223, 228, 229, 253
Linguistics, comparative, 271
Linguistics, structural, 223
Lippitt, R., 147, 149, 153-154, 160-161
Logic, 103, 108, 110
Logical Types, 63
Loomis, E., 309, 324

Love, 174, 176, 184, 219
Low, J.H., Jr., 125

McBurney, J.H., 154, 161
McCarthy, J., 247
McDavid, R.I., Jr., 14, 225-226, 249-251, 253
McDavid, V., 253
McGregor, S.M., 245
McGuckin, H., 204
McKay, V., 217
McKeon, R., 85, 86, 88, 90-91
McKinley, F., 342
McLachlan, D., Jr., 13, 20, 271
McNemar, Q., 142
McQuitty, L.L., 152, 161

Macauley, J.R., 144, 158
MacKay, D.M., 35
Management education, 211
Management theory, 172
Manic-depressive, 315
Mann, C.H., 151, 161
Mann, J.H., 151, 161
Map, 108, 330
Marathon training groups, 183
March, J.G., 147, 161, 216
Marquis, D.R.P., 170
Martin, W.E., 146, 160
Masserman, J., 309-310, 312, 323
Mathematics, 108
Mayer, L., 309, 324
Mayer, M., 97
Meaning, 47-48, 52, 56, 59, 71, 104
Medawar, P.B., 218
Meili, R., 24, 32
Meirowitz, B., 159
Melton, A.W., 152, 161
Memory, 76
Mencken, H.L., 253
Mental retardation, 330
Message, 62, 68
Meta-communication, 265, 268
Metaphor, 226, 295
Meyer, H.J., 142, 158
Middle-level managers, 204
Mill, J.S., 167
Miller, G.A., 151, 156, 160
Mills, T.M., 147, 153, 158, 161
Minor, G., 114, 125
Model, speech production, 326, 336
Models, 44, 93, 104, 105
    isomorphic, 45
    structural, 44
    transactional, 43
Moreno, J.L., 188, 192

Morphemes, 224, 278
Morphophonemic, 227, 237, 240, 271
Morris, C., 315, 323
Morris, R.T., 145-146, 161
Morse, H., 320, 323
Motivation, 181
Motor coordination, 330
Motor skills, 343
Mowrer, O.H., 124-125
Mueller, R.A., 145, 161
Muir, L., 311-312, 315, 318, 324
Multi-ordinal terms, 334
Munn, N., 22, 32
Murray, E., 9-12, 17, 73-77, 84, 93, 102, 114-123, 215, 295, 308, 324
Murray, H., 211
Mussen, P.H., 33
Mysticism, 103, 109

Naess, A., 146, 161
Nasality, 332
Need-mechanism, 187
Need system, 186
Negative reinforcement, 318
Nelson, D.D., 322, 324
Newcomb, T.N., 139, 161
Newman, J., 50
Newman, P.W., 329, 339
Nieman, L.J., 148, 161
Non-allness, 114-123, 332
Non-Aristotelian system, 114, 116-123, 329
Non-elementalism, 331
Non-directive clinician, 322
Non-directive therapy, 312-313
Non-identity, 332
Non-lexical interaction, 268
Norms, 146, 152
Norton, M., 114-145, 158

Observational level, 331
Ogden, C.K., 74
Oliver, R.T., 82, 90, 213-214, 218- 219
Olum, V., 32
Openness, 176
Operationalization, 140
Oral communication, 310, 321
Oration, 84
Order, 73, 127
Organization, 205, 216
Organizational education, 211
Organizational leadership, 207
Orthography, 226, 256
Osgood, C.E., 112, 117, 120, 122, 124-126
Oswald, L.H., 310

PERT, 18, 133

Paralinguistic, 310
Parsons, T., 158
Participation hypothesis, 151
Pattern, 69, 73-74
Pattern discrimination, 21
Patterning, 68
Paulson, S., 145, 161
Penn, W., 169
Perception, 206, 229, 230, 232, 235
Perceptual activity, 28-30
    constancy, 22
    organization, 26, 28
Permissiveness, 183
Personality, 150, 308-310, 314, 318
Personality disorders, 308-312, 314-317, 319
    321-322
Persuasion, 207, 213
Peters, R.W., 93
Peterson, G.E., 14, 226, 256
Phillips, G., 14, 306, 316, 324
Philologists, 223
Philp, H., 148, 161
Phonemes, 281, 287, 289
Phonemic analysis, 271
Phonemics, 230
Phonics, 228
Phonological development, 280
    distinctions, 280
    system, 277, 287
Phonology, 224-226, 228, 230, 245, 256
Physical sciences thinking, 38-40
Piaget, J., 22-24, 26, 30, 32
Pines, M., 309, 324
Pittenger, R.E., 252
Plato, 75, 90
Polansky, N., 147, 160-161
Political rhetoric, 215
Pollock, A.B., 211
Polysemia, 227, 295
Population, 141
Postal, P.M., 271
Power structure, 147-148, 152, 153
Preparation, 141
Problem-solving, 133, 154
Process, 73, 141
Product, 141
Programmer, 66
Prosthetic devices, 337
Protective phrases, 178
Psychiatrist, 313-315
Psycholinguistic, 18, 224, 228, 231, 240
Psychological distance, 176-177
Psychotherapy, 18, 308
Ptacek, P., 14, 307, 325
Public speaking, 312-313

Quintilian, 313
Quote, 334

Randomness, 73
Rapoport, A., 124-125, 216
Rating scales, 335
Raven, B.H., 140, 161
Reality testing, 217, 219
Rebstock, E.F., 13, 135-136, 204
Redundancy, 62, 67-69
Reduplication, 343
Reflective thinking, 133, 206
Reich, W., 66
Reinforcement, 62-63, 72
Repetition, 312-314, 343, 345
Reticence, 309-311, 313, 315-318, 320-321
Rhea, J., 142, 159
Rhetoric, 18, 78-83, 85-87, 89, 91, 94, 213, 214,
    317
Rhetoric of science, 213-215, 219-220
Rice, A.K., 212
Richard, P., 189
Richards, I.A., 74-75, 79-80
Richards, J.M., 59
Rickover, H., 96
Rieber, R.W., 321, 324
Riecken, H.W., 149, 161
Riegel, R.E., 247
Riesman, D., 316, 324
Robinson, D., 27, 32
Rockey, J.R., 114, 124-125
Rogers, C., 312, 324
Rogge, E., 90
Rogler, L., 309, 324
Rohrer, J.H., 161
Role-playing, 211
Roles, 148-150, 152-154, 208
Rommetveit, R., 145, 148, 161
Roseborough, M.E., 158
Rosen, S., 147, 161
Rosenberg, P., 306
Rosenzweig, A., 280
Rowley, V., 309, 324
Ruesch, J., 38, 65, 72, 87, 311, 324
Rush, G.P., 26, 32
Russell, B., 63, 68

Sakoda, J.I., 148, 161
Sanford, F.H., 161
Sanford, R.N., 157
Sapir, E., 341, 346
Saporta, S., 14, 227, 280, 284, 291
Saunders, D.R., 142, 151, 159
Sayles, L.W., 212
Schachter, F., 309, 324
Schacter, S., 145-147, 153, 161

Scher, J., 314
Schiedel, T.M., 150, 161
Schizophrenia, 305, 309, 320
Schneider, G., 27, 29, 30-31
Schneider, L.I., 149, 161
Schramm, W., 112, 125
Schutz, W.C., 150-151, 162
Science, 103, 107, 110
Scientific rhetoric, 213
Scott, L., 29, 32
Search patterns, 69-70, 72
Sebeok, T., 310, 324
Seiler, J.A., 212
Self-reflexiveness, 330
Semantic compatibility, 113
Semantic control, 295
    differential, 112-113, 115, 124
    equivalence, 260-262
    reactions, 104, 124
    space, 115
Semantics, 85, 231, 256
Semantogenic, 307, 309
Semology, 224
Set learning, 69
Seth, G., 320, 324
Sexon, M., 322
Shakespeare, W., 227, 295, 297
Shannon, C., 82
Shapiro, D., 310, 323
Shaw, M.E., 150, 156, 160-161
Sheats, P., 144, 148, 152, 158
Shepherd, J.R., 150, 161
Sherif, M., 145, 158, 161, 212
Shils, E.A., 158
Shriver, B., 150, 158
Siegel, S., 125
Similarities, 330, 333
Simon, H.A., 216
Simpson, G.G., 99, 102
Slater, P.E., 144-145, 148-149, 152, 158, 162
Sliding triad, 70
Slochower, M.Z., 26, 32
Small group research, 133, 138, 139, 143
Small groups, 141, 157, 207
Smith, B., 60
Smith, H.L., Jr., 239
Smith, R.G., 113, 125
Snidecor, J., 340, 346
Snow, C.P., 215
Snygg, D., 219, 309, 323
Sociability, 148
Social behavior, 265
    distance, 179
Socialization, 199, 344
Sociogram, 192-193
Sociograph, 194-195, 198

Sociometric data, 192
    method, 191
    questionnaire, 198
Sociometry, 136, 188, 190, 203
Sofer, C., 212
Sondel, B., 13, 19, 73, 88-89
SoRell, Z., 13, 225, 245
Southern Illinois University, 114
Speech, 9-12, 18-19, 80-81, 139 ff, 305-306, 308-312, 322
    abnormal, 308-309, 312-313
    normal, 309, 312-313
Speech behavior, 308, 310, 325
    clinician (correctionist, therapist), 305-306, 309, 311, 313
    defective, 328, 334
    defects (disorders), 305-306, 313, 316-317, 322, 328-329
    fluency, 321, 343
    impairment (problem), 325, 329
    pathologist, 308, 313, 320, 326, 328-330, 334-336, 338
    pathology, 305-306, 308, 325, 329, 331, 340
    teacher, 306, 309, 310-311, 313-314, 316-318, 320, 322
    training, 319
    variation, 330
Spriesterbach, D.C., 339
Sputnik, 97
Staats, A.W., 124-125
Staats, C.K., 124-125
Stage fright, 306, 309, 316, 319-322
Stampe, D.L., 271
Stanford-Binet Test, 21
Status achievement, 152
Status-consensus, 149
Stein, W., 312, 324
Steiner, G.A., 143, 158
Stevens, C., 280
Stewart, J.L., 14, 307, 340, 342, 346
Stice, G.F., 142, 151, 159
Stogdill, R.M., 140, 150, 162
Stone, S.B., 13, 224-225, 228
Stout, D.B., 340, 342
Stratton, G.M., 22, 32
Strauss, G., 212
Strodtbeck, F.L., 151, 153, 154, 158, 160, 162
Structure, 141
Studebaker, J.W., 164-165
Stutterer, 306, 310, 314, 321, 329, 341
Stuttering, 309, 312, 315-316, 321-322, 340-345
Subgroups, 195, 201
Subject-predicate, 243, 332
Sub-verbal levels, 333
Suci, G.J., 112, 125
Sundene, B., 124, 126

Supek, I., 214-215
Symbolization, 226, 257-258, 318, 326
Symbols, 103, 258, 263, 325
Syntality, 141
Syntax, 256
System, 68
Systems, reversible, 51
    spontaneous, 51
Systems-research, 155
Szaz, T., 310, 324

T-group training, 18, 134
TORI actualizing experiences, 183-184, 186
    processes, 173-174, 176, 181
Tactile channel, 328
Tannenbaum, P.H., 113, 117, 121, 125
Task achievement, 154
    dimensions, 151
Tautology, 64
Taylor, F.K., 147, 162
Teachers, 95-96, 98
Teaching, 96, 228
Territory, 108, 330
Thayer, L., 13, 19, 34-35
Theory-building, 34
Therapy, 213, 321
Thibaut, J., 50, 140, 146-147, 153, 159, 162
Thistle, M.W., 79
Thomas, C.K., 251
Thompson, W., 13, 78
Thonssen, L., 87
Thoreau, H.D., 169
Tobler, E., 24, 32
Toynbee, A., 168
Trager, G.L., 239
Trainer, 184
Transactional psychology, 205-206
Transceiver, 50
Transference, 65
Transports, 28
Travis, L.E., 308, 324
Treiner, J.C., 114, 125
Triandis, H.C., 112-113, 125-126
Trist, E.L., 211
Trust, 182, 184
    system, 187

Valences, 56, 58
Vancouver Island, 342-345
Van Doorninck, W., 30, 32
Van Riper, C., 308, 310, 324
Van Til, W., 102
Velten, H., 287, 289-291, 294

Venable, T.C., 140, 162
Verbal disorders, 320
    level, 331
    patterns, 318
    withdrawal, 320
Vernon, M.D., 23, 32
Vroom, V.H., 151, 162
Vurpillot, E., 29, 32

Waddington, C.H., 31-32
Wagner, R.H., 81
Walk, R.D., 22, 32
Walker L.C., 156, 160
Walter, W.G., 45-46
Wayne State University, 163
Weakland, J., 72
Weaver, C.M., 113, 126
Weaver, R., 81
Weaver, W., 82
Weinberg, H.L., 13, 103
Werner, H., 23, 33
Werner's law, 223
West, R., 321, 324
Whaley, R.M., 163
Whatmough, J., 80, 87, 93
Wheeler, D., 167
White, B.L., 22, 33
White, R.K., 149, 161-162
Whitman, W., 169
Whorf, B.L., 215
Whyte, L.L., 44, 48, 52
Wieman, H.N., 90
Wiener, N., 74-75
Wilkinson, E.J., 319, 324
Williams, F., 124, 126
Williams, W., 316, 324
Wilson, E.W., 309, 323
Wilson, M.O., 158
Wilson, T., 81
Wise, C.M., 245, 247-248, 251
Wispe, L.G., 142-143, 148, 159, 162
Wohlwill, J., 23, 33
Wood, G., 204
Woodward, J., 211
Words, 213, 332
Wright, H.F., 161
Wrigley, C., 152, 161

Zagreb University, 214
Zander, A., 140, 147, 150, 152, 159-160
Zaporozhetz, A.V., 21, 33
Zelko, H., 82
Zidonis, F.J., 244
Zoberman, N., 29, 32

ABOUT THE CONTRIBUTORS

DEAN C. BARNLAND, Ph.D. Professor, San Francisco State College. Authority on communication theory, group communication and interpersonal communication. Formerly on faculty of Northwestern University. Numerous publications in the area of communication and group dynamics. Co-author of *The Dynamics of Discussion*. Author of *Interpersonal Communication: Survey and Studies*.

GREGORY BATESON, M.A. Oceanic Institute, Hawaii. Leading ethnologist, anthropologist, and authority on communication. Has done anthropological field work in New Guinea and Bali. Co-author of *Communication: The Social Matrix of Psychiatry*, and *Balinese Character, A Photographic Analysis*. Author of *Naven*; and numerous articles for the scholarly journals.

RAY L. BIRDWHISTELL, Ph.D. Visiting Professor, Annehberg School of Communications, University of Pennsylvania and senior Research Scientist, Eastern Pennsylvania Psychiatric Institute. Author of *Introduction to Kinesics, Kinesics and Context* and co-author of *The Natural History of an Interview*. Author of numerous articles in the scholarly journals.

O. R. BONTRAGER, Ph.D. Professor of Education, Long Beach State College, California. Author of many scholarly articles. Chief lecturer for many years for Institute of general semantics summer workshops.

HELES CONTRERAS, Ph.D. Associate Professor of Linguistics and Romance Language, University of Washington. Authority in linguistic theory and Spanish syntax. Co-author of *A Phonological Grammar of Spanish*. Author of *Sobre Gramática Transformacional*. Cuadernos del Instituto Lingüístico Latinoamericano, Cuaderno No. 7, Montevideo, Uruguay, 1966.

RUPERT L. CORTRIGHT, Ph.D. Professor of Speech, Wayne State University. Past President of Speech Association of America. Co-author of *Creative Discussion* and *The New Training for Effective Speech*. Author of many articles in the area of discussion and public speaking.

DAVID ELKIND, Ph.D. Professor of Psychology and Director, Graduate Training in Developmental Psychology, Universtiy of Rochester, New York. Formerly Associate Professor and Director of the Child Study Center, University of Denver. Recently completed a year of study in Switzerland with Jean Piaget. Author of numerous articles in the field of child development.

SETH A. FESSENDEN, Ph.D. Professor and former Head of the Department of Speech and Drama, California State College at Fullerton. Co-author of *The Teacher Speaks; Basic Experiences; How to Read the Bible Aloud; Speech for the Creative Teacher; Speech for Today; Bonney — Fessenden Sociograph; Understanding and Being Understood*. Author of *Design for Listening* and *Speech and the Teacher*.

KENNETH D. FRANDSEN, Ph.D. Associate Professor of Speech and Research Associate, Computer Center, The Pennsylvania State University. Communication Research Specialist. Author of studies in information, persuasion and interpersonal communication processes.

JACK R. GIBB, Ph.D. An organizational consultant in private practice in La Jolla, California. Currently President of the American Association for Humanistic Psychology, and has been on the faculty of Brigham Young University, Michigan State University, and Stanford University. Has been director of the Group Process Laboratory at the University of Colorado, and has been Director of Research and member of the board of the National Training Laboratories. Best known for pioneering work with leaderless training groups and is co-editor of *T-Group Theory and Laboratory Method* (1964), the basic work on sensitivity training.

LORRAINE M. GIBB, M.A. An organizational consultant in private practice in La Jolla, California. With her husband she has originated the TORI theory of group and organizational development. The theory is presented in chapters co-authored by the Gibbs in Gazda's *Innovations to Group Psychotherapy* (1968), Bugental's *Challenges of Humanistic Psychology* (1967), and Otto and Mann's *Ways of Growth* (1968). Has been a member of the research and training staffs of the National Training Laboratories, and is a consultant to educational and volunteer organizations.

KIM GIFFIN, Ph.D. Professor of Speech Communication, and Director of the Communication Research Center, University of Kansas, Lawrence. Author of many articles in the area of interpersonal communication and group process.

LOUIS E. GLORFELD, Ph.D. Associate Professor of Speech, University of Denver. Formerly Director of Freshman English at Northern Illinois University. Author of books and articles dealing with language behavior and English composition. Editor of *A Short Unit on General Semantics; Language, Rhetoric and Idea;* and others. Co-author of *Concise Guide for Writers.*

WENDELL JOHNSON, Ph.D. (late) Professor of Speech Pathology and Psychology until 1963, then Louis W. Hill Research Professor, University of Iowa. Leading speech scientist, speech pathologist, and general semanticist. President of International Society for General Semantics from 1945 to 1947. Author of numerous scholarly articles. Author of *People in Quandaries; Stuttering and What You Can Do About It; Your Most Enchanted Listener; Stuttering in Children and Adults.* Co-author of *The Onset of Stuttering; Diagnostic Method in Speech Pathology;* co-author and editor of *Speech Handicapped School Children* and others.

ROBERT B. LEES, Ph.D. Professor of Linguistics and Head of Department, University of Illinois, Urbana, and Director, Division of English Linguistics, Tel-Aviv University, Israel. Author of *The Grammar of English Nominalizations* and numerous articles.

RAVEN I. McDAVID, Jr. Ph.D. University of Chicago. Fellow, American Council of Learned Societies; American Anthropological Association. Member of Linguistic Society of America, International Center of General Dialectology and others. Co-author of *Structure of American English in the Atlantic States.* Editor (H.L. Mencken) *The American Language.* Associate editor of the *Linguistic Atlas of The Middle and South Atlantic States* and numerous articles on sociolinguistics.

DAN McLACHLAN, Jr., Ph.D. Physicist, Chemist, Information Theorist, and Professor of Mineralogy, Ohio State University, Columbus. Former President of the American Crystalographic Association. Author of *X-Ray Crystal Structure* and numerous other publications. Devised machines for computing results of x-ray diffractions.

GORDON E. PETERSON, Ph.D. (late) Director of Speech Communications Research Laboratory, Santa Barbara, California. Formerly Director, Communication Sciences Laboratory, University of Michigan. Author of numerous articles in the area of speech science.

GERALD M. PHILLIPS, Ph.D. Professor of Speech, Pennsylvania State University. His interests and publications range from communication disorders to rhetoric and group communication. Co-author of *Speech: Science and Art,* author of *Communication and the Small Group.*

PAUL PTACEK, Ph.D. Professor and Chairman of Depaitment of Speech Communication, Case Western Reserve University, Cleveland. Author of numerous research publications in communication disorders and speech science.

EUGENE REBSTOCK, Ph.D. Professor at and former Chairman of Speech Department, San Francisco State College. Has had wide experience in management and communications training. Author of numerous articles dealing with the communication process.

SOL SAPORTA, Ph.D. Professor of Linguistics and Romance Languages, and Chairman of the Department of Linguistics, University of Washington. Fellow at the Center for Advanced Study in the Behavioral Sciences and in 1965 delivered the State of Oregon Condon Lectures. Publications reflect his interest in Spanish linguistics, linguistic theory, and psycholinguistics. Assistant Managing Editor, *Modern Language Journal.* Editor of *Psycholinguistics, A Book Of Readings.* Author of numerous articles and reviews.

BESS SONDEL, Ph.D. For many years faculty member of the University of Chicago and from 1957-59 Consultant in Communication to the Faculty of the Graduate School of Business, University of Chicago. From 1965, Adjunct Professor of Science Information in the Graduate School, Illinois Institute of Technology, in the Department of Language, Literature, and Philosophy. Books include *Are You Telling Them?; Everyday Speech, Speak; Up; Communication: A Field Theory; The Humanity of Words;* and *Power-Steering With Words.*

ZELL RODGERS SORELLE, Ph.D. Associate Professor of Speech, West Texas University. Author of articles in speech and communication. Parts of this paper read at the Second World Congress of Phonetics, Tokyo, Japan, 1965 and published in the *Proceedings.*

JOSEPH L. STEWART, Ph.D. Indian Health Service, U.S. Public Health Service, Washington, D.C. Formerly with School of Speech, University of Denver. Author of numerous articles in audiology and speech pathology.

SAMUEL STONE, Ph.D. College of Education, Wayne State University, Depaitment of Secondary English, Speech and Foreign Languages. Formerly with Department of Education, University of Denver. Author of numerous articles in linguistics and education.

LEE THAYER, Ph.D. Professor of Administrative Communication and Director of Business Administration, University of Missouri at Kansas City. Editor of *International Symposium on Communication Theory and Research.* Author of *Communication Systems in Organization Management and Interpersonal Relations.*

WAYNE THOMPSON, Ph.D. Professor, Department of Speech, University of Houston. Co-author of *Basic Experiences in Speech.* Author of *Quantitative Research in Public Address and Communication, Fundamentals of Communication,* and of numerous articles in speech and communication.

ALBERT UPTON, Ph.D. Professor of English and Director of General Studies, Whittier College, California. Semanticist and Linguist. Specialist in the written and spoken word. Co-author of *Creative Analysis.* Author of *Design for Thinking.* Contributor of Chapter XVIII, Communication and the Problem-Solving Process in *Communication,* Concept and Perspectives.

HARRY H. WEINBERG, Ph.D. (late) Temple University, Philadelphia. Extensive work in general semantics and communication theory. Author of Levels of Knowing and Existence: *Studies in General Semantics.*

JANUA LINGUARUM

STUDIA MEMORIAE NICOLAI VAN WIJK DEDICATA

Edited by C. H. van Schooneveld

SERIES MAIOR

2. Dean Stoddard Worth, *Kamchadal Texts Collected by W. Jochelson*. 1961. 284 pp.
f 75,—/$ 21.40

3. Peter Hartmann, *Theorie der Grammatik*. 1963. 552 pp.   f 108,—/$ 30.90

5. A. R. Luria, *Traumatic Aphasia: Its Syndromes, Psychology, and Treatment*. Translated from the Russian. 1970. 479 pp. 99 figs. and diagrams   f 96,—/$ 27.50

8. Thomas A. Sebeok and Valdis Zeps, *Concordance and Thesaurus of Cheremis Poetic Language*. 1961. 259 pp.   f 75,—/$ 21.40

9. Gustav Herdan, *The Calculus of Linguistic Observations*. 1962. 271 pp., 6 figs., 43 tables.
f 54,—/$ 15.45

10. Antti Sovijärvi and Pentti Aalto (eds.), *Proceedings of the Fourth International Congress of Phonetic Sciences, held at the University of Helsinki, 4-9 September 1961*. 1962. 854 pp., numerous figs. and plates.   f 162,—/$ 46.30

11. Werner Winter (ed.), *Evidence for Laryngeals*. 1965. 271 pp.   f 50,—/$ 14.30

12. Horace G. Lunt (ed.), *Proceedings of the Ninth International Congress of Linguists. Cambridge, Mass., August 27-31, 1962*. 1964. 1196 pp., plate   f 150,—/$ 42.00

13. N. I. Žinkin, *Mechanims of Speech*. Translated from the Russian. 1968. 475 pp., many figs.   f 96,—/$ 27.50

14. Ruth Hirsch Weir, *Language in the Crib*. 1970. 2nd Printing. 216 pp.   f 38.—/$ 10,75

15. Thomas A. Sebeok et al. (eds.), *Approaches to Semiotics: Cultural Anthropology*, Education, Linguistics, Psychiatry, Psychology. 1964. 294 pp.   f 40,—/$ 11.45

16. A. Rosetti, *Linguistica*. 1965. 268 pp.   f 65,—/$ 18.60

17. D. P. Blok (ed.), *Proceedings of the Eighth International Congress of Onomastic Sciences, Amsterdam, 1963*. 1966. 667 pp., 23 figs., 2 plates   f 120,—/$ 34.30

18. Pierre Delattre, *Studies in French and Comparative Phonetics: Selected Papers in French and English*. 1966. 286 pp., 2 tables, 35 figs.   f 53,—/$ 15.25

19. Jesse Levitt, *The "Grammaire des Grammaires" of Girault-Duvivier*. 1968. 338 pp.
f 64,—$ 18.30

20. William Bright (ed.), *Sociolinguistics: Papers of the UCLA Conference on Socio-linguistics.* 1966. 324 pp., figs. f 57,—/$ 16.30

21. Joshua A. Fishman et al. (eds.), *Language Loyalty in the United States: The Maintenance and Perpetuation of Non-English Mother Tongues by American Ethnic and Religious Groups.* 1966. 478 pp., figs, tables. f 69,—/$ 19.75

22. Allan H. Orrick, *Nordica et Anglica: Studies in Honor of Stefán Einarsson.* 1968. 196 pp. 8 ills. f 50,—/$ 14.30

23. Ruth Crymes, *Some Systems of Substitution Correlations in Modern American English.* 1968. 187 pp. f 34,—/$ 9,75

24. Kenneth L. Pike, *Language in Relation to a Unified Theory of the Structure of Human Behavior.* Second, revised edition. 1967. 762 pp. f 72,—/$ 20.60

25. William Austin (ed.), *Papers in Linguistics in Honor of Léon Dostert.* 1967. 180 pp. f 34,—/$ 9.75

27. David Cohen (ed.), *Mélanges Marcel Cohen.* 1970. xxxix + 461 pp. f 190.—/$ 54.00

29. Victor Egon Hanzeli, *Missionary Linguistics in New France: A Study of Seventeenth- and Eighteenth-Century Descriptions of American Indian Languages.* 1969. 141 pp. Ill. f 42,—/$ 12.00

30. Jitka Štindlova, *Les machines dans la linguistique: colloque international sur la mécanisa-tion et l'automation des recherches linguistiques.* 1968. 336 pp. f 66,—/$ 18.90

31-33. *To Honor Roman Jakobson: Essays on the Occasion of his 70th Birthday, 11 October 1966.* 3 vols. 1967. 2464 pp. f 450,—/$ 125.00

34. J. C. Heesterman *et al.* (eds.), *Pratidānam: Indian, Iranian, and Indo-European Studies Presented to Franciscus Bernardus Jacobus Kuiper on his 60th Birthday.* 1968. 654 pp., plates f 160,—/$ 45.45

36. Herbert E. Brekle und Leonhard Lipka, *Wortbildung, Syntax und Morphologie: Fest-schrift zum 60. Geburtstag von Hans Marchand.* 1968. 250 pp. f 75,—/$ 21.40

38. Rudolf P. Botha, *The Function of the Lexicon in Transformational Generative Grammar.* 1968. 368 pp. f 52,—/$ 14.85

MOUTON · PUBLISHERS · THE HAGUE

CPSIA information can be obtained
at www.ICGtesting.com
Printed in the USA
BVHW060048040320
573983BV00013B/277